E___ ...ering History

Engender

Caribbean
Women
in
Historical
Perspective

James Currey Publishers
London

ing

History

Editors: *Verene Shepherd*

Bridget Brereton

Barbara Bailey

IRP

Ian Randle Publishers
Kingston

First Published 1995 by
Ian Randle Publishers
206 Old Hope Road, Kingston 6, Jamaica

ISBN 976-8100-41-9 paperback

ISBN 976-8100-50-8 hardback

and

James Currey Publishers
54b Thornhill Square
Islington, London N1 1BE

ISBN 085255-726-4 paperback

ISBN 085255-727-2 hardback

Catalogue records for this book are available from the
National Library of Jamaica and the British Library.

Text and cover design by
Prodesign Publishing Services,
Kingston, Jamaica

Printed and bound in the USA by
Data Reproductions Corp

in memory of
ELSA GOVEIA
and for
LUCILLE MATHURIN–MAIR

CONTENTS

Preface

With the exception of the articles by Patricia Mohammed, Verene Shepherd, Swithin Wilmot and Hilary Beckles (whose symposium paper was on women in cricket), the articles included in this volume represent a selection of papers presented at an international symposium titled *'Engendering History: Current Directions in the Study of Women and Gender in Caribbean History'*, held at the University of the West Indies, Mona Campus from November 10–12, 1993. The symposium was hosted by the Department of History in association with the Mona Centre for Gender and Development; and we thank our colleagues sincerely for entrusting us with the responsibility of editing this selection of papers.

On behalf of the Department of History, we should like to acknowledge the financial assistance toward the publication of this selection of Symposium papers which was provided by *OXFAM, the Petroleum Corporation of Jamaica (PCJ), Petrojam* and the University of the West Indies Research and Publications Fund. We thank Carol Thompson for wordprocessing services and Florizel Allen, Augustin Charles, Jonathan Dalby and Waibinte Wariboko for assistance with proof-reading.

We are grateful to Dr Patrick Bryan, Head of the Department of History, Mona, and Verene's husband Bramwell Shepherd, for so kindly lending us their services in the editing and proofreading of articles which were translated from Spanish. We also thank Professor Barry Higman for his willingness to read and comment on draft sections of the book.

We wish to thank all who helped to make the symposium a success: Mrs. Linnette Vassell who did much to push the idea of this Symposium; other colleagues in the Department of History and the Centre for Gender and Development who worked tirelessly on various committees and sub-committees; Mrs. Hope Senior, Miss Juliet Williams and Miss Vanessa Ellis who had the mammoth task of producing 200 copies of each of the original 32 papers; members of staff of other Faculties and Departments of the UWI and the wider University Community; UWI students co-opted to help in preparatory work; presenters and other participants; sponsors from the University community, the private sector, women's organisations and international funding agencies. Without your support neither the symposium nor this book would have become a reality.

Finally, we would like to express our gratitude to the staff of Ian Randle Publishers for the professional way in which they went about the business of transforming the typescript into book form.

Verene Shepherd
Bridget Brereton
Barbara Bailey

Introduction

Since the emergence of women's history as a definable field in the last 25 years there has been an increase in the production of historical works on women, which have dramatically altered the epistemological foundations of history. Women's history is now an established area of discourse in many parts of the world. Its wide-ranging impact is evident in the fact that scholars from across the disciplines support the call for greater attention to the influence of historical processes on the lives of women and a more critical evaluation of the influence of historical contexts on the ideological production of notions about women.

In a sense, the emergence of women's history can be located within the context of the development of social history, with its 'democratic' tendencies and its call for the writing of history from the perspective of traditionally marginalised groups. Another impetus was the 1960s civil rights movement in the USA which in itself had its genesis in slavery and the resistance against slavery. This struggle was over the recognition of minority rights, mostly of African-Americans. During the same decade, the feminist movement in the USA and in Europe re-emerged on the public stage, sharing much of the discourse of the civil rights movement in its struggle for the rights of subordinated women. The revitalised feminist movement was thus able to fashion its appeal and its self-justification within the prevailing rhetoric of equality. The women's movement played a critical role in raising key questions such as what accounts for women's situation as 'other' and what perpetuates it historically. In answering these questions, academic feminists and other scholars used an explicitly historical approach as this could enable feminist theory to fulfill its potential for radically changing the existing epistemologies. Therefore women's history became regarded as central — not tangential — to feminism.

Women's history challenged the androcentric ideology inherent in historical discourse. Scholars claimed that to effect meaningful change it was not sufficient to add women to the existing history, thereby creating a parallel history. They urged the questioning of methodological assumptions and the modernist notions in which history was regarded as universal, with no attention to the differences between the historical experiences and realities of men and women. Scholars, and academic feminists in particular, called for a new history which would not only be about great people, government, diplomacy, state building, formal religions, trade and warfare, all of which were areas in which men were the principal actors, except of course where there was a powerful woman like Queen Isabella or Nanny of the Maroons who could not be ignored. Rather, they called for a history which would show that women's concerns and activities were different from men's; that women were not peripheral but were very much integral to history.

To correct this imbalance in historical discourse, historians of women developed a multiplicity of perspectives. Some adopted a more descriptive and compensatory approach in this reconstruction of historical knowledge. Some, viewing the neglect of women in historical discourse as part of women's experience of oppression, began by cataloguing areas of neglect and female oppression. Others wrote biographies of outstanding women; some narrated the history of women's contribution to political struggles like slave resistance, the suffrage movement, reform movements, the emancipatory struggles, all the time redefining the meaning of politics. Still others adopted a multidisciplinary approach, finding useful approaches in the methods of anthropologists, linguists, sociologists and literary writers.

Other historians went a step further and began to look for ways to include a type of analysis which had been omitted from historical discourse and which would produce a feminist standpoint and therefore a better picture of reality. These scholars challenged the existing paradigms and methodologies and the validity of existing canonical historical knowledge. They called for new empirical data and new analytical perspectives which could be used in the reconstruction and redefinition of historical knowledge to produce a gendered history. In this process of re-evaluation, the concept of gender began more and more to be used as an analytical tool not only to change the perspective of the traditional history, but to alter the historical epistemologies; for only by studying the social relations between the sexes could one begin to understand ideas about the division of labour, sexual difference and its construction, social organisation and political ideologies. In other words, gender analysis could lead to a rewriting of history which would re-evaluate the meaning of maleness and femaleness and restore a balance in the history of men and women.

As part of the mandate to question the assumptions which governed the study of history, scholars directed their scholarship to new fields of research which would provide heroines as well as heroes, challenge the traditional chronologies of historical events and employ gender analysis in understanding the relations between the sexes. They also identified the conceptual weakness of perceiving women's history as homogeneous and therefore also the danger of universalising the new discourse. They pointed to the need to take differences based on gender as well as race, class, colour, caste, nationality and occupation into account in reconstructing Caribbean history.

This heterogeneous approach, which gained wider appeal on account of the growing attention to multiculturalism, was even more crucial for understanding Caribbean women's experiences which often departed from the universalising discourse of western scholars.

The integration of a feminist empirical approach, which uses gender and other intersecting variables as an analytical tool, with the historical discourse on the Caribbean, developed only in the 1960s and 1970s. Caribbean historians were late in realising the epistemological and pedagogic importance of utilising this approach for the construction of women's history. Influenced by prevailing ideas in the discipline which saw women's experiences as trivial or non-historical, and by aspects of Marxist ideology which confined women to the private sphere in the division of labour, the pre-1960s texts tended to dichotomise the activities and experiences of men and women into the categories of: public vs. private; work vs family; and personal vs political. These approaches masked the true contribution of women to Caribbean history and not only left them out of the history books but resulted in a distorted historical account which only partially represented the reality.

The neglect of Afro-Caribbean and Asian women in Caribbean history was less understandable than that of middle-class, white and mixed-race women. While elite and middle-class women came under the influence of patriarchy and later the Victorian ideology, working-class women — before and after slavery — had never neatly fitted into the prevailing dichotomies which sought to create mutually exclusive categories of wage labour in the public sphere and non-compensatory labour in the private/domestic sphere.

Information on women in the Caribbean was not entirely absent, for historians possessed the contemporary writings of Europeans and others who observed Caribbean society from the late fifteenth century. These works, of course, utilised justificatory language, written as they were in a period when European colonisation efforts were at their zenith. Those written in the eighteenth and early nineteenth centuries were often couched in the language of the pro-slavery ideologue and were aimed at impeding the emancipation struggles on both sides of the Atlantic. These biased accounts therefore portrayed Caribbean enslaved women as physically unappealing, uncouth, lazy and in need of the 'civilising' influence of slavery. Other writings of the same era, by persons sympathetic to the anti-slavery movement, were less overtly hostile to slave women but still revealed racist and classist biases.

Since the 1960s, and beginning with the pioneer work of Lucille Mathurin-Mair, the androcentric biases of early Caribbean histor- iography and the racist and sexist ideologies of the contemporary literature have been increasingly challenged.

In addition to purely historical works, Caribbean historians have benefited from the work of sociologists and specialists in gender studies. In this regard, the Women in the Caribbean Project and the subsequent establishment of an academic Centre for Gender and Development Studies on each of the three campuses of the University of the West Indies were critical. The major objective of these two initiatives was to provide a database to further the understanding of the position of women in contemporary Caribbean society from a historical perspective and so influence the transformation of social structures and male-female relationships in all spheres of activity within the region. To this end scholars, particularly feminist scholars, in a number of disciplines became engaged in a process of testing established assumptions and theories and exploring phenomena of particular importance to women which had hitherto been ignored or marginalised. At the same time, they introduced a feminist methodological approach to this process of knowledge-building.

The establishment of gender studies as a legitimate area of academic discourse has facilitated the engendering of mainstream academic fields through more adequate and valid epistemologies. History is one of the disciplines which has benefited from this illumination.

These developments have yielded a solid body of research data about the historical experience of Caribbean women. It seems fair to say that the first or 'retrieval' phase of Caribbean women's history has made considerable progress. Less has been done in terms of the second phase, that of applying gender analysis to Caribbean history.

Of course, the research still does not reflect the historical experiences of all groups of women in the Caribbean. The primary focus of the research has been on the experiences of enslaved black women, with only limited attention to coloured women, white working-class and elite women, and nineteenth-century immigrant women. This research pattern is caused by several factors, among which are the increased focus of anthropologists and sociologists since the 1950s on black women's roles in Caribbean family structure during and after slavery and an earlier imperialist scholarship which conceptually subsumed white and coloured women to their male counterparts in assessments of agricultural and mercantile activities in colonial culture. Additionally, immigrant women, coming to the Caribbean after the abolition of slavery, especially from Asia, formed a comparatively small section of the total populations, particularly in Jamaica and the French and British Windward Islands, and as such were perceived as having been marginal to the larger historical process. Predictably, not much research effort has been applied to the study of their historical experience. This is despite the fact that they were crucial in the continuation of the capitalist plantation system in the post-slavery and post-indentureship periods. Recently, however, scholars have begun to address this imbalance in the research.

The articles in this volume testify to the remarkable amount of research effort which has been applied to the study of Caribbean women's history, and the ongoing attempts to rewrite history based on the ever-emerging new contexts. They seek not only to add new empirical data on women to the fund of historical knowledge, since that would simply be writing a compensatory history, but also to re-problematise existing theory, and critique the dominant systems of knowledge. The majority of articles, in the tradition of the prevailing scholarship, focus on African and African—Caribbean women, but there are also articles on white European, mixed-race (coloured) and Asian women, in the quest to avoid writing a totalising Caribbean women's history. The Caribbean, after all, represents a diversity of ethnic groups, the result of the great voluntary and involuntary migratory movements from the sixteenth century. Caribbean women's historiography must be cognisant of the different experiences of women according to race or ethnicity, caste, class, colour, age, nationality, language, location (rural vs. urban) and occupation.

The book is divided into six sections which cover, chronologically, the period of slavery to the modern historical period. Geographically, the articles relate primarily to the Anglophone Caribbean; but some effort has been made to adopt a pan-Caribbean approach, with material included that is representative of the experiences of women in the Hispanic and the Francophone Caribbean. Since the Caribbean also did not develop in a vacuum but was shaped by historical developments in Africa, North America and Europe, the book includes articles which adopt a comparative perspective, linking the experiences of Caribbean women to their counterparts in other parts of the world, particularly those equally influenced by European colonialism.

In the first section, which is devoted to theoretical perspectives, Terborg-Penn, Mohammed and Hall focus on the problematic issue of discursively constructing a women's history which is representative of the multiple experiences of national and racial groups in the Caribbean, Britain and North America. They argue that as much of western feminism is based on the experiences and agenda of white, European elite women, there is an urgent need for gender analysis to take on board the experiences of Africans and Indo-Caribbeans, particularly in the context of a post-colonial world. Thus Terborg-Penn proposes an African feminist theoretical approach which encompasses not only the experiences of women on the continent but also in the diaspora. This enables the forging of a link with women in the Caribbean and elsewhere and makes an opportunity for a cross-cultural analysis which can include issues of race, class, gender, religion, age and ethnicity. She examines the tenets and values of African feminism and demonstrates methods of application.

Mohammed posits another theoretical approach to the process of writing gender into history. Through the experiences of post-indenture migrant Indians in Trinidad, she examines how femininity and masculinity were reformulated in the period 1917–47. She argues that for each ethnic group or class in society, the construction of gender is carried out within the framework of a system of gender relations which may or may not be in the dominant system in that society at a given period.

Hall argues that historians of Britain and the British empire should urgently rethink ways of writing imperial histories. For centuries white British identities, both male and female, have been constructed through sets of assumptions about imperial power in relation to racialised 'others'. Imperial histories also contained negative images of women in the empire who were subjected to multiple forms of domination: imperialism, sexism and patriarchy. She argues that imperial relations have to be subjected to revision in a way which takes gender fully into account, and that there is a need to re-evaluate the ways in which men and women in the empire were conceptualised, particularly in the missionary discourse after the abolition of slavery.

In Section Two, (the title of which was inspired by a course developed at the UWI, Mona, by Barry Higman), the focus is on the variety of sources and methodological approaches to the study of Caribbean women's history. A concern of all the authors in this section is that in seeking to probe the gender dimension in the history of the Caribbean since European contact, one is largely dependent on documentary evidence generated by men. Some of this evidence represents a textual invention of the Caribbean, and demonstrates the dominative discourses of imperial powers such as Britain. There is a paucity of recorded testimony by women, as opposed to about women, which presents a difficulty in any attempt to reconstruct the social history of diverse groups of women in the region. Despite these difficulties, the three authors have been able to suggest new approaches and sources for the representation of the multiple experiences of women in the Caribbean. Brereton demonstrates the ways in which women's diaries, journals, private letters, autobiographies and female-authored texts can provide a rich source of evidence about women's historical experience in the Caribbean which can supplement the mainstream of documents generated by men and help provide a more nuanced view of Caribbean social history, its gender dimensions and its 'invisible women'. She examines nine sources, ranging chronologically from the 1770s to the 1920s and covering eight territories in the English-speaking Caribbean.

Chamberlain's article is based on oral history, the representation of the experiences of Barbadian emigrants to Britain. She shows how oral history has the potential to contribute to the interpretation of women's experiences and warns that this source should not be relegated to the periphery of historical enquiry and dismissed as untrustworthy and subjective. She shows that oral sources are different from conventional sources precisely because they deal with perception and subjectivity.

Robertson argues persuasively that dress is one of the most revealing mirrors of social attitudes and should be regarded as a serious source for social history rather than as a subject of marginal academic value. Dress is a mirror of class as it can set people of wealth and leisure apart from the middle and working classes. In the nineteenth century dress also mirrored differences in women's age, marriageability and marital status. Clothes at that period also reflected societies' general attitudes towards women as fragile and delicate. Changes in dress styles demonstrate socio-economic changes among the classes in society.

Section Three focuses on women during the slavery period and takes in the experiences of enslaved women in the Anglophone, Hispanophone and Francophone Caribbean. The articles demonstrate clearly that the enslaved woman was critical to the economic imperatives of the sugar plantation society which defined her life and experiences. The enslaved woman was acutely aware of her importance to the continuation of the capitalist plantation complex. It was armed with this realisation of her important role that she was able to devise strategies to subvert it.

The first article in Section Three is by Hilary Beckles who examines the implications of the recent historiographical shift from history to women's history and the conceptual and methodological problems which arise when a more gendered history is not pursued. This he demonstrates from data on the construction of the white and coloured women during slavery as opposed to the construction of the black woman. He argues convincingly that gender and race ideologies were principally at work in determining the division of labour and were responsible for the crystallisation of consciousness within the slave mode of production.

The second article is by Digna Castañeda who writes on the Cuban female slaves, particularly those in the western section of the island, in the first half of the nineteenth century. She argues that African slavery is seen with the greatest clarity and depth in the role and place of the Afro-Cuban woman in Cuban colonial society. She shows how the intersection of social class, race and gender manifested itself during slavery and how these elements became a means of exploitation. In the end the Cuban slave woman suffered from the multiple effects of being black, female and enslaved; yet they played critical economic and cultural roles in slave society.

Moitt's article analyses the social condition of enslaved black women in the plantation societies of the French Caribbean and the ways in which the organisation of labour had an impact on enslaved women's experiences, for enslaved women's occupations opened up to them a wide range of resistance strategies. To date, the majority of published studies on slave resistance have focused on the English-speaking Caribbean, so that this article will be essential for the development of a comparative, pan-Caribbean study of slave work and resistance strategies.

Matos-Rodríguez focuses on Puerto Rico, among the last outposts of slavery in the Caribbean. He shows the active participation and importance of women in lower sectors of retail, in domestic work, in food-selling and entertainment establishments in nineteenth-century San Juan. Unlike the other two articles in this section, Matos-Rodríguez' focus is on the urban sector and the discussion centres essentially on poor, coloured women. His objective is to show the solidarities and differences among working women in order to understand their lives from a historical perspective.

Section Four is located within the context of the post-slavery Caribbean, a fundamental period in the shaping of the social and economic experience of Caribbean women, the majority of whom were making the transition from slavery to freedom. The articles, by showing differences based on race, class and colour, reinforce the realisation by Caribbean historians that there is a homogenous Caribbean women's history. They also show that women were not peripheral to Caribbean post-slavery society; neither did they accept blithely attempts to marginalise them. While there were clear efforts to confine them to the private domestic sphere through a sex-discriminatory type of education, or to disadvantage them through dependence on male benefactors, and through the sex-typing of jobs where they remained in the public sphere of work, they clearly opposed such efforts of subordination. The articles by Kerr, Satchell, Shepherd and Mayers examine a range of issues, from coloured and black women's search for economic autonomy through property accumulation and peasant development and the running of taverns and lodging houses, to Indian women's participation in the labour force and the social experiences of female students who suffered from discrimination in the school system of Barbados.

Kerr explores the historical explanations for the evolution of a coloured female-dominated economic activity, that of lodging house keepers. She contends that the coloured woman emerged from a position relegated to her by dominant males where her opportunities were limited, with a number of avenues for social and economic success. Coloured females suffered from multiple oppression from the period of slavery on the basis of race, colour, gender and legal status. The main area of their victimisation, Kerr maintains, was their subservient and seemingly dependent relationship on white males for whom they were mistresses, lovers, and prostitutes, and who attempted to keep them in that bind by 'allowing' them to enter the occupation of lodging house keeper. But, as

Kerr shows, these women were strategists rather than victims, turning what seemed like a disadvantageous position into economic and social strength.

Satchell focuses on women's roles in peasant development and as buyers and sellers of land. It is clear that land transactions were not gender-specific, though men dominated them. He also examines the discriminatory land-holding laws which affected married women in particular down to 1882. Women facilitated the development of the peasantry by disposing of land to both men and women. But women received far less land than they were selling. Women transferred a total of 225,000 acres but bought just 70,000 acres, between 1866 and 1900.

Shepherd focuses on the little-studied area of female Indians' historical experience in Jamaica, arguing that they were not marginal to the larger historical development of post-slavery Jamaica but, as contract workers, (and later free settlers), contributed to the continuation of the capitalist plantation system. The central objective of her article, though, is to demonstrate the ways in which gender considerations conditioned the Indian female experience of migration, indentureship and settlement in the host society. She rationalises the elevation of gender over race and class to a position of primacy in the immigrant experience by positing that race and class conflicts were not the only forms of struggle which immigrant women had to undertake in the late nineteenth- and early twentieth-century Caribbean.

Mayers argues strongly that gender discrimination existed in the Barbados educational system in the period 1907–43 in terms of the physical facilities provided, as well as in the number of awards, which enabled winners to access education. The planter oligarchy dictated the pace of educational development in colonial societies as it had a vision of the needs of an agricultural society which would be ordered in their socio-economic interest. All the major reports on education seemed to recommend a structure organised to meet the requirements of a highly stratified society catering in different degrees to the upper, middle and working class. Race, class and gender were clearly factors which determined access to education in Barbados as in the rest of the Caribbean. The curriculum reflected the efforts to sex-type education so as to create in the Caribbean what European missionaries called the 'proper gender order'.

Section Five is devoted to the role of women in protest and political movements. The articles seek to reinterpret the meaning of politics, demonstrating clearly that despite the sexism and racism which initially denied black and coloured women the legal right to vote, the lack of the franchise did not exclude women from active participation in the public world of politics during slavery and in the post-slavery Caribbean. Women like Mariana Grajales of Cuba were active directly and indirectly in revolutionary struggles. Caribbean women, as Wilmot shows, opposed any attempt to impose upon them a 'proper gender order', according to which men worked for wages and the women were expected to retreat to the domestic arena to do uncompensated labour. As under slavery, they had an active role to play in the public sphere of work and acted as historical agents to refashion their economic role and protect their economic gains in post-slavery society. Denied access to the formal political process, the street became their political platform and they participated in street demonstrations and protests to protect their existing rights or claim new gains.

Stubbs focuses on the evolution and construction of the mother myth of Mariana Grajales Cuello, a symbol of Afro-Cuban resistance in the nineteenth century. Mariana is regarded as a strong revolutionary icon of Cuba and her role in Cuban history has taken on a political interpretation which ranges from liberal patriot to revolutionary. She has acquired legendary proportions as a heroic and valiant mother and her home was, indeed, a centre of social transformation. The mother of Antonio Maceo, the noted general in the Cuban revolutionary army in the war of 1868–78, she became noted for preparing her family for war during this period. She sacrificed home, husband and children to the war and nine of her children in fact died in it. She herself joined the insurrection and ran hospitals and provision grounds in Antonio Maceo's base camps.

Vassell presents a stirring analysis of the role of Daphne Campbell in the political activities of modern Jamaica. Her objective is to give the working class a space to speak and reflect their experiences in society and the ways in which they have acted in social and political terms. She argues that the testimonies of women can provide a window on the issue of class tensions among women within the women's movement; on how women have perceived their own personal autonomy and how working-class women, despite the attempts to confine them to the so-called 'private' sphere, have transcended these boundaries to enter the 'public' sphere of politics. Her article also provides scope for exploring issues raised explicitly in the new women's history, African diaspora women's history and issues related to the definition of women's political action.

The articles in the final section are not totally focused on the Caribbean but cover topics which are of interest to Caribbean women's history and which have the potential to provide comparative perspectives. These articles on African and European women are particularly crucial in view of the prevailing preoccupation with the external influences on gender roles and women's experiences 'after the crossing'.

Through over 80 infanticide prosecution dossiers of the assize courts of the Department of Cantal in Central France between 1791 and 1899, Dalby seeks to answer certain questions: what motivated the practice of infanticide among women in rural France in the nineteenth century? Why infanticide rather than other alternatives such as abandonment? To what extent were the motives of these women similar to those of other women in early modern Europe, and indeed the Caribbean? His analysis shows clearly that infanticide is quintessentially an issue of gender and a phenomenon which transcends the boundaries of culture. Infanticide is by definition a 'female crime' whose structural origins lie in women's subordination and alienation in a profoundly patriarchal society. In certain respects, as Dalby shows, infanticide was not only an act of self-justification, but almost one of emancipation, by which the mother in the absence of a support system sought to determine her own future.

Wariboko sheds new light on the historical development and transformation of New Calabar, one of the Eastern Delta States of Nigeria, by re-evaluating the influence, status and role of women as New Calabar responded to the tripartite forces of change: consular rule, transatlantic commerce and Christianity. He discusses, through a variety of documentary and oral sources, how New Calabar perceived the female image, potentials and capacities, through some of its extant myths and legends relating to the origins of communal socio-cultural and political institutions. His conclusions echo those of Caribbean writers: that while sexism, patriarchy and male domination existed in most societies, with women being given the opportunity to contribute to society in a subordinate position rather than as equals, women were not completely helpless, exploited and voiceless. They have sought redress for inequalities and have traditionally in all societies possessed the capacity to contribute to societal evolutionary development.

Finally, Goodridge looks at the general involvement of Cameroonian women in the socio-economic life of their communities and the impact on their lives of the intrusion of western, specifically British, colonial capitalism. A central aspect of his analysis is that, as in the Caribbean, the plantation provided the principal colonising agency in West Cameroon and is thus crucial to the study of the impact of colonialism upon women. By dealing with some of the more exploitative aspects of the plantation system, he counters aspects of the imperial tradition of African historiography which suggests that plantations were beneficial since they offered opportunities for women to take part in the modern economic sector through wage labour on, or sale of foodstuffs to, the plantations. While focusing on the impact on women of British colonial policies, Goodridge also examines women's responses to colonising agencies and institutions. Above all, Goodridge's article demonstrates the consistency in British colonial policies as they impinged on women, whether in the Caribbean or Africa, and their use of Victorian ideology and patriarchal notions to make decisions about women's economic and social roles.

The articles in this volume, then, build on the existing body of scholarship and seek to chart the development of an intellectual tradition which moves Caribbean and black women's experiences away fromthe margins of the historical discourse. It is hoped that the present volume, like the symposium from which it has emerged, will contribute to the second phase of Caribbean women's history, the 'engendering' of the region's past.

Verene Shepherd
Bridget Brereton
Barbara Bailey

Notes

For further reading on historiographical and conceptual issues in women's history, see works such as:

1. H. Beckles, 'White Women and Slavery in the Caribbean' *History Workshop*, 36, 1993.

2. Barbara Bush, *Slave Women in Caribbean Society, 1650-1838* (Heinemann/Indiana, 1990)

3. Patricia Hill Collins, *Black Feminist Thought* (Routeldge, New York, 1991)

4. Joan Kelly, *Women, History & Theory* (University of Chicago Press, Illinois, 1986)

5. S. Jay Kleinberg (ed), *Retrieving Women's History* (Berg/UNESCO, 1992)

6. P. Mohammed & C. Shepherd, [eds], *Gender in Caribbean Development* (UWI,WDS, 1988).

7. Linda J. Nicholson, *Feminism/Postmodernism* (Routeledge, New York, 1990)

8. *Gender and History: The Limits of Social Theory in the Age of the Family* (Columbia University Press, New York, 1986)

9. K. Offen, R.R. Pierson & J. Rendall, eds., *Writing Women's History: International Perspectives* (Indiana University Press, New York, 1986)

10. Joan W. Scott, *Gender and The Politics of History* (Columbia University Press, New York, 1988)

11. R. Terborg-Penn, S. Harley & A.B. Rushing, eds., *Women in Africa and the African Diaspora* (Howard University Press, Washington, 1987)

12. The 'dialogue' section of the *Journal of Women's History* (Indiana University Press)

SECTION ONE

History

and

Gender Analysis:

Theoretical

Perspectives

1.

Through an African Feminist Theoretical Lens:
Viewing Caribbean Women's History Cross-culturally

Rosalyn Terborg-Penn

African feminism is a theoretical approach developed in the early 1980s by anthropologist Filomina Chioma Steady, who herself is a child of the African diaspora. Born in Sierra Leone, Steady's ancestors were enslaved in another area of the African continent, trekked to the sea, then packed on a slave ship bound for the Americas. En route the vessel was captured by the British; the Africans were freed and returned to the African continent, but settled in Sierra Leone. However, this British colony was not their home of origin. Perhaps the legacy of her family experience influenced Steady in developing the African feminist theory, because it lends itself not only to the experiences of women of African descent on the continent, but also to women of the African diaspora worldwide.[1]

By definition, persons of African descent living in the Caribbean, like those in the United States who call themselves African Americans, are people of the African diaspora. Scholars of African diaspora history define the field as the study of 'Africans abroad', or the study of individuals who were forced to leave the African continent, primarily through the international slave trade, and scattered throughout other continents all over the globe. This multi-generational process involved Africans and their descendants, who actively attempted to recreate their own culture and practice their values and beliefs in the new worlds forced upon them. Through the over 300-year history of the transatlantic slave trade, newly arriving Africans continually nurtured the spread of the old culture and values. As a result, African culture was never crushed, just amended. In the diffusion process, a new world view began to develop among African diaspora people, which combined African, Indian, Amerindian and European customs, arts and beliefs. The degree to which Africanisms survived varied from jurisdiction to jurisdiction.

In researching African diaspora women's history, it is important to focus upon the Caribbean, because aside from Brazil, more Africans were brought to this region for longer periods of time than any other region. Although a greater diversity of people of mixed racial heritage in the United States consider themselves African American than do similar cohort groups in the Caribbean, as in the United States, much of the national experience of most Caribbean states reflects African diaspora heritage.

If one supports Melville Herskovits' thesis that women are the culture-bearers of most societies, then one may ask this question in relation to the Caribbean: how did African women and their female descendants, enslaved in the jurisdiction, carry the culture which enabled them to survive into the twentieth century?[2] Were there characteristics among enslaved women in other parts of the Caribbean and the western hemisphere generally that were similar? I argue that there were differences, but also similarities. There are enough similarities to analyse Caribbean women's history cross-culturally, inside and outside the region. I argue further that the way to view this cross-cultural analysis is through an African feminist lens, because the view achieved is all inclusive. African feminists concern themselves with race, gender, class, religion, age, and ethnicity, all factors in the cultural survival of the people.

Tenets of the African feminist theory

Filomina Steady's theory of African feminism can be used to approach the study of African-descended women's lives through an analysis of their own networks, which were used to overcome obstacles placed in the way of survival. Beginning with an examination of the values which foster the customs of free women in traditional African societies, historians can plot how these traits have changed, though the values have remained somewhat the same.

Perhaps the two most dominant values in African feminist theory, which are traceable through time are: encouraging self-reliance through female networks and developing survival strategies. These values have become institutionalised in many African and African-descended communities. Historically, this combination has not been present in institutionalised forms among females in Euro-centred world societies, but can be traced continually in time among women of African descent in New World societies as well as in Africa.[3]

When one examines the literature of slavery in the United States and the Caribbean, instances of self-reliance through female networks can be identified. Where these are examined, several common characteristics can be identified, including: (i) younger women relying on older women (of 40 years old or older); (ii) women looking to female kin, fictive kin and cohorts for support; and (iii) redefining household relations which may be primarily female. There are cases of self-reliance through female networks found in the literature of slavery in the United States and the Caribbean.

The narrative of Harriet Jacobs is an example from the era of slavery in the United States. Jacobs cites the assistance she received from her manumitted grandmother and an older slave woman in the North Carolina community where they all lived. In one way or another, each woman provided sanctuary for Harriet as she fled the sexual harassment and punishment of her male owner. Eventually, Harriet hid for several years in the attic of a shed outside her grandmother's house until she and another enslaved woman were able to escape north of slavery. Throughout the ordeal the African American women relied upon each other to feed and care for Harriet as well as to maintain the secret of her hiding place. Thus, all three characteristics can be observed in this case.[4]

Another example of self-reliance during the slavery period can be found in the story of Old Doll, a domestic slave on the Newton Estate in Barbados. Old Doll, born about 1736, was the senior female among at least three generations of slaves who lived and worked as housekeepers on the estate from the mid-1700s through till around 1830. Their struggle through self-reliance and networking to obtain privilege and freedom can be observed through the records left by the managers of the Newton Estate. Much of what these women achieved in property holdings, social status, literacy and even manumission resulted from their ability to pull together, both as a family and as an occupational group. Among the many privileges and indulgences the women managed to manoeuvre were positions for their children and grandchildren. Old Doll and her half-sister Mary Ann are good examples of this strategy. Several males in Old Doll's line became masons, whereas the males in Mary Ann's family became coopers. Old Doll and her daughter Jenny, both of whom were literate, successfully petitioned their absentee owner for their manumission.[5]

There are many examples of this tenet at work in the stories of women in both the USA and the Caribbean during the post-emancipation period and the early twentieth century. During the Civil War years in the United States, the majority of slaves were emancipated as a military strategy by president Lincoln in order to weaken the Confederate Army. African

American women and men saw the war as a means to improve their condition. For men this meant joining the Union Army. For women such as Harriet Tubman, Sojourner Truth and Susie King Taylor, this meant attaching themselves to black military units, where they worked with other women serving as laundresses, cooks, practical nurses and teachers. A major part of the work of all of these women was assisting the wives and children of the black soldiers. Networking with women who helped one another during this hectic time was a consistent story reported in the narratives of all three of these once-enslaved women. Elements of self-reliance were especially prominent in Harriet Tubman's reminiscences. She spoke of how she baked root beer pies at night and freed women sold them among the soldiers during the day, while she nursed the sick in the army hospital. In addition, Tubman, who was a woman in her 40s in the 1860s, taught the freed women folk medicine and instructed them in hygiene.[6] Here is an example of at least two of the characteristics of African feminism.

During the early twentieth century Puerto Rican women provided role models and networked for self-reliance in order to support their families and earn decent wages through union affiliations. Doña Adela was one such woman from Lares in the western part of the island. Although racial identity was not noted in her story, Adela, poor and widowed at 24, was no doubt a woman of colour. She became the head of a family of women and learned from others in her church to form a community of women networking together. She eventually organised a needlework factory in her home, a *pequeño taller*, teaching her seven daughters to sew and contracting the work in Mayaguez, the major western city. Although a multitude of problems including fires, disease and death plagued the family, the women in Doña Adela's church community provided the support needed for her to sustain her family. When Mayaguez became a major needlework centre on the island in the 1930s, Adela and her family moved there to work in a factory. There she joined a labour union of women, where women, once again, helped one another.[7] Here one sees all three of the characteristics.

The second tenet, that of women developing survival imperatives, can be characterised by: (i) resisting oppression; (ii) defining female leadership; and (iii) redefining economic and political roles for women. Examples of this can, as before, be found in the literature about women for the slavery periods in the Caribbean and the United States.

In Jamaica rebel slave women who attained leadership positions ordinarily reserved for males were examples of women redefining leadership roles. Times like these often came when slaves planned rebellions as resistance against the institution of slavery. Queen Cubah, who in 1760 featured prominently in organising slaves to revolt in six different parishes, involved nearly all of the Koromantyn people on the island. She had been crowned Queen of Kingston before planning the revolt. Lucille Mathurin has speculated that Cubah functioned in the role of traditional West African queen mothers. Several of these women were known to have assisted in organising efforts for military expeditions against ethnic enemies in West Africa. However, Cubah's role appears to have gone beyond the traditional women's role of exhorting the men and providing food needed for the campaign. Unfortunately the plot was discovered, and Cubah was captured and deported from the island. She returned, but was captured and executed.[8] Nonetheless, her efforts characterise at least two of the characteristics of this tenet: resisting oppression and defining female leadership.

During the last generation of slavery in the United States, African American female abolitionists worked in various traditional and radical ways to end slavery. The Forten Purvis family of women in Philadelphia is a good example of three generations of free black women who waged the anti-slavery war between the 1830s and 1860s. The group included Charlotte Forten, Sr, her three daughters, Harriet Forten Purvis, Marguerite Forten and Sarah Forten Purvis, and her two granddaughters, Hattie Purvis and Charlotte Forten, Jr. They joined the Philadelphia Female Anti-Slavery Society, signed anti-slavery petitions, boycotted slave-made products, bought free labour grown produce and hid runaway slaves. Although some of these activities were done in conjunction with the males of their families, the Forten Purvis women worked primarily in their women-led organisation, where they redefined the traditional roles for American women by entering the public arena.[9]

Examples in the literature about post-emancipation and early twentieth-century women apply to the Caribbean and to the United States as well. From the post-emancipation period in St Croix, Mary Thomas, known as Queen Mary, has been celebrated until today in folk songs as the leader of the Labour Rebellion of 1878. Discontented with the near-slavery labour contracts the workers on the estates and in the rum factories suffered, the people revolted and burned most of the great estate houses from Christiansted to Frederickstad, the two major cities on the island. All the men arrested and tried for participation were emigrants who had come to St Croix from other islands. Only Mary and the three other queens tried in the Denmark court case were indigenous to the island. Only they have been celebrated as leaders by the folk. Apparently, the females, all of whom were older women, were recognised leaders and were given titles, like Cubah in Jamaica 100 years before. In nineteenth- century St Croix, these women not only resisted oppression, but were defined as leaders who were redefining the economic roles that black women took on the island thereafter.[10]

In both the United States and in the Caribbean during the early twentieth century, women sought political equality with men through demanding the right to vote. Hence, they attempted to redefine political roles for women, often for reasons connected with reforming their communities and improving economic and social conditions for women and their families. Bertha Williams, an African-American woman from Rhode Island in the northeastern United States, was a leader of the woman suffrage movement among the women in her networking. She successfully organised women's political associations, mainly the suffrage club called the Political League, in which the women lobbied for and raised funds for the women's suffrage campaign. From beginnings in 1913 Williams fought for women's suffrage and for black women's political patronage, particularly once the Nineteenth Amendment to the United States' Constitution enfranchised all women in 1920. Williams believed that black women voters could wield power in their organisations, by pressing politicians to improve public schools for black children and by legislating to outlaw lynching, the execution of black people by mob violence. Both of these strategies were survival imperatives for black people.[11]

Among Puerto Rican women, especially the black working classes in the tobacco industry, women's suffrage was political leverage to fight economic oppression. Redefining women's economic and political roles were connected, as a result, in these women's call for universal suffrage. Genera Pagen exemplified the radical, confrontational suffragists in the early 1920s, who as a Puerto Rican, but also a United States citizen, demanded the right to vote once the Nineteenth Amendment had been ratified. A labour organiser (whose racial identity has not been found), Pagan organised working-class women in Puerto Rico and Puerto Rican women in New York City to seek political empowerment through the ballot box. Of the working-class women, many were females of colour. As New York residents they could vote, but the suffrage amendment did not cover Puerto Rican women living on the island. Pagan tried to vote nonetheless — unsuccessfully. Although the women's suffrage legislation passed in the Puerto Rican legislature in 1929 enfranchised only literate women or the white elite, the working-class suffragists of colour continued their suffrage struggle.[12] Pagan's resistance and assumption of political leadership in Puerto Rico exemplified two characteristics of the second tenet.

Similarly, women in St Thomas argued for the right to vote as United States citizens, but also as a means to improve social and educational conditions on the island. The women of the St Thomas Teachers Association, primarily a group of black women, took their case to court in 1935 and successfully sued the Board of Elections. By the 1930s citizenship for people in Puerto Rico and St Thomas included United States constitutional protection for citizens residing in the territories. As a result, the St Thomas women suffragists were able to achieve what Genera Pagan could not more than a decade earlier.[13] In St Thomas black women successfully redefined their political roles through resistance.

These examples reveal ways of applying the theory cross-culturally to women's experiences during and after slavery. In both periods, the ways in which heroines have been revered and remembered by later generations is important to the understanding of women's roles in carrying on the culture of black people. Black is the term I will use in referring to African-descended people regardless of colour. How female leaders were chosen is an important question also; however, the historical sources and the oral testimonies that survive rarely deal with this process. As a result, scholars researching women's history must return to the sources they have used in the past to re-examine them for clues to answer the questions. With this in mind, scholars searching for sources on women also may want to examine carefully the works about black women written by sociologists, anthropologists, ethnomusicologists, folklorists and others.

Colour stratification as an analytical variable

Before applying the theory to women's past, we must focus upon colour stratification as an analytical variable in the study of women of African descent. First, it is important to look at the term 'black', because not all women of African descent identify with this term. In the United States, for example, by law, people with any measurable degree of African ancestry are considered black. As a result, since slavery, women of African descent, regardless of skin colour, have been identified and often have identified themselves as black. In this sense, 'black' symbolises a cultural milieu more than colour. Today, when a person of obvious African descent attempts to take on the anti-black cultural behavioural mannerisms of mainstream American society, that person is called 'Negro' or 'coloured' by peers. In this context these are negative terms used to deride the individual for attempting to discard black heritage.

Although there are southern cities in the United States such as the District of Columbia where, until recently, social stratification by colour and class was prevalent in the African-American community, outside the community, as viewed by the majority, there is no middle ground. Similar patterns have and may still exist in some areas of the Caribbean, the Bahamas and Bermuda. Such variables must be considered when doing the research. Some people of African descent living in jurisdictions such as the Bahamas and Bermuda have told me that there is some colour polarisation. It appears that in jurisdictions where the white population has been in the majority since the early European colonial experience, people of colour find themselves with little middle ground. Furthermore, in jurisdictions governed by the United States such as Puerto Rico and the US Virgin Islands, racial identification has become polarised over the past century. One is either black or white.

On the other hand, in many Caribbean and South American societies women of African descent vary in colours that determine legal status as well as cultural association.[14] A mulatto woman in the British West Indies, for example, does not identify herself as black, whereas the same kind of woman born in the United States may choose to or may be forced to do so by American society. When the same type of mulatto woman emigrates to the United States, she may perceive herself to be non-black; however, after experiencing social and economic discrimination based upon colour, she will begin to identify with blacks because of her need for a survival network.

On the other hand, as many African-Americans know, for several generations in the United States, individuals who looked white and could assume the speech and mannerisms of the white world, "passed" for white. In so doing, however, they were forced to give up their family and friends who could not pass into the white world.[15] The sense of alienation that resulted often forced people of colour who passed for white to return to their black communities. Others passed for white on the job, but returned to being black when at home in their own communities.

An example of this is the story of Delia Bierman Terborg, my grandmother who immigrated to the United States from Suriname during the first decade of the twentieth century. In the 1920s she sought employment in the New York City garment district, an area where European and Caribbean immigrant women were employed as needle workers. African-American women migrating to the city from the South with similar skills could not find employment in these factories, except as menial workers at very low pay. For Caribbean women of colour with foreign accents, the only strategy that could gain them employment was passing for white.[16]

Differences in legal and cultural identification by race cause barriers to reconstructing the past and cross-cultural analysis, especially for researchers studying countries where blacks were not counted in the population censuses for several generations. The key to historical reconstruction in such cases must rest first upon how women identify themselves and second, on who they are identified as by the society in which they live. In addition, the perceptions about race and colour of scholars who have written previously about the subject must be considered also.

An example of how historical analysis can fool researchers is my reading of Lucille Mathurin Mair's 1986 Elsa Goveia Memorial Lecture. Her presentation was entitled: 'Women Field Workers in Jamaica During Slavery'. This classic work integrated gender into the new literature on slavery in the Caribbean which was fast growing in the 1980s. I began reading the essay with my own cultural notions about enslaved women in Jamaica, presuming that when Mair talked about black women she meant all women of African descent who were enslaved on the island. However, when she began to speak about the under-representation of "black" women in specialised labour positions, such as skilled and domestic work, I realised that she was using colour stratification in her quantitative as well as her conceptual analysis. As a result, she listed slave women in two categories: blacks and mulattos. In her analysis she found 62 per cent of the women doing specialised work to be mulatto. She noted that the female house servants in this group were not so much "skilled" as "favoured" workers.[17] I realised that colour was a dynamic conceptual framework of this discussion of slavery, one that was rarely used in the current literature about enslaved women workers in the United States, but one of which I needed to be aware in researching Caribbean scholarship.

Scholarly studies of Caribbean women and other African diaspora women

The works of other historians have not confronted the issues of African feminism directly. However, at least three historians and Filomina Steady herself have approached the study of black women's past in such a way that applies well to this theoretical path. The three historians are Lucille Mathurin Mair, Deborah Gray White and Bernice Johnson Reagon.

The examples of Mair's work which fit best into the African feminist model were studies she wrote earlier in her career, when she published as Lucille Mathurin.[18] Perhaps the best known of these works, cited earlier in this study, is *The Rebel Woman*, which was first published in 1975 as a book for young readers, though it is used by all types of Caribbean women's history students. This little book deals with the various ways African and creole women in the British West Indies resisted enslavement. A decade before the African feminist writers of today, Mathurin looked to African women's behaviour as the root of enslaved Caribbean women's militancy. Although Mathurin did not use an African feminist analysis, she touched on several of the tenets, including use of ridicule by women, in her chapter, 'Nanny - Rebel/Queen/Mother'. Both of these strategies are found in Steady's African feminist conceptualisation. Although Mathurin used traditional manuscript sources and documents and did not specifically deal with Steady's concept of women's networking, clues for researchers abound in Mathurin's work.[19]

Filomina Chioma Steady combined with fellow anthropologist Kenneth Bilby to write an article in the late 1970s about female roles among the maroons in Moore Town, Jamaica. Steady had conducted research among descendants of the maroons who had been resettled in Freetown, Sierra Leone. Bilby had engaged in field work in Moore Town, where he interviewed present-day inhabitants, and collected oral traditions. Together they combined his data and her theory. The idea they developed centred upon Nanny as the dominant figure in this maroon society, where the role of women was essential to ensuring community survival.

In their essay, first published in 1981, nearly all the tenets of African feminist theory can be observed and in particular, reliance on the skills of older women, like Grandy Nanny, who is still revered by descendants as a supernatural force. Bilby observed that to present-day maroons, Nanny is the heroine of Moore Town; she is the mythical, original ancestress from whom the Moore Town maroons are descended. Despite her mythical exploits, there is no doubt that Nanny existed. What institutionalises women's significant roles in Moore Town is the fact that there were important women other than Nanny as well, Molly, Diana and Mama Juba who, like Nanny, was considered to be a great 'science woman', versed in supernatural arts.[20] Bilby and Steady combined the anthropological methods of field work and oral traditions to research an historical topic, which also required them to use traditional sources. This methodological approach seems therefore useful for investigating the roles of women, which often appear to be invisible.

By the 1980s in the United States, African-American women historians such as Deborah Gray White and Bernice Johnson Reagon were laying the foundations for the historical framework of the African feminist theory.[21] Like Mathurin, neither scholar identified with the theory; nonetheless, their work speaks to issues and tenets raised by Steady. Their methodology included non-traditional means for data analysis.

White identified a number of issues which could be useful to Caribbeanists conducting a comparative analysis of women's enslavement. She looked at the question of reproductive policies and trends in the United States from 1800 to 1860 and concluded that the slave trade developed 100 years later in North America, unlike in the Caribbean. In both instances the preference for males remained until the early nineteenth century, when North American masters sought both men and women and encouraged slaves to reproduce themselves in family units.[22]

Reproduction as a function of enslaved women remains a controversy among African-Americanists, especially the issue of enslaved women resisting reproductive functions imposed by the master through abortion practices. White felt that the evidence to settle the debate has not yet surfaced, so she declined to make a judgement; however, she contended that enslaved women were often able to restrict pregnancy for several years after reaching puberty, despite the master's attempts to have them breed earlier as their life cycle enabled them. White argued that young slave women learned these practices from older, experienced women who networked with them in resisting slave policies and for community survival. White also looked to Africa for customs and practices collected by anthropologists. She dealt with the organisation of female societies and female initiations among various ethnic groups on the continent, to support her belief that African and creole women enslaved on plantations in the United States were able to retain many of their women-centred African beliefs through women's networks.

In Bernice Johnson Reagon's essay about African diaspora women as "culture workers", which was published in 1987, she related an experience she had when in 1976 she became the coordinator for the Smithsonian Institution African Diaspora Program. In this capacity she helped to organise the summer Festival of American Culture on the Mall near the Capitol building in Washington, DC. For the first time, the Smithsonian decided to broaden the term 'America' by inviting groups from outside the USA. It was in this area that Reagon witnessed the roles of women in the development of New World African diaspora societies.

Of the three women she met and worked with, all were heads of their communities, the keepers of the community traditions. Reagon said each was chosen by her community and each accepted the responsibility to meet the needs of her community and the people each served. One woman was the highest priestess of Condomble in Bahia, Brazil. The roots of this religious practice are found among the Yoruba in West Africa. Another woman was the spokeswoman for the Georgia Sea Island Singers of the United States. Each of the songs of this group had its roots in the African traditions maintained by the Gullah people of the Sea Islands.[23]

The third woman was Imogene Kennedy, queen of the Kuminas from Jamaica, and known as Queenie. According to Reagon, the Kuminas were a cult which blended European Christian religious concepts with those of West African religions, especially the concepts of Ashanti. Their ceremonies opened with songs and prayers which combined elements from the various religions. As her contribution to the Festival, Queenie performed a table ceremony, which Reagon viewed as a redefinition of the diaspora area. For a time, the place became a Kumina community where Queenie held the highest status as a spiritual leader. Reagon concluded that Queenie had assumed the responsibility of protecting and nurturing her community in order to work out ways to keep the traditions strong for the people. Like the Candomble in Brazil, the Kuminas' rituals were outlawed and maintained underground. Reagon was convinced that a comparative study of women in the African diaspora was imperative to collective survival.[24] A cultural historian, Reagon is also a performing artist, the founder of the a cappella singing group, Sweet Honey in the Rock, so it is not surprising that she observes and applies ethnomusical methods to her analysis, which she can use in her research of contemporary as well as historical events.

As an historian who believes in non-traditional and interdisciplinary methodology, my work still appears to be on the frontier of comparative African diaspora women's history. In 1986 my essay 'Black Women and

Resistance: A Cross-Cultural Perspective', was published in an anthology called *In Resistance: Studies in African, Caribbean and Afro-American History*.[25] To my surprise, it was the only comparative essay in the collection.

In viewing some of the ideas from and responses to my essay, note that it was controversial when I presented it at a conference at Stanford University in 1983. The conference topic was studies about resistance among oppressed people who are African, Afro-Caribbean and Afro-American. The occasion was the 40th anniversary of the publication of Herbert Aptheker's classic book *American Negro Slave Revolts*.

The conference gave me an opportunity to do a cross-cultural review of several manifestations of resistance among women of African descent, across time and place. Although I identified my theoretical perspective as African feminist, the editor of the anthology, Gary Okihiro, called my view 'Afrocentric'. The major problem I had with his summary of my essay was that he left out the feminist perspective. Despite the fact that he was very sympathetic to my work and admitted that many of the men who challenged my view were sexist, Okihiro was blind to the female focus of my analysis. As a result, he placed it correctly within the traditional African diaspora context, which holds that diaspora history is an extension of African history and that there is a tradition of identification with Africa among blacks in the diaspora. However, that identity, he said, contains common values originating in the African cultural context, one of which was self-reliance, which fostered the essential basis for the people's resistance to slavery.[26] What was missing in his summary was the whole point of my argument, that self-reliance is one of women's values, one that enables them to resist all kinds of oppression.

My aim was to exemplify the tenets of the theory by showing how historians can place African-descended women within the African feminist conceptual framework. In the essay the unifying themes were the focus upon analysis more than the events of the examples given. The categories cited included 'women as spiritual leaders and warriors', 'women in slave revolts and maroon societies' and 'women in post-emancipation resistance'. I cited examples from Africa, Brazil, the Caribbean and the United States. Among the unifying themes I identified were the leadership of older women, several of whom were revered because of their contributions to community survival and/or because of spiritual powers that sustained the community. In addition, I noted that the survival strategies used by women in resistance were rooted in African cosmology.[27]

I argued that within traditional societies throughout various regions of the African continent, common values in women's experiences provided a synthesis which can be used for establishing a model to view women of the diaspora. The prescription is as follows: combine the ideology of self-reliance among women who rely upon one another for various forms of support, and add the creation of survival imperatives designed by women. Then look through the lens to view how African-descended women in a variety of settings oppose social, economic and political threats to their communities. The process which results is the African feminist theoretical approach.

Among the several women and activities in my original presentation were three who have become representational icons for women freedom fighters: Queen Ann Nzinga (Angola), Grandy Nanny (Jamaica) and Harriet 'Moses' Tubman (United States). I used them because these women were universally known among students of the African diaspora, and because I could view them from the lens constructed. In sum, they appeared to have supernatural powers; they were older women whose leadership had been tested by members of their respective communities, and they attained honorific titles, if not in their lifetimes, in subsequent years. Despite the fact that I cited several other women such as Cherry Turner of the Nat Turner conspiracy in the USA, Queen Cubah of Jamaica and Filippa Paria Aranha of Minas Gerais, Brazil, the discussion after my paper focused upon Nzinga, Nanny and Tubman, and was led by the white male participants in the conference.

The major controversy was over my selection of 'heroines' like Nzinga and Nanny who the men challenged as not being real heroines because some questioned whether the women's behaviour had been honourable. There were accusations that Nzinga herself was a slave trader. There were accusations that Nanny returned runaway slaves to the colonists after the signing of the Moore Town treaty. The controversy heightened when the black female graduate students in the audience charged the men with attempting to discredit black women as a cover for the 'quilt' of white ancestors, 'the true slave traders'. Finally, the elder scholar, the anthropologist St Claire Drake, rose to speak. He had founded the black studies program at Stanford University where the conference was being held. Drake admonished the men for not understanding my argument, which he interpreted as a discussion of heroines who were selected by their own people, not by myself as researcher. He argued that nothing the men could say to detract from these women could diminish their status as heroines in the context of their own culture. Drake ended the controversy, as the male scholars deferred to him with respect.

Historian Bettina Aptheker, who attended the conference discussed the controversy with me later in amazement, expressing her opinion about the sexism in the academy. Later, in her book *Tapestries*, she revisited this scene from the conference, responding as she had to me about the problem of sexism among those in the academy who challenge women scholars when they analyse historical women found in non-traditional roles.[28]

The only other presentation at the conference which dealt with women was the one about slaves in the United States from Elizabeth Fox-Genovese. Her conclusions about African-American women's resistance were nearly the opposite of mine. Using a Marxist feminist approach, she found the resistance responses of enslaved women in the United States to be determined by changes in the world of the master class. As slave masters created harsher policies, she speculated, women's resistance increased. Fox-Genovese saw little collective identity among enslaved women. She determined that resistance was stimulated from outside, not inside the enslaved women's communities. As a result, she concluded that there was a danger in interpreting the resistance of females in terms of women's defined resistance. Her only concession was reproductive resistance, the one area I avoided in my presentation.[29] Our male peers at the conference seemed to have no problem with her analysis and did not challenge her.

My conclusion then and now is that feminist analysis will remain controversial until the threat it appears to create is dispelled. Ten years after the Stanford conference, I can say that the threat appears to be dissolving. Academics who resisted in the past are coming round to view women's experiences as having a wide range of implications for analysis, because they open the lens wider in order to include feminist interpretations.

Future methods and implications for African feminist analysis

Using traditional historical methods as well as non-traditional sources can allow for the writing of feminist histories, such as Barbara Bush's study of slave women in the Caribbean, and revisionist histories, such as Hilary Beckles' social history of enslaved women in Barbados.[30] African feminist theory requires the traditional and the non-traditional. Interdisciplinary sources and oral testimony still fall in the category of non-traditional applications among many historians. However, to make women's community visible, literary, musical, psychological, sociological and anthropological sources may be needed to provide clues in order to fill the gaps in the empirical data. Often records note women as either victims or victimisers, but do not include women's perceptions about their own condition. These may have to be obtained from the voices of the women themselves. An African feminist perspective cannot succeed if women are viewed from the outside in, rather than from the inside out. Finding paths for recreating women's views about their experiences is essential to the task. The book by Melton McLaurin about Celia, a sexually-abused US slave woman who murdered her master, used a variety of interdisciplinary approaches to telling the woman's story.[31] Although McLaurin did not use the African feminist approach, his research left the door open to create one.

Challenging the empirical data and revising the secondary sources can be important ways for reconstructing the history of black and other women of colour, whether their lives are lived in the Caribbean or in other areas of the diaspora. One of my former graduate students, Cassandra Costley, completed a master's thesis in African diaspora history in 1993. She wrote about the African roots of African-American birth-control practices, using an African feminist perspective.[32] In her research she revisited the secondary and primary data about reproductive strategies for resistance among enslaved women. Like Deborah White, she found that the evidence was not strong enough to confirm the opinion held by some that birth control was a widely practised form of resistance among enslaved women in the United States. However, she did find that fertility control, often through abstinence, but also through mechanical and botanical techniques, were strategies employed by African, Afro-Caribbean and African-American women for ordering their own lives. The other sources Costley used included studies by anthropologists and botanists. She revisited slave narratives, nineteenth-century African-American newspapers and studies by nineteenth-century historians, looking for clues about women's use of fertility control practices.

This type of inquiry about African-descended women's perceptions about themselves and their reproductive agency can be a model for not only individual jurisdictions in the African diaspora, but also for comparative analysis in the Caribbean, with African-American women in the United States and women on the continent of Africa as well. The African feminist lens accommodates all of these research objectives. Comparative African diaspora women's history is one of the trends for future historical development. Consequently, a new frontier is opening for engendering Caribbean history.

Endnotes

1. Filomina Chioma Steady, *The Black Woman Cross-Culturally*. (Cambridge, MA: Schenkman Publishers, 1981), Introduction.
2. Melville Herskovits, *The Myth of the Negro Past*. (Boston: Beacon Press, 1958; reprint, 1990), pp. 146, 166, 176.
3. Rosalyn Terborg-Penn, 'African feminism: a theoretical approach to the history of women in the African diaspora', in Rosalyn Terborg-Penn *et al.* (eds.), *Women in Africa and the African Diaspora*. (Washington DC: Howard University Press, 1987), pp. 44—45.
4. Harriet A. Jacobs (ed. Jean Fagan Yellin), *Incidents in the Life of a Slave Girl, Written by Herself*. (Cambridge, MA: Harvard University Press, 1987), Chapters XVII, XXI, XXIX.

5. Hilary McD. Beckles, *Natural Rebels: A Social History of Enslaved Black Women in Barbados* (New Brunswick, NJ: Rutgers University Press, 1989), pp. 65—68, 127.

6. Rosalyn Terborg-Penn, 'Black Women in Resistance: A Cross-Cultural Perspective', in Gary Y. Okihiro (ed.), *In Resistance: Studies in African, Caribbean and Afro-American History*. (Amherst: University of Massachusetts Press, 1986), pp. 203—204.

7. Blanca G. Silvestrini, 'Women and Resistance: Herstory in Contemporary Caribbean History', *The 1989 Elsa Goveia Memorial Lecture* (Mona: Department of History, University of the West Indies, 1990), pp. 6—8.

8. Lucille Mathurin, *The Rebel Woman in the British West Indies During Slavery* (Kingston: African-Caribbean Publications, 1975), p. 21.

9. Dorothy Sterling (ed.), *We Are Your Sisters: Black Women in the Nineteenth Century* (New York: W.W. Norton, 1984), pp. 119—21.

10. Terborg-Penn, 'African feminism', pp. 53—56.

11. *Ibid.*, pp. 56—58.

12. Yamila Azize-Vargas, 'The Roots of Puerto Rican Feminism: The Struggle for Universal Suffrage', *Radical America*, 32:1 (January—February 1989), pp. 70—79.

13. Terborg-Penn, 'African Feminism', pp. 59—60.

14. See Louise Spencer-Strachan, *Confronting the Colour Crisis in the Afrikan Diaspora, Emphasis Jamaica* (New York: Afrikan World Infosystems, 1992).

15. See Shirlee Taylor Haizlip, *The Sweeter the Juice: A Family Memoir in Black and White* (New York : Simon and Schuster, 1994).

16. Rosalyn Terborg-Penn, 'Survival Strategies Among African-American Women Workers: A Continuing Process', in Ruth Milkman (ed.), *Women, Work and Protest: A Century of US Women's Labour History* (London: Routledge and Kegan Paul, 1985), pp. 150—51.

17. Lucille Mathurin Mair, 'Women Field Workers in Jamaica During Slavery', *The 1986 Elsa Goveia Memorial Lecture* (Kingston: Department of History, University of the West Indies, Mona, 1987), p. 4.

18. Lucille Mathurin, 'The Arrivals of Black Women', *Jamaica Journal*, 9, 2&3 (1975), pp. 2—7; Lucille Mathurin, 'Reluctant Matriarchs', *Savacou*, 13, Gemini (1977), pp. 1—6.

19. Mathurin, *The Rebel Woman*, Introduction, Chapters 4 and 8.

20. Kenneth Bilby and Filomina Chioma Steady, 'Black Women and Survival : A Maroon Case', in Filomina Chioma Steady (ed.), *The Black Woman Cross-culturally*, pp. 457—64.

21. Deborah Gray White, *Arn't I A Woman? Females Slaves in the Plantation South* (New York: W.W. Norton, 1985); Bernice Johnson Reagon, 'My Black Mothers and Sisters or on Beginning a Cultural Autobiography', *Feminist Studies*, 8 (spring 1982), pp. 81—96; Bernice Johnson Reagon, 'African Diaspora Women: The Making of Cultural Workers', in Rosalyn Terborg-Penn *et al.*, *Women in Africa and the African Diaspora*, pp. 167—80.

22. White, *Arn't I A Woman*, pp. 67—69.

23. Bernice Johnson Reagon, 'African Diaspora Women: The Making of Cultural Workers', pp. 168—69, 174—75.

24. *Ibid.*, pp. 172—74.

25. Terborg-Penn, 'Black Women in Resistance', pp. 188—209.

26. Okihiro, (ed.), *In Resistance op. cit.*, p. 7.

27. Terborg-Penn, 'Black Women in Resistance', *op. cit.*, pp. 188—90.

28. Bettina Aptheker, *Tapestries of Life : Women's Work, Women's Consciousness and the Meaning of Daily Experience* (Amherst: University of Massachusetts Press, 1989), p. 18.
29. Elizabeth Fox-Genovese, 'Strategies and Forms of Resistance: Focus on Slave Women in the United States', in *In Resistance op. cit.*, pp. 143—44, 157—58.
30. Barbara Bush, *Slave Women in Caribbean Society* (Kingston: Heinemann Publishers, 1990); Hilary McD. Beckles, *Natural Rebels* (New Brunswick, NJ: Rutgers University Press, 1989).
31. Melton A. McLaurin, *Celia, A Slave* (Athens, GA: University of Georgia Press, 1991).
32. Cassandra R. Costley, 'The African Roots of Some African-American Birth Control Practices', (unpublished master's degree thesis, Morgan State University, 1993), Introduction.

2.

Writing Gender into History:

The Negotiation of Gender Relations among
Indian Men and Women in Post-indenture
Trinidad Society, 1917–47

Patricia Mohammed

Theorising gender as a category of historical analysis

The task of the feminist historian is not restricted to adding women, the
sex whose history has been denied, to historical accounts of society. In
order to engender history itself, the discipline must be challenged from
both theoretical and methodological perspectives. To write gender into
history, the historical construction of masculinity and femininity or the
construction of gender identities must itself be posed as the problem. In
this approach gender must be conceived of as another category of
historical analysis in which the cadences in gender relations are
juxtaposed and connected with the ongoing conflicts in society, especially
the confrontations of class, race and ethnicity.

To make gender a category of historical analysis we must envision
society continuously functioning around a recognisable gender system,
or a series of gender systems. The term gender in this article takes its
definition from Joan Wallach Scott: 'Gender is the social organisation of
sexual difference. But this does not mean that gender reflects or
implements fixed and natural physical differences between men and

women; rather gender is the knowledge that establishes meanings for bodily differences.'[1] A gender system is defined as that system of gender relations which is deemed to exist at any time and around which the cultural construction of masculinity and femininity proceeds. The term gender relations, as I use it, refers to the social relations, both structured and unstructured, between men and women which are 'guided by norms and values, underpinned by ideology, sanctioned by a range of mechanisms from social opprobrium to death.'[2] A gender system is best perceived as the rules governing the social, sexual and reproductive behaviour of both sexes in any given society. The components of a gender system include the social roles assigned to men and to women; the cultural definition of masculinity and femininity; the sexual division of labour; the rules regarding marriage and kinship behaviour between the sexes, as for example, whether monogamy or polygamy is an acceptable practice within a particular culture; the social significance of women's identification with the family; and women's position relative to men in political and economic life. Clearly these components vary with each society or culture so that the term 'gender system' itself defies precise definition, and like gender, remains an elusive concept.

Gender systems in general function around a notion of patriarchal dominance. The concept of patriarchy is often applied in popular usage in its literal meaning 'the rule of the father' and in its feminist usage as 'the hierarchical relationship between men and women in which men are dominant and women are subordinate.'[3] Patriarchy has also been used to distinguish the forces maintaining sexism from other social forces, such as capitalism. It has been introduced through psychoanalysis in terms of the psychic and symbolic context of oedipal socialisation as opposed to that of a political and economic domination of men over women. In addition, anthropological, archaeological, historical and sociological studies have demonstrated that there are manifold variations of patriarchal systems in which the spheres of domination between men and women within the same society differ. What is clear is that once patriarchal dominance was established by men, it needed to be maintained, and the ideology of patriarchy is constantly retained and is evident in the power relations between the sexes. It is important to understand that patriarchy is not only a relationship of power between men and women, but also exists in the relationship between men and men. Where and how this is manifested can only be illustrated with direct reference to the particular historical circumstances. In general most societies exhibit both the ideology and practice of male superordination and female subordination. Thus the ongoing construction of masculinity and femininity and the shifting definitions of gender identity involve rewriting the patriarchal contract through negotiations in the sphere of gender relations, a process which I refer to as the 'negotiation of gender relations'. For each ethnic group or class in society, the construction of gender and the negotiation of gender identities are carried out within the framework of a system of gender relations which may or may not be the dominant system in that society, depending on the historical circumstances of the society at a given period.

The primary aim of this article is to delineate another theoretical approach to writing gender into history. This requires first of all a challenge to traditional history. Conventional history has concerned itself with the individual, the event, the important social motors which in some way shaped the world. Since many of these important world-shaking events were orchestrated by men, traditional history tended to focus on men. The development of social history has facilitated the narration and analysis of other rhythms of history, of groups and groupings excluded from these momentous processes. When women's history was added to historiography in the heady days of the contemporary feminist movement, it was conceived initially as the way in which this neglected group could be included, and a necessary balance restored.

The wave of women's history which characterised the early phase of the contemporary feminist movement attempted to render the invisible visible. In carrying out these tasks, the writing of women's history also created new myths to serve the goals of the feminist movement; and understandably and justifiably so since in any social movement the knowledge of one's history is a liberating experience. If women had been marginalised in historical analyses, this being one manifestation of the wider subordination which they incurred in society, then a rewriting of history which represented their contributions was meant to recover both their dignity and their true roles in the development of society today. Stimulated by the political challenges which contemporary feminism represented, some writers of women's history, or 'herstory' as it was referred to at one point, tended to celebrate and romanticise women in history, resulting in 'volumes of sketches of great women, descriptions of their country childhood, and tributes to their mothers.'[4]

Feminism embodies two simultaneous processes: a consciousness of the subordinate position in which women are viewed in society; and the actions which those who regard themselves as feminist take to redefine this unequal position. In their earliest attempts to record women's contributions in history, some writers of women's history concentrated on the issue of women's subordinate status. As Linda Gordon observed, feminist historians 'felt impelled to document oppression, diagram the structures of domination, specify the agents and authors of domination, mourn the damages.'[5] Inadvertently they maintained the notion of women as victims of history rather than as active agents. Substituting women for men in history also did not rewrite conventional history. What was seen as the subject matter of conventional history and the methods by which the evidence was retrieved and articulated, remained unchanged for a while.[6]

The development of historiography from a gender perspective has demanded both a theoretical understanding of gender, as well as a notion of how gender works in history. In the last 15 years more complex approaches have begun to emerge, in which the study of one sex as opposed to the relations between the sexes has been questioned. Joan Kelly's essay entitled 'The Social Relation of the Sexes' was written at a period when the feminist debates centred on whether sex, like class, was a social category in which women were seen as comprising a distinctive social group. Kelly's inquiry into a new periodisation for feminist history led her to conclude that an assessment of historical change, in which sex is seen as a social category, should be broadened to include changes in the relation of the sexes. She suggested: 'The activity, power, cultural evaluation of women simply cannot be assessed except in relational terms: by comparison and contrast with the activity, power, cultural evaluation of men, and in relation to the institutions and social developments that shape the sexual order.'[7] Kelly cites a contribution of Natalie Zemon-Davis in support of her argument, a comprehensive statement which deserves full repetition:

> *It seems to me that we should be interested in the history of both women and men, that we should not be working only on the subjected sex any more than an historian of class can focus exclusively on peasants. Our goal is to understand the significance of the sexes, of gender groups in the historical past. Our goal is to discover the range in sex roles and in sexual symbolism in different societies and periods, to find out what meaning they had and how they functioned to maintain the social order or to promote its change.*[8]

Elizabeth Fox-Genovese has also cautioned that adding women to history as either victims or heroines has not challenged the discipline of history itself, but rather has carved out a space for another subject of history, assigning women to the status of the 'other' once more, in historical events which continuously shape the world.[9] Situating this task in the Caribbean context, Bridget Brereton has pointed to the limitations of a separate women's history and the need for understanding the shifts which occur in gender systems. She has observed: 'It is futile to try to pursue woman as an abstracted category, frozen in time, isolated from the great historical developments. There was never any single, uniform system of male dominance or female oppression nor any single gender system: each changes constantly as societies change.'[10] Fox-Genovese has stressed that 'we must adopt gender systems as a fundamental category of historical analysis, understanding that such systems are historically, not biologically, determined' and that 'the forms of male dominance vary historically and cannot be assimilated under the general rubric of patriarchy.'[10] Both Fox-Genovese and Brereton have also emphasised that gender systems are by no means fixed, but vary historically, and that they are continuously being constructed over time.

When we depart from the simplistic use of gender to refer to women, we move to a level of analysis which seeks to answer several fundamental questions: What constitutes gender? How is it to be recognised? Why does it take the form it does? And how does it change over time? What are the component parts of gender? What parts of the society are involved in the construction of gender identity? What parts of the body are implicated in the construction of gender identity? In essence, the question which has perplexed feminists has been the way in which masculinity and femininity — gender identity — is constructed out of biological sex and birth and how one's gender identity continues to be shaped by economic, political, social, psychological and cultural factors.

The ongoing conceptualisation of gender in feminist thought has involved an analysis of its relationship to sex and sexuality. The word sex has two connotations, one the biological base of gender, the other the colloquial use of the word which refers to an activity, not a person, hence the derivative term sexual relations which will be employed alongside that of gender relations in this article. The colloquial dimension of sex was very quickly dropped from feminist theory. Gerda Lerner suggests that the widespread public use of gender was 'probably due to it sounding a bit more "refined" than the plain word "sex" with its "nasty" connotations.'[12] Joan Scott also noted that gender has become a particularly useful word as studies of sexuality have mushroomed, as it offers a way in which sexual practice could be differentiated from the social roles assigned to men and women.[13]

The use of sex as the biological determinant of masculinity and femininity created immediate problems in feminist theory, as it placed greater emphasis on the biological and psychological features than on the cultural and social factors in shaping gender identity. Feminism was perhaps too easily dismissive of the arguments emerging from the school of biological determinism, for the shift to social and cultural determinants de-emphasised the importance of the relationship between sex and gender. The problem therefore with the conceptual shift from sex to gender, is that while sexuality[14] and sexual relations have been acknowledged as part of gender relations, they have not been sufficiently theorised or understood as involved in the process of the construction of gender identities.

Instead of making a distinction between sex and gender, Gayle Rubin employs the term 'sex/gender system' and describes this as 'a set of arrangements by which the biological raw material of human sex and procreation is shaped by human, social intervention and satisfied in a conventional manner.'[15] Even if we begin to think in terms of a definition of gender which is not framed in oppositional categories of masculine versus feminine, sex versus gender, such a definition still contains the notion of 'sexual difference'. Philosophically one can argue that it is not one's sex but sexual differences which create this skewed hierarchy between male and female positions in society. But the fact that it is the difference derived from sex and the sexual which is appropriated to create and maintain an ideology of difference and a skewed hierarchy, gives rise to further questions. Sexual difference is deeply embedded in subterranean aspects of a culture, in mythology and rite, thus least amenable to easy change. It is for that reason that contemporary feminist thought has not dealt sufficiently with the relationship between sex and gender. The idea of sex (as activity), sexual symbolism and imagery, are included implicitly, rather than explicitly, in the various definitions of gender. Through feminist initiatives, the area of sexuality has become a respectable area to research, and the amount of empirical data and theory which now exists on the subject is formidable. Yet for all our understanding, the area still remains elusive, not surprisingly, as Jeffrey Weeks has pointed out, 'The more expert we become in talking about sexuality, the greater the difficulties we seem to encounter in trying to understand it.'[16]

Michel Foucault's contribution to our understanding of sexuality has somewhat revolutionised the study of the subject and allowed us to see sexuality itself as an historical construction rather than as natural libido arising from biological urges "yearning to break free of social constraint". Rubin writes of Foucault's work on sexuality that 'he emphasises the generative aspects of the social organisation of sex rather than its repressive elements by pointing out that new sexualities are constantly produced.'[17] And he points to a major discontinuity between kinship-based systems of sexuality and more modern forms. Thus sex, sexuality and sexual relations must also be examined with historical specificity. For instance, what was perceived as socially acceptable sexual behaviour for a woman of the middle class in nineteenth-century England is vastly different from that allowed at the end of the twentieth century.

This means that both sex and gender as historical categories must be examined in context. As Joan Scott observes, we must consider it

> *a historical phenomenon, produced, reproduced, and transformed in different situations . . . The story is no longer about the things that have happened to women and men and how they have reacted to them; instead it is about how the subjective and collective meanings of women and men as categories of identity have been constructed. If identities change over time and are relative to different contexts, then we cannot use simple models of socialisation that see gender as the more or less stable product of early childhood education in the family and the school'.[18]

The process by which gender identities change over time is the cumulated result of shifts in ideological thinking about men and women by men and women. Men and women shape and define each other;

masculinity and femininity are categories which exist not only in opposition, but also in relation to each other.

Teresa de Lauretis, a feminist thinker in the school of post-modern feminism, has demonstrated how gender can be conceived of as a process of construction and thus how gender identity is continuously being reconstructed. De Lauretis attempts to theorise gender beyond 'sexual difference' and opposition, which she says have come to impose severe constraints on feminist thought. She approaches the construction of gender identity by using the method which Michel Foucault employed in developing his theory of sexuality, and which he referred to as the "technology of sex"[19], proposing that it is equally possible to apply Foucault's genealogical method to developing a "technology of gender". In explanation, de Lauretis makes several crucial contributions which illuminate the ongoing process of how gender is at work in society, and also how gender identity is simultaneously being constructed and deconstructed. She writes:

> The construction of gender is the product and the process of both
> representation and self-representation . . . The ambiguity of gender must be
> retained — and that is only seemingly a paradox . . . The construction of
> gender through its representation goes on today as much or more than in any
> other times . . . Paradoxically, the construction of gender is also effected by its
> deconstruction.[20]

Thus we have a notion of the construction of gender identity as an ongoing process, creating, shifting or recreating new gender systems. By seeing gender as both a process of representation (how accepted gender stereotypes are presented) and self-representation (how gender is represented in practice), de Lauretis makes a break with earlier thought which tended to view women primarily as victims of a patriarchal contract determined to keep them in subservience. In other words, patriarchy does not only exist as a concrete set of rules and regulations which confine women to a secondary status, but it is also dominant as an ideology in the perception and interpretation of gender relations for both sexes, thus reinforcing its hegemony over thought and action.

De Lauretis's technology of gender has two major weaknesses, especially for an understanding of the construction of gender and creation of identity under various historical periods or social circumstances. The weight placed on the possession of a feminist or gender consciousness, which could only have been derived from decades of feminist thought and struggle, diminishes the power of the analysis. The first assumption is that as human beings, men and women have a great deal of control over their construction of gender identity in any given time or space. Secondly, gender identity is perceived as somehow being pre-eminent over other dimensions of identity such as class and ethnicity, all of which, to use de Lauretis comment on gender, 'go on as busily today as they did in earlier times.'[21] While she is not unmindful of the fact that we are made up of multiple identities which coexist and may do so in contradiction to each other at one and the same time, her 'technology' of gender does not explicitly convey the fact that one's class and/or ethnic identity may be determinant factors in one's gender identity.

The problem of the feminist historian, therefore, is to discover how hierarchies of gender, like those of class, are constructed and legitimised under any historical period; how they vary by ethnic or racial group and are consciously being contested by individuals, institutions or structures. The implications of the discussion above are that both sex and gender must be viewed with historical specificity, and that we must see gender identities as continuously undergoing construction and deconstruction and forming new gender identities and new gender systems. In writing gender into history and employing gender as a category of historical analysis, we must view the construction of gender as a process operating at both the individual and collective levels and involving both material and ideological shifts.

The concept of negotiation in gender relations

The idea of 'patriarchal bargaining' suggested by Deniz Kandiyoti provides a critical point of departure from the accepted understanding of gender in terms of opposed sexual difference or as fixed non-malleable identities. Kandiyoti has supplied a tool of analysis which offers a way out of the impasse of de Lauretis's thought. She proposes a method by which women can deal with the patriarchal contract which they view as a fact of life. Kandiyoti interrupts the pessimistic grip of patriarchy on feminist thought by illustrating two active aspects of the concept. Firstly, while in general feminism has worked with a notion of classic patriarchy — the overarching rule of the father, the subordination of younger men by older men, the control which older women have over younger women and so on — she concludes from her analysis of concrete examples that the 'material bases of classic patriarchy crumble under the impact of new market forces, of capital penetration in rural areas.'[22] Secondly, Kandiyoti argues that while the patriarchal contract still influences women's gendered subjectivity and determines the prevailing gender ideology, women themselves 'strategise within a set of concrete constraints that reveal and define the blueprint of what I will term the patriarchal bargain of any given society, which may exhibit variations according to class, caste and ethnicity'. She concludes that 'patriarchal bargains are not timeless or immutable entities, but are susceptible to historical transformations that open up new areas of struggle and renegotiation of the relation between genders'.[23]

I have introduced, as Kandiyoti has done, the idea of a negotiation with patriarchy. The concept of negotiation, however, offers scope for different and more expansive configurations. This process is not only confined to a negotiation with patriarchy, but also to the negotiation of a new gender system, in which the patriarchal contract is being rewritten and in which the construction of new gender identities is taking place. The use of the term 'negotiation' is innovative in the feminist vocabulary. It first occurred to me in terms of a commonsense understanding of how people actually live their daily lives, but subsequently I found an application of the idea in Phyllis Rose's *Parallel Lives*. Rose recounts the life stories of five famous Victorian marriages 'as unsentimentally as possible, with attention to the shifting tides of power between a man and a woman joined, presumably for life.'[24] Admittedly, 'negotiation' brings to mind trade union bargaining, or even the class struggle, but in the case of gender relations, especially those being negotiated at the societal level, these negotiations are not geared towards the abolition of one sex because both have expressed needs of each other.[25]

The problem with negotiation is that it implies a rational rather than accretional process, in fact it hints at a cohesive rationality which many aspects of gender relations do not possess. But we must immediately conceive of a different setting for these negotiations, with different actors. It is not about sitting over a table in a conference room confronting each other. It is the compromises, the arguments, the conflicts in the domestic sphere which get ironed out over days of not speaking to each other. It is carried out in the wider society through legislation, media debates, representations of masculinity and femininity in popular culture, or it may be perceived in other organised or unorganised forms of female or male resistance. One can draw from experience to realise that these are the ongoing processes at work in most societies each day.

The negotiation of gender relations incorporates several dimensions. First is the idea that the negotiations are never static, but are always ongoing. Given that these negotiations are about gender relations and the construction of gender identity, they invariably start from basic premises about masculine and feminine roles in the specific class and culture, and from the knowledge of a system of gender relations, which in general, is familiar to all parties concerned. Thus one can theorise that negotiations in gender relations involve collusions, compromise and accommodation, resistance and subversion, between men and women, between individuals and institutions. We must see collusion, compromise and accommodation as part of the construction of gender identities, retaining many of the features from a gender system with which people are comfortable or familiar. Some of these may seem oppressive to those outside a particular class or ethnic group, but have their own internal rationale. For instance, the practice of polygamy among some tribes in

Africa may appear abhorrent to adherents of Christianity who promote monogamy.

Secondly, where do these negotiations take place in society? There is a subdivision here. Negotiations in gender relations can take place at the individual level where men and women, men and men or women and women, work out their own gender boundaries and norms, in the privacy of their homes, bedrooms or in their workplaces or social gatherings. This level of negotiations I shall term for purposes of analysis the micro-level. But there is also an ongoing set of negotiations being carried out at the cultural or aggregate level, where what is being negotiated are new components in the existing system of gender relations. For example, when a public debate is held about the passage of legislation which affects the rights of women, we see an instance of a negotiation carried out at a collective level. This level of negotiation involves a macro-level institution of the state, which often reflects the prevailing dominant ideology — and therefore the cultural structures which provide the accepted framework for masculinity and femininity. These include norms, laws, ways of seeing, structures of emotion, caste, politics, and religion, and they are above the individual man or woman. We are born into and grow with greater or lesser discomfort in such structures. Very rarely can we change them, and if we do it is hardly ever as individuals.

What is the relationship between the two levels: the individual and the institution, the micro and the macro? I argue that the sources of power in each sphere are differently allocated to men and women. Thus, for example, within the household and family, women appear to have more power, and negotiate within the frame of reference provided by household relations. As childbearers and child-rearers, their knowledge of children may give them greater bargaining power for themselves and for benefits on behalf of their children. On matters pertaining to religion, politics, and a wider social interaction with society, which has not been expected to be in women's knowledge, men have greater influence and through institutionalised frameworks such as religion and politics they have historically made decisions about women's well-being.

But how do the negotiations at the micro-level affect those at the macro-level? The rise of the women's movement in the 1960s and 1970s in the United States is a good example of how individual actions can and do affect the structural, not unlike termites eating away at the foundation of a building which must cause it to crumble. In the 1960s the expressed dissatisfaction of many individual women in homes, offices, universities, and so on, coalesced into a national organised women's movement, and collectively emerged in a slogan whose ideological message, 'The personal is political', was to have tremendous influence on many women in different societies. This came about from the attempt to arrive at new gender identities.

The theoretical formulation of the concept of negotiation is being articulated at two levels, therefore, which are connected. While institutions are built as a result of the accumulated decisions made by individual men and women, by history, by other metaphysical and material demands, there is a continuous dialectical relationship between individual action and group or community concerns. Theoretically, the relationship between the micro and macro disallows the tendency to 'reify subjectively originating antagonism between males and females as the central fact of gender'[26] and allows instead a focus on questions of how gender systems are formulated and reproduced. This approach to the explanation of structural change is supported by Christopher Lloyd, who points out that:

> Society is a macro structure that endures, has powerful effects, and is partly opaque to common-sense knowledge. But it also changes due to social actions and their mental/cultural antecedents. It cannot change spontaneously . . . In order to construct a viable approach to social change, therefore, it is essential to have a general theory of the dialectical interrelationships of the micro and macro 'moments' of the social totality (personality, consciousness, action, culture and social structure) and 'levels' of macro structure (economy, politics, state, culture, geography).[27]

The dialectic of negotiations assumes that there is no easy acceptance for desired changes and that there will be counter-attacks from those who actively seek to keep the patriarchy intact. Gender construction as a process is therefore a complex mix of material and mental factors; it is not stationary, nor is it uni-dimensional, and the multiple identities — class, ethnicity and gender — which men and women are comprised of, are being fashioned simultaneously, each interacting with the other. Women therefore have to constantly negotiate under a dominant patriarchal ideology for a position of greater equality. We need not see this in terms of present-day feminist consciousness of equality, but rather as a human response of rebellion when other less oppressive options are possible. Thus this negotiation may be viewed primarily as seeking greater freedoms of one kind or another within the confines of a patriarchal ideology. If these new ideas are inimicable to the traditional patriarchal contract, then those who are most threatened by its erosion will obviously find ways in which to quell resistance and subversion. Those threatened may include not only men but women of a particular class or age group.

An implicit assumption of the concept of negotiation is that there is power to negotiate. Thus one must be able to describe the nature of this power with regard to gender relations and to demarcate, if possible, what these sources of power are and how they are used as barter by men and women. Kate Young observes: 'One of the basic premises of feminism is that the relation between men and women is essentially a power relation in which, in the majority of societies known to us, women have less power than men.'[28] Marxist analyses suggested that power was structurally encoded in institutions, ideological superstructures and laws, and was part of an all-embracing system of relations dominated by the interests of capital. This approach revealed that both men and women were victims of some more encompassing forms of power, and within this was located the double oppression of women, in the family, through a sexual division of labour which appropriated female labour for the interests of capital, and through their sexuality and reproduction which ensured that they remained within the confines of a 'protective' male power.[29]

The nuances of power in gender relations are best understood through Michel Foucault's work. Quite early in his thinking he pointed to the elusiveness of the concept of power and to its many functions:

> *Power would be a fragile thing if its only function were to repress, if it only worked through the mode of censorship, exclusion, blockage and repression . . . . . If on the contrary, power is strong this is because, as we are beginning to realise, it produces effects at the level of desire — and also at the level of knowledge . . . .. The fact that power is so deeply rooted and the difficulty of eluding its embrace are effects of all these connections.*[30]

If patriarchal power in gender relations functioned only to repress, then the history of women in society would be one of a continuous slide into greater and greater oppression.

Foucault was attempting to derive a definition of the concept of power which would be useful in the analysis of social relationships. In this respect his disembodying of the power residing in a perceived omnipotence of the state is useful here. He argues that the state, like other relations of power, 'can only operate on the basis of other, already existing power relations. The state is superstructural in relation to a whole series of power networks that invest the body, sexuality, the family, kinship, knowledge, technology and so forth.'[31] Joan Scott brought all these issues into focus in her second proposition of a definition of gender when she states that '. . . gender is a primary way of signifying relationships of power'.[32]

In other words, I am asking, as Joan Scott has done, how significations of gender and power construct one another and how things change. The legitimising function of power can work in many ways: Fox-Genovese and Scott's theories conclude that how gender and power are interconnected and construct each other can only be determined by examining the specific historical circumstances in which these relationships are functioning. Nor is it wise to assume that there is always an immediate or direct connection between the power relations immanent in sexual difference and the state. Scott observes that the relationship between the state and power in sexual relations 'make little sense in themselves; in most instances the state had nothing immediate or material to gain from the control of women . . . Gender is one of the recurrent references by which political power has been conceived, legitimated, and criticised. It refers to but also establishes the meaning of the male/female opposition'.[33]

There is also the idea of a dominant ideology of a gender system which is wielded by those in positions of public power or authority (in religion or education, for example) and which is established as the normative base on which the gender system is premised. It is important to consider who determines the dominant knowledge of gender, for this feeds into the negotiations of all gender systems in the same country at the same time. For instance, it may reside in the authority of religion or the state institutions. The power of such institutions is that of the repression of individual actions which are outside the accepted norm, which itself is decided by tradition and upheld by a set of patriarchal rules.

In those instances of power, as for instance economic or political power, in which men are in general the main actors, we can find much clearer and direct lines between who presumably holds power, what kind of power is held and how it operates. The nuances of power in gender relations are far more difficult to locate as the ideology surrounding gender relations comes in a gift-wrapped package — notions of love, reciprocity, partnerships. It is difficult to separate where simple power ends and abuse begins, for instance, or what are the sources[34] of power most utilised in gender relations and in the construction of gender identities. An important corollary must be stated in examining the impact of power on gender relationships. In human society men and women have always expressed that need for each other, in pursuit of the larger goal of the preservation of the species. Power in this instance should not be perceived as an abstract, ephemeral thing, or in negative terms as portrayed in the cliché, 'the battle of the sexes', but should be viewed as a consciousness and a resource which can be brought to bear on the process of negotiation. Power can be viewed as the resources, strengths and consciousness which men and women are possessed of differently as a result of their different relationships to production and reproduction, and which each can exercise in the arena of sexual and gender relations in the development of human society.

How do these theoretical propositions translate into a method for writing gender into history? The fundamental question is what are the spheres of negotiation in gender relations under particular historical circumstances. Initially, this approach allows for a consideration of how women's resources and strengths have challenged the dominant order. This analysis, however, is not only confined to increasing women's visibility in history, but also allows for a continuous redefinition of concepts of femininity and masculinity in society. For instance, Lucille Mathurin Mair in her examination of women fieldworkers in Jamaica during slavery, observes that: 'Motherhood with its biological and customary social applications is frequently perceived as a conservative force which imposes constraints on female activism. It became, however, in this instance, a catalyst for much of women's subversive and aggressive strategies directed against the might of the plantation.'[35] Mathurin Mair describes how women not only deliberately depressed fertility, thus frustrating the planter's hopes for a self-reproducing labour force, but also withheld their labour and that of their children at crucial periods on the plantation. She notes: 'By their actions during slavery and apprenticeship, they placed themselves in the very eye of the storm of Jamaica's post-emancipation crisis'.[36]

Blanca Silvestrini analyses women's resistance to capitalism and multinational corporations in the first half of the twentieth century in Puerto Rico. She points out that women faced the new forms of capitalist growth in distinct ways from men, moving into factories before them. She writes:

> *Subordination was enforced in powerful ways by the capitalist organisations that moved to the island, the local intermediaries that facilitated their enterprises, and the bureaucratic apparatus at their service. Women looked inside themselves to resist the many incongruities involved in the new changes . . . They clung to traditional ways of understanding family and community relations, sexuality, language, education, and health among other things. At the same time they dared to speak, to break their silence, looking to other women's groups for support and action, and in many cases breaking into the ranks of political and labor organisations.*[37]

Both Silvestrini's and Mathurin Mair's contributions to 'herstory' of Caribbean women provide valuable insights and data on sites where Caribbean women have constantly forged new gender identities.

To fully exploit this new approach, however, we need also to investigate the dialectic inherent in the study of gender relations. If we ask what were the sites for accommodations, subversions, resistances and collusions of women in gender relations, then we need also to pursue the organised and unorganised resistances of the male patriarchy. What were the institutions or ideological instruments which ensured the persistence of patriarchy, as for example, areas of mythology, popular culture, religious doctrine and so on? And crucially in the process of negotiation, what were the sources of power which women had at their disposal to subvert or resist male control when there was a wider patriarchal contract at stake? For historians interested in using gender as a category of historical analysis and seeing this as a process in history, the theoretical considerations raised in the idea of a negotiation of gender relations provide both searching questions as well as tools for analysis. The methods by which this is carried out will vary for each historian and will also depend on the availability of data on the period being researched. Only repeated applications of this approach to writing gender in history will reveal its validity.

The spheres of negotiation between Indians in Trinidad, 1917–47

The final section of this article briefly illustrates the application of gender analyses to the study of the social history of post-migrant Indians in Trinidad from 1917 to 1947.[38] The study examines how a new system of gender relations was negotiated between Indian men and women, informed by the system which was left behind in India and the conditions in the new society which either facilitated or prevented change.

The system of indentured Indian labour introduced to Trinidad by the Crown Government began in 1845 and lasted for over 70 years. In 1917, when the transportation of indentured labourers was brought to an end, 143,000 Indians[39] had been taken from India[40] to Trinidad. Those who relinquished their right to repatriation and those who were born in Trinidad entered another phase of their history in this society. Trinidad was now their permanent home. From the time the indentured migrants chose to remain in Trinidad rather than to be repatriated at the end of their indentureship, they began the process of forging an Indian community in this new setting. The negotiations among Indian men and women, and between Indian men and women and the rest of the society, were carried out in the context of the consolidation of a largely impoverished group of migrants in a setting which may or may not have been hostile to them, but in which they felt and in fact were 'different'.[41] The construction of community was synonymous with the affirmation of ethnic identity in the new setting.[42]

Gerad Tikasingh's research reveals that the period 1870–1900 saw the emergence and establishment of an Indian community in Trinidad, 'the transformation of the Indians from a mere category of immigrants into a community.'[43] This process was both an economic and social one. First was the movement of Indians from essentially immigrant wage labourers in the export sector into a peasant proprietorship, and parallel with this was the social evolution of community as the Indians withdrew from estates into villages and here naturally attempted to reconstitute their known institutions and methods of social organisation, some of which had to be adapted to the new environment, others failing to survive.[44] Studied from a gender perspective, community can therefore be defined in terms of ethnicity and gender identity, both of which were interlocked in the affirmation of this emerging Indian community.

The period during indentureship was not characterised by sexual rivalry or intermarriage between Africans and Indians. However, from 1900 onwards this was no longer a dormant issue. Tikasingh reported that in 1901 'it was probably true that there was no intermarriage between Negroes and Indians,'[47] but by 1917 this had become another contentious issue in the struggle to preserve racial purity. The Indian men who were at the forefront of this national struggle were quite open about this, as seen in F.E.M. Hosein's exhortation to Indian men to marry within their race. Hosein lamented:

> *the growing tendency of cultured Indian gentlemen whom the impact of western influence has captivated to such an extent that they consider it the highest piece of wisdom to seek as suitable life partners ladies of a higher hue and of different race. . . . . Intermarriage in this Colony between Indians and others is becoming a social evil which must react on race.*[46]

The spectre before Indian men was the loss of a separate Indian identity, one which was linked to the notion of ethnic purity. This fear could only have been founded on new patterns in gender relations being recognised among both the male and female Indian population. As spokespersons for the Indian community, men were actively against racial miscegenation. For the Indian patriarchy this required control of their women in the various spheres of life.

What was the patriarchal contract in Trinidad in 1917? There coexisted three patriarchal systems simultaneously in Trinidad at this time, all competing with each other. These were: the dominant white patriarchy which controlled state power as it existed then; the 'creole' patriarchy of the Africans and the mixed group, functioning in and emerging from the dominant white group; and the Indian patriarchy found among the Indian population.

How did these three systems interact, and why did they affect the consolidation of an Indian community? I am proposing that there was a hierarchy to be found among these three coexisting patriarchal systems, and that Indian men found themselves at the bottom. They were still largely agricultural labourers, even though they had already begun to establish themselves as landowners and peasant farmers. They had just entered the arena of national political struggles, and only now began to produce a significant crop of educated or professional men who could compete evenly for resources on the wider social scale. Among the Indian population, both an idea of a dominant system and a group of men who presented these ideas were emerging in Trinidad by 1917, in the form of religious leaders, educated men and large landowners or entrepreneurs. They also epitomised a patriarchal dominance over Indian women. The records have substantiated a clear division between public and private spheres: Indian women were largely absent from the public records as mouthpieces of the Indian community.

The patriarchal contract was that of a competition between males of different racial groups, each jostling for power of one sort or the other — economic, political, social, and so on. In the face of the hegemony of the white and 'creole' population, and the increasing struggle on the part of the black and Indian populations to assert themselves, the contest was for a definition of masculinity between men of different races. For Indian men, this involved, as well, a retrieval of their masculine pride from the demeaned status it had suffered during indentureship, in which their classic patriarchy had suffered a severe dislocation. A consolidation of the traditional patriarchal system brought from India would place them in a better position to compete in the patriarchal race. The question is why a consolidation of an Indian patriarchy was so important to the Indian community as a whole.

The answer can be sought in the conditions which affected all Indians, male and female, despite their internal divisions by language, religion, caste and area of origin. It was important for the Indian community to constitute itself in Trinidad, since it was only now emerging from the derided positions it had been in during the system of indentureship. The symbolic boundaries which comprise community among migrants can very rarely be articulated in discrete categories as they emerge alongside and in conjunction with other struggles in the same society. In Trinidad the boundaries of a gender system based on the classic patriarchy from which Indians had emerged, became one of the significant markers which identified the difference of the Indian community from others in the society. Thus it was important for the Indian male to re-establish in the new society a system of power relations between the sexes which clearly reinforced the old patriarchal order: male dominance and female subservience.

It must be noted that the patriarchal bargaining between Indian men and women bears no direct relationship to the state's interest in this group of migrants. Under the system of indentureship, while the colonial state may have wielded a larger power over the community as a whole, as both Indian men and women were pawns in the chess game between capital and labour, the state continuously made adjustments to deal with the specific gender system which existed in the Indian community. For instance, although the legal system was comprised of magistracy by districts, it was accepted by the colonial legal system that the village *panchayat*[47] would have jurisdiction over some types of problems, especially those pertaining to sexual relations between men and women. In fact the broader spectrum of power in so far as it relates to gender relations were those articulated between a male/male patriarchal contest among different racial groups of men, and overriding these was a dominant ideal of gender relations prescribed by the ruling class which was comprised still of a European bourgeoisie. The primary negotiation was that between Indian men and women confined within their own patriarchal boundaries, while contending with the influences of the wider society.

During the period of indentureship the majority of Indians under contract had lived in barracks on the estates. In the post-indentureship period, villages and communities were reconstituted, and with this came the re-emergence or consolidation of many of the customs and traditions which had been brought from India. In this period the sex ratio had not evened out. Women were therefore important both to the physical reproduction of this group as well as the reproduction of ritual, part of which was indisputably female: their relegation to the domestic sphere had made them vital to some aspects of this culture, as for instance the cuisine. For all of these reasons it was necessary for a masculine assertion of power in Indian gender relations, and for a masculine definition of the Indian community to emerge clearly in the contestation of patriarchy in the wider society of Trinidad.

The original function of the kinship systems in India was to organise and control production and reproduction. This was carried out in the context of a defined gender system which regulated sexual activity within marriage. The legacy of kinship systems is that they constantly reproduce themselves, and the traditional gender systems are expected to be observed rather than those which are continuously emerging out of new material conditions by which society is governed as it changes. These legacies are not easily discarded, since procreation is necessary for human survival. But human society and the existential needs of men and women are constantly changing, such that male/female relations acquire additional functions to that of procreation, control of reproduction, exchange of resources, and so on. In the situation in which post-migrant Indians found themselves in Trinidad, in which they felt threatened by another culture, certain areas became defined as more important. Certainly, one would expect that the threatened group would tighten its hold on the most endangered aspects. Thus, it was necessary to re-establish rules which had governed the kinship and gender systems, in order to ensure the physical and cultural survival of the group. These rules upheld the preservation of a masculinity and femininity and a patriarchal order which both sexes were familiar with and which they would deem important for the continuity of Indian culture in Trinidad.

Some of the negotiations between men and women involved a great degree of collusion by Indian women with the classical patriarchy brought from the Indian subcontinent. From 1917 onwards, with the movement of Indians to peasant proprietorship, there were crucial concerns which impinged on gender negotiations and required other areas of compromise and accommodations between men and women. There were important areas of life to consolidate. Houses had to be built, food had to be grown, surpluses for the education and welfare of children had to be accumulated. In addition some migrants were India-born, some were first or second generation Indians socialised into the gender roles and norms which again being regulated by institutions such as religion, the *panchayat*, and, most of all, the emergent family forms as they were being reconstituted. The constitution of the Indian community in Trinidad required the co-operation between men and women in reconstructing homes and villages and the re-establishment of kinship rules. It is possible to understand that Indian women would also collude with many of the patriarchal norms being introduced by the dominant male Indian patriarchy, in which women were still viewed as subservient and passive creatures within a male-ordered world. Sheila Rowbotham observes that our need as human beings, whether male or female are 'not determined by our gender alone'.[48] Women were not indifferent to the re-establishment of their familiar culture and they colluded with men to a large extent, building institutions and re-establishing norms which appeared, to other groups in the society, to be particularly oppressive. For instance, child marriages were arranged by both parents, mothers-in-law controlled their daughters-in-law, and sons were still given the best opportunities for advancement in the family.

Both men and women had different sources of power in various areas of life and these were being negotiated each day in different spheres of interaction and at different levels. The economic survival of individual families depended on the joint efforts of man and wife when the extended family system which was part of the old kinship system was not yet in place to buttress their efforts. Thus female labour in the household and in the kitchen garden was an important economic source of power which women possessed, and which men, as a group, may have undervalued publicly but to which they acceded privately in their homes. In addition the economic contribution of women's labour was also vital to the production of surplus value in the Indian community and to the consolidation of male power, thus providing a rationale for further entrenchment of the patriarchal system. Women also possessed a knowledge of cuisine, domestic gardening, ritual practices of not only religion but also child-rearing and childbearing. Men did not have this knowledge simply because their knowledges were different. In such ways women were very important to the constitution of an Indian community in Trinidad and the history of the period 1917 to 1947 illustrates by and large the collusion and accommodations of Indian women in establishing this community in the new society.

Despite this, Indian women were not passive creatures, blindly accepting the oppressive features of the classic patriarchy from the original migrant culture. It is important, therefore, in defining gender in the context of the historical and cultural specificities of Indians and Trinidad in the early twentieth century, to appreciate the nuances of a gender system which did not separate sexuality from gender. Both were closely interlocked. The rules and regulations which governed members of Indian society, their expected behaviours to each other in general and in their sexuality, marriages and family forms, were clearly demarcated in the kinship systems as practised in India. This kinship system functioned in the context of a patriarchal system which regulated sex and sexuality within a closely controlled gender system. Within this system, sex as an activity did not exist out of marriage, and neither young men nor women had a choice in the matter. Their spouses were chosen for them by their male kin. For Hindus especially, the choice of marriage partner was carried out within the framework of another very tightly knit system which regulated all aspects of life, from birth to death: the caste system. Marriages were arranged only between persons of a similar caste. Monogamy was incumbent on women, while men had the option of remarriage on the death of their spouse. Fertility was an important signifier of feminine identity and female reproduction was closely controlled. The virginity of young girls was highly guarded.

Migration to Trinidad over a period of 70 years involving mostly single males or females, had created a major disruption in the kinship rules which before had been observed by both sexes. The newly formed society of Trinidad, peopled by diverse ethnic groups and dominated by a western culture, clearly did not provide a substitute kinship or family system to which Indians would easily assimilate. In their initial settlement into the new society it was expected that they would attempt to recreate the kinship and gender systems with which they were familiar. But in Trinidad, while a kinship system was being re-established, this was already gradually shifting from its rigid control over female (and male) sexuality to respond to conditions which Indian men and women encountered in the different 'Western' setting.

Significant modifications had already occurred in the pattern of gender relations among Indians during the period of indentureship. The system of indentureship had attracted many more males than it did females and women found themselves a very scarce resource. Along with another fundamental feature of Indian culture and customs which was tampered with in the crossing of the black water,[49] that of the caste system, gender relations immediately underwent a major and rapid transformation. So while some Indian women colluded with men to keep the system intact, other Indian women began to wield a power that they did not and could not possess under the conditions of the dominant gender system which defined life in India. They could and did challenge this system in Trinidad through their new wage-earning status and their sexuality, by moving from one male partner to another when it was in their own interests to do so. Again not without dire consequences, for this also led to violent retaliations on the part of men who had viewed women as personal property.

This investigation of sexual relations and sexuality provides a clue to unearthing the source of power which women in general possess and which Indian women clearly utilised in nineteenth and early twentieth-century Trinidad. A pertinent feature of the indentureship system, which was crucial for gender relations in the post-indentureship period, was an inordinate imbalance of male to female migrants. Table 1 shows the sex ratio of males per 1,000 females from 1891 until 1946, one year before this study terminates. Only by 1946 did the sex ratio in the Indian population in Trinidad begin to approximate a balance. The shortage of female migrants, from the first moment, provided Indian women with the most powerful tool for bargaining in sexual relations: an extreme scarcity of women among a migrant group which was largely averse to miscegenation.

Table 1. Sex Ratios (males per 1000 females) among Indian migrants to Trinidad, 1891—1946

Year	Sex ratio
1891	1,571
1901	1,410
1911	1,354
1921	1,234
1931	1,135
1946	1,066

Source: Jack Harewood, The Population of Trinidad and Tobago, 1975, Table 4H

Writing on conditions during indentureship (1845–1917), Tikasingh has drawn attention to the liberties which women could take at that time.

> Neither polygynous or polyandrous unions existed for long or to any great extent. The prevalent and extensive union was the keeper union, whose stability depended primarily upon the satisfaction of the female partner. For example, Mungaree had such an arrangement with Namoomarlala on Orange Field Estate who had given her $150 in silver and clothes and with whom she lived for eight years. She then went to live with Nageeroc with the understanding that she could return to her former keeper at any time; and at the time of her current court case, she was living with a shopkeeper. As soon as females were ill-treated by their 'papa' as Sarah Morton put it, they were quite ready to break the existing union and form another.[50]

This kind of behaviour and personal choice would have been unthinkable if Mungaree had remained in India. A marriage would have been arranged for her from childhood and, even if dissatisfied with her spouse, she would have been committed to endure this marriage until his death, not even with the option of remarrying then. Her sexuality would have been learnt within that marriage and she would have been confined to one sexual partner for the duration of her life. The disruptions to the gender system in Trinidad, which included radical shifts in sexual arrangements, allowed Mungaree opportunities to challenge this rigid set of rules.

The evidence available on female sexual 'misdemeanours' during and after the period of indentureship suggests that this trend in female behaviour persisted. Around 1915 or so, Batya, an only daughter of India-born parents of the Hindu religion, left the indentured man with whom she had had an arranged marriage. He was treating her badly and so she went to live with a man of African descent, who was then a driver at the McClean Estate in Rio Claro where she was employed. Shortly after, her father, mother, two brothers and her husband, armed with sticks, a flambeaux and a gun, arrived at her new home and called out to her new partner Mr Lewis, a man of African descent: 'We come for Batya.' Mr Lewis put up no resistance. 'Look she here. Come for she nah, look she here. She say she eh coming, I cyar drive she out.' They were unsuccessful that night and later in bringing her back to the fold, for she ceased all contact with her family.[51]

Indian women continued to challenge the traditional expectations of their sex in other ways and evoked mixed responses from males. Due to the shortage of women as well as the contradictions in emotional and pragmatic responses in the sphere of sexual relations, evidence such as the following could be noted in public notices placed by men in the newspaper:

> *Having been accused of ills treatment to my registered wife which she has failed to prove to the satisfaction of the court and no order of maintenance having been made against me in consequence, I beg to notify the public in general that although I am quite willing to receive her, she not consenting I shall have to take legal proceedings, not necessarily against her but against any other person who might harbour her later on, as I have not been cruel to her, nor have I divorced her.*[52]

This is not to suggest that all women were straying from traditional roles expected of them, nor that all men were so easily appeased. In fact the incidence of physical violence and murders of Indian women by Indian men suggests that violence was applied as a major method of control. Yet it is also true that a large number of men were led to take their own lives as a result of such confrontations to their masculinity in the face of their peers.

Indian sexuality was therefore undergoing redefinition in the context of a changing gender system in Trinidad. I have already argued that sex in the traditional system from which Indians had come was largely confined to the institution of marriage as the means of procreation. The method by which this was kept intact was by a system of arranged child marriages. In the new setting, the expression of another sexuality was one of the greatest challenges to the Indian patriarchy. But sexuality was not being redefined apart from the negotiations taking place in other spheres of life, as they all were intimately connected at various levels, and some, as for instance the *panchayat* and the reconstituted family, provided checks and balances on the extent to which any individual could challenge the norm. This challenge in sexual relations involved individual initiatives of change, and could be interpreted in one sense as the negotiation of a new concept of Indian femininity, and possibly masculinity, in the setting of Trinidad.

The examples cited above merely indicate the range of expressions which emerged as sexual arrangements were being negotiated among this group and the threats which were posed by the presence of another race of men who proved to be attractive partners to Indian women. The trajectory for Indian masculinity and femininity was the continued redefinition of sexual identity still framed within a notion of an Indian ethnic identity and the consolidation of an Indian community in Trinidad. While the organisation of the major religions of Hinduism and Islam in the early twentieth century, and the presence of the *panchayat*, could attempt to shape masculine and feminine identities into parallel versions of the Indian sub-continent, the greatest challenge to the received gender system which they sought to put back into place was that encountered in the shaping of sexual identities.

During the period 1917–47 of Indian history in Trinidad, it was the dissatisfaction of individual women with the structured patriarchy in the spheres of kinship obligations and sexual relations, as well as the later benefits of education, which allowed them to challenge the dominant patriarchal tendency, resulting in a redefinition of its boundaries. Indian women had already carried out a 'first negotiation' during the indentureship period, that of an affirmation of their sexual needs and the freedom of choice in partners. In addition, they had come to Trinidad not as dependent females but as wage-earners in their own right, and as such had other resources for bargaining for greater equality within the confines of a gender system.[53] And most importantly, they were not blind or indifferent to the other gender systems around them, thus incorporating new ideas into the map of possibilities for relations between the sexes. If these new ideas were inimical to the traditional patriarchal contract, then Indian men who were most threatened by its erosion would obviously find ways in which to quell resistance and subversion.

Two conditions of Indian women during indentureship — their scarcity as a sex and their wage-earning status — gave them certain freedoms; produced certain effects at the level of desire and knowledge. During the post-indentureship period this would resurface in other ways. During 1917–47, while collusion, accommodation and submission could be read into the actions of the majority of women who built houses and communities with their partners, their resistances could be more clearly seen in those negotiations they undertook for their daughters and sons, thus ensuring change in subsequent generations. For example the education of males used to take pre-eminence over that of females who, viewed primarily in roles of wife and mother, were not given opportunities for education in the earlier period. By the 1940s education had emerged as a major site for negotiation between men and women.

The project of writing gender into history in this instance, therefore, leads to an understanding of how masculinity and femininity, while being reconstituted in a traditional and accepted form, were also undergoing major transformations.

Conclusion

The conclusion towards which this approach to writing gender into history propels us is that gender systems are by no means fixed or immutable, but that they are constantly shifting and changing through each historical period, and with each set of historical circumstances in which men and women find themselves. Gender systems are therefore consistently recreating themselves in different formations over every historical period, persistently defining and reshaping versions of femininity and masculinity, and in fact, all facets of what is considered the purview of a gender system.

The question one might well ask though is how does this approach actually write gender into history. Perhaps it challenges fundamental questions posed by historians of gender relations. What comprises the discipline of history? Who were the main actors in human history and what were their contributions to historical development? What were the major themes with which history has concerned itself and what empirical evidence was considered the data of history? A writing of gender into history brings all of these questions into sharp focus and attempts to refute the traditional boundaries. Though still in its infancy, it seems to me that a history in which sexual inequality and sexual difference are posed as problematic, reveals another lens through which we can view the development of society. By unwrapping gender from the covers under which it has been hidden, we begin to disclose evidence which has hitherto not surfaced. Since gender allows us to make women the primary subjects of our enquiry, it sheds light on the contribution which women have invariably made to the development of a culture. By focusing on areas of life which are considered outside the conventional range of the discipline, we can deepen our analyses of the motors which lead to social change. By unearthing gender as another rhythm in society, we can lend an ear to the different conflicts and preoccupations which both sexes, of necessity, engage in, in the daily business of material existence. Most of all, writing gender into history can, optimistically, further the goal of the feminist struggle, which, in the final analysis, is to demonstrate that sexual difference should not provide a basis for yet another measure of inequality in human society.

Endnotes

1. Joan Wallach Scott, *Gender and the Politics of History* (New York: Columbia University Press, 1988), Introduction, p. 2.
2. Kate Young, 'Notes on the Social Relations of Gender', in Patricia Mohammed and Catherine Shepherd (eds), *Gender in Caribbean Development*, Women and Development Studies Project (Jamaica, Trinidad and Tobago and Barbados: University of the West Indies, 1988), p. 99.
3. Heidi Hartmann, 'The Unhappy Marriage between Marxism and Feminism: Towards a more Progressive Union', *Capital and Class*, No. 8 (1976), p. 138.
4. L. Gordon, 'Rewriting Women's History' in S. Gunew (ed.), *A Reader in Feminist Knowledge* (London and New York: Routledge, 1991), p. 74.
5. Gordon, 'Rewriting Women's History', *op. cit.*, p. 75.
6. This assessment of women's history is not at all meant to be dismissive of the real contribution that historians writing in this field have made thus far. The sheer quantity and approaches to writing women into history are themselves quite impressive. Two essays, Elizabeth Fox-Genovese's 'Placing Women's History in History', *New Left Review*, 133 (May-June 1982) and Olwen Hufton's 'Survey Articles Women in History — Early Modern Europe', *Past and Present*, 101 (1983), review the range of material presented in women's history over the past few decades.
7. J. Kelly-Gadol, 'The Social Relation of the Sexes: Methodological Implications of Women's History', *Signs: Journal of Woman in Culture and Society* (1976), (1) 4:809—23.
8. From an address by Natalie Zemon Davis to the Second Berkshire Conference on the History of Women, October 1975, later published in *Feminist Studies* (winter 1975/76).
9. E. Fox-Genovese, 'Placing Women's History in History', *New Left Review* (1982), 133:5—29.
10. B. Brereton, 'General Problems and Issues in Studying the History of Women' in P. Mohammed and C. Shepherd (eds), *op. cit.*, p. 125.
11. E. Fox-Genovese, 'Placing Women's History in History'.
12. G. Lerner, *The Creation of Patriarchy*, (New York and Oxford: Oxford University Press, 1986), p. 238.
13. Scott, *Gender and the Politics of History*, p. 32.
14. For clarification of its use in this study sexuality is best defined by Jeffrey Weeks in *Sexuality*, Key Ideas Series, Editor Peter Hamilton (Chichester: Ellis Horwood Ltd and London and New York: Tavistock Publications, 1986). He writes that sexuality is a 'historical construction which brings together a host of different biological and mental possibilities — gender identity, bodily differences, reproductive capacities, needs, desires and fantasies — which need not be linked together, and in other cultures have not been . . . but the capacities of the body and psyche are given meaning only in social relations'.
15. G. Rubin, 'The Traffic in Women: Notes on the "Political Economy" of Sex' in R. Reiter (ed.), *Toward an Anthropology of Women* (New York: Monthly Review Press, 1975), p. 165.
16. J. Weeks, *Sexuality*, p. 11.
17. G. Rubin, 'Thinking Sex: Notes for a Radical Theory of the Politics of

Sexuality', in C.S. Vance (ed.), *Pleasure and Danger: Exploring Female Sexuality* (London: Routledge and Kegan Paul, 1984), p. 276.

18. Scott, *Gender and the Politics of History*, Introduction, p. 6.
19. M. Foucault, *The History of Sexuality: An Introduction* (New York: Vintage Books, 1980), Vol. 1.
20. T. de Lauretis, *Technologies of Gender: Essays on Theory, Film, and Fiction* (Bloomington and Indianapolis: Indiana University Press, 1987).
21. de Lauretis, *Technologies of Gender*, p. 3.
22. D. Kandiyoti, 'Bargaining with patriarchy', *Gender and Society* (1988), (2), 3: 274—89.
23. D. Kandiyoti, 'Bargaining with patriarchy', p. 275.
24. P. Rose, *Parallel Lives: Five Victorian Marriages* (UK: Penguin, 1988), p. 13.
25. Two meanings of the word negotiation, as defined in the *Concise Oxford Dictionary* (1988), give another measure as to the way in which it is being employed here. These are 'confer with another with view to compromise or agreement', and 'get over or through obstacle or difficulty'.
26. Scott, *Gender and the Politics of History*, p. 39.
27. C. Lloyd, *Explanations in Social History* (UK: Basil Blackwell, 1986), p. 182.
28. K. Young, 'Towards a Theory of the Social Relations of Gender', London, *Womankind* (1988).
29. M. Barrett, *Women's Oppression Today: The Marxist/Feminist Encounter* (first ed. 1980) (London: Verso, 1988).
30. Colin Gordon, (ed.), *Power/Knowledge Selected Interviews and other Writings 1972—77, Michel Foucault*, (New York: Pantheon Books, 1979), p. 88.
31. Colin Gordon, (ed.), *Power/Knowledge*, p. 122.
32. Scott, *Gender and the Politics of History*, p. 42.
33. Scott, *Gender and the Politics of History*, p. 49.
34. I have introduced the notion of 'sources' of power into the concept of negotiation, in order to get away from the abstractions still evident in Foucault's brilliant insights. It is also based on my conviction that people, men and women, are sometimes very consciously aware of the sources of power which they possess which they can wield over a partner or colleague. For example, in gender relations, a knowledge of someone's emotional dependence on one can be used as a tool for manipulating the other. Economic power is also a major controlling element in gender relations, where in general women are deemed to be dependent on men, although this is not always the case since women's non-wage earning activities are equally important, even if undervalued. But I would also argue though that in gender relations these sources are not necessarily consciously or conspiratorially used.
35. Mathurin-Mair, 'Women Field Workers in Jamaica During Slavery', *The 1986 Elsa Goveia Memorial Lecture*, Department of History, University of the West Indies, Mona, 1987, pp. 11—12.
36. *Ibid.*
37. Silvestrini, 'Women and Resistance: Herstory in contemporary Caribbean History', *The 1989 Elsa Goveia Memorial Lecture*, (UWI, Mona, Department of History, 1990), p. 9.
38. The larger study from which this theoretical framework has been excerpted, analyses, with supporting historical evidence, the spheres of negotiations in gender relations between Indian men and women during the period 1917—47.

This discussion is extracted from a PhD. dissertation 'A Social History of Post-Migrant Indians in Trinidad, 1917—47: A Gender Perspective' (Institute of Social Studies, The Hague, 1994). The statements presented here are therefore summaries of the findings of the larger study which was based on documented histories, archival and oral history research for the period 1917 to 1945 and are not to be interpreted as impressionistic.

39. 'Indian' as used here refers to people who were either born in India or those whose ancestors were from India. It has been the custom in the Caribbean literature to describe this group as *East* Indians to distinguish them from other racial groups in the *West* Indies.

40. The large majority of Indian migrants who were brought to Trinidad came from the United Provinces (Uttar Pradesh) in North India. Where India is referred to, unless otherwise specified, it refers to North India and more directly to those regions from which the migrants originated.

41. To enter another discussion on the 'difference' of Indian culture from a Western culture here takes us into other dimensions of the study which it is not possible to develop fully, but a knowledge of their difference is important to convey when one considers the distinctive differences which existed between Indian culture, an Oriental culture, from that in which they were placed, which was primarily a Western setting.

42. Kelvin Singh's discussion in Chapters 1 and 2 of *Race and Class Struggles in a Colonial State: Trinidad 1917—45*, (Kingston: The Press, University of the West Indies, 1994), published after the completion of this study, serves to confirm the ideas expressed in this extract and in the dissertation that 1917—47 was a period in which there was little cooperation between the different racial groups in Trinidad and that each was involved in consolidating separate communities. His data also support my findings, expressed later in this article, that the Indian community had by 1917 begun to be represented by a group of men who represented the patriarchal front of this ethnic group. In addition, his listings of the various men who represented the other groups all confirm the point I am making here, that the confrontation between the different groups was, at one level, between the competing male patriarchies. Women of all races were nowhere to be seen in these struggles.

43. G. Tikasingh, 'The Establishment of the Indians in Trinidad, 1870—1900', PhD. dissertation, Trinidad, University of the West Indies, 1973.

44. *Ibid.*

45. *Ibid.*

46. F.E.M. Hosein, unpublished paper, 5 October 1928.

47. A council consisting of five male elders chosen from within the community. With the grouping of Indians into villages, the *panchayat* selected by the village or community functioned as arbiters of moral and social conduct.

48. S. Rowbotham, *Women in Movement: Feminism and Social Action*, (London & New York: Routledge, 1992), p. 12.

49. Indians referred to this as *kala pani*, the crossing of the black water which meant that once they had left their towns and villages in India and entered this sea journey they already had tampered with the rigid rules and regulations which governed the caste system, and which defined Indian life from birth to death. This was a fundamental shift in Indian life which would have repercussions in many other areas of life, especially those associated with rules

pertaining to gender. For instance caste endogamy was the rule. In Trinidad, where all castes were already polluted, the ideology of caste was immediately challenged when marriages or alliances on estates broke all caste rules of endogamy.

50. G. Tikasingh, 'The Establishment of the Indians in Trinidad, 1870—1900', p. 270.

51. This information was taken from one of the 65 oral history interviews carried out with Indian men and women in Trinidad as research material for this study. The reference is to be found in Tape 39 among the collection of tapes which is now lodged at the library of the University of the West Indies in St Augustine, Trinidad. For purposes of anonymity, the names of the respondents have been changed.

52. *Trinidad Guardian*, 29 November 1918.

53. Evidence of Indian women's struggles against patriarchy during indentureship can be found as well in Rhoda Reddock's 'Freedom Denied: Indian women and indentureship in Trinidad and Tobago 1845—1917', in *Economic and Political Review: Review of Women's Studies*, (1985), 20 (43): 79—87.

3.

Gender Politics and Imperial Politics:

Rethinking the Histories of Empire

Catherine Hall

There is an urgency in the current political conjuncture for historians of Britain and empire to rethink ways of writing imperial histories. For British historians the urgency comes from the difficult questions which face British society about the meanings now attached to the nation. What identities are possible as members of that imagined community? What ethnicities? What future is there for Britain as a multi-ethnic society?[1] For centuries white British identities, both male and female, have been constructed through sets of assumptions about imperial power in relation to racialised others. Those white identities are now in crisis, and are no longer possible in the same forms. Britain no longer has an empire; she is no longer the first industrial nation and forms of national sovereignty have shifted given the transfer of power to Brussels. Furthermore, the empire has 'come home', in the shape of those decolonised peoples from the Caribbean, from Asia and from Africa who have made their homes in Britain and whose children have been confronted by the difficulties of being black and British.[2]

All this has led to a profound destabilisation of white identities. A strongly negative aspect of this is the political success of the British National Party and the rise in racial violence and racial harassment, which is particularly marked in London. It is concern over the future of white identities, particularly in relation to black, which underpins the current debate on national identity, a term now regularly used by British politicians, and which has provided the backdrop for the discussions over the construction of 'Fortress Europe' whose boundaries are swiftly being put in place to prevent migrants from the East and the South penetrating the prosperous fastnesses of the North.

Historians have an important contribution to make to this debate. It is vital to challenge the ways in which history as a discipline has contributed to the narratives of empire and helped to maintain what Edward Said has recently described as the 'consolidated vision' of imperial culture.[3] In very different ways British historians from Macaulay to Edward Thompson, to current imperial and Commonwealth historians, have maintained unproblematised those white identities which have been so intimately linked to the histories of empire. It is an urgent task now for historians of Britain and empire to be more self-conscious about these issues, to confront the forms of complicity with an assumed white superiority, to engage with the politics of knowledge and to decolonise the discipline. New ways of understanding the history of empire are needed, informed by those traditions associated with decolonisation, with the post-colonial critics and with feminism. An understanding of the place of 'race' and ethnicity in the construction of white men's and white women's identities in the past can facilitate the grasping of those traces of former imperial identities which survive in the present and are a challenge to those contemporary forms and discourses which perpetuate such practices. By taking on the legacy of the past historians can contribute to the project of rethinking the future, imagining white identities which are not rooted in a sense of imperial power and of superiority but in a recognition of difference. The possibility of imagining a multi-ethnic, non-hierarchical community of the future, a new kind of nation, depends on the recognition of the place of empire in the construction of British identities. This means tackling the ways in which the histories of Britain and empire have been mutually dependent. It was the colonial encounter that made both colonisers and colonised, all of whom are subjects of the erstwhile British empire, sharing a common history, all post-colonial subjects, made by the relations of empire, with identities constituted through different relations to colonial and imperial hierarchies of power.

Such histories need to build on the work of theorists of decolonisation such as Frantz Fanon and C.L.R. James. Fanon's radical shift of perspective, his insistence on the margins as sources of knowledge as well as the objects of Western knowledge, his refusal of the history written by settlers, his critique of bourgeois ideology as 'the proclamation of an essential equality between men (which) manages to appear logical in its own eyes by inviting the sub-men to become human, and to take as their prototype Western humanity as incarnated in the Western bourgeoisie', his complex analysis of nationalism and its ambivalent legacies, his recognition of the cultural aspects of colonialism and the struggles which were possible within cultural politics, his focus on the mind of the colonised and the ambivalence of the colonised condition captured in his title *Black Skin, White Masks*, are all insights which have been richly developed since, particularly in post-colonial criticism.[4] C.L.R. James' understanding of black struggle and resistance, connecting as it did to the tradition of Marxist historiography with its focus on consciousness and agency, has been much more easily absorbed by historians and has clearly profoundly influenced the work of black historians in the Caribbean and the USA particularly. So far, however, James's influence on British historians has been extremely limited.

The group best known now as the post-colonial critics, most notably Said, Homi I. Bhabha and Gayatri C. Spivak, have maintained that commitment to the decolonisation of European knowledge and have insisted on the complicity of academic forms of knowledge with institutions of power. Said's most significant achievement, as Robert Young has commented, has been to establish an object of study called 'colonial discourse'.[5] Said's key argument concerns the ways in which the West discursively constructed the Orient. That 'Orient', the imaginative production of the West, provided a crucial weapon in the West's cultural imperialism and was integrally related to economic, political and military forms of imperialism.[6] Said's major intellectual debts have been to Michel Foucault and Antonio Gramsci. Since the publication of *Orientalism*, he has further developed and refined these arguments, taking on some of the criticisms which have been made particularly in relation to the absence of counter-narratives to the hegemonic project of empire, but still holding to a homogenising view of Western discourses which significantly weakens his case.[7]

Bhabha has drawn more directly on Fanon and Sigmund Freud for his inspiration and has taken questions of fantasy to the centre of his project. He has problematised the relation between coloniser and colonised and explored the ambiguities around power, conflict and resistance which lie at the heart of colonial discourse. He is concerned to break down any simple binary opposition between coloniser and colonised and focuses on the different kinds of powers and resistances which are in play in these relations. He explores the discrepant temporalities of the metropolis and the periphery, the ways in which mimicry and exaggeration, for example, express the ambivalent relations of hybridity and 'in-betweenness', spaces which are crucial to Bhabha's thinking. Relations between coloniser and colonised in his thinking are characterised by a deep ambivalence: the other is both an object of desire and derision, of delight and contempt, with the coloniser simultaneously projecting and disavowing difference in an essentially contradictory way, asserting mastery but constantly finding it slipping away.[8]

Like Bhabha, Spivak draws on post-structuralism and deconstruction, but her insights also derive from feminism, particularly third-world feminism. Imperialism is for her a 'subject constituting project' and she focuses on the ways in which different subject positions have been discursively constructed for women and for men, which are instrumental in relations of imperial power. Her discussion of *sati*, for example, explores it as an instance of the ways in which women are caught between two forms of domination, imperialism and patriarchy, and allowed no place from which they can speak. It is not possible, she argues, for the subaltern (a term which she adopts from Gramsci in dialogue with *Subaltern Studies*) to speak authentically, since she is only constituted as a subject through those positions which have been produced.[9] Such a bleak view is modified by Lata Mani, who argues that a careful reading against the grain of such sources as missionary reports and official documents makes it possible to reconstruct woman as subject and restore to the centre elements that are marginalised by these accounts.[10] Spivak also argues that part of the project of imperialism is to refract 'what might have been the absolutely Other into a domesticated Other that consolidates the imperialist self', an insight that can be illuminating in thinking about English nineteenth-century discourses on 'race'.[11]

Feminists such as Spivak and Mani are part of a collective project to rethink imperial relations in a way which takes gender fully into account. By now there is a considerable body of literature in this field, from feminist theorists, writers, critics and anthropologists as well as historians. Much of the work has been inspired by the black feminist critique of white, first-world feminism, and the insistence that recognising and confronting the racisms that permeate everyday life in the West have to be at the heart of developing new forms of feminisms which can speak to different women, in different places, with different cultures and experiences. Black and third-world feminists have themselves been vital in the struggle to provide tools with which to work. Chandra Talpade Mohanty, for example, analyses the ways in which the category of 'third-world woman' has been utilised by white Western feminists and draws attention to the ways in which 'native' women were constructed as narcissistic and self-consolidating others, a pattern with a very long history.[12] Toni Morrison's *Beloved* weaves together lost memories and histories and inspires us to think in new ways about the experience of slavery and its traces in contemporary American society.[13] Audre Lorde's injunction that 'the Master's tools will never dismantle the Master's house' and that white women must learn to think for themselves on the subject of 'race' has echoed across the last decade.[14]

The key feminist contribution to a new understanding of colonialism and imperialism lies in the recognition of the centrality of the gender order to the social, economic and political order. The first wave of feminist historical writing in Britain focused on the effort to put women into the historical frame, to discover the ways in which they had been 'hidden from history', their employment forgotten, their political participation ignored, their 'private' lives left private. In the 1980s the focus shifted for many feminist historians, from an emphasis on the 'discovery' of women to an analysis which centred on the category of gender. Gender emerged as a concept with which it was possible to think about the relations between the sexes, the differential positions of men and women within any society, the power relations that always operate between the sexes as well as between classes and ethnic or racialised groups.[15] Once gender is perceived as a key axis of the relations of power in any society, then the gender dimension of each aspect of those relations becomes a necessary site of historical investigation. Subject positions for men and women are constantly in the process of being constructed, reconstructed and contested.[16]

In the context of colonial history these processes can be traced in the official documents of the Colonial Office, through the records of missionary societies, through an examination of the practices of sugar plantations, or the May meetings of the serious Christians and philanthropists, in the travellers' tales of intrepid male and female explorers. Men and women are positioned as colonisers and colonised, with all the associated complexity and ambivalence, on any colonial site, or any site connected with the domestic consumption of colonialism. Their identities are constructed through a complex articulation of the hierarchies of power associated with class, with gender, with 'race' and with ethnicity. Those articulations are never simple and are frequently in contradictory relations to each other. To take an example, men's power over women, white men's over white women and black women, black men's more limited power over black women, were at the heart of both plantation society and post-emancipation society in Jamaica. The reworking of those forms of power was as central to the vision of a new society as was the renegotiation of the labour relation. It engaged the Colonial Office, planters and missionaries in a complex struggle over the freed peasantry. In the process white identities were being forged as much as black, men's identities as well as women's.

The first imperative of feminist politics — to put women back into the historical frame — has not been displaced, but a further set of questions and issues are now insistently on the agenda. What are the relations between women of different ethnic and racial groups, how are 'race' and gender articulated in specific historical instances, how do those relations of power connect with class hierarchies, how can historical work help in the analysis of the complexities of the post-colonial, and not so post-colonial, world?

Between the abolition of slavery in 1834 and the rebellion at Morant Bay in 1865, both moments at which Jamaica was a subject of central concern in British society and politics, the English 'produced' and imagined Jamaica and its peoples in a variety of ways.[17] In sermons and missionary publications, in novels and travellers' tales, in political pamphlets and speeches, the English represented Jamaica in diverse and contradictory ways. A crucial shift occurred in this period between abolition and Morant Bay, from the hegemony of the abolitionist discourse of universalism — 'Am I not a man and a brother' — to the discourse of racial difference. In the words of Thomas Carlyle, blacks were not black Anglo-Saxons and were born to be mastered.[18] Through an analysis of the changing constructions of 'blackness' and of 'race' in this period, it is possible to investigate the changing meanings of 'whiteness' for men and women of the English middle class, what it meant to be white and to be English, how different that was from being black and Jamaican. A brief example can illustrate how new theoretical insights about colonial relations can be illuminating, how a new historical narrative might begin to be constructed.[19]

In the period after the abolition of slavery and particularly after the ending of apprenticeship in 1838, the Baptist missionaries in Jamaica, who had been intimately connected with the struggle over slavery, were hated by the planters and were powerfully, if ambivalently, identified with freed blacks, recognised that the planters would now use their control over housing to impose a new variety of forced labour.[20] The essence of the 'great experiment' of emancipation for abolitionists was the dream of building a new society based on free labour which would demonstrate that blacks could work like whites, could be like whites. Slavery, in their view, had produced an unnatural phenomenon, male slaves who were entirely dependent on their masters, who could not truly be *men* since the essence of manhood was independence. Emancipation marked the moment at which those previously enslaved could cast off their dependence and learn from the missionaries how to be men — in the image of the middle-class Englishman. That meant being married, being independent in 'pecuniary affairs', working for wages, being a householder, paying for medical care and education, celebrating the voluntary principle which was at the heart of dissenting politics, refusing state intervention in church, school and welfare, becoming 'domesticated Others' who consolidated the imperialist self.

Jamaica offered an exceptional opportunity to carry this vision into effect since there was a weak established church, a strong dissenting presence and a state which had depended on the plantations to provide welfare. The potential for the missionaries lay in the linked moment of emancipation and conversion, for emancipation gave men and women social, economic and potentially political freedom while conversion offered a new life in Christ, the possibility to be born anew as a new man or a new woman. This was the abolitionist dream, that black men would become like white men, not the white men of the plantation but the white men of the abolitionist movement, responsible, independent, industrious, domesticated Christians. The black women would become like white women, not the white women of plantation society locked into their debasing acceptance of concubinage but the white women of the English middle-class imagination, occupying their small but satisfying sphere, married and living in regular households. A new gender order was central to the vision of the abolitionists. In their new Jamaica black men would survey their families with pride, black women would no longer be sexually subjugated to their masters but properly dependent on their husbands.

The Baptist missionaries and their allies in England, realising the continued problems with the planters as they forcibly evicted their tenants and linked wages to rents, decided they would have to turn to dramatic solutions. They began to borrow capital from England and buy up extensive tracts of land in order to establish new villages, free villages, where blacks could live unmolested.[21] Many of the first villages were named after heroes of the anti-slavery movement as well as centres of abolitionist support: thus Wilberforce, Buxton, Clarksontown, Sturge Town, after Joseph Sturge the Birmingham corn merchant and dedicated supporter of emancipation, as well as New Birmingham and Kettering. In 1840 William Knibb, the best known of the Jamaica Baptist missionaries, celebrated these free villages in his speech at the great anti-slavery convention held in London. 'One of them', he reported to the assembled dignitaries of the movement:

> bearing the name of their venerable President Clarkson, another was called Birmingham, and a third they had named Victoria. (Enthusiastic cheers) To show their respect for that esteemed man Joseph Sturge (loud cheers) — they had a town which bore his honoured name, although that was not needed, for it was deeply engraven on every negro's heart. (Renewed cheers).

As Knibb concluded, 'We have the germ of a noble free peasantry.' In his view the results of emancipation should not be judged by the poundage of sugar, 'but by the cottager's comfortable home, by the wife's proper release from toil, by the instructed child'.[22]

The missionaries bought land, they surveyed and laid it out, they superintended the construction of roads and streets, they directed the settlers in the building of their cottages and the cultivation of their grounds, they supplied them with deeds, they married them before they moved in, they educated their children, they formed societies among them for the improvement of agriculture, they gave them — in the words of James Murcell Phillippo, one of the most active of the missionaries — a 'relish for the comforts and conveniences of civilised life, and improved their domestic economy'. They worked to convince 'these simple minded people' that their own prosperity depended on working for moderate wages.[23] The vision was of a society of wage labourers who could supplement their modest earnings with home-grown fruit and vegetables. The plots of land would be adequate for this but not sufficient to support a family. They would, however, be large enough to earn a right to vote so that eventually planter power would be displaced. The women would stay at home, the children would be at the mission school.

At the heart of the vision was missionary influence, symbolised by the church and the mission house standing at the top of the hill, overlooking the village. Through the pulpit and the *Baptist Herald and Friend of Africa* the missionaries and their wives instructed the freed men and women on how to keep their houses clean, how to create a garden which might even sport rose bushes, how to eat as families with sit-down meals at a table provided with clean cloth, knives and forks, how to train their children sexually by making sure boys and girls had separate bedrooms.[24] They were concerned to create a new social order with its gender order firmly in place, a social hierarchy with the white missionary, the patriarchal father, at the apex, then 'his' wife, then 'his' deacons, then the rest of the congregation.

But this vision depended on a white dream which erased black culture. The new world was to have no connection with the 'barbarism' and 'savagery' of Africa, as the missionaries saw it. Myalism and obeah were to be repressed, together with concubinage, illegitimacy and gaudy clothes. When in 1859, however, Edward Bean Underhill, the secretary of the Baptist Missionary Society, went to Jamaica to see how the experiment of emancipation was working and whether the disturbing reports which were reaching England of poverty, of economic failure, of loss of religious enthusiasm, of a decline in morality, were true, he found troubling evidence of superstition and irregularity. Visiting Sturge Town he questioned those he met, 'on their habits, their social condition, what England expects of them, and what is said about them'. He was disturbed to find that the native minister had indeed gone native, he had formed a breakaway chapel which was said to have links with obeahism. Underhill found small congregations, a decline in the number of marriages and a reduction in missionary influence. He returned to England even more convinced of the need for the white missionary presence if civilisation were to develop amongst the blacks.[25]

The free villages represented the missionary fantasy of a good society. That good society was formed in part by the missionaries' displacement from their own society. As dissenting ministers their class position was uneasy, their relation to conventional forms of political power marginal. In Jamaica they glimpsed new possibilities of power. As Knibb put it, 'the whole island had to begin the world at once', for in his vision there was no world as yet.[26] White missionaries and black freedmen could build this new world together, a black society led by white men. The missionary discourse on blacks, like abolitionist discourse more generally, was profoundly ambivalent. The language of familiarism by which it was framed, the universal family of God, provided the perfect rhetoric for such an ambivalence. Phillippo's image of himself as the father of the mission, guiding and correcting his white pastor brethren, instructing his native sons and preparing them for their responsibilities in the future, relying on his wife to do her sisterly and maternal work by his side, provides an eloquent instance of the class, the racial and the gendered hierarchies of abolitionist discourse and the ways in which it could be articulated to the 'consolidating vision' of empire.

Missionary discourse both gave and denied black people equality in the present, while promising it for the future. Missionaries fought for equality before the law and equality in political representation, yet they constructed 'their' people as their children and pupils, learning from them the ways of civilisation. Such a conception was underpinned by deep-rooted assumptions about white civilisation which worked on the premise that the corruption of some whites could be redeemed by the action of others, that a particular version of English 'freedom' must be at the heart of any civilised society. Such a conception jostled in Knibb's own head with his knowledge and experience of both black and white societies. The instability of the missionary identity, caught between two cultures, the interpreter of the one to the other, produced the dream of a third where blacks and whites would live harmoniously in a missionary regime of truth.

Such a dream was built on a fatal flaw, the refusal to recognise an existing black culture. For once established, the free villages could not be maintained in the missionary image. Phillippo's fantasy of his all-seeing, all-regulating, all-supervising hand and eye — buying land, designing houses, marrying parents, educating children — reckoned without the inhabitants of 'his' villages. For they were populated by black men and women and their children, who brought their own culture, shaped by slavery, the middle passage and the plantation, and honed through their encounter with Christianity and with missionaries, to build their own syncretic forms of religion, their own rituals, their own practices, their own Afro-Jamaican way of life.

Missionary understandings of 'the negro' and the 'race' depended on the assumption that 'negroes' who were not Christians were savage and barbaric, whereas those who had been converted and had experienced the discipline of the missionary church, particularly with a white pastor, were new men, respectful, industrious, domesticated, aware of their responsibilities to authority, rightly seeking their political, economic and legal rights as subjects. Their conception of the new black woman was one which focused on marriage, child-rearing and domestic duties and side-stepped the extensive evidence of the failure of marriage to become popular, the high levels of illegitimacy, the incidence of women's labour and of women's importance to patterns of landholding.

These imagined figures of the black man and woman depended on a denial of the different forms of family which were becoming characteristic of black culture, a denial of the different masculinities and femininities which were celebrated, a denial of the place of obeah and myalism in village life, a denial of the syncretic forms which so many black Baptists adopted. But these denials were increasingly built on fears of what lay hidden and threatening to erupt. Since 'Africa' meant only savagery and barbarism, the potential for civilising new black subjects lay in missionary zeal and the hard work of decades. Without whites blacks were locked in the dark and degradation, intellectually at zero, with no memories, traditions or culture to build on.[27]

The significance of the missionary project, to 'colonise the interior'[28] and create a civilisation of a new kind, was overtaken by the emergence of other black identities, articulated most powerfully in the rebellion at Morant Bay. That rebellion shattered the missionary dream and marked the moment at which the language of racial difference, always inflected with classed and gendered meanings, was powerfully re-articulated in Britain. Jamaican black people were no longer 'domesticated Others' who could learn to be 'like us'. Rather they were expelled to the realm of 'absolute other', to be controlled and mastered rather than educated and regulated within a paternalist regime.

Endnotes

1. For the concept of nation as an 'imagined community' see Benedict Anderson, *Imagined Communities. Reflections on the Origin and Spread of Nationalism*, (London: Verso, 1983).
2. In the question of the difficult relation between black and British see Paul Gilroy, *There Ain't No Black In the Union Jack*, (London: Hutchinson, 1987).
3. Edward Said, *Culture and Imperialism*, (London: Chatto and Windus, 1993).
4. Frantz Fanon, *The Wretched of the Earth*, (Harmondsworth: Penguin, 1967); *Black Skins, White Masks*, (London: Pluto Press, 1986).
5. Robert Young, *White Mythologies. Writing History and the West*, (London and New York: Routledge, 1990).
6. Edward Said, *Orientalism*, (Harmondsworth: Penguin, 1985).
7. See particularly *Culture and Imperialism*.
8. Homi K. Bhabha, 'Difference, Discrimination, and the Discourse of Colonialism', in Francis Barker *et al.* (eds), *The Politics of Theory*, (Colchester: University of Essex Press, 1983); 'The Other Question', *Screen*, 24, 6 (1983); 'Of Mimicry and Man: the Ambivalence of Colonial Discourse', October, 28 (1984); 'Signs Taken for Wonders: Questions of Ambivalence and Authority under a tree outside Delhi, May 1817', in Francis Barker *et al.* (eds), *Europe and Its Others*, (Colchester: University of Essex Press, 1985).
9. Gayatri C. Spivak, 'Can the Subaltern Speak?', in Cary Nelson and Lawrence Grossberg (eds), *Marxism and the Interpretation of Culture* (London: Macmillan, 1988); *In Other Worlds*, (London and New York: Routledge, 1992).

10. Lata Mani, 'Cultural Theory, Colonial Texts: Reading Eyewitness Accounts of Widow Burning', in Lawrence Grossberg, Cary Nelson and Paula Treichler, (eds.), *Cultural Studies* (London and New York: Routledge, 1992).

11. Gayatri C. Spivak, 'Three Women's Texts and a Critique of Imperialism', *Critical Inquiry*, 12, 1 (1985), p. 253; and for a historical essay which makes use of this insight see Catherine Hall, 'From Greenland's Icy Mountains . . . to Africa's Golden Sand: Ethnicity, Race and Nation in mid-nineteenth century England', *Gender and History*, Special issue on 'Gender, Nationalisms and National Identities', Vol. 5, No. 2, (summer 1993).

12. Chandra Talpade Mohanty, 'Under Western Eyes: Feminist Scholarship and Colonial Discourses', *Feminist Review*, 30 (autumn 1988); Chandra Talpade Mohanty, Ann Russo and Lourdes Torres, (eds.), *Third-World Women and the Politics of Feminism*, (Indiana: Indiana University Press, 1991).

13. Toni Morrison, *Beloved*, (London: Picador, 1988).

14. Audre Lorde, 'The Master's Tools Will Never Dismantle the Master's House', in Cherrie Moraga, Gloria Anzaldua and Toni Cade Bambara (eds.), *This Bridge Called My Back. Writings by Radical Women of Color* (New York: Kitchen Table Women of Color Press, 1981).

15. For a longer account of this shift in perspective in the British context see Catherine Hall, 'Feminism and Feminist History' in *White, Male and Middle Class: Explorations in Feminism and History*, (Cambridge: Polity, 1992).

16. For an analysis of the centrality of gender to English society in the nineteenth century see Leonore Davidoff and Catherine Hall, *Family Fortunes: Men and Women of the English Middle Class 1780—1850*, (London and Chicago: Hutchinson and Chicago, 1987).

17. The research from which this paper is drawn was funded from 1990 to 1992 by the Economic and Social Research Council, Ref. R000232169.

18. Catherine Hall, 'Competing Masculinities: Thomas Carlyle, John Stuart Mill and the Case of Governor Eyre', in *White, Male and Middle Class*.

19. For a much longer version of the argument which follows see Catherine Hall, 'White Visions, Black Lives: The Free Villages of Jamaica', *History Workshop*, No. 36 (autumn 1993).

20. Mary Turner, *Slaves and Missionaries: The Disintegration of Jamaican Slave Society 1787—1834*, (Urbana: University of Illinois Press, 1982); Thomas C. Holt, *The Problem of Freedom. Race, Labor and Politics in Jamaica and Britain, 1832—1938*, (Baltimore: The Johns Hopkins University Press, 1992); Robert Stewart, *Religion and Society in Post-Emancipation Jamaica*, (Knoxville: University of Tennessee Press, 1992).

21. For secondary sources on the free villages see Sidney Mintz, *Caribbean Transformations*, (Chicago: Aldine Publishing Co, 1974); Swithin Wilmot, 'Baptist Missionaries and Jamaican Politics 1838—54', paper presented at the 12th Conference of Caribbean Historians (April 1980); 'The Peacemakers: Baptist Missionaries and Ex-Slaves in West Jamaica', *Jamaica Historical Review*, Vol. 13, (1982); Alex Tyrrell, *Joseph Sturge and the Moral Radical Party in Early Victorian Britain*, (London: Christopher Helm, 1987); Hugh Paget, 'The Free Village System in Jamaica', *Caribbean Quarterly*, Vol. 10, No. 1 (March 1964); George E. Cumper, 'A Modern Jamaican Sugar Estate', *Social and Economic Studies*, No. 3 (1954).

22. *Anti Slavery Reporter*, 29 July 1840.

23. James Murcell Phillippo, *Jamaica: Its Past and Present State*, (London: John Snow, 1843), pp. 430—31.
24. See, for example, *The Baptist Herald and Friend of Africa*, 15 January 1840, 14 December 1842.
25. Edward Bean Underhill, *The West Indies: Their Social and Religious Condition*, (London: Jackson, Walford and Hodder, 1862), pp. 243, 295, 312, 315—16.
26. *Missionary Herald*, June 1845.
27. Underhill, pp. 315—16.
28. *The Baptist Herald and Friend of Africa*, 14 December 1842.

SECTION TWO

Text and Testimony:

Sources and Methods

for 'Engendering'

Caribbean History

4.

Text, Testimony and Gender:

An Examination of some Texts by Women on the English-speaking Caribbean from the 1770s to the 1920s

Bridget Brereton

In seeking to probe the gender dimension in the history of the Caribbean since European contact, one is largely dependent on documentary evidence generated by men. Whether one relies on official records of different kinds, newspapers and periodicals, correspondence and other materials produced by private citizens, missionaries or travellers, or published accounts by residents and visitors, the sources are mostly written by men.[1] There is little recorded testimony from women. This creates a methodological problem not very different from the issue which has concerned historians of the Caribbean for decades: how to approach the social history of the majority of the region's peoples — Amerindians, Africans and East Indians, creoles of African or Indian or mixed descent — on the basis of evidence largely created by Europeans (expatriate or creole) separated from the majority by deep gulfs of ethnicity, culture (including, often, language and religion) and class. Clearly, documents generated by men will always be crucially important to the reconstruction of the history of women and gender in the Caribbean precisely because they form by far the greatest part of what has survived. But there are a few precious texts by women who recorded their experiences as residents of, or visitors to, the islands. Did these articulate and literate (often literary) women express feminine perspectives on Caribbean society? In short, is there gendered testimony in these female-authored texts? I propose to examine nine such texts, ranging chronologically from the 1770s to the 1920s, and providing evidence from Jamaica, Antigua, St Kitts, Bermuda, the Turks Islands, St Vincent, Barbados and Trinidad.[2]

Five of the authors were women from Britain resident in, or visiting, the Caribbean, with family and social connections with the islands' white elite. Only one, however, was simply a 'tourist' passing through: this was Janet Schaw, an aristocratic and cultured Scottish lady who visited Antigua and St Kitts with her brother in 1774. Maria Nugent, the best known of our authors, was the American-born wife of George Nugent who served as governor of Jamaica in 1801—06, and her journal was written over a period of nearly five years in the island. Elizabeth Fenwick lived in Barbados between 1814 and 1821; she was a well-educated Englishwoman who had gone there to join her married daughter, with whom she ran a successful girls' school. Schaw, Nugent and Fenwick wrote letters to friends, or private journals, not intended for publication (and not in fact published until long after they had died), but Mrs A.C. Carmichael (we do not know her first name) and Frances Lanaghan wrote elaborate and lengthy books published in 1833 and 1844. Carmichael was the wife of a Scottish planter who lived in St Vincent and Trinidad in the 1820s. Her book had a strong polemical element: it was a passionate defence of the planters and of slavery and an attack on the British government's slave policies in the 1820s. Lanaghan's book on Antigua was published anonymously, but the 'Author's Preface' indicates that she was British, that she had 'Antigua connections' and that she had lived there for many years, both before and after 1834.

All these authors bring to their texts a strongly British, and aristocratic (or, at least, upper-middle-class) consciousness. By contrast, Mary Prince, Mary Seacole, Yseult Bridges and Anna Mahase were all Caribbean women, representing the range of ethnic and class diversity found in the nineteenth-century Caribbean. Mary Prince's short text enjoys a unique position in Caribbean historiography. It is the only extant work written by an enslaved woman from the British Caribbean colonies; no comparable account is known to exist. Prince was the first African-Caribbean woman 'to write an autobiography and a polemic against slavery'. She was born a slave in Bermuda around 1788, and worked in Bermuda, the Turks Islands and Antigua, before coming with her owners to Britain in 1828. In London she walked out of slavery and made contact with the Anti-Slavery Society. Its secretary employed her as a domestic, and it was in his house that she dictated her *History*, so that, (in her words), 'good people in England might hear from a slave what a slave had felt and suffered.'[3]

Mary Seacole was a Jamaican of mixed race, born between 1805 and 1810 to a Scottish army officer and a free black woman. Her autobiography, called by its modern editors 'one of the most important personal histories to be written by a Caribbean-born woman', describes an extraordinary career and a very modern personality, though much of the action takes place outside the region.

Yseult Bridges, née Guppy, was also a creole, born into Trinidad's local white elite in 1888. Her nostalgic memoir recalls a sheltered girlhood with its privileges and restrictions around the turn of the century.

At about the time that Yseult was shipped off to England to be 'finished', Anna Mahase (née Chandisingh) was born into Trinidad's rapidly growing Indian community. The daughter of India-born parents who had both converted to Christianity, Anna's autobiography chronicles a pioneering career as a teacher who quietly yet persistently challenged many of the gender values and codes of her own Indo-Trinidadian group as well as of the wider colonial society.[4]

These texts will be examined for evidence of a gendered perception of Caribbean society between the 1770s and the 1920s. How did these women view slave and post-slave society? Can one get a sense of diverging historical experiences of women as opposed to men? Can we find evidence about the life stories and life chances of Caribbean women (while never ignoring the vast differences created by ethnicity, legal status, class and chronology)?

Slavery and its systemic brutalities engendered a deep-seated insecurity among whites resident in the Caribbean: the 'terrified consciousness' of West Indian whites, which, of course, outlived slavery itself. For women, these fears were probably reinforced by dominant values which saw them as helpless, defenceless, peculiarly vulnerable because of their close, uneasy contact with hordes of slave domestics. Nugent, Fenwick and Carmichael, living in the islands during the turbulent last three decades of British colonial slavery, all express a strong sense of personal insecurity, of living surrounded by alien and potentially menacing people.

Nugent's consciousness was haunted by the spectre of Haiti, and she dreaded its effects on the domestic slaves: 'The splendour of the black chiefs of Santo Domingo, their superior strength, their firmness of character, and their living so much longer in these climates, and enjoying so much better health, are the common topics at dinner; and the blackies in attendance seem so much interested, that they hardly change a plate, or do anything but listen.' With the French fleet near Jamaica (in 1805) and the governor away organising the defence of the island, she tried to fight off panic; the 'bad Negroes' took advantage of the scare to roam about and to steal; when she went for a walk in Port Henderson, she met 'a horrid looking' black man, who failed to bow to her, but instead grinned, and gave 'a fierce look, that struck me with a terror I could not shake off.' Fenwick, who was in Barbados during the 1816 rebellion, dreaded another 'fatal insurrection' and wrote that this terror prevented her ever feeling 'the soothing consciousness of being at home.' Living in

St Vincent in the 1820s, Carmichael stressed the insecurity of white families on remote plantations, surrounded by untrustworthy slaves. In any crisis, with all the white adult men called out to militia service, the planter's wife would be utterly alone, often with small children, entirely in the slaves' power. Even in normal times, with estate houses quite open and impossible to secure, she notes, you might spend half the night awake, uneasy, listening. Moreover, personal insecurity had increased with the new slave policies after 1823; the slaves now looked on their owner as their enemy, and even the 'good negroes' had become insolent and unruly, including the domestics.[5]

Slavery was terminated in 1834 in Antigua, but Lanaghan, writing in the early 1840s, was also made uneasy by fear of potential harm from the black domestics, the hostile inmates of the household. Citing a recent incident where servants had tried to burn down a house with the white family inside because of a minor squabble, she asked: 'Who would not think himself safe within the precincts of his own home? — where but in that fortress would we look for rest? Alas! . . . even in our own domestic circle, revenge' might lead to the destruction of 'that great blessing, family peace!' And fear — not, indeed, of the household domestics, but of blacks outside the home — remained a part of the consciousness of the white child in the Caribbean long after the end of slavery.

Yseult Guppy, born in 1888, recounted what was, perhaps, the classic nightmare of the white creole girl. As a child of about nine or ten, she was walking alone in a rough part of Port of Spain, when:

> to my horror a huge negro stepped in front of me, grinning, and barred my way. 'Let me pass', I said, trying to assume an imperious air . . . The negro grinned still more widely . . . I was now getting frightened. He gave a loud guffaw, echoed from all sides from the crowd that was collecting now, hemming me in, from the ragged children prancing around me. They gaped and jabbered, and the smell of their unwashed skin and clothes was rank and nauseating. My knees went weak, my stomach seemed to cleave to my spine. With all my heart I longed for Estelle [her black nanny] to appear. The big negro man took a step towards me with his hand outstretched, intending to grip me by the arm. I felt my face grow stiff as though it was moulded in cement, while everything began to spin about me. I think I must have been on the point of fainting'

when she was 'rescued' by a kindly (and masterful) Englishman.[6]

A sense of personal insecurity was combined with apprehensions about the physical and moral safety of young children in slave society. Nugent gave birth to two infants in Jamaica; her fears about their health were reinforced by her acute perception of the moral dangers of a West Indian childhood. She saw how hard it would be to prevent her son, surrounded by domestics obliged to gratify his every whim, from 'thinking himself a little king at least, and then will come arrogance, I fear, and all the petty vices of little tyrants.' Fenwick's married daughter 'pines to rear her boys in England, & dreads for them the sensual indulgences & luxury that most Children here [Barbados] are allowed.' Carmichael thought that as soon as the child was weaned, 'a destructive kind of accidental education commences' at the hands of the domestic slaves. Their influence made children undisciplined and rude, and sending them 'home' at 10 or 12 was the only remedy.[7]

Up to the middle of the nineteenth century at least, the Caribbean remained a dangerous place for European residents, and fear of illness and sudden death pervades the journal entries and letters of Maria Nugent and Elizabeth Fenwick. The latter was preoccupied with the health problems of her small grandchildren — fevers, mysterious 'eruptions almost as virulent as smallpox' — and the sudden deaths of friends and young pupils. Her daughter was in constant ill health — only a 'change of Climate', the doctors thought, 'could renovate her impaired constitution' — and her beloved son Orlando, a young man of around 20, succumbed to yellow fever after an illness of just three days. No wonder, she wrote sombrely, 'we who seek for gain in these climates have terrible penalties awaiting us.' Nugent, too, worried endlessly about her husband's and infants' health; a very large number of journal entries recorded the illnesses and sudden deaths of white people personally known to her, especially military and naval officers and their families. The many doctors who attended at King's House in Spanish Town are familiar characters in her journal. She noticed soon after arrival that white women in Jamaica were far more successful in keeping their health than the men, which explained the number of white widows in the island; unlike the women, who were generally temperate in their habits, the men 'really eat like cormorants and drink like porpoises.' Fenwick found exactly the same situation in Barbados, noting, 'nothing is so common here as old Ladies of from 80 to 100 years of age. The men shorten their period by intemperance & sensuality.' Indeed, she was terrified that Orlando might slip into the universal 'habit of drinking', and her son-in-law was a drunkard.[8]

For white women resident in the Caribbean, the management of the household domestics, whether slave or free, was pivotal to their daily existence. Control of the domestics was one of the few forms of power they possessed, and defiance of their authority by the servants was seen as an assault on their power and privileges as women of the elite. Several of the texts under review are rich sources on domestic life and management, and the troubled and troublesome relationship between mistress and servants. A rare positive note was struck by Janet Schaw, who visited Antigua and St Kitts in 1774 (but never managed a West Indian household). She was delighted with Memboe, the slave assigned to her as a personal maid in Antigua, and was immensely impressed with the superb servants and the domestic order and comfort found in the household of Samuel Martin, the island's 'patriarch'. Nugent, faced with managing the vast household at King's House, was less optimistic, though she was generally tolerant of her 'poor blackies'. The house was in chaos when she arrived, and her English maid had to 'set the black ladies to work, that our rooms may be a little less filthy', but they were merry and good humoured, and became more energetic after she met with them and promised them 'every kindness'. An evangelically minded Christian who was deeply shocked by the irreligion of white Jamaica, Nugent devoted a great deal of time to religious instruction of the King's House domestics, preparing a 'little Catechism' for them, and seeing to their baptism. When she left the island, she recorded 'now I shall not leave one, belonging to [the household], unbaptised.' She delighted the King's House domestics by dancing with 'an old negro man' at a fete for the servants held to celebrate the governor's return, 'exactly the same as I would have done at a servants' hall birthday in England.' This deeply shocked two creole ladies who were her guests, who nearly fainted at the spectacle and were convinced that insurrection was bound to folow such a display of familiarity; but Nugent was unrepentant. A British aristocrat, she dealt with her slave domestics with a degree of tolerance and civility. But as she travelled around Jamaica, staying on plantations, she found many disorderly, uncomfortable houses, with crowds of awkward, dirty servants and badly managed children. The creole ladies constantly abused their domestics: 'the continual scolding at the servants is to me the most distressing thing in the world'.[9]

Elizabeth Fenwick records that she found dealing with black domestics, both slave and free, an appalling task. The management of a Barbadian household, she wrote, involved 'annoyances & fatigue . . . that the mistress of an English family, with even the worst of English servants, can form no idea of.' These were slaves hired from their owners (for an 'exorbitant' sum), 'a sluggish, inert, self-willed race of people, apparently inaccessible to gentle & kindly impulses. Nothing but the dread of the whip seems capable of rousing them to exertion, & not even that can make them honest. Pilfering seems habitual & instinctive among domestic slaves.' Since the Fenwicks did not flog, their hired hands 'pursue a regular course of negligence, lies & plunder':

> When I kept house for Eliza during her confinement, I was several times almost mad with the provocations their dirt, disobedience & dishonesty caused me.. . . You would be astonished to hear me scold, I do so, I assure you, & that with a vehemence which on reflection surprises & pains me. Yet every instance of kindness, remonstrance, persuasion, or gentle reproof are so determinedly scoffed at by the greater part of this wretched race, that an excessive propensity to indolence can alone preserve any degree of equanimity of temper.

With no sense of irony, Fenwick wrote of 'the slavery of managing a family in the West Indies with Negro Domestics'.[10]

Carmichael, who managed plantation households in St Vincent and Trinidad, struck the same note. In a decade in the Caribbean she declared that she never encountered a servant, man or woman, who would have been 'reckoned even passable in England.' Even in the grandest houses hordes of untrained and dirty domestics abounded. A moderate family, which would need only three maids, one 'man' and 'washing put out' in England, required ten adults and five or six youths in the West Indies; and still the work would be badly done. Laundry work was abominably done: 'of all your troublesome establishment, the washerwomen are the most discontented, unmanageable, and idle.' Their destruction of clothes and linens was 'past belief'; everything was 'ill washed' and badly ironed in the West Indies. No lady had ever managed to get her washerwomen, her own slaves, to stop starching everything, even handkerchiefs. The domestics became even more unruly with the 'Amelioration' reforms of the 1820s; they decided not to work on Saturday evenings because 'Massa Buxton' had said they were free then. 'I am not quite sure', Carmichael wrote bitterly, 'if all the females who sign petitions, and sigh over the distresses of the poor negroes, would much relish doing their work for them.'[11]

Writing of Antigua just after the end of slavery, Lanaghan considered most of the domestics to be idle, dishonest and negligent; 'one English servant will do twice the work two creoles will.' She thought that male domestics were generally better than the women, and praised the skills of the cooks, so long as they were left entirely to their own devices and no attempt was made by the mistress to impose European methods. Pilfering of food was universal, and no domestic felt any shame on being detected. Lanaghan noted that since emancipation, Antiguan domestics 'think themselves upon an equality with the highest in the land', refusing to accept any reproof or direction from the employer. She saw that they did not behave with the class-based 'propriety' of English servants:

If you keep them at their proper distance, they become dissatisfied, and complain of your being harsh to them, if, on the contrary, you shew them any degree of attention and try to make their situation as comfortable as possible, they then assume too much, and entirely forget the difference of rank. Try to serve them, and it is ten chances to one you make them your enemy; do them ninety-nine favours, and refuse the hundredth, and you are reviled and blamed as if you had injured them.

This uneasy web of class/racial antagonisms, Lanaghan thought, was the result of the 'pestilential influence' of slavery.[12]

It is Mary Prince, of course, who provides a unique view of the mistress-domestic relationship from the other side of the barricades. She was employed mainly as a domestic for most of her working life in the

Caribbean (*c.* 1788—1828). Three of her four owners treated her, and her fellow domestics, with extreme brutality. Captain and Mrs I— of Bermuda, who bought her when she was about 12, routinely tortured their domestics, including two little slave boys. Hetty, a 'French' slave, was constantly flogged with both whip and cow-skin. After an especially atrocious flogging, Hetty went into premature labour, delivering a dead infant, and never recovered; she died soon after. 'The manner of it filled me with horror', Prince records tersely. She herself was physically abused by both Captain and Mrs I—. The latter

> caused me to know the exact difference between the rope, the cart-whip, and
> the cow-skin, when applied to my naked body by her own cruel hand. And
> there was scarcely any punishment more dreadful than the blows I received on
> my face and head from her hard heavy fist. She was a fearful woman and a
> savage mistress to her slaves.

When Hetty died, the teenaged Prince inherited all her chores, milking and looking after the cows, minding the children, cleaning and general housework: 'there was no end to my toils - no end to my blows'.[13]

Prince's last owners were the Woods, with whom she lived in Antigua as nursemaid, washerwoman and chambermaid. Mrs Wood constantly abused her in vile language — one recalls Nugent's comment — and threatened soon after she was purchased, 'You have been used to the whip [i.e. in Bermuda], and you shall have it here.' Unlike Mrs I—, Mrs Wood seems to have left the actual floggings to her husband. The Woods' relationship with Prince was complex. She was constantly abused both verbally and physically, yet she was their chief 'confidential' servant who was left in sole charge of the household during their frequent absences from home, and they refused to sell her despite several offers: 'she sold five slaves whilst I was with her; but though she was always finding fault with me, she would not part with me.' The ability to control Prince, a woman of manifest courage, intelligence and dignity, was clearly critical to the Woods' sense of power and self-worth in a slaveholding society. When Prince got married at the age of 38 to a free black, both the Woods were furious: they could not tolerate her assertion of a right to a separate and autonomous sexual and personal life. Mr Wood flogged her, and Mrs Wood said: 'she would not have nigger men about the yards and premises, or allow a nigger man's clothes to be washed in the same tub where hers were washed.' When she went with the family to London, new tensions entered the relationship, for Prince could not be held a slave there against her will, yet she knew no one in London and wanted to return to her husband in Antigua. On three occasions, after bitter confrontations, the Woods told her to leave and she refused; the fourth time, 'I took courage and resolved that I would not be longer thus treated, but would go and trust to Providence.' After 13 years of 'working like a horse' for the Woods, she was turned out into an alien city like a beggar.[14]

Fifty years after the end of slavery, at least in the nostalgic memory of Yseult Bridges, a white creole child in Port of Spain, the black domestics, pensioners and retainers who moved in and out of her home were friendly, gentle, supportive presences. Her mother (Alice Rostant Guppy, a French creole) was a domestic tyrant, obsessively critical of her servants' performance (11 in all, plus sundry, less permanent hangers-on), directing their lives with the arrogant self-confidence of a slave-owner's daughter. When the family moved from Port of Spain to the country, she decided the servants' fate unilaterally: who was uprooted to accompany them to the new house, who was pensioned off, who was handed over to relatives. She freely interfered with the servants' personal lives: she forced the estate overseer to go through a church marriage with his common-law wife, with whom he had several children, despite the warnings of her husband and the strong objections of the couple. The formerly happy family soon disintegrated, the overseer was dismissed, and he abandoned his wife and five children to fend for themselves. 'My mother was much mortified', Bridges writes; but consoled herself with the certainty that she had saved the wife from mortal sin.

Bridges recalls the servants of her childhood as affectionate, utterly loyal retainers of the old world; her memoirs contain no hint of the degradation and self-contempt at the heart of these traditional relationships. Zabette, for instance, born a slave, rose to be head domestic in the Rostant country house; she had delivered and nursed Rostant babies, and was now a dignified pensioner. She called Alice Guppy and her siblings 'me white chillum' and her own children 'me black fambly'; and it comes as no surprise to learn that she delighted in telling stories of the 'wonderful old days of slavery' and high living on the patriarchal French creole estates. Mary Hodge, the laundress, had been born and reared at the Guppy mansion in San Fernando. By the 1890s she was elderly, but handled all the family's washing with the help of her daughter, as well as doing other tasks when needed. Only rarely does a darker note creep into Bridges' nostalgic memories of the servants. When her mother's maid was 'seduced' by the handyman's wayward son, both were instantly dismissed, the girl evicted pregnant and penniless: so much for paternalism. While most of the servants are affectionately described, Lizzie Waldron, who had been Yseult's grandmother's maid, is not: she was 'a strange mulatto woman, holding herself aloof from everyone . . . something sinister about her', for she was a proud woman who never fitted into the paternalist mode of servitude. She had a house in town and her own servant, and came and went as she pleased. A retainer who never fawned and was completely unservile, she is recalled as 'bitter' and 'shifty', contrasted with the loyal and warm-hearted domestics who knew and cherished 'their born positions in life'.[15]

As these authors were women, assigned the gender role of household management, or, in one case, a domestic slave herself, some of their texts are excellent sources for the history of domesticity in the slave and post-slave societies of the Caribbean, and it seems fair to conclude that they bring a gendered perspective to this topic (mediated, of course, by ethnicity and class). One might also expect that they would bring a feminine consciousness to bear on the subject of sexuality and sexual relationships. By the early 1800s, the concerns of middle-class British women about their lack of sexual autonomy and their vulnerability to male power over their bodies had spilled over into writings produced by anti-slavery women. A concern for female slaves' sexual jeopardy became a salient theme in the anti-slavery literature generally, and it was a striking aspect of the Caribbean slave regime everywhere. Several of the authors are acutely aware of these matters, though they are often reticent presumably because of the gender and class conventions of the time.

No observer of slave society, however superficial, could fail to note the ubiquity of liaisons between white men and black and brown women, enslaved and free. Antiguan men, Janet Schaw noted in 1774, indulged freely in 'licentious and even unnatural amours, which appears too plainly from the crouds of Mullatoes, which you meet in the streets, houses and indeed everywhere.' Showing no sympathy for the sexual predicament of enslaved women, Schaw went on:

> The young black wenches lay themselves out for white lovers, in which they
> are but too successful . . . These wenches become licentious and insolent past
> all bearing, and as even a mulattoe child interrupts their pleasures and is
> troublesome they have certain herbs and medicines, that free them from such
> an incumbrance, but which seldom fails to cut short their own lives, as well as
> that of their offspring. By this many of them perish every year.

Writing in 1815, no doubt influenced by the humanitarianism (or uneasy conscience) which had spread widely in educated British circles since Schaw's day, and probably also by the frequent allusions to the sexual abuse suffered by female slaves in the anti-slavery literature, Elizabeth Fenwick was capable of empathy with both the women involved in these 'amours' and their offspring. 'It is a horrid & disgraceful System', she wrote, 'the female slaves are really encouraged to prostitution because their children are the property of the owner of the mothers.'

> What is still more horrible, the Gentlemen are greatly addicted to their women
> slaves, & give the fruit of their licentiousness to their white children as slaves.
> I strongly suspect that a very fine Mulatto boy about 14 who comes here to
> help wait on two young Ladies, our pupils, is their own brother, from the
> likeness he bears to their father. It is a common case & not thought of as an

enormity. It gives me a disgusted antipathy & I am ready to hail the Slave &
reject the Master.

No wonder that she feared that her adult son would acquire, not only a drinking habit, but also 'those vices of Manhood' so universal in Barbados white society.[16]

Maria Nugent swiftly became aware of the sexual politics of Jamaica, for on her second day at King's House she was told 'strange stories of the influence of the black and yellow women', and on one of her first visits to an estate (Hope) she met the overseer's 'chere amie, and no man here is without one, a tall black woman, well made', with her three 'yellow children'. Indeed, Governor Nugent's immediate predecessor, Balcarres, had maintained a 'profligate and disgusting' menage at King's House. Some planters had mistresses and children on all their numerous properties; Nugent met 'mulatto ladies' at St Mary's who said they were 'daughters of Members of the Assembly, officers, etc, etc.' She concluded that 'white men of all descriptions, married or single, live in a state of licentiousness with their female slaves' and that there was no hope for any moral improvement among the slaves while this situation continued. Though Nugent was sympathetic towards the offspring of these unions, especially the daughters, most of her concern was directed to the young white men who risked 'ruin' from their 'horrid connections' and 'improper lives'. Many journal entries describe her unsuccessful efforts to keep 'our young men' [the British officers who formed the governor's staff] from these entanglements. 'Poor foolish Captain Johnson', for instance, the governor's military secretary, was 'in great distress, about an ugly mulatto favourite, who has been accused of theft.' Driving around Spanish Town, Nugent encountered 'several of the unfortunate half-black progeny of some of our staff; all of fine muslin, lace etc . . . What ruin for these worse than thoughtless young men!' 'This is, indeed, a sad immoral country', she pondered; but, on the evidence of her journal, she spared few thoughts for the young men's willing or coerced prey.[17]

Both Nugent and Fenwick thought that 'immorality' was rife even among men of the elite in Jamaica and Barbados. By contrast, Carmichael stated that the immorality said to exist in the 'best' society 'I nowhere found' in the course of a decade's residence in Trinidad and St Vincent. (There is, of course, abundant evidence to the contrary, and one recalls that Carmichael had a strongly polemical agenda in publishing her book: to vindicate the planters from the humanitarian attacks on their world.) She insisted that lower-order whites were the principal sinners, overseers and managers of small estates who could never afford to marry and who lived with black women, becoming degraded to 'a white negro'. As for the free coloured women, 'to allure young men who are newly come to the country, or entice the inexperienced, may be said to be their principal object.' The European men are made the almost innocent victims, their lovers become the predators.[18] For all her sympathy for her 'young men', Nugent was more honest about Caribbean sexual politics.

Sexual abuse is a submerged subtext in Mary Prince's narrative. As her modern editor explains, the conventions of evangelical anti-slavery literatures dictated that female slaves be presented as 'pure' beings, without an autonomous sexual life, though often the passive victims of brutal white males. Extreme reticence characterises Prince's treatment of the subject. Though the reader suspects that both Captain I— and Mr Wood may have been sexually involved with their female chattel, she openly describes only one episode of sexual abuse, when she defied the advances of Mr D—, her third owner: 'He had an ugly fashion of stripping himself quite naked and ordering me then to wash him in a tub of water. This was worse to me than all the licks.' If she refused, he beat her. At last she 'defended myself, for I thought it was high time to do so. I then told him I would not live longer with him, for he was a very indecent man . . . with no shame for his servants, no shame for his own flesh.' After this act of defiance, she got herself sold to the Woods: 'the truth is, I did not wish to be any longer the slave of my indecent master.' Prince presents herself as the active and courageous defender of her 'virtue', not a passive victim. She hints at an affair with a white man, Captain Abbot, who lent her money; and after her conversion to evangelical (Moravian) Christianity, she came to realise she was 'a great sinner' — presumably, sexual sins. After conversion, she entered into a religious marriage with a free widower. She presents herself as an autonomous person with responsibility for her sexual life, slave or not. Her account shows that female slaves were capable, despite their own sexual jeopardy, of empathising with white women victimised by male power. All her domestics pitied Mrs Williams (Prince's kind childhood owner) because her husband was harsh and often left her for long periods to live with other women. Prince herself risked serious injury to defend Mr D—'s daughter from her father's brutal beatings.[19]

Writing in the more strait-laced 1840s, Lanaghan was generally reticent about white Antiguans' sex life, though she did state that 'the root of all West Indian misery [was] illicit love.' But she says unequivocally that during slavery the 'polished and urbane white masters had no objection to making the negroes the partners of their illicit intercourse' and then condemned the resulting children to a life of degradation. The daughters became 'housekeepers' to white men as a matter of course, and were educated to think it better 'to inhabit the harem of a white man, than to be the lawful wife of a man of colour.' Most of the time, though, the 'fearful immorality' Lanaghan describes as the legacy of slavery had to do with the blacks, and their reluctance to enter into lifelong, Christian marriages. She is a stern moralist with little sympathy for sexual irregularities by women of any ethnic or class background, though optimistic that the blacks would gradually transform themselves into well-behaved Christian peasants. In one interesting though puzzling passage, Lanaghan claimed that infanticide had become fairly frequent in Antigua since the end of slavery: semi-educated young black or brown girls, with ideas well above their station, entered into 'illicit unions' and then sought to conceal their 'follies or errors' by destroying the innocent evidence. She does not reveal whether the fathers of these little victims were generally white, nor explain why the birth of a child outside legal marriage should, in a West Indian island after the end of slavery, drive its mother to infanticide.[20]

The gender values of eighteenth- and especially nineteenth-century Europe dictated that women were more tender-hearted, more sympathetic to suffering humanity, than men. It may be interesting to examine the texts to see how far (if at all) their authors exemplified these traits in their approach to slavery and racial oppression in the Caribbean. Of course chronology is important too: upper- and middle-class ideas about slavery were transformed in Britain between the 1770s and the 1820s or 1830s.

Indeed, Janet Schaw seems to exemplify the callous indifference of the 1770s, even in a cultured and refined lady. In St Kitts, she constantly saw virtually naked slaves, men and women, toiling in the fields, the marks of the whip plainly visible on their backs. This seemed 'dreadful' to the 'humane European', but:

> *when one comes to be better acquainted with the nature of the Negroes, the horrour of it must wear off. It is the suffering of the human mind that constitutes the greatest misery of punishment, but with them it is merely corporeal. As to the brutes it inflicts no wound on their mind, whose Natures seem made to bear it, and whose sufferings are not attended with shame or pain beyond the present moment.*

She felt even better when she saw a group of 'new Negroes' just off the boat awaiting sale at the market; she had no doubt that they were 'perfectly indifferent to their fate . . . laughing and jumping, making faces at each other.' As a refined woman with the normative sense of modesty and propriety, Schaw acknowledged her initial shock and repugnance at the notion of female slaves especially being brutalised; but she was swiftly — and with no obvious conflict — brought to see the Africans as sub-human brutes, outside her frame of reference and therefore unworthy of pity, let alone empathy.[21]

Maria Nugent, at the turn of the century, has little to say about slavery as an institution, though a degree of sympathy for the slaves might be deduced from her constant use of the term 'poor blackies' and (perhaps) from her kindness to the King's House domestics and her concern for their spiritual welfare. She expressed concern when she heard that pregnant slaves worked in the fields up to six weeks before delivery and were back two weeks after; but she seems to have accepted uncritically the assurance that 'it was astonishing how fast these black women bred, what healthy children they had, and how soon they recovered after lying-in.' Fenwick, in the early 1820s, is clearly far more uneasy in her mind about the slave system than Schaw or Nugent. She often expressed pity for the slaves, especially the women, and the children brought up in the master's home like 'pets', only to be ruthlessly thrown out into the fields when old enough to work. For several years, too, she and her daughter refused to buy slaves — it was 'repugnant' and 'revolting' to her mind — and when she finally did purchase domestics, she gave the news to her English correspondent with obvious embarrassment. When a teenaged free coloured domestic was caught stealing a large sum of money, Fenwick let her go unpunished; because she was free, she could only have been arrested on a capital charge (these were the days before penal reform) and Fenwick 'could not bear to prosecute to death.' The robust callousness of Janet Schaw is quite absent in Fenwick's private letters, which were not intended for publication, though she mastered her squeamishness sufficiently to own several slaves and to employ even more. Mrs Lanaghan, who lived in Antigua before and after 1834, condemns slavery unequivocally as an inhumane and indefensible institution. Though in general an admirer of the Antiguan plantocracy, to which she was connected, she states that she 'has no doubt' that cruelties against the slaves took place in the island even during the last years of slavery, when she was resident, though she never personally witnessed any. Her account of the atrocities of the past — in other words, before the 1820s — is sober in tone, factual yet indignant. There is no attempt here to justify slavery in the manner of the late nineteenth-century writers. And Lanaghan was too close in time to its end to project the romantic myth of a paternalist, kindly regime which suffuses Yseult Bridges' musings on Trinidad's slave past.[22]

Mary Prince was the only one of the authors who could testify to 'what a slave had felt and suffered.' Her sober account of atrocities suffered by herself or inflicted on others in her sight and hearing spoke directly to the concerns of the British anti-slavery movement (and especially of women writers and activists) about corporal punishment of female slaves. Women in general did not control their own bodies; female slaves could be stripped naked and flogged in public by male owners or managers (as Prince was, notably by Mr D— in the Turks Islands); at slave auctions girls and women might be 'examined and handled in the same manner that a butcher would a calf or a lamb' (as she was at the age of 12). Hetty was tortured and murdered (with her infant) by Prince's second owners. Mr D—, her third owner, used to watch brutal floggings 'walking about and taking snuff with the greatest composure.' He was also responsible for the murder of Sarah, old, infirm and not quite right in the head, who was beaten and then flung into prickly-pear bushes; she died soon after when her cuts became infected. Hetty and Sarah, like Prince herself, emerge in the *History* as real people, as named women killed by their owners.[23]

Prince not only presented an individuated narrative, her own life story; she also consciously spoke for all slaves: 'In telling of my own sorrows, I cannot pass by those of my fellow-slaves — for when I think of my own griefs, I remember theirs.' She appeals to her (British) readers to reject the myth (so easily accepted by Janet Schaw) that Africans were brutes without feelings. 'The Buckra people who keep slaves think that black people are like cattle, without natural affection,' she wrote, 'but my heart tells me it is far otherwise.' They tried to make English people believe that slaves were happy and had no desire to escape slavery.

> But they put a cloak about the truth. It is not so. All slaves want to be free —
> to be free is very sweet . . . The man that says slaves be quite happy in slavery
> — that they don't want to be free — that man is either ignorant or a lying
> person. I never heard a slave say so. I never heard a Buckra man say so, till I
> heard tell of it in England . . . I tell it to let English people know the truth;
> and I hope they will never leave off to pray God, and call loud to the great
> King of England, till all the poor blacks be given free, and slavery done up for
> evermore.[24]

The situation of the free coloureds and their strictly inferior status in slave (and even post-slave) society were noted by several of the authors. Nugent seems generally to have accepted the rigid colour line without much difficulty; she often met with free coloured women when visiting estate houses, but always privately in her bedroom, and probably never dined with a non-white Jamaican throughout her stay in the island. But Fenwick expressed dismay at the 'impassable boundary' which in Barbados separated 'the white from the coloured people (many of whom are a fair, light haired people); & those [coloured] creoles whose wealth would introduce them to the first circles in England a white beggar would not speak to here. We cannot admit a creole pupil [to her school], yet some creole families on this Island live splendidly & are very rich . . . All this puts me out of temper.' The view implicit here, that wealth and life style ought to entitle coloured families to social equality with elite whites, was articulated even more strongly by Mrs Lanaghan. She believed that it was, at the very least, 'illiberal' to despise people merely because they had darker skins, and she condemned the 'prejudice' of white Antiguans in the 1840s. 'It is said,' she noted, 'that the white ladies are the strongest upholders of prejudice'; they argued that they could not mix with coloureds on grounds of morality, because they were 'illegitimate'. But Lanaghan pointed out that these ladies would mix freely with illegitimate whites, and in any case, many of the younger coloureds were both legitimate and highly respectable. No one would expect upper-class whites to mix socially with coloureds of inferior rank, she concluded, but why should they not accept their equals in wealth, education and respectability? They did not, of course; and Yseult Bridges' book shows that by the end of the nineteenth century the caste lines were almost as rigid as ever. No non-white persons appear in her childhood memories except domestics, labourers or employees there are hints of racism in her descriptions of the servants ('fat hips', 'thick lips', 'startling grimaces', 'half-castes').[25]

It is Mary Seacole, of all the authors, who unequivocally rejects racism and racial discrimination (though she is something of a class snob). Born early in the century, of mixed race, she has little to say about prejudice or discrimination in Jamaica; but she encountered plenty of both at the hands of Americans in Panama, where she worked for some years in the 1840s and 1850s:

> *I think, if I have a little prejudice against our cousins across the Atlantic — and I do confess to a little — it is not unreasonable. I have a few shades of deeper brown upon my skin which shows me related — and I am proud of the relationship — to those poor mortals whom you [the British] once held enslaved, and whose bodies America still owns. And having this bond, and knowing what slavery is; having seen with my eyes and heard with my ears proof positive enough of its horrors — let others affect to doubt them if they will — is it surprising that I should be somewhat impatient of the airs of superiority which many Americans have endeavoured to assume over me?*

When Seacole left Cruces, she was thanked for her services during a cholera outbreak by an American whose little speech included an expression of regret that she had been born 'a yaller woman' and a generous wish that she could be 'bleached'. Seacole replied:

> *I must say that I don't altogether appreciate your friend's kind wishes with respect to my complexion. If it had been as dark as any nigger's, I should have been just as happy and as useful, and as much respected by those whose respect I value; and as to his offer of bleaching me, I should, even it if were practicable, decline it without any thanks. As to the society which the process might gain me admission to, all I can say is, that, judging from the specimens I have met with here and elsewhere, I don't think that I shall lose much from being excluded from it. So, gentlemen, I drink to you and the general reformation of American manners.[26]*

Here, as in so much else, Seacole defied gender norms in her forthright denunciation of racism to a masculine gathering in a rough frontier community.

In writing about the island societies they knew, several of the authors paid special attention to describing the lives of women, particularly but not exclusively women of the elite with whom they had social contact. These texts, therefore, provide valuable evidence about women in slave and post-slave society.

Janet Schaw noted that the white Antiguan ladies never walked, took hardly any exercise other than dancing, and never let the sun touch their skin, covering up with masks and bonnets 'that absolutely make them look as if they were stewed.' But she was delighted with them, finding them amiable and intelligent, excellent wives and mothers, and devoted housewives: 'even those of the first fortune and fashion keep their own keys and look after every thing within doors; the domestick Economy is entirely left to them.' Though they loved fine houses, lavish entertainments, expensive carriages and 'crouds of mullattoe servants', they were 'modest, genteel, reserved and temperate' in their personal habits (unlike the men, who were 'gay, luxurious and amorous'). Stretching credibility to the limit, Schaw described these creole ladies as entirely indifferent to all scandal-mongering and gossip; moreover, 'jealousy is a passion with which they are entirely unacquainted, and a jealous wife would be here a most ridiculous character indeed.' Perhaps this was a discreet hint that the Antiguan ladies were expected to ignore their 'amorous' husbands' entanglements with black and brown women. In any case, Schaw's description of these paragons of virtue was based on a very brief visit.[27]

Maria Nugent's opinion of the Jamaican women she met was more astringent. There were few white women, outside the main towns, in Jamaica in 1801; Nugent went on a tour of country estates, staying at different houses, and did not encounter a single one for the first eight days. Those she met she thought generally idle, ignorant, and horrible to their domestics. Mrs C, for instance, was 'a perfect creole, says little, and drawls out that little, and has not an idea beyond her own Penn.' She commented of a group of Spanish Town ladies 'all I could get out of them was "yes, ma'am — no, ma'am", with now and then a simper or a giggle. At last, I set them to work stringing beads . . .' Throughout her journal, Nugent complained of the narrow interests and lack of refinement among the white Jamaicans, like Mrs Israell of Clarendon, who had been to Kingston a few times and was forever talking about 'when I was in town.' She was also shocked, as we saw, at their treatment of the domestics: 'As for the ladies, they appear to me perfect viragos; they never speak but in the most imperious manner to their servants, and are constantly finding fault.' What upset Nugent about the Jamaican white women — their constant abuse of their domestics — was life and death to Prince. Mrs I— of Bermuda and Mrs Wood of Bermuda and Antigua were (we saw) abusive and brutal slave-owners. Mrs I— meted out corporal punishment with her own hands, while Mrs Wood went in for verbal and mental abuse, encouraging her husband to inflict the whippings. For these women, control of slave domestics was central to their lives. Only Mrs Williams, Prince's childhood owner, was a kind mistress, and even she had to pretend to be severe when her brutish husband was home (fortunately not often). White women inflicted immeasurable pain on their slaves, and might themselves be the victims of tyrannical fathers and husbands.[28]

Mrs Carmichael agreed with Nugent that white creole women were often undereducated and lacking in refinement. 'In society,' she noted, 'the ladies are too generally found distinguished for that listlessness, and meagreness of conversation, which arise from an uninformed mind.' But while Nugent thought the women were ignorant because they were idle, Carmichael believed the exact opposite: 'the constant domestic drudgery of a female's life in the West Indies, married or unmarried, . . . leaves them no time for improving the mind.' She was concerned to stress the heavy work load of the planter's wife, who managed the estate's stock-raising operation and the kitchen garden, dealt with all the quarrels of 'the people', watched over the slave children and cared for the sick, sewed clothes for the domestics, supervised the laundry and fixed the clothing after its punishment by the washerwomen, and did the patching and mending. Because the pantry and store-room of an estate house were always away from the main building, numerous trips each day added to her burden, and even simple tasks like laying the table for dinner had to be personally supervised and checked. This description of the estate lady's round in the 1820s (which may have contained a propaganda element) is at considerable variance with the impression given by Nugent, or by Lanaghan in the early 1840s. The latter writes of listless creole women spending much of the day on their sofas, neglecting their children and letting the domestics do what they pleased. Her description of the daily routine of the elite country lady in Antigua suggests a life of idleness and monotony: the women 'amuse themselves with various feminine and elegant employments' such as music and light reading in the morning; after lunch, the 'toilet' occupied them until it was time for a walk or a drive; then they dressed for dinner, following which there was music, conversation and perhaps dancing. Presumably the lady of the house managed the servants, but there is no hint of the heroic strugles of Carmichael's estate wife. Picnics, bazaars, balls, tea parties and drives were the diversions of the Antiguan ladies, according to Lanaghan. Her picture of the country lady's life is much the same as Yseult Bridges' account of the women of the Rostant family on their Santa Cruz (Trinidad) estate in the 1890s.[29]

Of the four pre-1838 texts (other than Prince's), it is Mrs Carmichael's which pays by far the most attention to the female slave; but unfortunately, the propaganda element in her descriptions is so strong as to lessen their value as evidence. Her slave women were mostly prosperous people with plenty of fine clothes and jewels; if they worked in the fields half naked it was by choice. They were bad mothers who preferred to go out in the fields for the 'fun and gossip' rather than stay at home to nurse their infants (she implies that they had a free choice). They were cruel to their children, merciless beaters for trifles. When the 1824

Trinidad Order-in-Council prohibited corporal punishment of females by the owner, good parents complained, knowing that they themselves would beat their daughters far more severely than the owner ever would. F, a middle aged, respectable woman, begged Mr Carmichael to flog her 14-year-old daughter; when he explained that he could not, she beat the child cruelly, yet she was a creole and a Christian. The women were liars and thieves; the domestics brazenly wore stolen clothing and lied fluently, always 'swearing on the book' when detected and reproached. Girls and women of all ages were constantly quarrelling and fighting each other in the most violent ways. Carmichael reports at length on interviews she says she conducted with five African-born women on her St Vincent estate, identified only by initials. Though there are some convincing details about them, the dialogue is only too obviously designed to convey an image of Africa as a hell from which these women were happy to escape into a benign Caribbean slavery; one does not get a sense of real individuals. It is fortunate that Prince's spare but telling life history of a domestic slave (a creole) exists to counter Carmichael's propaganda portraits. The only woman who emerges as a fully rounded person from her text is C, a slave on the Trinidad estate who refused to do any useful work for massa but was a successful and prosperous ntrepreneur who purchased her own freedom long before 1834.[30]

Mrs Lanaghan, writing just after the end of slavery, was fascinated by the black Antiguan women, and she provides detailed and lively accounts of their dress, their social behaviour, their entertainments and their occupations, accounts which are suffused with a class-based snobbery but are generally free from racism and are quite sympathetic. Writing of coloured or mixed-race women, she carefully distinguished between those of the elite and those who belonged to a lower status group. Girls of the latter were often affected in manners, idle, ignorant and interested in nothing but show, with no ambition but to wear clothes 'utterly unbefitting their station' and to spend their lives 'brushing and dressing their hair'. This characterisation is quite close to Carmichael's. But Lanaghan, always acutely sensitive to class differences, stressed that elite coloured women were polished and cultured, some of the younger ones educated in England, 'and although, perhaps, rather more silent than in the present age is expected of women, what they do say is generally to the purpose.' Her account of the lives of coloured estate ladies is identical to the one she gives of their white counterparts.[31]

Mary Seacole, daughter of a white man and a free black Jamaican woman, could not have been more different from the elegantly idle coloured ladies described by Mrs Lanaghan. Her mother, Mrs Grant, was a noted 'doctress', a traditional healer, held in high esteem by Kingston's military men who frequented her lodging-house as much for medical care as for accommodation. Seacole learned most of her medical skills from her, acting as her assistant from the age of 12, and took over the hotel on her death. Her mother exemplified the enterprising, independent free coloured or free black woman, making her way in a racist and sexist society, and her own remarkable career must have owed far more to this woman than to her father, even if she did say that she owed her energy to her 'good Scotch blood'. Seacole's whole life was a challenge to nineteenth-century gender roles, and she is explicit in her pride that she always earned her own bread and succeeded in life, despite tragedies and difficult struggles, on her own. After her husband's death when she was still a young woman, she refused several offers of marriage: 'And here I may take the opportunity of explaining that it was from a confidence in my own powers, and not at all from necessity, that I remained an unprotected female.' Yet as a woman of her time, writing for the British public, she makes several concessions in her narrative to gender values. 'Though a hearty, strong woman,' she wrote, 'I think my heart is soft enough'; her mission in life was 'to be of service to those who need a woman's help . . . wherever the need arises — on whatever distant shore.' In Panama, she was an independent female entrepreneur dealing with the roughest of customers and patients, but she carefully disassociated herself from the 'low' women she encountered: 'My present life was not agreeable for a woman with the least delicacy or refinement; and of female society I had none. Indeed, the females who crossed my path were about as unpleasant specimens of the fair sex as one could well wish to avoid.' From the prevailing Western gender perspective, she was a pretty dubious specimen herself.[32]

In the autobiography of Anna Mahase one glimpses a brief but poignant portrait of a woman, or rather a child, who made the perilous journey from India to the Caribbean on her own. Anna's mother, Rookabai, ran away from her new husband and emigrated in the 1880s as a 12-year old girl. Born into a Brahmin family, and well-educated in the Hindi language and literature, she was married to a much older man. The little girl was distressed when she was handed over to him, was afraid of his moustaches, and ran away from her in-laws' home, ending up in the emigrant depot in Calcutta and then in Trinidad. This child had defied the whole social and gender structure of traditional India in her desperate escape to another world. Here she was placed as a domestic in an English family, and then came under the influence of the Canadian Presbyterian Mission to the Trinidad Indians. Rookabai became Elizabeth Burns, a Christian, and was married off to the promising Christian teacher George Chandisingh in 1891. But she remained a rebel. Strong-willed, 'a born leader of women and children', she clashed with her husband, the family split up, and she returned to India, 'which had always been her desire', leaving her husband and all her children except the youngest girl who went with her. Her daughter Anna had life chances never open to Rookabai, for all her courage: a fulfilling career as a teacher, and a marriage entered into freely as an adult.[33]

Several of the authors provide interesting evidence about the rearing and education of girls in the Caribbean. Only Mary Prince gives us a glimpse of the childhood of a slave girl (in Bermuda). In the relatively benevolent household of Mrs Williams, she grew up in some security and comfort with her mother, also a domestic, and her siblings. Mrs Williams' daughter made her a pet; 'she used to lead me about by the hand, and call me her little nigger. This was the happiest period of my life; for I was too young to understand rightly my condition as a slave, and too thoughtless and full of spirits to look forward to the days of toil and sorrow.' Prince's 'education' consisted of instruction in the full range of domestic tasks, as well as care of livestock, from her various mistresses and fellow domestics. In her late 30s, she was taught to read by the wives of Moravian missionaries in Antigua; she records, with pride, 'I got on very fast.' The texts reveal much about the rearing of elite children. Maria Nugent, for example, was acutely aware of how white Jamaican children were turned into little tyrants; her own creole niece was a good (or bad) example. Children were 'injudiciously treated' in every respect, allowed to eat anything, made 'truly unamiable, by being most absurdly indulged.' Even Mrs Carmichael, concerned to depict planters' wives as devoted mothers, admitted that they neglected their children's 'moral' education.[34]

Elite girls were educated in various ways. Carmichael's young children were taught by a British governess, but theirs was a wealthy family, and she pointed out that governesses tended not to stay for long in the West Indies. Mrs Lanaghan implied that the average English 'governess' in Antigua was an impoverished and ill-educated female down on her luck. Lanaghan also tartly noted that 'not long ago', white girls not of the elite received very little education of any kind; girls of 14 would spend their days sitting on the floor with their black attendants, sucking canes and gossiping, while their mothers lounged on the sofa. But many attended schools for 'young ladies', of the kind run by Elizabeth Fenwick and her daughter in Bridgetown between 1814 and 1821. This successful school was attended by girls from rich families who chose not to send them to England; no coloured children were admitted, and girls stayed until about 17. They attended between 7 am and 4 pm, learning writing, arithmetic, geography, history, music, dancing and (sometimes) French. Fenwick seems usually to have had between 40 and 60 pupils, and made a good income, though she complained of rivals setting up shop and cutting into her market. Generally, though, elite or would-be elite parents tried to send their girls to England for a 'polish'. Nugent noted how Miss Israell of Clarendon, educated at a 'fashionable' London school, was forever consumed with anxiety lest her country-bumpkin parents embarrass her. Lanaghan described upwardly mobile white families in Antigua who sent their daughters to 'some suburban seminary', to learn 'to sketch a landscape, complete a butterfly in Poonah painting, play fashionable airs upon a piano, speak Anglicised French, dance a quadrille, and perhaps embroider a footstool.' They then returned in triumph, 'to astonish papa and mamma' and to 'swell the ranks of the female coterie.'[35]

Things had hardly changed by the 1890s. Yseult Guppy went first to a little kindergarten in Port of Spain, run by two French creole spinsters who had failed in the marriage sweepstakes. Then she was taught by the English daughter of the Principal of Queen's Royal College, along with two English children, in the latter's house. Finally she went to Miss Bunkle's school, then the only private girls' school in the island. (St Joseph's Convent, run by French nuns, was presumably ruled out by Yseult's father who was strongly anti-Catholic.) Miss Bunkle was an English spinster. She coached the few older girls taking British examinations, while all the other pupils were taught by five or six young creole women, badly paid, undereducated, and lacking any notion of discipline or pedagogy. There were between 50 and 60 girls. At first they were all from elite French creole or English families; later Bunkle took in all who could pay — Portuguese, Venezuelan, 'Greek' — though these girls would all have been defined as 'white'. When the family moved into the country Yseult received desultory (though fascinating) tuition at home from her scholarly father. Then, at 14, came the inevitable: she was shipped off to England to be 'finished' before entering 'Society', to eradicate 'the insidious singsong creole accent and acquire that poise and complexion, that cachet, which would enhance her chance of making a "good match" . . . the whole object of a woman's existence.'[36]

Anna Chandisingh, second-generation Indo-Trinidadian born into a Christian home, received a far more useful education from the Canadian Mission than that to which her near-contemporary was exposed. She attended the mission-run primary school of which her father was headmaster, then spent four years in the mission's Home for Girls in Tunapuna. Anna was ambitious academically and studied hard. At 15 she began to teach needlework in various primary schools. Then she went in 1915 to the Girls' High School in San Fernando as a boarder, studying for the teaching examinations; she and four other teenagers were the nucleus of the female section of the Naparima Training College. They studied along with the young men: 'To me it was a novelty, young East Indian men and girls in their teens, sitting and studying in one common room. It was the first of its kind . . . These were the days of the beginning of the emancipation of our East Indian girls and women.' After a hard struggle, Anna eventually passed the Third Class Teachers' Examination, and could begin her career as a certified teacher in mission schools.[37]

Maria Nugent provides some useful evidence about the experience of motherhood for elite women in the Caribbean during the early nineteenth century. Nugent gave birth to two infants in Jamaica. She wrote a lively account of her first 'creole confinement' in 1802. As if a labour of two and a half days, oppressive heat, semi-darkness and mosquitoes were not misery enough, 'the old black nurse brought a cargo of herbs, and wished to try various charms, to expedite the birth of the child, and told me so many stories of pinching and tying women to the bed-post, to hasten matters, that sometimes, in spite of my agony, I could not help laughing, and, at others, I was really in a fright, for fear she would try some of her experiments upon me. But the [English] maids took all her herbs from her, and made her remove all the smoking apparatus she had prepared for my benefit.' On the morning after the birth of her son, she was allowed a warm bath (which suggests that she had an enlightened doctor), and she bathed each day during the three weeks she remained in her bedroom; then she resumed normal life. She had previously engaged the wife of an Irish soldier as a wet nurse, though she was upset that the heat, and her public duties as governor's wife, made it unlikely that she could nurse herself ('why should I not be a mother indeed?'). The inoculation of the baby against smallpox at six weeks was a source of great anxiety; it had to be repeated and, when finally successful, made the infant quite ill (this was not the milder vaccination). Nugent seems to have tried to keep her baby away from black domestics as much as possible and vowed that 'none of the blackies' should ever give him 'a morsel'. Her second confinement, in 1803, was short and easy; 'my illness was literally nothing, for I was actually speaking and walking towards the sofa, the instant before it was all over.' Her infant daughter was handed over to the Irish wet nurse and little George (aged 11 months) was rather abruptly weaned to make room for hr. The little girl was vaccinated in both legs using vaccine taken from 'a nice little mulatto child', probably one of the earliest attempts at vaccination in Jamaica. Both babies were reasonably healthy during their time in Jamaica, but her journal shows that Nugent was increasingly preoccupied by the perceived dangers to their health posed by residence in the Caribbean, an anxiety echoed in Elizabeth Fenwick's letters, which are full of concern about her four Barbados-born grandchildren.[38]

Mary Prince was childless; at least, there is no mention of her ever giving birth or being pregnant. Was she made sterile by the repeated physical abuse to which she was subjected all through her childbearing years? As a teenager she witnessed the murderous flogging of pregnant Hetty, followed by the birth of a dead infant and Hetty's own death. Motherhood, in Prince's narrative, is pure tragedy. In her spare prose, she describes her mother's misery when she (along with two sisters) was sold away at the age of 12:

> *The black morning at length came; it came too soon for my poor mother and*
> *us. Whilst she was putting on us the new osnaburgs in which we were to be*

sold, she said, in a sorrowful voice, (I shall never forget it!) 'See, I am
shrouding my poor children; what a task for a mother!' . . . 'I am going to
carry my little chickens to market' (these were her exact words) 'take your last
look of them . . .

Slave mothers, Prince knew, 'could only weep and mourn over their children, they could not save them from cruel masters.' Marriage of the morally responsible kind was difficult for slaves, but at the age of 38, Prince married Daniel James, a hard-working carpenter who had purchased his freedom. The Woods thwarted all their efforts to buy hers, and Prince records: 'I had not much happiness in my marriage, owing to my being a slave. It made my husband sad to see me so ill-treated.' After only two years of marriage, she left him in Antigua when (still a slave) she accompanied the Woods to Britain, and seems never to have been reunited with him.[39]

Marriage was, of course, the accepted destiny for women — that is, for whites — and Fenwick gives us a glimpse of her daughter Eliza's unhappy marriage to a man who had succumbed to the Barbadian habit of excessive drinking. After years of mental anguish, she finally told 'Mr R.' to mend his ways, or leave Barbados and try to sober up; he departed for England 'exactly one hour after she had been put to Bed of her fourth Child', leaving his financial affairs in confusion. Once Eliza had recovered from all this, she felt profound relief: 'the relief of no longer being exhausted with nights of watching, shame & terror of what evils intoxication might involve her in before the dawn of the morning; & what still more reconciles her to her hard destiny is that her children are saved from witnessing the errors of their father & that she shall bring no more little beings into life to have but one protecting parent.' Three years later, Mr R. had made no contact with his wife and children; 'what quarter of the world contains him, or whether he be living or dead, we know not.' Elizabeth Fenwick herself had left, or had been left by, her husband, and passed in Barbados as a widow.[40]

For the elite Trinidadian girl of the 1890s, marriage was 'the whole object' of her life. Failure meant relegation 'to the background of the home, there to live parasitically or to eke out a genteel existence in some ladylike way.' For the matriarch of the Guppy household, Alice Rostant Guppy, a 'good marriage' was the only proper destiny of her daughters. She monitored likely white bachelors with meticulous care, concerned equally with social status, money and career prospects; age or national origins (once they were 'white') mattered less. She firmly believed that marriage, children and home were 'the very foundations' of a woman's life, and that love would follow marriage and children, not the reverse. Hence she encouraged the marriage of Ruth, aged 18, to an Englishman 17 years her senior, whom she did not love (he was supposed to be 'in love' with her), because of his private means, good (English) family background and promising career in the colonial service. The elite girls entered the marriage sweepstake at the annual debutantes' ball at Governor's House, and Yseult Bridges gives an amusing description of the drama surrounding Ruth's preparation for this event, on which her 'whole future' might depend. Ruth (aged 17) was carefully made up: her shoulders and arms were whitened by a mixture of French chalk and gin, while another concoction of gin with a pink ribbon soaked in it was applied to her cheeks; this was essential because, having returned from her 'finishing' in England some months back, she was sallow, 'washed out', in comparison with girls just back with rosy cheeks. Both Ruth, and later Yseult herself, were married at 18 to Englishmen working in Trinidad who were considerably older than them. Not getting married meant failure; Mary Seacole's deliberate rejection of remarriage in favour of making her own way in the world was apparently unheard of among the Trinidad white elite, except for the women who opted for the Catholic religious orders.[41]

The experiences of the young Anna Chandisingh (born in 1899) illustrate the changes in marriage patterns and life chances for girls of the Indo-Caribbean community. Rookabai, her mother, had been a Hindu child bride in India, and after baptism in Trinidad, underwent what was, in effect, a second arranged marriage, this time organised by the Canadian Presbyterian Mission, which actively sponsored (or vetoed) matches among its young converts who were seen as 'promising'. The teenagers at the Home for Girls, for instance, were married off at 15 or 16, by their parents, the missionaries or the home's Canadian supervisor. This might well have happened to Anna. A young teacher working in Princes Town 'asked for' her, but the missionaries vetoed the match because their policy was not to permit 'Tunapuna girls' to marry 'in the Princes Town field.' At 16 she was still single. Then the missionary's wife arranged a match with a teacher from a Tunapuna family. She had never spoken to the young man, but 'I did not mind because he had belonged to a Christian family . . . so I decided in my mind that all would be well.' Nothing came of this, however, and Anna subsequently refused another offer of marriage, saying she was not ready to marry. Now aged 18, she got her first job as an assistant teacher at Sangre Chiquito. Here she met Kenneth Mahase, then a pupil teacher, and a discreet romance began. This was a Western-type courtship, involving unchaperoned walks at night and long conversations alone together, as well as a correspondence against the rules of the Presbyterian Training College where Kenneth was studying. The two studied together and passed the teachers' examinations together. Once Kenneth secured an appointment as a headteacher, they were married; Anna was 20. The missionaries approved of the match, but this was no arranged marriage.[42]

The texts provide considerable evidence about the working lives of women in the Caribbean. Nugent says very little about the field slaves —

no doubt she had virtually no contact with them — but the life style of domestic slaves is often described, admittedly in passing, in her journal. Carmichael, a planter's wife, has more material on the women field hands and their work regime, though her testimony on this subject may be of limited value because of the propaganda element in her book. Prince was never a field hand, but in Bermuda and Antigua she performed a wide range of tasks in and around the household: care of livestock, laundry, cleaning and general housework, child care. In the Turks Islands she worked in the salt ponds, giving a rare first-hand account of the appalling conditions endured by the men and women slave labourers. In addition to the unpaid labour for her owners, Prince earned cash by taking in other people's washing, buying provisions cheaply and selling them to ship captains, and generally doing own-account trading. Lanaghan noted that many black Antiguan women still worked on the sugar estates in the early 1840s, but she was especially interested in those who had left the plantations and gone to live in town, and she devoted a whole chapter to a lively account of their occupations as washerwomen, hucksters, porters and general labourers. This is a sympathetic account on the whole, but she reveals her class and gender values in the following passage:

> Many of the negro women . . . are so very masculine in their voice, manners and appearance, that it is at times a matter of doubt to say to which sex they belong. This may be attributed to the general system of treatment during slavery: they were required to work the same as the men; and when punishment was thought necessary, no regard was paid to their feelings, but their persons were equally exposed as those of the other sex. Of course, these proceedings in time rendered them callous, and in the end, divested them of all those principles of modesty which are so great an ornament to the feminine character, whether in high or low condition of life . . . While employed in their daily avocations, it is customary to tie up their garments almost — if not quite — as high as their knees; and even when walking about the streets of the capital, if it is rather wet weather, the same degree of indelicacy is practised. All these causes combined, tend to lessen the women in the eyes of strangers; although the creoles appear to see no indecorum in their style of dress, or manners.[43]

There was little scope for women of the elite to engage in remunerative or interesting work, during or after slavery. As has been noted, Elizabeth and Eliza Fenwick ran a successful school in Bridgetown, but they were well educated and clearly enterprising Englishwomen (Eliza had been an actress before marriage). According to Yseult Bridges' memoirs, white creole women had few options if they remained unmarried and did not take the veil. The Misses Cadiz ran a kindergarten, and young local white women taught in Miss Bunkle's school (she was English), but they had no training and were inefficient teachers. Genteel poverty was the usual fate of the unmarried white woman. A sad example was Yseult's talented aunt, Eugenie (Nini) Rostant. Slightly deformed, she could not marry, and she had sacrificed her small legacy to help a brother in trouble. To support her young sister, she announced she would work for a living, to the scandal of the whole family. A brilliant musician, she refused to prostitute her talent by teaching music to children. Instead she got a job as postmistress and registrar of births and deaths for a Port of Spain suburb, to the disapproval of all the Rostants. She was rescued from this social humiliation when her sister married a foreigner and she went abroad to live with the couple.[44]

Mary Seacole and Anna Mahase, by contrast, carved out satisfying careers for themselves which defied many prevailing gender rules and expectations. Seacole's career, of course, was nothing short of extraordinary, and is too well known to need to be described here. What emerges strongly from her autobiography is the determined way in which she systematically prepared herself for her work as a doctor and (in effect) matron/proprietor of a private nursing home. Though her mother, as we saw, was her first and most important teacher, she carefully learned everything she could from medical men she met in Jamaica, Panama, and later England and the Crimea. In Panama she dissected the body of a small cholera victim in order to understand the disease better, and she became a recognised expert in its treatment, saving many lives in Jamaica and Panama, and she saved others during a yellow fever epidemic in Jamaica. A woman alone in Panama during an especially lawless time in its history (the early 1850s), she learned to manage unruly and often racist men who dined at her restaurant. Many tried to cheat her, but only the 'cutest Yankee' had a chance of outwitting her. In Panama and in Jamaica, she prepared herself for her famous intervention in the Crimea. Seacole's career was certainly unique, yet she came out of a tradition of independent, often entrepreneurial, free coloured and free black women in her native island.[45]

Mahase, too, broke out from gender norms in her career, as she was well aware. She studied hard and systematically to prepare herself for teaching in the Canadian mission schools. At 18 she took up her first position as Fourth Class Assistant Teacher in a small rural primary school; she was then the first Indo-Trinidadian to be employed as Assistant Teacher in a school in north Trinidad, and in 1919 she became the first female Indo-Trinidadian qualified (certified) teacher in the whole island. When she got married in 1919, the government's rules required that she resign from teaching, but the head of the mission argued with the Director of Education and she was allowed to stay on as Assistant Teacher in the school of which her new husband was headmaster. She was the first woman in Trinidad to be part of a husband and wife team of qualified teachers. The gender biases of the Canadian mission (as well as the colonial government) ensured that in a teaching career of 35 years she never rose above Assistant Teacher. Anna Mahase makes no complaint about this injustice in her autobiography, and it seems likely that her position in the partnership with her husband (Assistant Teacher and Headteacher) satisfied her. But her text makes it clear that she knew that she was a pioneer who had opened doors for others, that she had broken through gender restrictions and asserted (always quietly, and in a ladylike way) a right to autonomy, just as her mother, the refugee from a child marriage in India, had done in the ancestral land.[46]

These female-authored texts do not provide a consistently gendered testimony, nor do they always bring a clearly feminine perspective to bear on the Caribbean societies with which they deal. The authors' ethnicity and class, the values and limitations of the societies and eras to which they belonged, make this inevitable. But these women often show a feminine consciousness in the things they chose to write about and in the way they often focused on women and women's concerns. They are a rich source of evidence about women's historical experience in the Caribbean which can supplement the mainstream of documents generated by men, and they can help provide a more nuanced view of Caribbean social history, its gender dimensions and its 'invisible women'.

Endnotes

1. It seems fair to say that the three best-known studies on women in the slave societies of the British Caribbean all depend largely on male-authored sources: H. Beckles, *Natural Rebels: A Social History of Enslaved Black Women in Barbados* (London: Zed Press, 1989), B. Bush, *Slave Women in Caribbean Society, 1650—1838* (London: James Currey, 1990); M. Morrissey, *Slave Women in the New World* (Lawrence: University Press of Kansas, 1990). Of course all three scholars are sensitive to the issues of evidence and methodology involved in using androcentric (as well as ethnocentric) sources.

2. The texts, in chronological order, are: Janet Schaw, *Journal of a Lady of Quality; being the Narrative of a Journey from Scotland to the West Indies, North Carolina, and Portugal, in the years 1774 to 1776*, edited by E.W. Andrews and C.M. Andrews (New Haven: Yale University Press, 1939); Maria Nugent, *Lady Nugent's Journal of her Residence in Jamaica from 1801 to 1805*, edited by P. Wright (Kingston: Institute of Jamaica, 1966); A.F. Fenwick (ed.), *The Fate of the Fenwicks: Letters to Mary Hays, 1798—1828* (London: Methuen, 1927), pp. 161—217 contain letters written by Elizabeth Fenwick while living in Barbados between 1814 and 1821; Mary Prince, *The History of Mary Prince, a West Indian Slave Related by Herself*, edited by Moira Ferguson (London: Pandora, 1987; originally published London and Edinburgh: Westley and David, 1831); Mrs A.C. Carmichael, *Domestic Manners and Social Condition of the White, Coloured, and Negro Population of the West Indies*, 2 vols (New York: Negro Universities Press, 1969; originally published London: Whittaker, Treacher, 1833), Carmichael lived in St Vincent and Trinidad between 1820 and about 1830; Frances Lanaghan, *Antigua and the Antiguans*, 2 vols (London: Spottiswoode, 1967; originally

published anonymously, London: Saunders and Otley, 1844); M. Seacole, *Wonderful Adventures of Mrs Seacole in Many Lands*, edited by Z. Alexander and A. Dewjee (Bristol: Falling Wall Press, 1984; originally published London: James Blackwood, 1857); Y. Bridges, *Child of the Tropics, Victorian Memoirs*, edited by N. Guppy (London: Collins and Harvill, 1980) which deals with the author's childhood in Trinidad between 1888 and 1902; A. Mahase, *My Mother's Daughter. The Autobiography of Anna Mahase Snr 1899—1978* (Claxton Bay, Trinidad: Royards, 1992). All page references are to the editions cited above; I am grateful to Hilary Beckles for telling me about the Fenwick letters and providing a copy. A tenth work by a woman — Maria Riddell, *Voyages to the Madeira, and Leeward Caribbean Isles* (1792) — was examined, but it dealt exclusively with landscape, flora and fauna. Of course, I am aware that other 'women's texts' might be considered; Edna Manley's *Diaries* come immediately to mind. And after revising this essay for publication, I came across M. Ferguson (ed.), *The Hart Sisters: Early African-Caribbean Writers, Evangelicals and Radicals* (Lincoln, Nebraska and London: University of Nebraska Press, 1993). This includes various writings by Anne Hart Gilbert and Elizabeth Hart Thwaites, free coloured Antiguans prominent in the Methodist movement in the last three decades of the slave period. This article makes no claims to being a comprehensive survey.

3. See Introduction by M. Ferguson, pp. 1—41, and Preface to first 1831 edition by Thomas Pringle, p. 45. Prince's work is also discussed in Ferguson, *Subject to Others: British Women Writers and Colonial Slavery, 1670—1834* (Routledge: New York: 1992), pp. 281—98. Prince's text may be usefully compared with the celebrated book by the American, Harriet A. Jacobs: *Incidents in the Life of a Slave Girl, Written by Herself* (edited by Jean F. Yellin,Cambridge, MA: Harvard University Press, Harvard, 1987; originally published anonymously in 1861).

4. None of the texts was written as fiction: they are letters, a journal, autobiographical works or 'factual' accounts of Caribbean societies. But one should note that autobiographical fiction by Caribbean women constitutes another, potentially rich source of women's testimony about the region's past. *Wide Sargasso Sea*, by Dominica-born Jean Rhys, is justly famous, and several of Rhys' short stories are set in the Caribbean. Two other examples, interesting but far less known, may be mentioned here. Eliot Bliss was born in Jamaica in 1903 of English parents and spent her early childhood in the island, later returning as a young adult for a few years in the early 1920s. Her *Luminous Isle* (London: Virago, 1984; originally published London, 1934) is the story of her return to the island and her struggles with the narrow prejudices of expatriate society and of her own relatives. Lakshmi Persad's *Butterfly in the Wind* (Leeds: Peepal Tree Books, 1990) describes her childhood in the 1930s and 1940s in a wealthy upper-caste Hindu family of Trinidad. Her portrayal of the child's socialisation as a Brahmin, as a well-to-do Indo-Trinidadian and (above all) as a girl in a rapidly changing colonial society, is a valuable personal history in novel form. For a recent discussion of Toni Morrison's *Beloved* as a 'story of women's experience of slavery', see Elizabeth Fox-Genovese, 'Unspeakable things unspoken: ghosts and memories in the narratives of African-American women', *The 1992 Elsa Goveia Memorial Lecture*, (University of the West Indies, Mona).

5. Nugent, pp. 64, 198, 225—27; Fenwick, pp. 212—13; Carmichael, I, pp. 56—58, 245—46.

6. Lanaghan, II, pp. 95—96; Bridges, pp. 112—13.

7. Nugent, p. 146; Fenwick, p. 200; Carmichael, I, p. 25.

8. Nugent, pp. 186, 59, 81; Fenwick, pp. 182—87, 196—97, 204, 171, 173—74, 193.

9. Schaw, pp. 86—87, 105; Nugent, pp. 11, 12, 243, 156, 80, 82.

10. Fenwick, pp. 163—64, 167, 168, 175, 188—89.

11. Carmichael, I, pp. 20, 33—40, 118—19, 120; II, pp. 207, 268. T.F. Buxton was the main leader of the parliamentary anti-slavery movement in the 1820s.

12. Lanaghan, II, pp. 77—78, 137—41. She gives a spirited account of washerwomen at work, II, pp. 142—44.

13. Prince, pp. 52—60.

14. Prince, pp. 69—78.

15. For this and the preceding paragraph, see Bridges, pp. 27, 32, 46—64, 82, 181, 188-91. A sensitive fictional portrayal of the Madame-servant relationship in a French creole family very like that of Yseult Bridges can be found in *Witchbroom* (London, 1992) by the (male) Trinidadian writer Lawrence Scott.

16. Schaw, pp. 112—13; Fenwick, pp. 169—70. It is interesting that Fenwick's correspondent, Mary Hays, a radical British writer, had herself published an anti-slavery novel, *The Memoirs of Emma Courtney*, in 1796. See Ferguson, *Subject to Others*, pp. 194—96.

17. Nugent, pp. 12, 29, 30, 68, 78, 86—87, 172—73, 214.

18. Carmichael, I, pp. 59—62, 71.

19. Prince, pp. 67—68, 71—74, 48.

20. Lanaghan, I, p. 259; II, pp. 177—78, 180—81, 96—99, 93—95.

21.Schaw, pp. 127—28, 103—05. Cf. Ferguson, *Subject to Others*, pp. 6—7.

22. Nugent, p. 69; Fenwick, pp. 169, 207, 203– 4; Lanaghan, I, Chapters XXX and XXX1; Bridges, pp. 81—82.

23. Prince, pp. 52, 61—65. Cf. Ferguson, *Subject to Others*, pp. 262—64.

24. Prince, pp. 65, 62, 83—84.

25. Fenwick, p. 169; Lanaghan, II, pp. 177—82; Bridges, pp. 39, 112—13. Bridges' account of her encounter with the menacing black man in Port of Spain has a clear racist undertone.

26. Seacole, pp. 67, 97—98; cf also pp. 105—07. On Seacole, see C. Craig, 'Wonderful Adventures of Mrs Seacole in Many Lands: Autobiography as literary genre and a window to character', *Caribbean Quarterly*, 30 (2), (June 1984), pp. 33—47.

27. Schaw, pp. 87, 113—14, 125.

28. Nugent, pp. 72, 52, 55, 58, 59. A 'penn', or pen, was an estate devoted to livestock rearing. Prince, *passim*, pp. 47—84.

29. Carmichael, I, pp. 39, 21—23; Lanaghan, II, pp. 78, 200, 206—13; Bridges, pp. 128—31.

30. Carmichael, I, pp. 145—49, 154—59, 188, 265—81, 302—12; II, pp. 145—58, 181—86, 199—201.

31. Lanaghan, II, pp. 109—12, 118—21, 126—28, 142—47, 166—71, 182—86; Carmichael, I, pp. 69—75.

32. Seacole, pp. 55—57, 59—61, 78, 100. For the Jamaican tradition of brown and black women keeping lodging houses which doubled as private nursing

homes, see A. Josephs, 'Mary Seacole: Jamaican nurse and "doctress", 1805/10—1881', *Jamaican Historical Review* XV11 (1991), pp. 48—65.

33. Mahase, pp. 3—5, 11—20. The spelling Rookbai is also used by Mahase.
34. Prince, pp. 47—48, 73; Nugent, pp. 146—47; Carmichael, I, pp. 25—26.
35. Carmichael, I, p. 26; Lanaghan, II, pp. 198—201; Fenwick, pp. 167—69, 191, 202; Nugent, p. 58.
36. Bridges, pp. 97, 116—20, 157.
37. Mahase, pp. 20—28, 32—34.
38. Nugent, pp. 123—32, 118—22, 198—99, 174—79; Fenwick, for instance, p. 196.
39. Prince, pp. 50—53, 74—75.
40. Fenwick, pp. 193—95, 212.
41. Bridges, pp. 157—66.
42. Mahase, pp. 3—5, 22—44.
43. Prince, pp. 61—65, 71; Lanaghan, II, pp. 142—47; quotation, p. 146.
44. Bridges, pp. 97, 17—20, 94.
45. Seacole, pp. 55—108; see Josephs, pp. 48—65.
46. Mahase, pp. 37—46, 34.

5.

Gender and Memory:
Oral History and Women's History

Mary Chamberlain

Introduction

Precisely because memory is malleable, is susceptible to confusion and
conflation, to lapses and lying, to suggestion and sensation, and always to
the role of the imagination, oral sources have been dismissed by many
traditional historians as untrustworthy, or relegated to the periphery of
historical enquiry. 'For some areas of historical study,' Arthur Marwick
reluctantly conceded in the 1989 edition of his student primer, *The Nature
of History*, 'relating to the poor and the underprivileged, this kind of source
may be the main one available . . . for Black Americans in the Deep South,
working class wives in Edwardian Britain, Italian peasants in the First
World War, and for much recent Third World history'.[1]

This is the only reference Marwick makes to oral history, black history
or women's history. In some ways his assessment is correct. Oral
testimonies have been used as a prime, or supplementary, source in
constructing histories of certain social groups who, by reason of gender,
class, education, race or culture, have left few other, if any, conventional
sources. Unless engaged in contemporary political history (where their
informants are likely to be key political players), historians who use oral
sources have been forced to argue not only for the value and validity of

their *sources* but equally the value and validity of their *subjects* within the historiographic taxonomy. The task of the academic historian has not been made easier by the association of 'oral history' with both political and consumer populism. 'Oral history' 'empowers' and, in the right hands, 'sells'.

The issue, however, is not to do with whether oral sources are good or bad, true or false, or whether they enhance the supply side or empirical research, or offer an antidote to historical elitism.[2] It rests in what Alessandro Portelli identified as the 'peculiarities' of oral history.[3] In his view, oral sources tell us less about events as such than about their meaning, and their value lies in the areas of language, narrative and subjectivity. Oral sources are different from conventional sources, precisely because they deal with perception and subjectivity. But if those differences and problems are recognised not as limitations, but as representative of a 'different credibility', then their evidential value takes second place to their potential value of signification. I wish here to use Portelli's argument and insights, but to focus on some of the characteristics of oral sources which offer particular insights into the history of gender.

Memory and culture

The first, obvious and most vital feature of oral sources is that they rely on memory. The relationship between memory and the imagination has been a constant feature in the history of both rationalist philosophy and romanticism, in which memory plays a non-rational role as inferior image, or subconscious prompt, to the imagination.[4] At the same time, memory and the imagination have been perceived as unique to the individual. Indeed, what constitutes the 'individual' has been defined by the specific properties of memory. Memory and the individual are indivisible. This notion, central to much western philosophy since the eighteenth century, was given added impetus by psychoanalysis in the nineteenth century, which highlighted the role of memory in the construction of individuality. Yet, obvious though it may seem, the synonymity between memory and individuality is an epistemological, and therefore cultural, construct. Many of the criticism of oral sources *qua* sources rest on this notion. Memory, as a function of the imagination, is both volatile and inferior; at the same time, the individual, peculiarly identified by memory, cannot speak for the collective.

Yet the language, images, priorities and expectations which shape memory and give it structure and meaning derive from shared, that is social, languages, images, priorities and expectations. In this sense, although the *voice* may be individual, and differs from one to another, the form memory assumes, the ways in which it is collated and expressed, is collective. It is culturally and socially determined.

If we recognise that memory rather than being confined to, and by the individual, manifests elements of a shared consciousness and is part of the process of social production, then oral sources offer the potential for entering into a wider cultural milieu. In that sense, the individual voice may be representative of the collective voice and provide evidence of broader attitudes, values and patterns of behaviour. Several such voices may confirm cultural practices. They become objectively self-validating and are the stock-in-trade of ethnographic studies in which comparative research argues forcefully that what appear to be universal principles of human behaviour are always culturally determined. In this sense, the historian who uses oral sources enters the terrain of what may be termed 'historical ethnography'. What may appear to be an individual and fragmented account, is representative of the totality and it is the totality which provides, through affirmation or denial, meaning.

Memory, language and gender

The second obvious, and related, feature of oral evidence is that it is spoken evidence. The form of medium for expressing memory is language. Historians cannot study the substance of their oral evidence without taking account of the form on which it is structured, and the ways in which language itself structures meaning. Again, the relationship of language to meaning has been one of the predominant concerns of Western philosophy, although it is only relatively recently that gender has entered into the philosophical debate. Language[5] itself is gendered. The internal categories employed to structure perception are man-made. Women's experience, in that sense, is already alienated. Moreover, the broader socialisation of men and women encourages them to use language in particular ways. For women, this stresses personal, rather than public, categories. 'Men talk but women gossip' may be a stereotype; but evidence for gendered linguistic subcultures has been supported by research in both the social and behavioural sciences and noted by educationalists.

The first task, therefore, for the feminist historian using oral sources is to enter into this gendered subculture by acknowledging its linguistic roles and its subtexts, and by recognising that women are, as it were, culturally bilingual, that they inhabit simultaneously, not sequentially, a domestic and a public world, and it is this which shapes their experience, the language which expresses it and the priorities allocated within it. In dealing with memory and language, one must deal with gender.

Compare, for instance, these narrative extracts from recent interviews with Barbadians. They are responses to the question, 'tell me about your mother'. I have deleted references to names, but the extracts are otherwise unedited.

> Mrs A., born Barbados, 1908: *My mother, my grandmother, we live together . . . My grandmother, when she took sick in 1921, hair, enough hair pretty white hair like silk cotton, and me and my sister would pick her hair, and we did fair size children at the time, so my mother had the last baby she had born, and my grandmother took sick so. After she took sick, we had to go and pick porn grass and let my mother stay at her mother, that is how it was. Yes, we had to went and pick porn grass and then my mother stay with my grandmother.[6]*

> Mr. B, born Barbados, 1906: *I came along and find my mother . . . had five children when I made six, and she had one more after me then, seven. That was all she had did then. Well, them all, [she] do different work coming on, cor [because] it was for people, do enough field work and about servants and so on, from time to time . . . do while for do, you see time it didn't use a lot of money.[7]*

The respondents were a married couple. The wife's response was badly ordered. It jumped erratically between six subject categories within a short narrative space. Alternatively, her narrative may be interpreted not as a catalogue of subject areas ('indirect-style' or 'topic-associating' response) but in terms of a single unitary vision, as a graphic, textual and sensual description of her grandmother and mother within the totality of their relationship.[8] By contrast, her husband's response listed sequentially the functions performed by his mother. It had segregated, selected and ordered data. In that sense, it could be perceived as the more 'logical' response. Yet to my mind, there is no question that the woman's response expressed an integrated, holistic description of the context in which her mother lived and the context in which, as children, they went out to work. Her husband, on the other hand, while perceiving the integrative world inhabited by his mother, had difficulty expressing it, preferring instead to list methodically two functions performed by his mother and measuring her role against outside referents of class with which, as historians, we are already familiar. His mother worked 'for people'; her earnings 'didn't use a lot of money'. For his wife, the reference points are internal to the family. Her narrative conveys the meaning of her mother's life, implicitly acknowledging the relationship across the generations, the values and attitudes inherent within it, and the emotions generated by it. Her grandmother's 'pretty white hair' privileges us to this. For the historian, the husband's response may offer the most useful evidence, for his wife's response appears too confused and illogical to be of any (conventional) empirical value.

Contrast these two accounts also.

> Mr B, born Barbados, 1917: *She was a very hard working peasant of Barbados. Very poor, but very honest. She worked at various estate plantation, work in St Joseph, St Andrew, St Lucy. And agriculture. Heading cane, working, the dumping, cutting grass, cutting bush, is to make, doing the cane that they make, dung, you know, nutritious dead or the soil.*[9] *(emphasis added)*

> Mrs. B, born Barbados, 1919: *My mother was a very hard working woman. She had thirteen children, but only six of us live. I was the eldest of them all . . So she married, but not to my father, so I, her husband die only, then the last boy was four months old and she had to work, go out to work, hard and hard and I was the only one to help her. I has to go out early and work, in the third class and when I work, I gets twenty cents a day, then it raise to twenty four cent. I used to try to do the same work as the older women that older than I, so to help her and I would bring all my money and give her. So she used to say I was her husband, yes.*[10] *(emphasis added)*

Again, the first response contains external reference points. His mother he describes as a gender-neutral 'peasant', her ascribed role. He offers a sequential and compartmentalised description of her work. His wife's response foregrounds gender. Her mother was a woman. Mrs B. does not distinguish between her mother's domestic and public roles and her own position within the family. Clearly, in all these narratives, class and education enter into the nature of the language. This is 'working-class' speech. Yet all informants had attained the same educational level at school (standard four). In theory, the gender differences cannot be accounted for by differing access to education, although there may have been (though this is beyond the scope of this article) different and perhaps unconscious emphasis on gender attainment in the education process.

In addition to structure, language also contains what Portelli labels 'orality', which embraces not merely the linguistic framework, but such para-linguistic features as timbre, volume, rhythm and velocity, which equally convey meaning. Such 'meanings' often provide a subtext, a set of aural symbols which can convey obvious clues to class or emotion, but also less obvious ones to identity and perception. The 'subject' is lost in the process of transcription, but can contribute significantly to interpretation.

Let me offer another example, from a non-Caribbean context. A poor London woman in the 1920s pawned her wedding ring in order to make ends meet. To prevent her husband finding out, she replaced the gold wedding ring with a brass one from Woolworth's.

Eventually, she was able to redeem the original ring, but, as her daughters recalled:

we couldn't get the Woolworth's ring off . . . she was saying 'Your father'll kill me, your father'll kill me.' And she had a big red finger, because it was her paralysed hand, you see. And every time you pulled the finger out (straight), after a while it would take your hand and close up with your hand on it . . .[11]

They eventually succeeded in removing the ring. It is a story of urban poverty, within a context of domestic violence. In many ways it is sufficient. Yet this story was told not 'straight' by her two daughters, but within a context of laughter. They could barely talk. They repeated themselves, emphasising and illustrating the narrative by mimicking the movements of their mother's paralysed hand. What meaning does this subtext of mirth and mimicry offer? First, it signalled collusion, a recognition that the act of pawning the wedding ring was an implicit subversion not only of male authority in the home but in the broader society, which defined working-class women as feckless and fecund. Second, it signalled judgement, an indication that they had evaluated the road they had travelled from childhood to the present and were able to measure the distance and locate it within its historical context. This subtext signalled a gap between the available codes and conventions of description, and the meaning which these women ascribed to their behaviour. As Anderson and Jack suggested:

A woman's discussion of her life may combine two separate, often conflicting perspectives: one framed in concepts and values that reflect men's dominant position in the culture, and one informed by the more immediate realities of a woman's personal experience. Where experience does not 'fit' dominant meanings, alternative concepts may not readily be available.

As a result, they argue, 'To hear women's perspectives accurately, we have to listen in stereo.'[12]

Historians, like informants, are required to exercise distance and objectivity. Logicality and rationality are the required hallmarks of the historian's trade. Historians are trained to investigate what is explicit, either 'wittingly' or 'unwittingly'; any other 'readings' lead to conjecture only. Nevertheless, although this aural 'para-language' may not exist in literary communication, it does in oral communication. The meanings suggested are implicit. They are not articulated. My understanding of the 'subtext,' of which this is one example, alerted me to how a 'para-language' can offer a contradictory meaning, and/or suggest a position of unarticulated dissonance, or discomfort, with prevailing norms and values. Further questioning on the theme of subversion confirmed my initial hunch. But it was the para-language, not the language, which alerted me to this, and led, finally to a wider interpretation of the culture of working-class women in London, which emphasised the role of deception and subversion in the construction of self and collective identity.

If one looks at language, as these small examples show, gendered language — both women's and men's — needs to be understood precisely because it is gendered and therefore makes different connections and priorities. This does not invalidate either 'language'; but it does recognise that the memories of men and women provide different insights, motivations and reference points which must be accommodated within an interviewer's framework and should not be dismissed when they fail to do so. Historians have been trained in the positivism of their profession. Looking at language and gender may require skills and insights which take them beyond the limits of their profession, limits which are, arguably, gendered themselves, but which may offer valuable insight into how identities and memories are constructed, and the role these play in the process of historical socialisation and social change.

Memory and subjectivity

And yet oral evidence is also subjective evidence. Oral sources are first-hand, personal accounts. However much one may wish to 'read' them as assertions of a wider set of social relations, it flies in the face of 'common sense'. Memory is autobiographical. It remains doggedly 'individual'. In the historian's pursuit of objectivity, the value of oral evidence can, it is assumed, be upheld only when it can be corroborated with evidence from other sources, or by accounts of analogous similar experiences. Oral history offers facts. In the examples quoted above, the man's evidence is easy to comprehend and to corroborate: the primary emphasis is on their mother's working lives outside the home, defined by familiar social and economic reference points and confirmed by analogy. The women also refer to their mother's work beyond the home, but their descriptions interweave their mother's workplace role with her domestic role, and their own place and role within the family. It is difficult to disentangle the subject-ordering from the content. All that can be validated by analogy is evidence of 'muddled thinking', an apparent confusion and conflation within the texts, a chaos, substantiating a broader mythology that women are overlaid with what appears extraneous information. How do phrases such as 'pretty white hair' (Mrs A), or 'she called me her husband' (Mrs B), offer insight into the material structures which provide the context for these women's lives, other than as thicker, more flowery description? This evidence is impressionistic. It lies within the imaginative. It is, above all, subjective. It belongs more appropriately within the realms of fiction and romanticism than a rationalist, positivist tradition.

Should one then dismiss subjectivity when it intrudes into the collective memory, for diminishing the value of 'hard' empirical evidence? What use can it be to the historian? Subjectivity, as the Italian historian, Luisa Passerini, summarised it, is: 'both the aspects of spontaneous subjective being contained and represented by *attitude, behaviour and language* as well as other forms of awareness such as the sense of *identity, consciousness of oneself* and more considered forms of intellectual identity.'[13] (emphasis added)

Memory is both collective and subjective. Thus, what is said can be taken as representative of a culture, but this culture is reflected not only in its material world of artifacts and spatial arrangements, and in its ordered world of social relations and shared structures, including language, but also in the symbols and myths, the dreams which reflect and reproduce that culture and which give expression to otherwise abstract values of hopes and desires, failure and envy. These values are socially (and therefore historically) constructed; they all play a role in the shaping of identity and behaviour; they are, however, gendered in that they are the product of particular sets of relationships and ascribed behaviour.

In order to understand society, it is essential to understand first the construction and operation of gender as acted out in the relations (attitudes and behaviour) between men and women, and in the cracks and niches within those relationships, in the subversions and deceptions; and second, how gender is represented in consciousness and expressed in notions of identity. Men and women's narratives are constructed differently. This is reflected in their use of language and para-language and the intrusion of seemingly irrelevant information. But if the premise of a gendered subculture is extended, such extraneous detail may offer further clues into this subculture. Rather than dismiss what appear to be frivolous and subjective embellishments, one should perhaps look at them as the mechanisms by which the individual negotiated with the social, although always within the categories of the latter. Indeed, they may offer vital clues into an historical understanding of gender.

Precisely because one listens to memories in their oral expression (for otherwise one shares no access to it) one should, therefore, mark out the points of subjectivity, in the extraneous detail, in the flights of imaginative fancy, that the often inarticulate world of the senses, of passions and dreams, of disappointments, discordancies and the restrictions of human life and human identity, as experienced by women, find expression.

Thus the sensual world of hair 'like silk cotton,' suggests intimacy offered, provided and valued. It suggests the importance of hair as a symbol of (female) gender and sexuality. It suggests also a recognition of chronology, of growing up, of getting old. There may be other interpretations. But this is an insight into the world which women value, and is no less important for doing so. Equally, the phrase 'she called me her husband' is not just an indication of the accepted role of the male as provider. It indicates also a broader mythology, accepted by both generations, of the fallibility of all husbands. That her daughter tried to work as hard as the older women is not only a symbol of the daughter's pride in assuming the role of provider but implicit acknowledgement of women's role as providers as well as nurturers.

But there is more to subjectivity. Let me offer another example. In response to the question: 'When you landed in England, what was your first impression?' Mrs C, born in 1930, replied:

> When I was leaving, I got a tailor to make me a nice jacket, and I made a skirt, so I had a nice outfit. And when I came to Victoria, my brother bought a lovely red coat, fitted one. And I was this pretty young girl, this lovely red coat. Well, I first look at the house, and I wonder, what's these things on the roof for? And I said, 'All these factories!' 'Cos I only knew factories had chimneys, you know, and I sais . . . 'they must got a big shortage here for labour, with all these factories.'[14]

Mrs C answered the question by locating herself, as subject, in this new country, by identifying herself in terms of her gender, in the guise by which, perhaps stereotypically or mythically, female gender is most conspicuously identified, in terms of clothes and appearances. The chimneys represented (mistaken) opportunities, of equal importance to her as appearance. Subjectivity and gender awareness were interlaced. Above all, she was 'this pretty young girl, in this lovely red coat.' She was feminine. This was her identity and it demarcated difference. Her (erstwhile) partner (born 1929) on the other hand replied:

> Gloomy, but that didn't surprise me because I was told about the weather conditions and it was in the season, the cold season, gloomy, gloomy, very gloom, you walk, you going in, you see the chimneys, every house has a chimney stick up and the smoke going up and smog and what have you.[15]

It is significant that in his response, England was identified 'objectively'; this world conformed to what he had been told about. His own subjectivity, his sense of self, was missing in this extract, although it emerged in different ways later in his narrative, as he recounted his life story, building up a chronological account of his career. But nowhere was there any overt statement that he was masculine, that his self-identity was linked with gender. It was taken as implicit, in the work he undertook, in the roles he performed. But for his erstwhile partner, her subjectivity, her sense of self, was central to being feminine. She was there. Again, should one dismiss this as evidence of frivolity, edit it out of her account, focus instead on her career, force her narrative to conform to a male-ordered world of objectively defined categories and roles? To do so invalidates her perception. If the historian must be true to the sources, then what emerges in oral sources, even if it does not conform to historical categories, must be accounted for.

In these extracts, I am favouring the women's account by suggesting that their potential is richer than that of men's. I do so for two reasons. First, because I understand what women tell me and can relate to it. As a woman, I have no problem with their spiralling descriptions, although as an academic historian I do. There is a temptation to dismiss such memories as too difficult to disentangle, or too frivolous to be of historical value. What does it matter what she wore? Yet as this and the earlier examples show, the problem of compartmentalising women's memories should not invalidate those memories, but alert us to what may be of significance. Equally, when an informant emphasises her subjectivity, her femininity, this should be taken not as an uncomfortable intrusion into the historian's objectivity, but accepted as a vital indicator of the difference in which she lived her life. Second, I think that it is necessary in the spirit of positive discrimination and equal opportunities to investigate these issues. Although many feminist historians have used oral sources, on the whole they use them within masculine academic categories of class, power, and so on. I said in my introduction to *Fenwomen*[16] that 'the women's story must be told, but it must be seen in a perspective of its own.' I believe that oral history should go beyond the story, and explore how those stories are perceived, received and transmitted.

Women's subjectivity, as Sally Alexander reminds us:

> *is only one element in the relation of sexual difference, but one fraught with difficulties of interpretation because it opens up not only behaviour, thought, opinion and family stories to historical enquiry, but also the unconscious mental processes. That is, we listen to fantasies about desire and loss, the compelling inner directives of the structure of sexual difference.*[17]

In this view, sexuality and the politics of gender must be considered a powerful determinant of human behaviour, at least as powerful as the more familiar materialist determinant of class. This requires not only a fresh interrogation of sources, but the courage to argue that subjectivity matters, precisely because it may provide clues to the private, personal and often unconscious 'directives' with which an individual negotiates a life course. This is particularly important in the case of women where the bargaining points are not in her control, when the perceptions of 'logicality' and 'illogicality' are gendered, when the values implicit in her evidence are marginalised in both general and academic convention. If memories contain gender differences in structure and content, then those differences require exposure and explanation. They may contribute to an alternative interpretation of the historical process and present a fundamental challenge to interpretation. Indeed, gender should offer a challenge to the reading not merely of oral sources, but of all sources.

With each generation and with each layer of subjectivity, the past moves on. Memory, too, has a history, but the history it offers is a generational history. Nevertheless, it is a vital part of the process of socialisation, for the structures, themes and shifting meanings of memory are inherited, passed down through the generations. Studying memories across generations may be used as an exercise in 'micro-history', to chronicle the ways in which people cope and change, reject and reflect, inherit and construct their sense of self, and with what effect.

Oral sources provide an opportunity to approach history, in which gender should be a determining characteristic, from the inside out, to recognise that men and women's memories are different, and differently expressed, and that these differences are important agents in historical transmission. This idea is not new. The social and behavioural sciences and the growing field of family therapy all point to the importance of the family, and a family 'ethos' in shaping the life courses of subsequent generations.[18] Historians, however, have been slow to accommodate these insights. But a focus on gender, on questions of subjectivity, necessarily orientates our understanding towards the family, and the ways in which gender is represented and transmitted (or transformed), and with what effect.

Mrs C, this 'pretty young girl in a lovely red coat', signalled her identity through emphasising her femininity. Her daughter was seven when her mother left for England. 'I can remember her going . . . I can remember my mother had on a white organza blouse on the day she left. And I always remember thinking how pretty she looked. But I was devastated.'[19]

Why should both mother and daughter describe arrival and departure in terms of clothes? Given the trauma of the separation, clothes (say the rationalists) should be the last, not the first, item on the agenda of recall. Mrs C goes further:

> my mother was very smart. Half of her money went on clothes . . . (I was) young, free and happy. I was always a kind of happy woman, you know? . . . I used to make (my daughter's) clothes and she was happy, she was happy, she was a happy little girl . . . I used to make her so pretty . . . and she was a good child. No problems with [her].[20]

A love of clothes may have been inherited from her mother and was projected on to her daughter. More particularly, Mrs C emphasises happiness, of which clothes were the outward expression. It is a perception corroborated by her daughter:

> One of the memories I have of my mother is a fun person. Nothing seemed to make her cross . . . I think I was a grandmother child, firstborns in Barbados usually are. So I remember my grandmother being the focal point of my life, and my mother was this woman who wafted in, smelling of perfume, with nail polish, wide skirts, thin waist, made a lot of noise in the house, laughing . . .

Fun and clothes were part of Mrs C's sense of self and the *persona* was directly perceived and interpreted by her daughter. But there was more. Her daughter recalls her father visiting and taking her:

> to his family in St Lucy, and I used to feel like a little treasure, because my mother was a dressmaker and she, when she knew he was coming, she would dress me up in the prettiest dress . . . I think she used to show off about me and I think he also is the passion of her life. He was her first lover . . . both of them are always telling me, and I'm very conscious of it, that I was a love child, and very much a love child for both of them . . . he would collect me, and carry me down to St Lucy, to my grandmother, who would then parade me through the village . . . she'd just show me off, she'd take me to the village shop and she'd put me on the counter and my dress would fan out . . .[21]

Clothes were an expression of her mother's (and her father's) sexuality, of which she, as the daughter, was the living embodiment. Her early sense of self was not only vividly connected with appearances, but also inseparable from her mother's love and sexuality. Throughout her narrative, her mother's clothes are a recurrent theme. When her father left for England,

> I must have been probably five. I remember my stepmother, and my mother and a couple of other girlfriends that my father had . . . all at the quayside . . . He was kissing all of them. And they all adored him, although he'd obviously done dirties on most of them . . . and they started to quarrel . . . I can remember all of this. I can actually remember the dress my mother had on that day. And she was laughing . . .[22]

Equally, when her mother re-migrated to Canada,

> I was devastated . . . she has an old dressing gown that she left in the house the morning she left. And I picked it up, and when I'm upset, I put it on, and I sleep in it. Sometimes I go and I wrap it round my neck. I can smell her on this dressing gown, which is ridiculous. I am forty two years old.[23]

Far from being a frivolous accessory, in this mother/daughter relationship, clothes were an expression and a symbol of their relationship, with all the complexities of absence, of loss, of sexuality, of happiness and of love. Clothes, in other words, conveyed a set of meanings which were integral to the various identities of both mother and daughter.

Yet historians are not supposed to view appearances as important. A history of fashion features low on the historian's agenda. Worse, why should feminist historians emphasise appearances, when most of their endeavours have been on denying, personally and politically, the gendered meanings inherent in appearances? What can the historian make of these sources, which are couched in highly subjective terms and which carry a conspicuous amount of emotional weight? First, a recognition that personal relationships are a central and unifying feature of human life. In women's memories, as these testimonies show, the family nexus is prominent. If one is to understand gender historically, then the centrality of passions, of relationships, and their role in directing attitudes and behaviour needs to be accommodated even though the evidence is awkward, charged with emotion and seemingly irrational. If one takes sufficient notice of these subjective sources, emblematic themes may emerge which could illuminate what I described earlier as the cracks and niches in gender relations, the means by which women create, sustain and transmit identity in a culture which daily disadvantages and discredits identity.

As an illustration, I have highlighted how in two (possibly three) generations of one family, clothes are a significant theme for the women. More generally, in the interviews with Barbadian migrants, and over the years in interviews with others, women refer again and again to the clothes they wore. Appearances represent identity; they signal femininity. On a broader level, clothes are part of the iconography of womanhood. But they also indulge the imagination and the senses. Clothes represent a definition or statement of difference, independence and autonomy. They may also signal defiance and deception. 'I ent show poor', another informant told me. Such definitions may be illusory, but dressing well places women in the centre, as creators of the illusion, as appropriating one set of male-derived meanings and investing them with their own. The signal may be subtle, but then the best deceptions are.

The dialectic of memory

But, the critics say, memory is multi-layered and multi-faceted. It may be subjective, but it is not pure. Memory contains vicarious as well as experientially derived experience. It is mobile and fluid, and subject to influences which may be traced vertically across the generations and horizontally within the generations. Memories change and distort as other social and cultural influences — film images, song, dance, literature, politics, and so forth — and personal factors, such as the life cycle itself, enter into perception and alter or adjust those memories. Memories, therefore, offer shifting interpretations. People live through and with memories which have already mapped out a territory in the social imagination, in whose paths they walk. At the same time, the form which memory takes, the way people remember, shapes not only the content, but what is revealed to others, and how it is revealed. In addition, in narration, there is always an element of genre and a notion of audience. The mentality or orality of memory is necessarily complex, subject constantly to revision and interpretation.

Rather than this being a limitation, it can be used positively to enrich the analysis. For example, Mrs C's daughter was left in Barbados when her mother migrated to England. In this unedited extract she describes how her mother

> *sent me a blonde dolly, which I hated. She sent her sister, who would have been a lot younger than her, a brunette. It was smaller than mine, and bit by bit, I couldn't do it for my grandmother to see, but over a period of probably a month, I had completely destroyed this dolly, because I hated the blonde hair. Interestingly, because now I can see it in intellectual terms, the blonde dolly was alien to me, as a black child who had never seen a blonde person. But my mother, thinking I was her little girl, she had sent me the biggest, prettiest doll England had to offer. I hated it. I resented my mother. I was angry with her for sending M. the pretty little brunette, which was more to what I was used to. And I, in turn, resented M. for having this dolly, not parting with it, to let me borrow it. And bit by bit, I used to have accidents with this dolly, the big one. I remember another day hitting it with a stone. Then I remember, another time, being extremely angry and I actually took a rock and bashed its face in. By the time I was finished with it, you couldn't recognise it as a dolly. But I hated it. Isn't it strange how you remember!*[24]

Recalling and narrating this event required interpretation and reinterpretation: to make sense of her antagonism to the doll, to account for the anger and resentment towards her mother, to accommodate her mother's motives and exonerate her, to articulate her jealousy of her aunt, and to explain deceiving her grandmother in whose charge she had been left. The story operates on a range of psychological, social, emotional and racial levels. More particularly, it was not mere hindsight which enabled this understanding. The daughter joined her mother in England when she was ten years old, and her interpretation is necessarily overlaid with her subsequent experiences of racism in England and the means she developed to cope with this. Until prompted, she had 'forgotten' the doll; once prompted, that memory was necessarily evaluated and explained. The doll was both a symbol of abandonment, and a prefigurement of alienation. This single memory, therefore, was recounted in a multi-layered fashion, mobile, fluid and conveying a complicated arrangement of 'meanings'. It is also reminiscent of Maya Angelou (who received a similar gift of a white doll from her absent mother[25]) and perhaps broader cultural archetypes: the moment of time when the child's sense of abandonment is synchronised and symbolised in a gift which was alien to her experience, understanding and culture. The doll was an intrusion and an insult. But she cannot be sure. The daughter was a university-educated woman. She was well-read in both Caribbean and black American literature. Its symbolic importance may have been given meaning by external influences.

It does not matter. The individual is not immutable. There is no single, authoritative centre. There is no autonomy. Instead, there are, as Gwendolyn Etter-Lewis described it, 'multiple and differing images of a black female self.'[26] And it is these 'multiple and differing images' which need to be reinvestigated in any history of gender.

Oral evidence offers one way forward, by providing a three-dimensional source which can be interrogated at a range of levels, not least of which will be the points at which memory is both revised and/or blends personal experience with the language and images of a more public world. Oral sources cannot be examined as narratives, and can be located within genres, in terms of grammar, structure and theme. For memories are narratives; they are biographical and as such are shaped by particular conventions; they require selection and simplification; there is a constant dialectic between internal experience and external categories, between the personal and the public, between private space and symbolic space and symbols. Even time is constructed not on linear or chronological lines, but in terms of priorities. It is possible to look for archetypes, or for particular recurrent mythologies which contribute towards and shape how a life is interpreted. Such analysis is beyond the ambition of this article; yet the pointers cannot be abandoned. Even within this short piece, the white doll/absent black mother emerges as one possible archetypal theme. Equally, the grammar of memory divides on the faultline of gender. The totality of mothers and grandmothers may be representative of an ideal, rather than a literal, type. Holistic memories, incapable of corroboration or analogy, may reflect in structure and form, a more universal way of perceiving and acting. If one looks at narratives partly through the lens of a cultural fiction, then their force and role — in conveying moral values, in ordering forms of heroism or neglect or even brutality, as systems which convey meanings rather than truth, as powerful didactic elements in the historical construction of self and identity — may be recognised as central to an understanding of how gender is both determined and acts as a determinant. They may suggest a way in which such seemingly disparate sources can be collectively validated. It may be necessary to look to literary criticism, to folklore, to ethnography, to find paradigms, to be more interdisciplinary in the interpretation of sources. But out of the chaos of gendered memories some order may be found. It may not conform to the more familiar rational conventions, but that could release, rather than inhibit, further insights.

Conclusion

Oral sources are neither true nor false, and to pursue them as either is to pursue a chimera. What is needed is an interrogation of oral sources to arrive at a different set of historical evidence. The language of memory is the means by which tradition is transmitted, the means by which structure and values are internalised, passed on and inherited. Memories are imaginative recountings, representative of a set of meanings by which and through which lives are interpreted and transmitted, constructed and changed. Rather than relegate gender and memory to the edges of history, they should be foregrounded as one of a set of central, interpretative tools for understanding the nature and process of historical change.

Endnotes

I am grateful to the Nuffield Foundation whose grant enabled me to undertake research into the social history of migration from Barbados to Britain. This article has drawn on examples from that research.

1. Arthur Marwick, *The Nature of History* (3rd edn, London: Macmillan, 1989; first published 1970).
2. Mike Frisch, *A Shared Autobiography: Essays on the Craft and Meaning of Oral History* (New York: Albany, 1990).
3. Alessandro Portelli, 'The Peculiarities of Oral History', *History Workshop Journal*, No. 12 (autumn 1981).
4. For the relationship between memory and imagination in philosophy, see Mary Warnock, *Imagination* (London: Faber, 1976).
5. Dale Spender, *Man Made Language* (London: Routledge, 1985).
6. Ref: B28. All such references from the Barbados Migration Project (Mary Chamberlain). Tapes and transcripts deposited with the National Life Story Collection of the National Sound Archive of the British Library.
7. Ref: B30.
8. I am grateful to Dr Velma Pollard for offering me this insight. See Velma Pollard, 'Indirectness in Afro-American Speech Communities — Some Implications for Classroom Practice', Faculty of Education, University of the West Indies, Mona, Jamaica.
9. Ref: B4.
10. Ref: B10.
11. Mary Chamberlain, *Growing Up In Lambeth* (London: Virago, 1989), p. 117.
12. Kathryn Anderson and Dana Jack, 'Learning to Listen: Interview Techniques and Analyses', in Sherna Berger Gluck and Daphne Patai (eds.), *Women's Words: The Feminist Practice of Oral History* (London & New York: Routledge, 1991).
13. Luisa Passerini, 'Work Ideology and Consensus under Italian Fascism', *History Workshop Journal*, No. 8 (autumn 1979).
14. Ref: BB29.
15. Ref: B34.
16. Mary Chamberlain, *Fenwomen* (1st edn, London: Virago, 1975).
17. Sally Alexander, 'Becoming a Woman in London in the 1920s and 1930s', in D. Feldman and G. Stedman Jones (eds.), *Metropolis* (London: Routledge, 1990).
18. See Mary Chamberlain, 'Family and Identity: Barbadian Migrants to Britain', *The Yearbook of Oral History and Life Stories*, (Oxford: Oxford University Press, 1994); and 'Motive and Myth in Migration: Barbadians to Britain', paper presented to 25th Annual Conference of the Association of Caribbean Historians, (UWI, Jamaica, 1993).

19. Ref: BB45.
20. Ref: BB29.
21. Ref: BB45, p. 31.
22. Ref: BB45, pp. 11—12.
23. *Ibid*.
24. Ref: B45.
25. Maya Angelou, *I Know Why the Caged Bird Sings* (London: Virago, 1984).
26. Gwendolyn Etter-Lewis, 'Black Women's Life Stories: Reclaiming Self in Narrative Texts', in *Women's Words, op. cit.*

6.

Pictorial Sources for Nineteenth-Century Women's History:

Dress as a Mirror of Attitudes to Women

Glory Robertson

Dress is one of the most revealing mirrors of the social attitudes of any society. It has strongly reflected attitudes to class, to youth and age, to male and female roles. Clothes until quite recently were intended to set people of birth, affluence and leisure apart from the rest. Dressing above one's station in life earned disapproval and ridicule from those of higher rank. This disapproval in Jamaica sometimes mirrored racist as well as class attitudes. A visitor in 1900 wrote, 'Next morning everyone turned out in their Sunday best. Big hulking negresses were attired in gorgeous silks and satins, and truly wonderful hats with broad brims and feathers, and ribbon . . . The woolly locks under all this fashionable headgear were pathetically ludicrous.'[1]

It is only fair to record that another observer was able to see that the people he thought ludicrous might disapprove of him, and that some visitors thought that black working-class women wore their best attire with dignity. They looked more at home in it than English housemaids and haymakers in similar garments, according to Anthony Trollope, the well-known English novelist.[2]

At the end of the twentieth century, fashion is aimed at the mass market rather than at the elite, so that clothes are no longer the social indicator that they once were and it can be difficult to discern the class origin of a student in faded jeans and T-shirt. But in the nineteenth century there were many class indicators in women's clothes. For example, in the 1840s shoulder seams and armholes of fashionable European dresses were so made that it was difficult to lift the arms, a method of clothes construction that was unwearable by women who had to engage in strenuous physical work. The sheer weight of middle-class clothes — the numerous petticoats of the 1840s and early 1850s, the elaborate draped skirts of the 1880s — was tiring. The appropriate walking length for a lady's dress in the 1880s was not very much above the ground at a time when Jamaican peasant women could hitch up their skirts and leave their legs bare as high as the knee.[3] In the 1890s, photographs show working-class women dressed in their best at weddings in simple round skirts, not the fashionable gored and flared skirts which required more skillful dressmakers. Shoes and stockings were a social indicator throughout the nineteenth century and into the early years of the

Figure 1. *1869. Clear indications of working class status are the headtie, short sleeves for day wear, the simple skirt and the bare feet. The shape like a third foot at the back is a photographer's stand, used to keep the subject from fidgeting during the long exposures that were necessary.*

twentieth; many working-class people wore shoes only to church and for special occasions; some never wore shoes at all. Most working-class women did without corsets and it was only they who wore headties. The quantity of material needed for some of the fashionable styles must also have been a factor. Dress lengths advertised in Jamaica in 1857 and 1860, when the crinoline was fashionable in Europe, vary from 8 to 18 yards.[4] A circumference of 3-3½ yards at the hem was recommended for the tied-back skirts of 1876. Norah Waugh describes their construction as one width of the fabric for the centre front, two or four widths for the side gores and two or three widths at the back.[5] An 1880s dress with its draped apron front and a cascade of drapery over the bustle at the back also took more material than a simple skirt.

Ideas concerning youth, age and marital status of women were also reflected in what was considered appropriate wear. Throughout the nineteenth century there were clearly defined stages: a very young girl wore skirts short enough to show the lace-edged ends of her drawers; as she grew older this garment became not only invisible but unmentionable. At 16 or 17, a girl put up her hair, lowered her hemline and became an adult, but it was unthinkable that she should show the degree of decolletage allowed to married women of mature years. One of the Jeffery-Smith sisters of Spanish Town recollects that at the turn of the century, 'At formal balls ... the dowagers rustled in, . . . with bodices cut remarkable low, considering how strict they were on us girls!'[6] Certain colours and materials were considered inappropriate to young unmarried girls but could be worn by married women of exactly the same age, to whom they gave 'the touch of stateliness and the settled air' becoming to the matron. So throughout the period women's magazines gave advice similar to this: 'very young unmarried ladies, whom fashion will not permit to dress expensively, wear organdy and tarlatane, very simply trimmed; while gauze, crepe, satin, tulle and lace all of the richest description and with splendid garnitures, are adopted by married belles.'[7] Marriage was the most important change in status that could happen to a woman, and it was signalled by the clothes she wore.

In the eighteenth century an interest in fashion had been as much the province of men as of women among the European upper classes, for whom, as Aileen Ribero says, 'the art of dressing well was not just a part of good manners but a necessary prop to established society'.[8] Men were expected to take an interest in clothes and both sexes dressed to convey the idea of a leisured class. Silks, embroidery and lace were all part of men's wear though the nobility and gentry of England, with their much greater emphasis on living in the country, always tended to be more plainly dressed than those of France, the fashion leaders of Europe, who revolved around the royal court. An important factor in the decrease of male finery in the nineteenth century was the feeling, coming from the rising middle class of the Industrial Revolution, that to be worthy of respect a man should earn his living in some way. One result of this was that the plain garments suitable to a place of business became necessary for all men who did not wish to appear frivolous. The subdued clothes of a professional or a businessman, to quote Pos and Smith, 'reflected and reinforced his social role. He was not an aristocrat at leisure but a hard-working, self-disciplined man, daily meeting the responsibilities of the marketplace.'[9] Thereafter, it was through the dress of their women that nineteenth-century men displayed their rank and affluence and an interest in fashion became, by definition, both feminine and frivolous.

In the mid-nineteenth century middle- and upper-class women were regarded as fragile and dependent, with a role restricted to the home; by the end of the century the rights of women, the 'women question' as it was called, had become an issue. This change was also reflected in clothes. Alison Gernsheim has said that 'Never before or since has Western women's costume expressed respectability, acquiescence and dependence to such a degree as in the 1840s.'[10] Women's movements were restricted by their clothes, but they were also sheltered and protected by them from the touch or even (at any rate, in day clothes) from the gaze of men. The fashions of the 1840s featured a full skirt, long enough to hide the feet, and held out by numerous petticoats; bonnets which were so low at the sides of the face and projected so far in front that the face was screened from view except from directly in front; the back of

Figure 2. *c. 1886. Walking length for a niddle class lady on the right and for a working class woman on the left. The skirt that appears short has been pulled up over a cord round the hips for greater freedom of movement.*

the neck was covered by a veil attached to the bonnet; large shawls or mantles covered the upper part of the figure when outdoors and gloves covered the hands. In the 1870s a very narrow, sheath-like line was worn and bodices were most carefully cut to mould the figure, but a fashion writer of the time observed that 'The hard casings, the whalebone coffin worn inside it, deprived the visible surface of the vivid suggestion of the living and breathing body.'[11] The eventual introduction of more practical clothing from about 1890 went hand in hand with the entry of middle-class women into the work force and the general emancipation of women. This will be discussed in more detail below.

The question of women wearing men's clothes has been a sensitive issue since biblical times. Although women had already adopted masculine-style coats, neckcloths and hats for wear with riding habits and for travelling, the 1890s 'new woman' going out to work in her tailor-mades (which we would call suits) worn with 'mannish' collars and ties attracted criticism and ridicule precisely because she was wearing these masculine-type styles in her new role as working woman. But the greatest condemnation was reserved for women in any garment which publicly revealed that they had legs. Such exposure was regarded as indecent; it was also seen as an invasion of the man's role. It is not by accident that the phrase, 'she wears the pants', signifies a wife who dominated her husband. An American, Amelia Bloomer, in the 1850s attempted to reform women's dress by introducing an outfit consisting of knee-length tunic and Turkish trousers, very full and gathered to a band at the ankles. Women who wore it in public met with so much abuse and ridicule that very few dared to do so.

I have not found any mention of Jamaican women in the Bloomer costume, but the reaction to trousers is illustrated by two newspaper stories. In one story, two middle-class Kingston girls, simply as a prank, one evening in 1884 donned their father's trousers and masqueraded as men, walking from their home in Kingston Gardens to their uncle's house in the same suburb, then a 'good' residential district. They were recognised, and the consequences began to be apparent when the male friend who had recognised them exhibited marked disrespect for them in their own house. He was thrown out by their father and sued him on a charge of assault. The way in which the case was publicised in a newspaper shows clearly that the girls were indeed regarded as having forfeited respect by 'unsexing themselves'. They had been unwomanly, 'disgusting' and guilty of 'indecent exposures'. At a different class level, in 1857 a woman accused of stealing a goat tried to escape arrest by leaving her yard clad in pantaloons, a shirt, a white jacket and a hat. She passed through the crowd 'taking snuff all the while', but suspicion was aroused, she was pursued and caught and the spectators 'commenced to exult . . . in a manner almost unendurable.' Idlers

Figure 3. *c. 1862. Two crinoline styles for day wear. Contrast these skirts, held stiffly out by the steel hoops beneath, with that of the peasant woman in Figure 2.*

waited outside the courthouse in Kingston for about two hours to see her brought there in her 'peculiar dress.'[12]

In the early 1850s the skirt became even wider and to support it some of the petticoats were lined with horsehair or even straw.[13] In 1853 hoops began to be stitched into the lining and skirts appeared even more voluminous because of the stiffened flounces with which they were often trimmed. In 1856 the cage crinoline was invented in France, consisting of rows of hoops made of flexible steel connected by tapes, the hoops increasing in size from waist to hem. It freed women from the burden of hot and heavy petticoats clinging to their legs and was an immediate success in Europe and America. Even Amelia Bloomer stopped wearing her tunic and trousers because she found the cage crinoline light and comfortable.[14] It achieved a more elegant line than the bulky petticoats, and swayed gracefully as the wearer walked. However, it was inconvenient in crowded rooms, unmanageable in a breeze, dangerous at times, and offered great scope to cartoonists and other wits. For example, the *Falmouth Post* took the trouble to reprint a non-Jamaican tale of a disappointed bride whose wedding did not take place because her hoops were too wide to pass through the church door.[15] The cage crinoline reached its greatest popularity and size about 1859—64; in the early 1860s the shape changed somewhat as the front became slightly flattened and the fullness swelled out behind. By 1865—66 fashion magazines were predicting the end of the crinoline but it did not disappear till about 1868.

Crinoline dresses were simple in comparison with the complex styles that followed in the next 20 years. Although the cage crinoline was abandoned at the end of the 1860s, the basic shape of the skirt, a flattened front with fullness behind, was retained; the fullness, often provided by a peplum or overskirt, was bunched at waist level at the back and supported by a pad tied round the waist. This was called a bustle or 'dress improver' or tournure. Alternatively, the required shape could be created by wearing a half-crinoline. From about 1874 tapes sewn on the inside pulled the front of the skirt back against the legs to create a more slender effect, called the tied-back skirt. The bodice by 1876 was made much longer, fitting very tightly over the stomach and hips and ending in a point at front and back; it was, says Alison Gernsheim, 'practically a corset, made of shaped pieces of material with sometimes as many as seventeen seams so that it should tightly mould the curves of the body',[16] and was appropriately named the cuirasse bodice. As the length of this bodice made a bustle at waist level impossible, the back drapery was moved downwards, to a position between the hips and the knees, fanning out into a train. The Princess line without a seam at the waist became a characteristic style for bodices. There was also a close-fitting but not corset-like jacket bodice ending just below the hips in a straight line instead of points. The emphasis was on the slenderness of the line, but trimming of every kind could be added to the narrow foundation skirt, often in a different colour or a different material. The sheath-like shape remained fashionable until 1880—82 when it was succeeded by a revival of the bustle, placed some inches lower than in the 1870s and projecting more prominently, with deep folds curving across the skirt in front, forming an apron-like effect. Later in the 1880s asymmetrically placed vertical pleats were popular. The bustle outline was high fashion till about 1887.

At the end of the 1880s there was another change of line in women's dress. The most obvious difference was that decorative emphasis moved from the skirt to the bodice or blouse. The bustle, the overskirt and all the draped folds of 1880s skirts disappeared; the new plain skirts fitted closely over the hips, flaring out below, or the same effect could be achieved by a yoke at the top of the skirt or a flounce at the knee.

The most significant developments in women's clothes in the 1880s and 1890s were in retrospect not the details of decoration and shape, but the rise to fashionable prominence of a matching coat and skirt called the tailor-made, and of the separate blouse. Garments called tailor-made had existed in the 1870s but they were dresses with jackets or simulated waistcoats; separate jackets and skirts did not appear till the 1880s and became high fashion in the 1890s. They could be worn to society weddings and afternoon functions but also in different materials in the country and for travelling. A loose, informal blouse worn with a contrasting skirt had existed in the 1860s as informal house wear but in the 1890s it became fashionable. A dressy blouse became acceptable even for informal evening wear, but a blouse worn with the tailor-made often had a masculine-type collar and tie.

Changes in women's roles in European society were taking place at the same time the development in style occurred. Women were winning the right to university education and aspiring to the right to vote. Middle-class women were beginning to seek paid employment outside the traditional fields of governess and companion. Just as it had become necessary for men to look business-like earlier in the century, so a business-like appearance became necessary for the working middle-class woman, the 'new woman' of the 1880s and 1890s. The new styles had not been created for such women; tailor-mades and blouses were worn by the leaders of society, including royalty, but they became associated with the 'new woman' for they were believed to be more appropriate to the

13 DUKE ST,

KINGSTON JA.

Figure 4. *c. 1891–92.*
Two young schoolteachers in the new three-piece suit for women.

workplace than the fashions which emphasised femininity. A women's magazine advised that 'The correct business attire for the modern woman suggest the best tailoring worn by men with just the touch of femininity which will save the woman from a certain hardness and harshness.'[17]

England and America were the leaders in the women's movement and the ripples spread to Jamaica, where in both education and employment there were new opportunities at this time. The establishment of Shortwood Training College for Women in 1865 marked the decision to allow trained women teachers into the government schools. In the 1890s a university graduate became head of a non-government girls' school; she was not a Jamaican but she was proof that women could get degrees. In 1896, when the Cambridge Higher Local Examination was extended to Jamaica for the first time, the only candidate was Anna Hollar of Barbican High School,[18] who some years later was finally able to go to university.

Figure 5. *1912. The winner (with her husband) of the mixed doubles in the tennis tournament at the Liguanea Club in 1912. She also won the ladies doubles. Women's clothes still had a long way to go for athletic freedom.*

The Jamaica Scholarship, given annually by the colonial government to enable students to go abroad to university, was awarded to a girl for the first time in 1912. Women in the 1880s and 1890s were finding employment in offices as clerks, formerly a male occupation, to operate the newly invented typewriters; shorthand, typing, book-keeping and business correspondence began to be taught in girls' schools. This expansion in office opportunities was not entirely accidental. When typewriters were first introduced they were used by men as well as women. Pos and Smith have pointed out that to justify the entry of women to the work force, their jobs had to be represented as 'extensions of a woman's "natural" role,' and that 'many "experts" claimed that women's "natural" manual dexterity, their patience and docility made them superior typists to men'.[19] Women were employed as clerks in the civil service; the nursing profession was expanding. Aleric Josephs has shown in a recent paper that postmistresses outnumbered postmasters in the Jamaican postal service, and that women were found in 25 of the 64 job types classified as professional by the census of 1911 compared with only 13 out of 58 in 1891. The actual numbers, 2,400 in 1911 compared with 1,095 in 1891, were pitifully small, nonetheless the total had more than doubled.[20]

Available Jamaican photographs seem to indicate that the blouse and skirt were more worn in the island than the tailor-made, but this may be due to the accidents of photograph survival rather than to rejection of the style. A tailor-made from the illustrated advertisement of an English firm offering to supply ready-mades by mail order to Jamaican women shows what may be called a modern dress.[21] With a shorter skirt and probably without the 'mannish' collar and tie, anyone could wear this style to work today without looking odd, whereas if one were to go to work wearing a bustle! Photographs show that the blouse and skirt were worn at every social level and every type of occasion, for example, by a rural woman sorting coffee beans, a butleress, a hatmaker, teachers at Westwood School and guests at a wedding,[22] indicating a fashion that was beginning to have a levelling, 'democratic' effect.

A factor in the gradual nineteenth-century emancipation of women was their increased participation in sports. Women's participation in sports in Jamaica in the late nineteenth century has yet to be researched. Did special golf courses for women exist in Jamaica, as they did at some places in England, with shorter holes because the tight armholes of women's dresses made a vigorous swing impossible? This difficulty was removed in 1904 when the now famous London firm of Burberry's invented a special pivot sleeve for their women's golfing jackets.[23] From the 1860s a costume very similar to Bloomer's was acceptable for sea bathing; later the trouser part of this outfit was discarded and women wore a knee-length tunic, with their legs covered by dark stockings. Cycling was a popular craze in the 1890s and gave more mobility to people who could not afford a horse and carriage. A few bold spirits in England and the United States cycled in knickerbockers, full knee-length trousers fastened by a band at the knee, others wore skirts with some kind of special adaptation. Pawsey's in Kingston advertised in 1897 'absolutely necessary for every lady cyclist the new patent dress clip keeps the skirt in position in the windiest weather', and Hancomb's had cycling skirts, but most women found that an ordinary pleated skirt was quite adequate. The Beehive, one of the largest Kingston shops, advertised special cycling corsets in 1897, but unfortunately without an illustration so we cannot see in what way they were different.[24] A photograph in the *Daily Gleaner* of the lady who won the mixed doubles and the ladies doubles tennis tournament at Liguanea Club in 1912 shows her wearing a hat, a standing collar almost up to her chin, long sleeves and a skirt not more than half an inch above the ground.[25] Clearly by 1912, progress towards emancipation had been made, but women still had a long way to go to full freedom.

Endnotes

1. E.A. Hastings , *A Glimpse of the Tropics* (London: 1900), pp. 241—42.
2. Anthony Trollope, *The West Indies and the Spanish Main* (London: Chapman and Hall, 1860), pp. 69—70. Another writer who wrote favourably was Sir David Sibbald Scott, *To the West Indies and Back: 100 days* (Dalziel, Scotland, 1908), pp. 229—30. Robert Elwes, *W.S.W.: A Voyage in that Direction in the West Indies* (London: Kerby & Son, 1866), pp. 46—47 was the visitor who realised that his own attire might be criticised by those he thought ludicrous.
3. Scott, p. 78 and the writer of an unsigned article in the *Daily Gleaner*, 23 April 1884, p. 2, both noticed this hitching up of skirts which also appears in photographs from *c*. 1890.
4. *Daily Advertiser*, Cardoza and Son's advertisement, 2 February 1857, p. 3; *Falmouth Post*, Abraham Morales, 24 April 1860, p. 3 and 19 June 1860, p. 3; David Brandon, 1 June 1860, p. 3.
5. Penelope Byrde, *Nineteenth-Century Fashion* (London: Batsford, 1992), p. 72; Norah Waugh, *The Art of Women's Clothes 1600 to 1930* (London: Faber, 1968), p. 150.
6. 'Jamaican memories'. Essay by Daisy Jeffery-Smith in Jamaica Archives, Spanish Town.
7. Women's magazines quoted in Byrde, pp. 117—18.
8. Aileen Ribeiro, *Dress in Eighteenth-Century Europe* (London: Batsford, 1984), p. 115.
9. Kathy Pos and Barbara Clarke Smith, *Men & Women: A History of Costume, Gender and Power* (Washington, DC: National Museum of American History, 1989), pp. 15—16.
10. Alison Gernsheim, *Fashion and Reality* (London: Faber, 1963), p. 25.
11. Quoted in C. Willett Cunnington, *English Women's Clothing in the Nineteenth Century* (London: Faber, 1937), p. 289.
12. *Gall's Newsletter* serialized their report of this case, which lasted only one day,

over several issues in October 1884, so great, apparently, was the interest in the 'scandal' of women dressed as men; *Falmouth Post*, 18 September 1857, p. 1.

13. For the history of nineteenth-century dress I have relied mainly on Anne Buck, *Victorian Costume and Costume Accessories* (Bedford: R. Bean, 1984), Byrde and Gernsheim, *op. cit.*

14. Byrde, p. 170.

15. *Falmouth Post*, 4 November 1856, p. 7.

16. Gernsheim, p. 62.

17. Quoted in Pos and Smith, p. 45, from the *Women's Home Companion* of 1908.

18. *Handbook of Jamaica* (1897), p. 314.

19. Pos and Smith, pp. 44—45.

20. Patrick Bryan, *The Jamaican People 1880—1902* (London: Macmillan Caribbean, 1991), pp. 233—36; Aleric Josephs, 'Gender and occupation in labour force statistics', paper presented at the 25th Conference of the Association of Caribbean Historians (UWI, Mona, 1993).

21. In the *Daily Gleaner*, 19 May 1900, p. 5.

22. The woman sorting coffee beans in W. Bellows, *In Fair Jamaica*, (Kingston: Educational Supply, 1907); the butleress, Alfred Leader, *Through Jamaica With a Kodak* (Bristol: Wright, 1907); the hatmaker, James Johnson, *Jamaica: The Riviera* (London: Cassell & Co., 1903); Westwood teachers, E.A. Wilson, *Men With Backbone* (2nd edn, Kingston: Educational Supply, 1913); the fashionable wedding, National Library of Jamaica photo files.

23. Elizabeth Ewing, *History of 20th-Century Fashion* (2nd edn, London: Batsford, 1975), p. 41.

24. *Daily Gleaner*, 23 April 1897, p. 2, and 5 November 1897, p. 1; the corsets, 4 January 1987, p. 1.

25. Mrs S.R. Cargill in the *Daily Gleaner*, 13 May 1912.

SECTION THREE

Women and Slavery

7.

Sex and Gender in the Historiography of Caribbean Slavery

Hilary Beckles

History and 'Womens' History'

The recent historiographical departure from 'History' to 'Women's History' in the Caribbean segment of the north atlantic slave mode of production cannot be described as a mass movement. Throughout the methodologically turbulent 1960s and 1970s excess conceptual inertia in the Caribbean historiographic tradition shaped and limited the culture of criticism and therefore theoretical enquiry. This was so in spite of a pervasive ideological practice by some nationalist scholars to discredit academically elements of what was considered the politicised historiography of a fractured and retreating colonising mentality.[1]

The radical character of the anti-colonial discourse in the Caribbean, strengthened and supported by ideological imperatives of black redemption and worker empowerment, had the effect of removing from centre stage the essential maleness of the targeted colonial historiography. Some feminist historians were swept along by the compelling tide of a hegemonic male representation of the nationalist project. While their participation in the discourse was guided by considerations of intellectual decolonisation and nation-building, they applied brakes to the advancing theoretical critique of patriarchy in order to facilitate the suppression of political dissonance. The result of this politic has been a paucity of texts within the emergent literature that examine specifically women's history, and therefore the existence of an undeveloped theoretical terrain that has inhibited movement towards a rigorous feminist critique.[2]

The pioneering work on women's history by Lucille Mair has had the effect of confirming the basic correctness of this development. For Mair, post-Columbian plantation slavery was the scene of the punishment — the crime having taken place at an earlier time. She called for an examination of sexual attitudes and values within the 'living country' of slavery in order to set out the circumstances and moments under which gender identities and ideologies were constructed and represented as relations of power. Furthermore, she insisted that the discursive practice enters in a pathological sort of way, the social lives of different 'types' of women in order to clinically assess the degree of space that separated them as well as the experiences that held them together.[3]

Subsequent work by Kamau Brathwaite, Verena Martinez-Alier, Arlette Gautier, and more recently by Hilary Beckles, Barbara Bush, Marietta Morrissey, Barry Higman, and Bernard Moitt has significantly advanced the study of women's history in many directions across imperial divisions of the slave mode of production.[4] These contributions were made in a manner that avoided conceptual conflict and hostility; historiographic criticisms have not featured in what seemed to be rather low-pitched academic engagements. It is entirely possible that this state of affairs is indicative of Caribbean historians' cautious appreciation of the directions of post-structuralist theorists especially as Michel Foucault and Jacques Derrida have been read as negating the primacy of human agency in anti-establishment struggles. Certainly, there is no developed discussion of gender as conceptual representation within the texts and subtexts of Gautier, Bush and Higman, neither is there a discourse on the manner in which gender relations, in the context of slavery, operated through the instrument of language. Also, the post-structuralist assertion that the term 'woman' is but a social construct that has no basis in nature has struck no central nerve, an insensitivity which says a great deal about the theoretical state of this recent historiography.

From History to 'Women's History' to 'Gender History'

If the movement from 'History' to 'Women's History' was at best a minor historiographical current, though potentially transformative in its intellectual implication, then it is also correct to suggest that the advance from 'Women's History' to 'Gender History' and feminist criticism is still at the stage of gathering the troops, or perhaps in a state of uncertainty with respect to the academic and discursive politics of the project.

Historians of slavery have tended to use the term 'gender' in reference to the complex social organisation through which the relations between males and females are understood and expressed. That is, it indicates the power of language in the interpretative framework that offers distinct social meanings which are understood to have a basis in bio-sexual differences. These social meanings are considered as culture products. They are socially constructed, internalised through communicative systems, and depend for their legitimacy upon hegemonic power. Gender therefore, as an analytical tool, requires academic specification, and ought not to be used interchangeably with 'sex' which is arguably rooted in nature rather than politics and culture.

Evidence of the tension within the historiography of slavery then, can be found at two junctures; one, where feminist scholars who adopt methodologies from post-modernist theorists meet with historians of women; two, between empiricist and marxist scholars who continue to debate the validity of sex and gender as useful categories. 'Gender history,' meanwhile, is received by sceptics as the privileged domain of literary critics, cultural anthropologists, and theoretical sociologists — all of whom they claim share a common measure of conceptual suspicions, if not contempt, for what is termed the 'objective canons of historiography'. For this group of reluctants however, it would be useful to suggest a visit to Linda Gordan's perceptive assertion that there 'may be no objective canons of historiography, but these are degrees of accuracy' since it is 'wrong to conclude that because there may be no objective truths... there are no objective lies.'[5]

Implicit in the research of Mair, Gautier, Morrissey, and Brathwaite, however, are the signposts for the crossing from 'women's history' to 'gender history'; in Beckles' work there is the suggestion that the time is ripe for a 'kind' of crossing. In outlining a framework for detailed historical investigation of the slavery period Mair projected categories for analysis that are typically those used in women's history; these are 'experience', 'identity', and 'relations' to the means of production, exchange and consumption. Here she states in very moving language that 'in Caribbean slave societies the black woman produced, the brown woman served, and the white woman consumed' — a typology which calls for an investigation of real life experiences across the social structure boundaries of race, class and colour.[6]

In addition, Mair signals the need for a more rigorous and conceptually informed gender analysis when she asserts that the textual representations of these three categories of 'woman' tell us very little about them as living beings, but much more about the purposes that such representations were invented and designed to serve. In discussing the socio-sexual manipulation and exploitation of all women by superordinately empowered slaveowning white men, Mair highlights the common terrain where womanhood and maternity were targeted and preyed upon by patriarchal authority and interest. There is however, no specific discussion of the range of representations that are present or absent within the texts; neither is there a discourse on how subjects are constructed, and of gender as that which gives social meaning to sexual differences. 'Woman' then, as social concept, whether described culturally as white, brown, or black, is not seen through poststructural lens; hence we are not told how gender operates through specific slave-based intellectual forms. This is also true for the work of Brathwaite, Beckles, Bush, and Gautier, which is tilted in the direction of the social, political, and labour experiences of women — both enslaved and free.

The tendency then, has been for historians of Caribbean slavery to subject women's experiences to investigations with respect to caste, class, race, colour and material relations — rather than to explore how such representations and discourses are internally organised by patriarchal mobilisations of gender ideologies. The result of this historiographical practice makes for a fascinating social history that identifies, even if in a limited way, the material and social conditions of women's oppression. In addition, by virtue of locating the terms and conditions of oppression in the area of socio-material denial and marginalisation, this literature suggests the ways in which women can and did seek ways of empowerment in order to resist and escape from that which oppressed them.

Historiographic patterns: The white woman

To date, the primary focus of research, and this is reflected in the structure of the historiography, is the black woman with the brown (coloured!) woman running a competitive second, and the white woman trailing behind at a distance. The texts on black women's enslavement by Gautier, Beckles, Bush, and Morrissey addressed directly, but with significant variation in empirical detail and conceptual concerns, aspects of brown women's experiences and identity, but did not explore systematically the lives of white creole and European women.[7] Subsequent essays by Beckles and Bush have outlined the paradoxical but privileged nature of their experiences with suggestions for discussions into the character of their social identities.[8]

By way of contrast, and this is very critical to a close conceptual reading of the historiography, a major subject of imperial and national(ist) historians has been the study of white male slaveowners. In these texts the slave-based colonial economy is seen as an expression of an elite merchant-planter accumulationalist vision within the rise of hegemonic Atlantic capitalism — non-propertied white males being pressed into their service as labourers, bureaucrats, and military defenders of the enterprise. This historiography focusses primarily on the entrepreneurship and politics of ruling class white males who are represented as having succeeded in fashioning with slave systems a modern, rational economic order from the chaos and backwardness of a precapitalist, indigenous primitivism. Caribbean colonisation and slavery for the European, says Brathwaite, was essentially 'a male enterprise'. 'It was not a joint enterprise', nor a 'family enterprise' he insists, but a 'family-stunted and male- oriented enterprise with the wife replaced by housekeeper or mistress'.[9] The white woman therefore, whether as wife, mother and sister to male slaveowners, or as slaveowner in her own right, is represented as supportive rather than innovative in the material and ideological reproduction of the colonial project.

These historiographic patterns and trends can be accounted for in three principal ways. First, they are endemic to an earlier proslavery imperial scholarship that conceptually subsumed the white woman to a patriarchal hegemony in the projection and assessment of colonial culture. Second, historians and social anthropologists, inspired by considerations of systemic decolonisation and nation-building, targeted the black woman's history in search of general explanations for social and cultural processes identified as endemic to the legacies of slavery. In this literature, the black woman is represented as 'culture carriers' and 'morality bearers' of a disenfranchised people seeking cohesion and upliftment. These alleged problems include matters such as the perceived instability and problematic matrifocality of the black family, and its inability to rise to the challenges of community development. Third, emerging from these two representations is the notion that the ideological formation of the modern Caribbean is in some way best explained in terms of a central paradigm that juxtaposes the white male and the black female as binary signifiers. This paradigm however, says little about the social logic and systems of representation within the slave mode of production which, it must be emphasised, was constructed as a show piece expression of renaisance rationality within the irrational colonial sphere.

Emerging from these historiographic patterns and trends are significant conceptual issues that require a further discussion. These are: the dangers involved in not clearly perceiving the roles and functions of the white woman as a pro-slavery agent within the reproduction of slave systems — its patriarchal superstructure especially; over-emphasis upon the experiences of enslaved black women as labourers and insufficient conceptual attention upon their biological and constitutional function as the conduits of slavery; and the retreat from a systematic use of gender ideology in which 'woman', as a category in history, is seen as constructed and reproduced by patriarchal systems of representation.

The tendency has been to see the white woman and the enslaved black woman as constituting a bi-polarity within a fragmented notion of womanhood that assured the reproduction of the slave system. Considerations of race however, privileged the white woman. In 1797,

Moreau de Saint Méry, noted with respect to the eightenth century developments at St. Dominique, that the white woman, who was in fact a 'passenger' in the formative years of the colonial mission — an ideological victim of a male-centred enterprise — later surfaced as a principal participant in its internal logic and reproduction, and became inseparable from its cultural legacy.[10] Conceivably, labouring white women saw the slave system as '*the*' avenue to betterment while their elite 'sistren' understood their privileged distance from labour in much the same way. Yet, 'united by their common sex', they were divided by a dichotomous gender ideology in which the latter were presented as the embodiment of purity and liberty, and the former as social evidence of decay and degeneration at the colonial frontier.

At the centre of the recent women's history literature then, is the notion of the elite white woman's removal from the process of sugar plantation production and her reintegration principally at the level of social reproduction — as mothers and wives within the household. From this location, she is understood to have functioned as a critical ideological legitimiser of the slavery system in so far as she exerted a pro-slavery influence on infant socialisation, imposed on household divisions of labour a conservative value system, and altogether reassured the planter-merchant socio-economic model of its development integrity and leadership. According to Brathwaite, the 'activities of these women appeared to be mainly entertainment on behalf of the establishment. They were very conscious of the establishment and their place within it. Basically, she was concerned with supporting the establishment and looking after her husband's welfare'. Quoting Mair, Brathwaite continues: 'One could not expect otherwise of the white female. She was the second sex, taking the cue from her man. The whole thrust of her upbringing had been to make her "pretty polly, pretty parrot", to add sweetness and charm to public life if she could, but not to interfere or to agitate.'[11] More recent work by Beckles, Trevor Burnard, and Mary Butler, however, shows the autonomous market activities of propertied white women as significant, and indicates that the "pretty polly, pretty parrot" representation constitutes a marked departure from known social circumstances.[12]

The provisions of the slave laws were quite explicit on the concepts and methods governing the reproduction of the status of slavery. This matter was central to the entire colonial enterprise and was specified in both statute and social convention. They provided that the offspring of white women were born free, irrespective of the father's status, and that the offspring of enslaved women were born into slavery regardless of the status of the father. White women could not be enslaved, and blacks were presumed enslaved until proof could be provided to the contrary. White women and black women were legally constructed as the vehicles on which freedom and slavery, respectively, travelled from the sixteenth century frontier to the matured, creole nineteenth century slave culture. Womanhood, then, came to represent the reproduction of two extreme social conditions; maternity, in turn, constituted the soil in which slavery grew and gave life to capitalist accumulation on a grand scale.

The linking of white womanhood and black womanhood to freedom and slavery respectively meant that the entire ideological fabric of the slave system was conceived in terms of race, sex and gender. The superordinate position of the white male patriarch however, ensured the marginalisation of all women, and sought the corresponding social emasculation of the black male. This social geometry was carefully constructed and fully articulated in different ways, within the ideological superstructure. The major proslavery campaign of the sixteenth century and seventeenth century, led by mercantile pamphleteers, clergymen, historians, and literary critics, won an impressive following, so that by the mid-eighteenth century the need for slavery had been received by majority opinion in Europe as having a basis in common-sense. Furthermore, that opinion came to expect that white women in Caribbean slave societies would support the structures and ideas established by 'their' men, and that black women would reproduce the conditions of slavery and seek contentment in whatever ameliorative measures 'benevolent' slaveowners offered.

Logically then, 'woman', both black and white, had to be socially constructed — engineered and re-engineered to facilitate the agro-commercial enterprise and its supportive social environment. It is here that in spite of some useful starts, more intense work needs to be done by historians of Caribbean slavery. What does it mean, for example, that representations of 'woman', reproduced during the slavery period say more about the origins and character of representation than about the actual lives, experiences, and identity of women? This is a question asked more often by historians of gender than by historians of women. But it is one that warrants no analytical or methodological contention and should inform all social history enquiries.

From the point of view of the hegemonic expansion of the slave mode of production the seventeenth century is the common place for an analytical beginning. It is a time and place generally associated with the proliferation of the sugar plantation and its revolutionary absorption of enslaved Africans. It was also a moment when propertyless white women constituted a significant element within the ganged labour force of the sugar estates. These women were recruited from the British Isles under the indentureship system, transported to the colonies and engaged as bonded labourers. Most were recruited as voluntary servants, but many were defenseless persons — convicts, vagrants, political prisoners and victims of religious persecution — 'sold' by the state that conceived their greater relative value to the imperium in terms of colonial servitude. Considerable evidence suggest the slave-like social existence of these plantation labourers, and indicate that their general treatment, measured in terms of material care and loss of civil liberties, was consistent with that experienced by enslaved Africans.[13] They were considered satisfactory workers at the frontier, and the nature of demand for their labour both for field work and domestic duties, indicates their much admired flexibility and versatility.

In addition to being catapulted into the deep end of the labour system, indentured white women adjusted in much the same way as men to the cruder moral and aesthetic aspect of the slave-management culture. The sight for example, of white women examining the genitals of black males on the slave market, which offended the sensibilities of some visitors, was not considered in the formative years as evidence of social degeneration. Rather, it was held as indicative of market rationality, and in no way seen as hostile to their roles as good mothers and wives. Indeed, the dialectical relations between social and economic forces demanded such actions as they were fully within the epistemological framework of the slave mode of production.

Manual labour, slave trading, and domesticity were not considered locked in contradictory orbit during the formative stages of gender representation. In fact, these practices were held together in determining the elements that constituted the images of the colonial white woman. There were many images and representations which in turn reflected the recognition of complexity and diversity in colonial social life. These are to be found in the early narratives, histories, travel accounts and biographies. In them, labouring white women are described variously as 'loose wenches', 'whores', 'sluts' and 'white niggers', and designated as suited mainly to field labour.

Considered unfit for marriage by propertied white males, and disqualified for domestic service, landless white women were dismissed to manual labour in plantations, public construction works, and the urban service sector. In these worlds they socialised intimately with the slave community, and with enslaved black men established households and produced children. The 1715 census of Barbados, for example, lists a number of free born mulattos who were parented by white women and 'black' and 'coloured' men; (see Table 1)

It is reasonable to suggest that these persons were specially listed in order to draw attention to their free status rather than to indicate the specific race of their parents.

By the early eighteenth century, however, the evidence indicates a significant shift in the ideological and social representation of the white woman. By this time the migration of white women to the islands had greatly contracted, and with the rapid expansion of the plantation culture throughout the Antilles, the question of sexual imbalance within the white community assumed new dimension. The shortage of white women was said to threaten the colonial mission since it rendered the

Table 1. The Inter-racial family of ties of white women in the parish of St. Phillip, Barbados, in 1715

Name	Age	Description given in Census
John Goddard	40	A mulatto, born of a white woman
Jane Goddard	32	White, husband a mulatto
Elizabeth Shepherd	52	White, husband a mulatto
Thomas Goddard	30	Mulatto, born of a white woman
Ann Goddard	30	White woman, husband a mulatto
Mary Shepherd	13	Mother a white woman, father a negro
John Wake	5	Father negro, mother white
Elizabeth Wake	8	Father negro, mother white
Simon Kitteridge	18	Son of a white woman and coloured man
Sarah Avery	15	Mulatto, born of a white woman
Charles Sergent	36	Mother white, father a mulatto
Mary Sergent	31	White woman, husband a negro
Elizabeth Sinckler	48	Born of a white and negro man

Source: Census of Barbados, 1715: Barbados Archives

white community unable to reproduce itself naturally. Meanwhile, plantation inventories were indicating clearly that black women had become the majority in the labour gangs of Martinique, St. Dominique, Barbados and other sugar producing colonies. Also, references to their greater relative productivity were seeping into accounting calculations which had the effect of consolidating the idea in planter managerial ideology that slave women were a more profitable investment.

Within the context of these changed socio-economic circumstances a new (and the most enduring) representation of the white woman was constructed. The resident creole elite patriarchy had consolidated its hegemonic rule as creators of a legitimate world and prepared to redefine white womanhood in light of its future interests. Within the restructured ideological sphere of the secure patriarchy the white woman was represented in clearly defined semiotic terms. She was now considered unfit for manual labour on account of her endemic fragility; unsuited to physical exertion in the tropic as a consequence of her possession of a faint heart and delicate skin; terrified of black male sexuality on account of her chaste, virginal, and jet-white purity; and devoid of lust, gaiety and passion, having embraced in its fullness the importance of ordered moral discipline and self-denial.

The white woman, then, marginalised within the culture of private capital, disenfranchised by colonial constitutions, and socially oppressed, now found herself cocooned within another system of representation that denied her social identity and right to autonomous self-expression. Eighteenth century texts in which these representations were formulated — the canons of the imperialist historiographic tradition — also indicate their mythical nature and illustrate clearly the ideological need within patriarchy for the reconstruction. The authors of these narratives — ideological engineers in their own right — were as much privately concerned with representations of this kind as they were with historical accuracy and authenticity, hence the entry of considerable fiction into the storehouse of historical writing.

The discrepancy between the social reality of everyday life and behavioural expectations embedded within these representations was oftentimes explored (and exploded!) in quite remarkable ways. A demonstrative case can be extracted from the records of eighteenth century Jamaica. It concerns the life of Elizabeth Moore-Manning, wife of Edward Manning, Member of the House of Assembly. In 1739, Elizabeth was brought by her husband before the Legislature in an attempt to settle a divorce case. Mr. Manning's case against his wife had to do with evidence surrounding (and high society's reactions) allegations that she was sexually involved with a number of black men on the estate. The 'burden of the evidence' supplied by slaves, white servants, and others, says Brathwaite, suggests that she was 'something of a nymphomaniac.'[14] This evidence indicated that the 'sheepboy', the 'watchman', the 'cookboy' and others had 'laid with Mrs. M.'.

Mrs. Manning, of course, claimed that much of this was untrue and that she lived a 'normal' life in the absence and presence of her husband who demonstrated no sexual interests in her whatsoever. The case, which soon became an attractive soap opera for Jamaican slave society, dragged on for months, with slaves — male and female — white housekeepers, managers, friends and family all having their say on Mrs. Manning's sexual taste, interests and style. White males, however, made of the same social material as the distraught Mr. Manning, had long considered unrestricted sexual access to the slave women as a 'right' of mastery, and the refusal to exercise it on their part was considered strange if not irresponsible.

Historiographic patterns: The black woman

At the same time, the social reconstruction of the black woman also began to take shape after nearly one hundred years of ideological vagueness and unspecification. As the labour gangs became increasingly female in composition and the fertility of black women was propelled into the market economy as the key to an internal reproduction of labour, frequent references appeared in texts to the black woman as superordinate amazons who could be called upon to labour all day, perform sex all night, and be quite satisfied morally and culturally to exist outside the formal structures of marriage and family. She was now projected by the white proslavery literary imagination as lacking a developed sense of emotional attachment to progeny and spouse, and indifferent to the values of virtue and high moral sensitivity.

The relations between the black woman's labour power and her reproductive capability were represented as exclusively confined to the culture of market forces. As property her worth was associated with productivity measurements that were calculated in terms of material output and childbearing — a child being accounted for at birth in the plantation inventories as an additional capital unit. Black womanhood and motherhood, then, existed at the same nexus of the market economy as factors in the production and reproductions process.

The predominate image associated with the representation of the black woman was that of great strength — the symbol of blackness, masculinity and absence of finer feelings. Her sexuality was projected as overtly physical (no broken hearts here!) — hence brutish and best suited to the frontier world of the far-flung plantation. Out there, social immorality, perversity and promiscuity were maintained by her on account of her possession of satanic powers that lured white men away from association with their virtuous white females — hence the existence of the mulatto community within the slave society.

Here, then, was the alleged moral crisis of slavery. A perfectly 'horrid system', says Mrs. Fenwick, an English school teacher and 'reluctant' slave owner in early nineteenth century Barbados.[15] Horrid because in no way was it conducive to the proper cultivation of white manhood and the refinement of a gentleman. The presence of black women in white households, she confessed, was the principal corrupting factor. White men simply could not resist them, but desired them, bought and brought them into their beds, and produced children with them. Edward Long's late eighteenth century explanation of this development in Jamaican slave society also identified the black woman as the threat to civilisation's advance:

> In a place where, by custom, so little restraint is laid on the passions, the
> Europeans, who at home have always been used to greater purity and
> strictness of manners, are too easily led aside to give loose to every kind of
> sensual delight: on this account some black or yellow quasheba is fought for,
> by whom a tawney breed is produced.[16]

Only 'a proper education' for the generality of white woman, he argued, would make them more 'agreeable companions', and hence more competitive for the company of white men. The cultured upliftment of the white woman, he believed, was necessary to encourage them to reject the 'goatish embrace' of black women, and crave for 'pure and lawful bliss' with white women.[17] Coloured children, says Mrs. Fenwick, born of open and shameless licentiousness, were kept in the household, raised by their white stepmothers as 'pet' and dismissed to the field gangs on reaching adulthood, there to labour with their mothers of whom they knew little or cared nothing.[18]

Black females, then, in eighteenth century gender representations, were not 'women' since they knew not how to nourish and care for their young, showed no loyalty and subservience to a male spouse, and could not construct a binding and building culture of domesticity. They were the 'other females' in the society whose potential claim to the status of 'woman' existed only with respect to their capacity for miscegenation with white males through which route the 'coloured' woman — liberated from the oppression of blackness — was created and idealised.

Once again, in the same texts within which these ideological configurations and structures were made, are to be found evidence of events and circumstances of a contrary nature. The textual juxtaposition produces no interpretative tension since a critical reading indicates that no close correspondence was ever expected between the two levels of communication. Representations were designed with ideological missions in mind, and they served very well such objectives, regardless of textual references to seemingly opposing evidence. This allows for an interpretation of the text as fictive, temporal discourses, rather than authoritative, objective social history.

The history of representations of women can be seen as the recreation of gendered political subjects, which allows us to redefine narrative history as the politics of a process by which power and knowledge are perpetually constituted. Indeed, the question of how power and knowledge are conceptualised resides at the core of much of the contention between those who are divided on the relative usefulness of 'women's history' and 'gender history' as analytical instruments. While historians of women demand that the real lives of women during the slavery period be carefully and systematically detailed before issues of meaning and identity are settled, historians of gender prefer to cast attention to assessing how 'woman' was redefined and reengineered under changing political and material circumstances. The problem of politics here is critical. Historians of women are critical of the gender approach precisely because it overemphasises the role of power which some poststructuralists attribute to language. Here, poststructualism is considered a new conceptual imperialism that negates the real world in which black women's struggle against oppression and injustice was endemic.

The politics of slavery, and women's forging of an anti-slavery ideology from experience, consciousness and identity, throws up the concept of 'rebel woman', as used by Mair, and the 'natural rebel' as conceived by Beckles. Two separate and distinct epistemological traditions inform these seemingly similar concepts of the slave woman in politics. The rebel woman is essentially a cultural icon whose central location within the slave community — the politicised space — is derived from the ascribed matrifocality of the African social legacy. She is 'nanny', 'Queen Mother' and 'priestess'. She is therefore culturally invested with political leadership, and the community rallies around her magical and spiritual powers. Men follow because of her claim to the vision that results from the possession of such powers. Freedom is the water that quenches the thirst of power, and anti-slavery is the jar from which the water is taken.

By necessity, the rebel woman is the 'special' central figure whose transformative powers are embodied in her singular capabilities. She can be replaced, but the apex remains. She leads those below but her powers and system of organisation are from above. The power she has is used for the liberation of the community of enslaved, but it is not derived from it. In essence, it is an elitist leadership in the tradition of divine authority, and therefore is not reproduced within the context of popular social change.

The 'natural rebel', however, is your typical 'woman in the fields', who possesses no claim to distinct individuality and is therefore one of the masses. Her identity, and the level of consciousness that informs her politics, have been conceptualised and defined by Brathwaite in his 'discovery' of the 'inner plantation'. The everyday experience of her enslavement represents the basis of a culture of refusal and resistance through which she claims a 'self' and an 'identity'.

The search for the 'natural rebel', then, begins with Brathwaite's claim that the slavery system impacted upon the black women in deeper and more profound ways than was the case with black men. The slave mode of production by virtue of placing the black woman's 'inner world' — her fertility, sexuality and maternity — on the market as capital assets, produced in them a 'natural' propensity to resist and to refuse as part of a basic self protective and survival response.

From this world of ideas, attitudes, and actions flowed a constant stream of rebellious sentiment that infused the slave community with an endemic anti-slavery ethos. Furthermore, since it was she in whom the seeds of slavery were planted and expected to germinate, she was also likely to be the conduit through whom anti-slavery flowed naturally.

The affirmation in this dialectic of pro-slavery and anti-slavery forces indicates the complex nature of the black woman's experiences and consciousness. It is here, it seems, that historians of Caribbean slavery have made some headway by refusing to dichotomise the methodologies of women's history and gender history, and by insisting that the two occupy different levels of the same habitat.

The implication of this stance is clear; the analysis of 'real experience' and the theorising of 'constructed representation' constitute part of the same intellectual project in the search for meaning and truth. 'History' and 'Politics', then, may constitute coded terms for 'experience' and 'representation', respectively, but only an integrative discursive practice can adequately tackle epistemological questions arising from the notion of meaning. Furthermore, the problem for the enslaved black woman in getting the slave master off her back in the day time and off her belly in the night time was very real, and not resolvable by psychoanalysis. Rather, it had origins in the way she was historically constructed and rendered vulnerable by a consequently liberated masculinity.

Conclusion

Concepts of gender and race were central to how persons interfaced by the relations of slavery, established meaning that determined social order and shaped everyday life. The ideological practice of gender determination contributed significantly to managerial values that focused attention away from class conflict to gender and race differences and inequalities. Gender and race ideologies were principally at work in determining the sexual and racial division of labour and were responsible for the crystallisation of consciousness within the slave mode of production.

There is an acceptance, therefore, of Joan Scott's assertion that historians of social life should examine carefully how, at given stages in the development of a social formation, people construct meaning and how difference operates in the construction of meaning.[19] Here, we tracked down the trajectory of gender construction of white and black women during slavery and examined how the language generated by pro-slavery agents gave potency to gender ideologies. The slave mode of production was conceived and held together by an ideological defense in which a gendered and racist order was considered paramount. Gender ideology soon found an enduring home in natural and moral codes, and was enforced by the judicial structure of the empowered patriarchy and the supportive social conventions it forged.

The tendency to privilege race above gender as an analytical category has no basis, therefore, in the logic and culture of the slave mode of production. Certainly, the slaveowner whose legal and ideological superstructure empowered him for unrestricted socio-sexual access to the slave woman as an expected return on capital, and at the same time imposed sexual constraints and curfews upon white women, interpreted this authority as having its roots in sex, gender, and race differences. The slave woman's location at the base of the power pyramid of the slave order, below that of the male slave, was secured essentially by sex and gender representation. It was in this politically imposed position, where the requirement of production and reproduction merged , that the black woman's experience, identity, and consciousness gave structural form to what represents the essential characteristic features of the slave mode of production.

NOTES

1. See Blanca Silvestrini, *Women and Resistance: Her story in Contemporary Caribbean History;* Dept. of History, U.W.I. Mona, 1989; Rhoda Reddock, 'Women and Slavery in the Caribbean: A Feminist Perspective', *Latin American Perspectives*, Issues 40, 12:1, 1985, pp.63-80; Arlette Gautier, 'Les Esclaves femmes aux Antilles Francaises, 1635-1848'. *Reflexions Historiques, 10:3*, Fall, 1983, pp.409-35.

2. See Bridget Brereton, 'Text, Testimony and Gender: An Examination of some Texts by Women on the English-Speaking Caribbean, 1770s to 1920s', a paper presented at the Symposium - Engendering History: Current Directions in the Study of Women and Gender in Caribbean History', U.W.I, Mona, 1993, and her article in this volume. Marietta Morrissey,'Women's Work, Family Formation and Reproduction among Caribbean Slaves', *Review* 9 (1986) pp.339-67.

3. Lucille Mair, 'Women Field Workers in Jamaica During Slavery', Department of History, U.W.I., Mona, 1989; 'An Historical Study of Women in Jamaica from 1655 to 1844 (Ph.D, U.W.I., Mona, Jamaica, 1974); *The Rebel Woman in the British West Indies during Slavery* (Kingston, 1975); 'The Arrival of Black Woman', *Jamaica Journal,* 9: nos 2-3, (1975).

4. Kamau Brathwaite, 'Caribbean Woman during the Period of Slavery', 1984 Elsa Goveia Memorial Lecture, Cave Hill Campus, Barbados; Verena Martinez-Alier, *Marriage, Class and Colour in Nineteenth Century Cuba: A Study of Racial Attitudes and Sexual Values in Slave Society (Cambridge, U.K. 1974); Arlette Gautier, Les Soeurs de Solitude: La condition feminine dans l'esclavage aux Antilles du XVIIe as XIX e* siecle (Paris, Editions Caribbeennes, 1985); Hilary Beckles, *Natural Rebels: A Social History of Enslaved Black Women in Barbados* (Rutgers Univ. Press, New Brunswick, 1989); Barbara Bush, *Slave Women in Caribbean Society, 1650-1838* (Indiana Univ. Press, Bloomington, 1990); Marietta Morrissey, *Slave Women in the New World: Gender Stratification in the Caribbean* (Kansas Univ. Press, Lawrence, 1989); Barry Higman, Household Structures and Fertility on Jamaican Slave Plantations: A nineteenth Century Example', *Population Studies*, vol. 27, 1993; and 'The Slave Family and Household in the British West Indies, 1800-1834', *Journal of Interdisciplinary History*, vol. 6, 1976; Bernard Moitt,'*Women, Work and resistance in the French Caribbean during Slavery, 1700-1848*', unpublished paper (1993); and '*Behind the Sugar Fortunes:* Women, Labour, and the development of Caribbean Plantations during Slavery'. in S. Chilungu and S. Niang (eds) *African Continuities* (Toronto, Teribi Publications, 1989).

5. Linda Gordon, 'What's New in Women's History', in Teresa de Lauretis (ed) *Feminist Studies/Critical Studies*, Indiana Univ. Press, Bloomington, 1986) p.22; See also, Louise M. Newman, 'Critical Theory and the History of Women: What's at Stake in Deconstructing Women's History', *Journal of Women's History*, vol. 2, no. 3, 1991; Mary Poovey,"Feminism and Deconstruction', *Feminist Studies*, vol. 14, 1988.

6. Cited in Bush, *Slave Women*, p.xii.

7. See Gautier, 1975; Beckles, 1989; Bush, 1989, and Morrissey, 1990.

8. Hilary Beckles, 'White Women and Slavery in the Caribbean', *History Workshop Journal*, issue 36, 1993; Barbara Bush, 'White "Ladies", Coloured "Favourites"

and Black "wenches": Some considerations on Sex, Race and Class Factors in Social Relations in white Creole Society in the British Caribbean', *Slavery and Abolition*, 2, 1991, pp.245-62.

9. Brathwaite, 'Caribbean Woman'.

10. Moreau de Saint Méry (1797), *Description Topographique Physique, Civile, Politique et Historique de la Partie Francaise de l'isle Saint Domingue* (Paris, 1958 reprint) p.10.

11. Brathwaite, 'Caribbean Woman'.

12. Beckles, 'White Women', op.cit; Trevor Burnard, "Family Continuity and Female Independence in Jamaica, 1665-1734', *Continuity and Change*, 7, (2) 1992; and, 'Inheritance and Independence: Women's Status in early colonial Jamaica', *William and Mary Quarterly*, vol.xxxiv (1977); Mary Butler, 'White Women and Property in early Nineteenth Century Barbados', Conference Paper: Engendering History - U.W.I, Mona, 1993.

13. See Hilary Beckles, *White Servitude and Black Slavery in Barbados, 1627-1715* (Knoxville, Tennessee Univ. Press, 1989); and 'Black Men in White Skins: The Formation of a White Proletariat in West Indian Slave Society', *Journal of Imperial and Commonwealth History*, 15:1, 1986.

14. Brathwaite, 'Caribbean Women'.

15. A.F. Fenwick (ed) *The Fate of the Fenwicks: Letters to Mary Hays, 1798-1828* (Methuen, Lon. 1927) p.164.

16. Cited in Veronica Gregg,'The Caribbean (As A Certain Kind of) Woman'; paper presented at conference - *Engendering History*, (1993), p.25.

17. *Ibid*.

18. Fenwick, *The Fate of the Fenwicks*, p. 164.

19. Joan Wallach Scott, *Gender and the Politics of History* (New York, Columbia, Univ. Press, 1988).

8.

The Female Slave in Cuba during the first half of the Nineteenth Century

Digna Castañeda

African slavery, a historical phenomenon of the New World, is seen with the greatest clarity and depth in Cuban colonial society, in the role and place of the slave woman. The African slave women, despite the great suffering they endured, managed to keep in their minds their native land and part of their culture. As a consequence, they not only fed and protected their offspring, but also taught them about Africa, life, freedom and survival. In this way, they ensured that the slaves would not become mere biological fuel[1] for the economic and cultural development of Europe but helped to establish the slaves' biological and cultural footprints. In brief, they guaranteed the survival of their race, and even more, they played an outstanding part in the wars for national independence in Cuba.

In the Caribbean, and therefore in Cuba, it is impossible to evaluate properly the black woman's present position if her slave predecessors are not taken into account. The study of slavery points towards the future; there is no alternative for those who study this form of oppression but to denounce continuously its evils as well as to find in it the inspiration that can identify ideas for any type of social change.

In this article, the first section of a major work about the black slave woman in Cuba, the examples discussed are drawn mainly from the western regions of the island during the first half of the nineteenth century. It is argued that the coincidence of social class, race and gender came about and manifested itself within African slavery at the same time that these three elements became a means of exploitation. In this context, the black female slave is triply discriminated against: for being black, for being a slave, and for being a woman.

Historical framework: first half of the nineteenth century

During the first quarter of the nineteenth century in Cuba, there were traces of the initial symptoms of a revolutionary consciousness expressed by, among others, Captain General Marqués de Someruelos, who led a local autonomist movement in which the representatives of the Cuban oligarchy demanded judicial and political equality for all Americans, Antilleans and *peninsulares*; the sending of deputies to the Spanish *Cortés*, and the autonomy of the colony, a task in which the Cuban priest Felix Varela stood out. Also, the political atmosphere prevailing was clearly seen in the publication of the first constitutional draft document of the island of Cuba, written in Venezuela in 1812 by the Cuban Joaquín Infante.

Consequently, when Captain General Dionisio Vives assumed command of the island in 1823, the conspiratorial activity which was the normal and permanent state of a large number of young Cubans was no longer confined to them.[2] The unrest also affected almost all social classes, and this is the time when the Masonic lodges and secret societies achieved their golden age. A good example was the 'Suns and Rays of Bolívar' conspiracy, founded in 1821, which sought to create the Republic of Cubanacán. To this atmosphere of political unrest can be added the threat of liberating expeditions initiated by Cubans from Colombia and Mexico, such as the one organised by the conspirators of the secret society named 'Great Legion of the Black Eagle', which collapsed in 1829.

Other symptoms that foretold the end of the colonial era in Cuba were the subversive writings of José Antonio Saco in *The Weekly Messenger*, published from 1828 to 1830, the writings of Félix Varela, published in *El Habanero* between 1824 and 1826, and the patriotic verses written by José María Heredia.

Nevertheless, from the 1830s, there was a period — that did not end until the second half of the nineteenth century — characterised by the weakening of the independence movement, as a result, among other reasons, of the effective work of Captain General Francisco Dionisio Vives.[3] Vives managed to guarantee the failure of Cuban separatism and to silence the opposition, to the extent that on 17 May 1824 Fernando VII described the island of Cuba as 'ever faithful' in a *Real Ordenanza*. There were also other events that influenced the new situation: the end of the independence movements against Spain on the continent, and the attitude of England and the United States who lessened their anti-Spain activities because they preferred Cuba to remain Spanish for the time being. Coincidentally, for the rising creole bourgeois aristocracy, independence was not a necessity because they had already achieved the right to free trade. At the same time, their position was strengthened by that of the landowners who tried to preserve their wealth, of which slave ownership formed a part.

In this part of the century, classic marronage and slave revolts suddenly became the 'black peril', so that slavery constituted a source of social and ideological contradiction, giving a new shade of meaning to the political trends prevailing in that epoch.[4] The frequent revolts had the new characteristics of insubordination, premeditation and coordination.[5] Among the most noted conspiracies was the Aponte Conspiracy of 1812, the first conspiracy of free blacks, and '*La Escalera*' in 1843.

In short, blacks were feared, whether free[6] or slave. This alarmist notion will be understood if the happenings around Cuba between 1789 and 1850 are examined in time and space. First, the Haitian Revolution[7] became known in Cuba and was seen as a concrete threat.[8] Second, fear increased when the ruling sector became aware of the numerical increase of the black population, whether free or slave, which in 1817 represented 57 per cent of the population. This increased to 59 per cent in 1847 and 61 per cent in 1855.[9] In addition to this, during the years 1842 and 1843, the English, under the pretext of fighting against the slave trade, stimulated several slave revolts through their consul in Havana, David Turnbull.

Also during this period, the activities of abolitionists like William Wilberforce, Victor Schoelcher and Abraham Lincoln, inspired by the abolitionist ideas of the philosophers Charles-Louis de Secondat Montesquieu, François-Marie Arouet, who called himself Voltaire and Abbe Raynal, contributed to the abolition of slavery in the English-speaking Caribbean colonies (1834), the French-speaking colonies (1848) and in the United States of America (1865). Thus, in the 1840s the internal situation of the colony, in addition to the factors stated above, led to the breakdown of the slave system in Cuba.[10]

The Cuban abolitionist movement found its followers among individuals of liberal thinking and, in general, among writers. The first Cuban novels, like *Autobiography* by Juan Francisco Manzano, *Francisco* by Anselmo Suárez Romero, *Sab* by Gertrude Gómez de Avellaneda and especially *Cecilia Valdés*, by Cirilo Villaverde, had a pronounced anti-slavery character. These works became primary sources of information on slavery in Cuba.

These were the main socio-political features of the period. The Spanish governors, pressed by the international situation mentioned above as well as by the slave rebelliousness, had been forced almost since the beginning of slavery to pass laws aimed at ameliorating slavery. But although most of those laws remained dead letters in some way, they allowed the slaves to defend themselves against their owners. The female slaves played critical roles in these activities.

During the first centuries of the slave trade, few female slaves were imported. Although on 5 May 1523, the solicitors of the already founded cities expressed their interest in introducing black females, the landowners refused to do so, basically because they could get male slaves on the African coasts relatively easily, and they never thought that the trade would end. Only in Baracoa did the Belemnite monks admit black females in their sugar mill, and married them to their male slaves.[11]

Nevertheless, at the beginning of the nineteenth century, after the slave trade was restricted, landowners began to acknowledge the need to bring female slaves from Africa in order to increase their slave stock through natural reproduction. This line of action was strongly supported by the creole economist Francisco de Arango y Parreño, who proposed at a meeting of the *Consulado* of Havana, of which he was a *síndico*,[12] an increase in the number of slaves by encouraging *hacendados* to ensure that one-third of the slaves introduced on to the estates should be female. To facilitate the process, their importation to the island would be exempt from all import duties.

At another meeting of the same institution, the deputies proposed, among other things,

> *that the master of a male slave married to a female slave of another master will be obliged to sell the male slave after valuation, if the owner of the female slave would like to buy, also taking into consideration the male slave's wishes and with the understanding that the owner of the male slave did not have one-third female slaves on his estate and the owner of the male slave did not allow him to marry.*[13]

Within this framework the Royal Decree of 27 April 1804 was promulgated, and it stated: 'The sugar mills and estates where there were only male slaves, should also include female slaves, restricting the license for the introduction of slaves to those properties to that sex [female] only until all the male slaves who wanted to, got married.'[14]

Although this was not totally fulfilled, in the mid-nineteenth century, there were black female slaves on all the estates sharing the harsh tasks of the plantation with their male partners. The fulfilment of the assignments given to black female slaves was done with such effectiveness that some foremen could say, 'black female slaves are hardier and more consistent than males . . .'[15]

This assertion was based on the fact that the duties of female slaves were not limited to agricultural tasks, but consisted also of others both in the city and in the countryside. They served their owners directly or were hired as wet-nurses or dressmakers, and performed other domestic chores, such as ironing and cooking. They also became midwives.[16] Most of these tasks, especially being midwives, helped enslaved women to acquire their freedom, which could also be obtained through ordinary sexual life with a white man.

Apart from the rigours of the regime of work to which female slaves were subjected in city and countryside, they were also victims of the most cruel and outrageous punishments like lashing, being sent to the stocks, or being whipped with their face downward even during pregnancy.[17] At the same time they were the targets of some sadist masters who manifested their sexual aberrations through activities that were inconceivable for the mentally sound. Don Ramón Saíz, from Havana, for example, promised his 14-year-old female slave, the mulatto Florencia Rodríguez or Hernandez,[18] to grant her freedom if she had sexual relations with him. Once his goal was achieved, he withheld her freedom and more than that, he punished her very often and forced her to work in the blacksmith's shop and even, according to the slave's own words, 'he tried to place silver rings in the most secret parts of her nature'.

In the face of this situation in October 1834, she complained to the mayor who asked if she was wearing the rings, to which the accuser answered no, but that her master had tried to put the rings on her, as he had previously with her friend, the *mulata* Inés, after he had had her as his woman for some time.

Despite these facts, the mayor did not do a thing except to offer to talk to the master and to send her home. In the circumstances, she continued urging her claims by other petitions as nobody paid attention to her in the village because, as she declared, the master had money and, she added, she sought help because if they were to send her back to him, she would die.[19]

The female slaves were also victims of such abuses as their owners stealing their belongings. Thus, for example, in Guanabacoa village on 1 March 1828, María del Carmen Gangá made an accusation against her master to the first mayor of the village, because her master had stolen 21 ounces of gold from her as well as some jewellery that was the product of her husband's savings. Although the master was summoned to appear in court many times, the records indicate that he never showed up.[20] Meanwhile the fact that the female slave remained in the hands of the *síndico* testified to the partiality of the colonial authorities.

In August 1860, the female slave Rosa Novantes presented to the *síndico* a document that credited her right to the money obtained for a lottery bill that she had bought with her mistress Doña Rosa Fuentes, priced at 50,000 pesos in 1855. According to the plaintiff, Don José Puentes had not given the corresponding share either to her or to her mistress. Having lost the case at the Nueva Bermeja Court, she went to see the Regent of the Royal Audience where owing to the delay, she insisted on having a defence attorney, or the necessary means for her defence and on the taking of testimony from witnesses.[21]

Of all these abuses, the most outrageous was the separation of the slave family. During the first half of the nineteenth century in Cuba, the slave family had unique characteristics, and although the family was recognised[22] and theoretically protected by the Hispanic legislation that ruled the colony, its capacity to survive under such inhumane conditions was truly dramatic.

Within this slave colonial context, the role of the black female, whether enslaved or free, was outstanding. In accordance with her possibilities, she fought boldly with all the means at her disposal, including legal ones, to protect her relatives; she helped them to obtain their freedom or get it back, and to keep them united. This was a hard and complex struggle, because generally the family nucleus was dispersed, subject to the will of different slaveholders who violated the laws with impunity, almost always with the connivance of the colonial authorities who were supposedly responsible for defending the slaves.

One of the methods used by the owners of slaves to violate the laws established to protect the slaves and the integrity of their families was to send the urban slaves to the countryside and hide them there. Thus, for instance, a document of the Superior Government Secretariat of the island of Cuba (12 September 1837) revealed, based on the story of the plaintiff, María Dolores Fría, that her daughter Ana María, slave of Marcos Podrón, came to her 15 days before and complained that her master habitually ill-treated her. She therefore asked the *síndico* for a licence to find a new master. But when a potential purchaser turned up, the master discouraged him by accusing her of being a runaway and of having several shortcomings. After achieving his objective, he sent the slave to Alquizar where she continued to be equally ill-treated and although she had been assessed[23] at 350 pesos, the master managed to prevent her from being sold. As a consequence, when in 1838 the master, Podrón, was commanded to allow the slave to go to the capital to find a new master because there was a potential buyer, he said she had already been sold to the administrator of Dolores sugar mill a few days before.[24]

The same method was used against the brown slave, María de la Cruz Pedroso, age 25, slave of Don Joaquín García, who was sent to the countryside to prevent her from being bought by the purchaser, whom Rosalía Pedroso, an African native who was her mother and a free brown, had found for her. This was the reason for her decision to approach the authorities.[25]

Slave mothers had also to face other arbitrary acts. For example, their children who had been born free were sold as slaves. They were separated from their small offspring, or their owners failed to protect them according to the stipulation of the colonial laws. There are many such examples: among them is the situation faced by the female slave María Dolores Español, property of Don Juan Peraza. She presented a claim to the *síndico* in 1851 because her daughter, María Francisca, a free brown, was unfairly enslaved. This young woman was born in Madrid in 1832, the year in which her mother travelled to the Peninsula, and in which the girl was baptised in the San Sebastián parish church. On coming back to Cuba, they stole her daughter and sold her as a slave for 6 ounces of gold, which her mother discovered after some time; and although she did all she could to obtain the baptismal certificate from the Spanish capital, she never succeeded.

Likewise, although the *síndico* from Bejucal filed a suit against Don Isidro Fernández who had bought the said freed slave, he could only get her sent in deposit to the Royal House of Welfare, where she was hired like the other slaves. This decision did not resolve the problems because it did not restore her freedom.[26]

Something similar happened to María Francisca Cañedo, free brown, whose daughter was in Doña Loreta García's possession for 22 years, out of which the slave spent more than 12 as a *coartada*, leaving only 5 ounces of gold to pay for her freedom. But the young slave got sick and she was given to her mother, for two years, to cure her. In this span of time, the free brown woman not only assisted her sick daughter at her own expense, and without receiving any help from the mistress, but also raised the mistress' son, which led her to believe that out of gratitude for her services plus the small amount of money left to pay for the young slave's freedom, her daughter would be granted her letter of freedom. Instead, she was cheated and as soon as her daughter recovered, she was taken away to the Malverde coffee plantation in Quivicán, where she was in 1849 when her mother took the case to the colonial authorities to claim payment for her services and for her daughter to be placed in deposit. To conclude, the young female slave was valued at 85 pesos, but the process could not continue because the slave did not appear in court, naturally, because she was in captivity.[27]

The violation of the colonial laws was constant, therefore the *coartación* process was violated constantly. This happened to María Justina, slave of Don José Came, who received 50 pesos from the slave's mother, the free brown Josefa Ramírez, as a payment for her freedom. Later on, the master sold her to Doña María Ana Betancourt without the requirements of a valuation. The new mistress, in turn, also tried to sell her to someone who was going to take her abroad. That was the reason why the slave's mother took the case to the *síndico* to request that her daughter be assessed at 50 pesos to allow her to find a new master of her choice.[28]

The constant increase in the slave's estimated price was another method used to hinder the sale of slaves already assessed. This is the reason why generally the female relatives, mothers, wives and daughters went to the court room to seek justice. This was the case of María Encarnación, a free brown from Cárdenas who in 1835 complained to the authorities in Havana because Doña Rosalía del Corral, owner of her mother Joaquina Gonga, did not want to accept the amount of money she offered to free her mother. She explained that the owner wanted 200 pesos for someone whose value was barely 100 pesos, because her mother was so gravely ill that she was unable to stand up straight, but still the mistress insisted on the same price.[29]

The marriage of the brown slaves, Hilario and Inés, who belonged to the slave crew of the Nazareno sugar mill, property of Juan de Larrinaga, in Guanajay, furnishes another example of the abuses suffered by the slave family. This couple, in 1852, asked that their four-year-old son, Juan Criollo, be given back to them. They explained that Don Juan Benítez, declaring himself the owner of the little black boy, had taken him away to another place; they said that they did not want to live without their son who constituted all their happiness. The *síndico*, arguing on the basis of the Slave Regulations of 1842, said that this set of rules tended, in all its articles, to develop the principles of morality and family among slaves and that Article 31 said: 'When the master of the male slave husband buys the woman, he should also buy along with her, the children who are under three years old, based on the right that up to this age the children should be breast-fed and nurtured.'[30]

For this reason, Don Juan Benítez was asked to come to the captain's office with the little boy, Juan, to sign the bill of sale with Jan de Larrinaga, in accordance with the previous valuation by the *síndico*, and because the parents wanted Larrinaga to buy their little son. Juan Benítez refused, arguing that he had raised the little boy as his own son and would not therefore, under any circumstances, sell him; that with him, the boy was better fed and cared for him and that, besides, he wanted to give him his letter of freedom so that by the time he became an adult, he would inherit it. Moreover, he proposed to buy for 2,000 pesos the boy's parents, his sister Eulogía, and by valuation, another slave, to collect from Jan de Larrinaga who owed him and thereby unite the whole family. To conclude, it appears that there was an agreement between the masters, because the authorities gave Juan Benítez the opportunity to buy the little boy who was given his freedom letter and it was decided that the boy should remain under the care of Juan Benítez, who was obliged to feed him. To sum up all these facts, the family remained separated.[31]

The kidnapping or sale of slaves was also another type of abuse suffered by blacks, including black women. Testimony presented by the United States' consul in Santiago de Cuba on behalf of the black woman Carolina, born in Savannah City, Georgia, gives further evidence. Carolina declared in her testimony that she was the daughter of free parents, and that she had been sold, together with her children and a sister, by Mr Francisco Fabars, businessman of the city, who also kept her brother as a slave. In the face of this situation, the consul demanded that the law be respected, because although he was not authorised to explain the measures the United States government would take if he got no response to his claim, he was sure that this crime would be mercilessly punished. Moreover, the female slave stated that her mother had her letter of freedom, given to her in payment for having raised Fabars himself in Baracoa, and that she went to the United States to accompany Fabar's mother; once there, she decided, being free, to go to Charleston. After some time she wrote back to her mistress because she wanted to return. The mistress immediately sent a cousin for her, but on their way back, they experienced shipwreck and in the accident the female slave lost her letter of freedom, the original copy of which must have been in Baracoa city. She also made it clear that the father of her children was Don Francisco de Mesa Garibaldo, who had bought their freedom. Therefore all three of them were free. Since she was short of money, she had claimed for the money that belonged to her, but Fabars had not given it to her, so she took the matter to court.

Fabar's defence was that Carolina's mother was the property of his mother; that they came from Santo Domingo and that on arriving in Cuba she decided to send some of her slaves to the United States, where Carolina was born. He also declared that the plaintiff's mother got pregnant in Cuba and died as a slave. Based on these circumstances, the authorities agreed to send Carolina to the slave depot. In the mistress's will she and her children were registered as slaves, and no letter of freedom was found. However, the Military-Political Government of Santiago de Cuba, taking into consideration the fact that her freedom had been paid for, acknowledged Carolina Fabar's free status and gave her her letter of freedom.[32]

Maybe the most famous case of deception in the nineteenth century, and one which became an international lawsuit, was that of Plassy Lawrence. This brown woman, also known in Havana as María del Carmen, was the slave of Don Pedro Pino when the claim was first presented to the English consul on 15 February 1851. The female slave stated that she had been unfairly submitted to slavery for over 30 years, although she was a native of the British island of Nevis.

According to her statement, in 1819 or 1820, counselled by Juan Scabraugh, she ran away from her mother who was a slave at the Farm. This man took her to the island of St Thomas, at that time a Danish island, where they were caught and handed over by the governor to be sent back to Nevis. But as she did not want to go back, she ran away from the detaining officers, and hid in the house of a native of that island named Jane Huggins, who took her to another black female from whose house she was placed in a boat captained by a white man, heading for Fagard Port in the island of Puerto Rico. From there, she travelled on horseback to another point called Cadgoa, and was taken to the house of Captain Florencio. She ran away from this place and went to the judges of the village, but found no mercy, and was put in jail under the custody of the mayor, Don Victoriano Sancalo, who sold her for 200 pesos to Don Joaquín Delgado. She defied this master because he wanted to send her to the field; so he exchanged her for a French cook from Don Leopoldo

Román, who enslaved her for two years. She refused to work or to be sold, insisting that she was free, so this master sent her to Havana on a ship with a group of African blacks and a shipment of wood that was unloaded in Talla Piedra, where she was warned not to say where she was coming from. From there, she was taken to the house of Don Antonio Vidá o Vilá on Cuba Street. Upon the latter's death, his butler Don Pablo Soler, in the light of her refusal to work on the grounds that she was free, sent her to the consulate where she stayed for approximately six months. She was then sold to Don Francisco Muñoz, who lived in front of the consulate on the road to Cerro. He, in his turn, sold her to Ramón Hérnandez in Jesús del Monte, who gave her to Don José Buciano, who was murdered shortly afterwards, but his papers went to Pedro Rizo who made her his slave. Plassy commented that his intentions were not clear.

María del Carmen or Plácida Lawrence or Plassy Lawrence — as her name appears interchangeably — wanted to go back to her family in Nevis; which is why she went to the consul of England in Cuba, who took up her case and presented a claim to the government of the island. While the investigations were going on as usual the slave was kept in the Paula hospital where she was forced to assist all patients and was exposed to infections. The consul pointed out this situation in a letter to the captain general and requested that she be removed from that place and freed because she had committed no crime.

Six months after all this began, the English consul again wrote to the captain general asking him to wrap up the case since, in his opinion, sufficient time had passed for the proper searches abroad. He added that at that moment, moreover, (2 February 1852) Plassy was in the Royal House of Welfare, but they wanted to send her back to the Hospital of San Lázaro to work as a hired slave there. In addition, the diplomat insisted on speeding up the investigation and freeing her from slave work, because she should be considered a British subject. In May 1852 the black male Fippo Laurence, an adult and relative of the slave, arrived from Nevis to identify her officially, which he did before the authorities, adding that he knew Plassy's mother, Elsie.

Meanwhile, the English consul made investigations in Nevis and received documents that gave credibility to Plassy's statements. They even checked the lists of slaves on the Farm estate as of 14 July 1817. This estate, which belonged to William Lawrence, listed Plassy as number 70, and 14 years old, and in the Nevis slave register of 1 January 1825, Plácida was mentioned as missing. The British diplomat sent the evidence to the Spanish governor of the island, and also insisted that she had been taken out of the island as a slave and sold with impunity, and that Plácida was a subject of Her Majesty Queen Victoria by birth. It was also proved by the scars on her leg, arm and body, that Plácida and María del Carmen were one and the same person. The consul demanded monetary compensation for his client for more than 30 years of enslavement in

Cuba and Puerto Rico. The compensation would take the form of a salary of 10 pesos per month, although she had earned more for her master, which amounted to 3,600 pesos. The consul was, however, willing to accept 2,000 pesos.

In the investigations carried out in Cuba, some masters denied Plassy was their slave. Other masters had died. The governor of the Danish island, St Thomas, also sent a report stating that there was no trace of Plassy's stay there. In these circumstances, the British consul declared in a letter to the captain general, dated 15 June 1852, that once she was properly identified as Plassy Lawrence, belonging to the Nevis island, she should be freed and allowed to go back in the ship that would leave Havana harbour on the 22nd of that month. As he received no answer, he sent another letter on July 1, in which he asked the captain general to send back the witness together with Plassy in the ship that was to leave on 10 July 1852. Finally, the diplomat sent another letter on 4 December 1852, indicating that the process had been too prolonged, therefore he considered the captain general had had time enough to consult his government.

Plassy then ran away on board an English frigate, *La Vestal*. The event became an international scandal that was reported in the English press, mainly by the *Morning Post*, whose article was reproduced by *La Gaceta de la Habana* on Wednesday, 23 February 1853. In one of its paragraphs, it stated:

> [On] *The 10th of December there was great excitement in Havana owing to the kidnapping from Nevis island, belonging to Great Britain, of a subject of her Majesty the Queen, the female black Plassy Laurence, who was sold as a slave in Havana. The British Government had demanded the return of this poor woman who found refuge on Her Majesty's frigate La Vestal, whose gallant Captain kept her safe under the British flag and ignored all proposals to restore Plassy to her masters, despite being under the cannons of the Spanish batteries and surrounded by the Spanish squadron.*

The reporter from *La Gaceta de la Habana*, the official newspaper of the Spanish government, said the delay of the Spanish authorities was:

> *not only just but also indispensable in a country where the sacred right of property is guaranteed by the law and under the custody of zealous authorities, who before presenting the desires of the Government of Her Majesty the Queen of Great Britain, in relation to the handing over of the mentioned Plácida Lorenza, should firstly find out the facts on which such a claim was based, and that it was also necessary even when her place of birth was positively identified, to answer a matter of international law of such importance for the interests of this Antillean island.*

Furthermore, the article stated, 'We consider no less worthy of praise the correct decision of our government to submit such behaviour to the resolution of His Majesty, because as we had said before, it was a matter of international law and in such matters only the Supreme Power can decide.'

In another paragraph, the article accused the people from the ship of performing a despicable act which favoured the escape of a person whose case was before the courts, pending a sovereign's resolution. In addition, the reporter asked what could be expected of a person who ran away from home at the age of 17.

The piece of news was also published by the French and American newspapers, for instance, the *Journal des Debats Politiques et Literaire* of 18 January 1853, *The Morning Courier* and *The New York Enquirer*. The last two under the title, 'Importante de la Havana', reported Plassy's escape, and featured *La Vestal*, commanded by Captain Cospabrick Baillie Hamilton, as a ship that served in the naval station of North America and the West Indies. The press defended Plassy and even referred to the fact that she was forced to become a prostitute and that her children were sold as slaves.

Further investigations proved that Plassy had run away, after she had conversed (in English) with the British consul, who had gone to the House of Welfare to talk to her. After Plassy's escape, the Captain general replied to the British consul on 15 December, telling him he had not yet received a decision from Her Majesty the Queen.

As a consequence of the international scandal provoked by Plassy's escape, the captain general of the island of Cuba suggested in a letter to the President of the Council of Ministers Overseas, the convenience of 'declaring the freedom of the forementioned black slave, so they could show a clear sample of disinterest and respect for the most severe and strict justice'. He also criticised the behaviour of the English consul, who, as the captain general said, offended the dignity and good faith of the Spanish government and abused the immunities and privileges that went with his position.

Finally, the search of the Spanish government to find the fugitive proved fruitless, as the letter sent on 29 August 1853 from the Spanish consulate in Nassau to Havana demonstrated, stating that they could not find Plassy either in Nevis or in the surrounding islands.[33]

To conclude, this unhappy women was in the hands of nine persons, had eight masters, was sold four times, bartered once and inherited once, all within the context of fraud and deceit in four Caribbean countries. The case became notorious not only because of the human significance, but mainly because by that date slavery had already been abolished in the British and French Caribbean colonies. Therefore, England and France did not give away this opportunity to harass publicly, the slaveholding Spain.

Conclusions

In conclusion, the black African and creole female slaves during the first half of the nineteenth century played an important role in the entire society of Cuba. They not only helped the masters' families with their work on the plantations and in the cities, but were also the foundation of their households, because they breast-fed the children, fed the adults, sewed their clothes, took good care of them when they were ill, and were even — as has been related — frequently forced to satisfy the sexual needs of their masters.

In the slave community, the role of women was all the more outstanding because apart from procreating, they were the centre of their homes. They were responsible for all the domestic chores and they were also the ones who fought all the legal battles, based on slave legislation, to defend their rights and those of their relatives and even to keep united the battered family, which is well known to have been the target of multiple disruptive attacks.

The tremendous battle that the slave women must have fought forced them to encounter complex judicial processes, the violation of the law and other arbitrary acts that reduced the possibilities of victory. However, their demands were far from being in vain, because not only did they serve to secure their rights, but they also allowed them to reveal, for posterity, the horrors of slavery and the true situation of the black female slave.

Endnotes

1. The term is used by René Depestre in 'Buenos Días y Adiós a la Negritud', *Cuaderno Casa de las Américas*, Havana, No. 29, p. 9.
2. See Cirilo Villaverde, *Cecilia Valdés*, p. 266, quoted by Alain Yacou in *Esclavage et Conscience Revolutionnaire à Cuba (Dans la Prémière Moitie du XIXe Siècle)*, (Pointe-à-Pitre: April 1969), p. 3.
3. *Ibid.*, p. 5
4. That is, integrism, autonomism, annexionism and independentism.
5. See Alain Yacou, *Esclavage et Conscience*, p. 16.
6. *Ibid.*, p. 18.
7. See Digna Casteñada Fuertes, *La Revolución Haitiana, 1791—1804*, (Havana City: Social Sciences Publishing House, 1992).
8. See Alain Yacou, *Esclavage et Conscience*, p. 9.
9. *Ibid.*, p. 13.
10. See Fernando Portuondo, *Historia de Cuba*, (Havana: National Publishing House, 1975), p. 196.
11. Fernando Ortíz, *Los Negros Esclavos*, (Havana: Social Sciences Publishing House, 1975), p. 196.

12. He was the official appointed in the cities to protect the rights of the slaves and to administer justice.
13. Ortíz, *Los Negros*, p. 197.
14. *Ibid.*, p. 198.
15. Anselmo, Suárez Romero, quoted by Ortíz, *Los Negros*, pp. 193—99.
16. See Pedro y Deschamps Chapeaux, *El Negro en la Economía Habanera del Siglo XIX*, pp. 169—84.
17. Ortíz, *Los Negros*, p. 285.
18. In the documents, these surnames are used interchangeably.
19. Fondo Gobierno Superior Civil, Sheaf 936, no. 33109, Cuban National Archives (ANC).
20. *Ibid.*, Sheaf 938, no. 33655.
21. *Ibid.*, Sheaf 953, no. 33655.
22. Supporting the family were the Royal Provision of Emperor Charles V and Cardinal Cisneros, dated 11 May 1527, confirmed repeatedly. See Fernando Ortíz, *Los Negros*, p. 401.
23. According to Fernando Ortíz, 'The *coartación* consisted of the right granted by the slave by giving his/her master a given amount of money if he/she was not sold at an agreed price, from which such an amount was discounted; and so the slave could become free by giving to his/her master the difference in money between the one already handed to the master as estimated and the fixed price.' For more information, see, Ortíz, *Los Negros*, pp. 285—90.
24. Fondo Gobierno Civil Superior, Sheaf 938, no. 33087.
25. *Ibid.*, Sheaf 946, no. 33353.
26. *Ibid.*, Sheaf 946, no. 33376.
27. *Ibid.*, Sheaf 946, no. 33365.
28. *Ibid.*, Sheaf 948, no. 33497.
29. *Ibid.*, Sheaf 937, no. 33060.
30. *Ibid.*, Sheaf 948, no. 33487.
31. *Ibid.*, Sheaf 947, no. 33312.
32. *Ibid.*, Sheaf 944, no. 33312.
33. *Ibid.*, Sheaf 947, no. 33381.

9.

Women, Work and Resistance in the French Caribbean during Slavery, 1700–1848

Bernard Moitt

This article details and analyses the social condition of enslaved black women in the plantation societies of the French Caribbean from 1700 to 1848, when slavery was abolished in the French colonial empire. It focuses primarily on the organisation of labour and its impact on slave women in Martinique, Guadeloupe, Saint-Domingue and French Guiana. It shows that gender was not a consideration in the allocation of most tasks; that women did proportionately more hard labour than men; and that the allocation of tasks conditioned women's responses to slavery, including resistance.

Research on slave women in the French Antilles is still in its infancy. Among other factors, the lack of good historical studies of the French colonies, itself the result of the paucity and unevenness of the data, especially for the *ancien régime*, is primary. This situation has led to an over-reliance on too few sources. For the seventeenth century, one of the few notable works we have is that of Jean-Baptiste (Père) Du Tertre[1] which provides an important window on the early lives of the slaves, though it falls into Lucien Abénon's category of works promoting exoticism.[2] The documentation for the eighteenth century is extensive in some cases, and includes valuable studies centred on slave law by Moreau de Saint-Méry and Lucien Petraud.[3] In general, however, the eighteenth-century works have focused heavily on Saint-Domingue, the most productive and richest colony in the Caribbean, indeed the world, in this period. Even so, gaining access to primary sources not in the French archives is difficult, and those which are housed in the archives are often in poor condition. In general, the quality of the data is spotty and often suspect. For most of the century, statistics are often widely divergent from source to source for any given year, and reveal mathematical errors. There is a lack of precision in the sources as well. Thus, Jean-Baptiste (Père) Labat's multi-volume work on slavery[4] remains indispensable because of its detailed, precise and valuable accounts of slave plantation life, including gender-specific labour. This is the case in spite of the fact that Labat, a priest and proprietor of Fond Saint Jacques plantation in Martinique was, in Gordon Lewis' words, 'the epitome of racial bigotry'.[5]

Were it not for the monumental contribution of Gabriel Debien, who spent much of his scholarly life working on slavery in Saint-Domingue, it would be much more difficult to reconstruct the lives of slave women in that colony. In addition to tapping traditional sources, Debien collected data from private archives and papers in the possession of families whose relatives owned plantations in the colony. Debien, a pioneer, did not focus on women, but it has been possible to extract a great deal of information about their lives from the rich historical legacy he has left us. Many of the studies on slavery in the French Antilles have been inspired by him, and the magnitude of his intellectual contribution is reflected in this article as well.

After 1804, when Saint-Domingue was already the independent Republic of Haiti, scholars began to concentrate on other colonies, especially Guadeloupe where resistance to slavery was more openly demonstrated than in Martinique and French Guiana. Many anti-slavery works appeared during this century, especially in the 1840s, as a counter to works promoting the view that slavery was beneficial and worth preserving. But, as with the historiography of earlier centuries, scholars have come to rely on too few sources.

In the twentieth century, French scholars have not been much concerned with research on slavery in the French Antilles, although important works by Debien and others have been produced.[6] Over the last decade or so, there has also been an increasing development of indigenous scholarship on slavery, no doubt due in part to the outlet provided by the publishing house Editions Caribéennes in Paris. Arlette Gautier's pioneering study on women and slavery in the French colonies[7] is an important beginning, though its treatment of gender is very general.

Women and labour

Women on plantations in the French Antilles performed a variety of tasks, but they were mostly relegated to the fields where they outnumbered men in the gangs. Gender was not a consideration in the allocation of most tasks requiring hard labour, as women were required to do the same work as men. But some occupations like midwifery were the preserve of women, and were thus gender-specific. On the other hand, plantation owners allocated virtually all of the specialised tasks, most of which were artisanal, to men. Thus, as in Africa, slave men maintained their traditional spheres of influence as coopers, carpenters, masons and blacksmiths. But slave owners also gave certain non-specialised tasks to men, such as being driver of the first gang, sugar boiler, messenger and coachdriver. In this way, the allocation of tasks placed the burden of hard labour on women. Thus, though women were generally outnumbered by men for most of the slavery period, they performed proportionately more hard labour than men.

Women formed the greater numbers of slaves in the field gangs whose members performed the bulk of the arduous labour upon which the economic viability of the plantations depended. Only recently has this aspect of women's labour been given the recognition it deserves. Indeed, much has been written about the economic prowess of Caribbean plantation economies during slavery, but only in the last decade or so has the historiography begun to reflect the significant role women played in the process.[8] This is hardly surprising. From the outset, the sugar plantation was associated with hard, intensive labour[9] and its failure to become a successful enterprise before it became entrenched in the Caribbean from the 1640s, has always been attributed to the lack of it. As black slave labour displaced white, European indentured labour throughout the Caribbean in the ensuing decades, sugar production became inextricably linked to slavery. After purchasing 12 slaves for 5,700 francs for the Fond Saint-Jacques plantation in Martinique in 1698, Père Labat assured his Superior General that it was 'absolutely necessary to have slaves unless we wish to discontinue the work of the sugar operations.'[10] Likewise, hard labour became synonymous with male labour. A primary reason is the preference expressed by Caribbean planters for male slaves as opposed to female slaves. Though not always respected by slavers, this preference nonetheless served to reinforce traditional and sexist views about women and labour on the plantations.

The preference implied that black women (perhaps women in general) were incapable of the hard labour upon which the fortunes of Caribbean planters depended in the seventeenth, eighteenth and nineteenth centuries. Similarly, it fostered the view that black men were naturally suited to the role of hewers of wood and drawers of water. Indeed, this view was articulated by Rose Price, owner of the Worthy Park plantation in Jamaica in a pamphlet he published in 1832. Aimed at members of the House of Commons where the abolition of British slavery was being debated, Price's pamphlet pronounced that the black man (and woman by inference) was 'destined by Providence to labour in a state of slavery, of some sort or other, till the curse of Adam is removed from the face of the earth, and from the brow of man in God's appointed time.'[11]

Field labour

On sugar plantations in the Caribbean, labour, it is said, was allocated based on the planter's needs and the slave's capacity to work.[12] In reality, need was the primary factor; and need was blind to sexual differentiation. Thus, slave women on Caribbean plantations performed, with few exceptions, the same tasks as men from an early stage. The majority of slaves, males and females, worked in the fields, where labour was most intensive. They also worked in the manufacturing end of the sugar operation, since the plantation was an agro-industrial complex. Male slaves were the sugar boilers and distillers, but on some estates, women distillers were preferred. Planters also gave the job of mill-feeding to women, who also performed general labour around the sugar works.

Field slaves were at the bottom of the slave hierarchy where women and men laboured like beasts. Père Labat observed that 'slaves performed the work of horses, transporting merchandise from one place to the other.'[13] Justin Girod-Chantrans, a Swiss traveller who visited Saint-Domingue in the eighteenth century, also captured the association between slaves and beasts of burden when he remarked that 'there is no domestic animal from which as much work is required as slaves and to which as little care is given.'[14] He also noted that the slave driver used his whip 'indiscriminately on animals and blacks'.[15] Girod-Chantrans brought out the realities of gender-neutral labour when he described a slave gang at work:

> They were about a hundred men and women of different ages, all occupied in digging ditches in a cane-field, the majority of them naked or covered with rags. The sun shone down with full force on their heads. Sweat rolled from all parts of their bodies. Their limbs, weighed down by the heat, fatigued with the weight of their picks and by the resistance of the clayey soil baked hard enough to break their implements, strained themselves to overcome every obstacle. A mournful silence reigned. Exhaustion was stamped on every face, but the hour of rest had not yet come. The pitiless eye of the manager patrolled the gang of several foremen armed with long whips moving periodically between them, giving stinging blows to all who, worn out by fatigue, were compelled to take a rest - men or women - young or old without distinction.[16]

The gang which Girod-Chantrans observed probably contained more women than men, given the pattern of task allocation. It was almost certainly the first gang, judging from the tasks in which its members were engaged. In the French Antilles, there were two or three field gangs on sugar plantations, depending on need. The first gang, the great gang, consisted of the strongest male and female slaves who performed the most arduous tasks such as preparing the soil for planting, weeding, cutting canes and manufacturing sugar.17 It was always led by a male slave driver. Less robust slaves, newly arrived slaves who had to be acclimatised, pregnant slaves and nursing mothers comprised the second gang which performed lighter and more varied tasks than those of the first gang, including the cultivation of food crops. On some sugar plantations weeding was the preoccupation of women in the second gang.[18] The third gang was made up of children between the ages of 8 and 13 years who picked weeds and gathered cane trash from around the mill. At age 13 or 14, young slaves moved up to the great gang.[19]

The driver of the third gang was a woman who normally served a dual purpose. She not only administered discipline but was able, according to Poyen de Saint-Marie, to care for younger slaves. Although the plantation did not pay much attention to the third gang, Poyen de Saint-Marie underlined its importance by stressing the tender care which he felt only women could provide because of their sex, and the knowledge which they were in a position to impart to young slaves. De Saint-Marie was inadvertently saying that the plantation depended on women to socialise young slaves into slavery. He writes:

> The primary task of the female driver of the child gang must be the preservation of the children's health. She must monitor them constantly and prevent them from eating harmful substances. She must teach them how to perform their duties well . . . She must also instruct them to obey orders without question and to resist bickering among themselves. As nothing accounts more for laziness among blacks than chigoe infection, she must inspect, clean and remove chigoes from their feet daily. At a young age, children are very receptive. Thus, much depends on authority figures who mold them into either good or bad subjects. Those who execute their tasks well merit much from their masters. On the other hand, those who neglect their tasks and shatter the planters' confidence are guilty.[20]

Women outnumbered men in the field gangs, as the following examples from Saint-Domingue demonstrate. On the plantation Beaulieu, there were 141 slaves in 1768 of whom 87 were males and 54 females. But only 9 males worked in the fields as opposed to 20 females. Similarly, on the Galbaud du Fort plantation female slaves slightly outnumbered male slaves but performed almost all the field work. Of the 54 males on the plantation, only 9 were in the fields. But 44 of the 58 females were field workers.[21] Also, on the Fleuriau plantation in the late eighteenth century, 60 of the 80 slaves (that is, 75 per cent) working in the fields were women.[22]

The association between women and field work began with the rise of the slave plantation economies in the seventeenth century and lasted until emancipation in 1848. Thus the working lives of most slave women changed little over time. Plantation records which list the occupation of slaves confirm that most women worked in the fields while men monopolised the specialised tasks. Of the 83 active men on the Breda plantation in the North Plain of Saint-Domingue in 1785, just after the owner had increased the male work force, about half fell into the category of skilled workers. Thirty-six men worked in the fields, while 6 were inactive. On the contrary, 73 of the 78 active women were in the fields and 5 were inactive. Thus, 'Except for the [two] domestics, the 51-year-old nurse and the 53-year-old nurse maid — a position reserved for the aged — all the able-bodied women were field workers, even the 15 creole women among them.'[23]

A list of 218 state-owned slaves, mostly from Martinique, Guadeloupe and French Guiana, who were granted freedom en masse in 1847, contains mainly women field slaves. French grammar makes it possible to make this assertion as the slaves were listed by professions in the masculine and feminine. Moreover, there are instances of two and three generations of women slaves, all confined to field work. For example, Genviève, 52, of Martinique, is listed along with her three daughters, Marthe-Louise, 32, Augustine, 24, and Jeanne-Rose, 11, all field workers. While the women worked in the fields, Auge, 53, Genviève's husband, cracked the whip in his role as slave driver. Likewise, Célestre, 40, of Guadeloupe, was a field worker, while her husband Pierre-Louis, 58, was a slave driver. Another Guadeloupean woman slave, Séverine, 46, was also a field worker and her husband, Pierre-Noël, 51, was a sugar boiler.[24]

Given the rigours of slave life, it would be difficult to overlook the case of Félicie, 40, yet another field slave from Guadeloupe. She had eight children ranging in age from 1 to 15 years. Her 15-year-old daughter, Célaine, also worked in the fields, as did her other daughters Eugénie, 14, Angélina, 11, and Marie-Gabrielle, 9. Her only son Félix, 9, was a field slave as well, but the fields would have been the only place for him at that age. Her other children, aged 5 and under, were too young to work.

Many other such cases were common among women slaves from French Guiana like Mémée, 38, a field slave married to 38-year-old Wacoulé, also known as Emder, a slave driver. But there were also women slaves such as Marie-Rose the sixth, 79, who gave religious instruction to young slaves on the Gabrielle plantation.[25]

French scholars have acknowledged the numerical superiority of female over male slaves in the field gangs, but have generally accepted this labour division as the natural order of things. Like Michael Craton who has found it 'a curious society, as well as an inefficient agricultural economy, in which women for the most part were the labourers and men the specialist workers',[26] and Hilary Beckles who advances the argument that West African women were 'acculturised to agricultural tasks, more so than men, and might have been considered more adaptable, at least in the short run,'[27] they have adopted different positions on this issue. In the nineteenth century, André Lacharière expressed the opinion that such a labour division

> *will become more serious and will have a negative effect on reproduction. For this reason, there is no issue more important and worthy for the legislature to concentrate upon than on the increase by reproduction of the agricultural population whose maintenance is indispensable to the existence of the colonies.*[28]

Lacharière inadvertently placed the continued existence of the French colonies in slave women's hands. Sexist as his comment may be, it strengthens the view that though slave women were primarily used as labour units, they were still expected to reproduce.

Victor Schoelcher, a philanthropist who sought to dramatise the plight of the slaves in the French colonies during the nineteenth century as a way of strengthening the argument for abolition, believed that slave 'women were perfectly suited to field work' and attributed the larger presence of women in the fields to the systematic promotion of young male slaves from field work to artisanal and other types of specialised labour, leaving the heavy tasks which required no skills to women. As he explained:

> *It is often the case in the field gangs that there are more women than men. This is how it can be explained. A plantation is, in itself, a small village. As it is usually established a considerable distance from major centres, it must provide all of its needs . . . masons and blacksmiths as well as animal watchmen. All the apprentices who are destined to replace them are now in the field gangs (the [slave] driver included), and this diminishes the male population available for field work.*[29]

This explanation has come down through time. Indeed, Gabriel Debien notes that there were always roofs rent by the wind, broken walls to repair, roads to improve and bridges to build. Planters aimed to get much of this work done after the canes had been cut, but the work often dragged on for many weeks due to interruptions by hurricanes and other problems.[30] On the plantations Boucassin and Vases in Saint-Domingue between 1774 and 1798, men did external work such as road repair, forced labour for the state on public works projects, and loaded barrels of sugar on to vessels. But whereas the ablest and strongest men were promoted in time to acquire enviable positions, becoming boilers, makers of animal-drawn carts and other specialists, women had few such distinctive positions which would have required an exemption from field labour. Debien holds the view that women

> *were better adapted than men to continuous work in the fields, perhaps because work outside the plantation and cane cutting — a task reserved for men — were considered to be the most demanding. As much as possible, it*

was seen as desirable for women to stay on the plantations . . . They were
never conscripted for forced labour required by the state. It may also be that
women were easier to subjugate or were less subject to illness.[31]

Debien is suggesting that by virtue of their gender, women's mobility and occupational categories were restricted. This is more plausible than his assertion that men did more strenuous work. Cane-cutting, for example, was not a male occupation in all the colonies. Women also did corvée labour in some colonies, though it is not clear what type. A list of dead slaves from the sugar plantation Noël in Remire in French Guiana includes the slave woman Doué, who went to perform corvée labour on 12 April 1690 and contracted a fever which forced her to return two days later. On 28 April she gave birth prematurely to a stillborn boy.[32] This suggests that she was in an advanced state of pregnancy, but this did not exempt her from hard labour. Corvée labour usually involved public works projects such as the construction of forts and roads, and plantations had to send a proportion of their slaves, sometimes just the men. During corvée planters did not feed slaves, so they had to manage how they could. Epidemics were therefore prevalent among corvée gangs, as was *marronage* or flight.

It should be emphasised that the structure of plantation society was sexist and that this sexism was reflected in the organisation of labour. Thus the slave women's plight resulted largely from patriarchy and the sexist orientation of Caribbean slave plantation society which put them into structural slots that had no bearing on their abilities. This means that women were not permitted to move into roles traditionally ascribed to males. As Debien notes, 'At about the same age, there was no differential in the work performed by either sex', yet 'all their life, women remained in the fields'.[33]

After a field was cleared and prepared for planting sugar cane, field slaves, mostly women, planted cane cuttings using either the holing or trenching method, either of which was equally laborious. Using bills and cutlasses, women also cut canes, a long, back-breaking task which had to be done once the canes were ripe, irrespective of illness among the slaves, epidemics and the inevitable hurricanes. As cane-cutting had to be synchronised with other phases of the sugar operations, labour needs were at their maximum during the harvest and the pressure on women slaves was likely to be severe from January to about July each year. Indeed, Père Labat noted that it was customary to begin cutting canes on Saturdays so that the grinding process could begin at midnight on Mondays.[34] He assigned 25 slaves to cut canes on Fond Saint-Jacques, arguing that since it 'was the lightest of tasks, women do just as much of it as men'. This may well have been his reason for assigning mostly women to this task.[35] But during the harvest the sugar operations often ran for 24 hours and field slaves worked up to 18 hours per day[36] between the cane fields and the mill where the manufacturing process took place. The labour of first gang slaves was therefore heavily drawn upon to supplement mill labour and was rewarded with glasses of *tafia* (local rum) from the planters.

Mill-feeding

Sugar manufacturing involved the transformation of sugar cane juice into crystallised sugar through a process of heating. It required a number of mill workers, some of whom fed the canes into the sugar mills. In the French Antilles, mill-feeders were usually women. Much has been made of the role of the boiler who, in Richard Dunn's words, was 'the most valued laborer on the plantation staff'[37] in that he skillfully turned raw cane juice into sugar by means of a long, tedious and complicated process requiring sound judgement and an acute sense of timing. Simply put, if the planter had no sugar to sell, or if the sugar was of poor quality, revenue would decline. Though true, this argument minimises the contribution of women in the field and in sugar manufacturing.

In making sugar, Caribbean planters used three roller vertical mills powered by wind, water or animals. There was no technological advancement in this system, which, according to Christian Schnakenbourg, remained practically unmodified for close to two centuries after 1640.[38] This is not surprising as technological advancement is not usually encouraged in areas where labour is abundant, if not dispensable. Schnakenbourg has found that the vertical mills were highly inefficient, poor energy users and spun either too fast or too slowly.[39] The technology was the same, in all regions of the Caribbean as were the problems, especially those related to mill-feeding.

Père Labat has left a detailed description of mill-feeding which reveals a great deal about women's labour. On many estates in the French Antilles, four women usually worked at the mill, but most often the nature of the work really required five. Women's labour at the mill was particularly taxed when the canes from the fields arrived at the mill so rapidly that there was hardly time to clean the equipment - a necessary measure which ensured the smooth running of the operations. Women also had to labour more extensively when working with water-driven mills which ground the canes much faster than wind or animal-driven mills, or when the huts in which they stored bagasse (cane residue) to dry was far from the mill.

One woman transported bundles of canes brought close to the mill by animal-driven carts to the principal woman mill-feeder. If time permitted, she arranged them in piles to the left of the mill-feeder who then put them on the mill table in a feeding position. If she was pressed for time, she simply dumped the bundles and moved on to fetch others.

Among other things, the principal mill-feeder had to decide how much cane could safely be fed into the rollers. When the work piled up and she was in a hurry, she cut the two cords which held the bundles of cane together with a bill and pushed an entire load between the first two rollers.

The mill-feeder took greater risks when working with water-driven mills. The speed of the mills meant that she seldom had the time to untie the bundles of cane, and fed one untied bundle after another as a consequence. Labat believed that such a practice should have been discouraged as too many canes passing through the mill put enormous stress on it, forcing the rollers to expand in which case they extracted less juice. He insisted that mills be constantly and steadily fed, however.[40]

A third woman folded the residue (bagasse) and fed it back between the first and third rollers to extract the maximum juice. One, sometimes two, other women assembled the residue into bundles which they carried into a large shed to be stored, dried and used as firewood for the coppers. They gathered small pieces which could not be bundled in baskets made from *laines*, locally grown reeds, and dumped them near the mill as animal feed, especially for horses, cows and pigs.[41] When the storage huts were too far from the mill, the women were often too pressed to bundle the residue and resorted to dumping it as animal feed in order to rush back to the mill. This deprived the operations of valuable, highly combustible firewood and points up an important dimension of women's labour.

Planters considered mill-feeding not only women's work, but work which dishonoured male slaves. In fact, Labat used it as a form of punishment. He gave male slaves, whom he deemed slack or lazy, the work the second woman mill-feeder performed, a task normally given to the weakest woman slave employed at the mill.[42] This view minimises the hazards of mill-feeding, however.

The grinding process was fraught with danger. Apart from miscarriages and other misfortunes which women alone experienced, female slaves invariably suffered numerous accidents, many of which resulted in infirmity, while working at the mill. To be sure, the danger of being crushed by the rollers was very real. As soon as the canes touched the edge of the rollers they were drawn into the machinery rapidly. Finger tips which came into contact with the rollers produced deadly results, but the conditions under which slave women laboured at the mill made such accidents inevitable. Accidents were frequent at night when women were tired and drowsy after labouring in the fields all day. Labat's description of the accidents which resulted in the maiming and death of such slave women is a very graphic, but realistic picture of the dangers to which the slave system subjected them, year after year. For this reason, it is worth citing in full. He noted that accidents were:

certainly frequent among female slaves . . . particularly at night, when, exhausted by hard labour during the daytime, they fall asleep while passing the canes. Dragged towards the machinery which they follow involuntarily still clutching the canes in their hands, they thus become caught up in it and crushed before they can be rescued. This is particularly the case when the mill is water-driven where the movement is so rapid that it is physically impossible to stop it in time to save the lives of those whose fingers are already drawn in. On such occasions, the quickest remedy is to promptly sever the arm with a bill (which is why it makes sense to always keep one without the curved tip at the head of the table, sharp and ready to use if needed.) It is better to cut off the arm than to see a person passing through the rollers of a mill. This precaution has been very useful to us at Fond S[aint] Jacques where one of our women slaves was drawn into the mill. Fortunately for her, . . . a male slave was able to stop the mill in time to give us the opportunity to sever half of the mangled arm, and thus save the rest of her body.

A woman slave belonging to the Jesuits was not as fortunate. In attempting to pass something to the woman on the other side of the mill, her shirt sleeves became caught in the cogs, and her arm, followed by the rest of her body was drawn into the machinery in an instant, before she could be given help. Only the head does not pass; it separates from the neck and falls on the side where the body entered.[43]

Planters did not focus on these accidents, perhaps because they considered slaves indispensable for most of the slavery period, but it is highly probable that they occurred in all the French colonies. In 1699 the hand of a woman slave belonging to Sieur Gressier of Trois Rivières in Guadeloupe became caught in the machinery. She attempted to free it by pulling at it with the other hand, but both became entangled. Hearing her cries, the sugar boiler on duty rushed to her assistance, pulling her arms away from the rollers. Another male slave wedged a piece of metal between the rotating cogs of the mill to stop it. But the force of the water-driven mill cracked a cog, forcing out the piece of metal which then lodged between the spinning rollers. The pieces of shrapnel which this explosion produced were so forcefully ejected that they punctured the stomach and fractured the head of the slave who installed the wedge. Meanwhile, backed by the increased force of the water, the rollers drew the sugar boiler in along with the woman mill-feeder, both meeting their deaths in this way.[44]

Writing in 1845, Jean-Baptiste Rouvellat de Cussac mentioned that a woman slave on a plantation in Fort Royal in Guadeloupe had a hand crushed by the mill. In another incident, a 12-year-old girl was crushed by the rollers, and her head fell on the mill table. These occurrences which, according to him, occurred on other plantations,[45] indicate that working conditions around the mill remained horrendous and continued to take a toll on women's lives down to the end of slavery. Also, while

Rouvellat de Cussac and others might have highlighted such cases to enhance the struggle for abolition, the use of young women slaves as mill-feeders suggests that they were moved into the first gang arbitrarily, without regard for age.

Some planters believed that slave women could avoid accidents at the mill if they took certain precautions. Women mill-feeders, especially the second mill-feeder, had to avoid standing on racks or other objects to gain a height advantage. Also, since slumber was the principal cause of accidents, planters had to ensure that women smoked and sang as they worked.[46] How this was to be achieved, it is not clear. Normally, the sugar boiler was considered the head of operations, but he was not necessarily in sight of the women. Planters put the emphasis on preventing women from slumbering, but the problem was fatigue and unsafe working conditions. Indeed, during the harvest the sugar mill operated around the clock. This was also the case in other areas such as Jamaica where women suffered similar accidents.[47]

Arlette Gautier may well be right in attributing the high incidences of infirmity among women to mill-feeding,[48] although she cites no evidence. Records from the Breda plantation in Saint-Domingue show a larger number of old women than men, but there was a higher level of infirmity among the women. There were also more women, mainly field slaves, than men who were considered old and worn-out though they had not yet reached the age of 60. Of 89 adult males in 1784, 9 were incapacitated; of 82 adult women, 15 were infirmed. What is particularly revealing about these statistics is that the Breda estate was considered better than most in terms of the treatment of slaves. For many years, Bayon de Libertat, Toussaint L'Ouverture's mentor who had a reputation for being fairer than others in working slaves, was the overseer.[49]

Rum distillation

The distillation of local rum was another important labour activity performed by slave women in the French Antilles. Indeed, the Rochechouart plantation in Martinique had two women distillers.[50] This strong rum, which the slaves called *tafia* or *guldive*, was made at the *vinaigrerie*, a place which Labat correctly acknowledged should have been more appropriately called the *distillatoire*. Local usage of the word *vinaigrerie* had become so ingrained, however, that it remained in vogue. The fact is that women made rum, not vinegar. The label *vinaigrerie* may well have diminished, in the minds of many, the skills required to make this economic activity a success.

The reasons why planters preferred women distillers are cynical, if not patronising, however. They assumed that women were less apt to drink than men. Even so, they had no confidence in women's ability to abstain.

Thus, according to Labat, they selected slave women 'considered loyal, and carefully monitored their reliability in an attempt to prevent them from yielding to the temptation of overindulgence, thereby risking insanity.' To guard against this possibility, and to deter them from stealing, Labat gave women distillers a jar of *tafia* each.[51] It would be interesting to find out whether this form of bribery was successful, since there was a local market for *tafia*.

The sale of *tafia* was an important part of a planter's revenue.[52] Besides being shipped abroad, it was sold in the colonies. In late seventeenth-century Martinique it fetched 6 *sols* per jar, more in areas not engaged in sugar production, and at times when wines and liquor from France were either rare or scarce. With 120 slaves working steadily for 45 days per year, Labat calculated that the Fond Saint-Jacques plantation produced 60 barrels of *tafia*, of which at least 54 could be sold. It is no wonder that the distillery was off limits to unauthorised slaves.[53]

Women's labour in the distillery enabled planters to defray costs and shirk their responsibilities to slaves, an aspect of the women's contribution which has been overlooked by scholars. Indeed, some masters gave slaves a quantity of *tafia* per week in place of flour and meat, a clear violation of the *Code Noir*. Such slaves were sometimes forced 'to roam about on Sundays trying to trade their liquor for flour and other essentials. This they use as a pretext for arriving very late and tired for work on Mondays. Those who drink their supplies are forced to steal from their masters at the risk of being killed or imprisoned.'[54]

Besides distilling *tafia*, women also did a number of odd jobs around the mill and distillery, many of which required heavy lifting. Women transported cane syrup and scum from the mill to the woman distiller. Women also changed the hot coppers and lifted and loaded merchandise into small boats. They swept the sugar works, washed and cleaned the vertical rollers and washed the muslin used to strain the cane juice. The boiler had to ensure that the muslin was properly washed and dried by the sun, not by the heat generated by the hot coppers which destroyed the fabric. Planters gave the fabric to the slaves when it was worn and no longer useful to the boiler. The slaves used it as blankets for themselves and their children.[55]

Domestic labour

Not all slave women were subjected to the harsh conditions characteristic of field-related work. The social reality of women in domestic labour must be seen from a different angle. Indeed, Pierre de Vassière viewed domestics as the fortunate lot,[5] but it is worth reiterating that, whether in the field or in the house, all black women were oppressed by slavery.

When Moreau de Saint-Méry wrote that 'in Saint-Domingue

everything takes on an air of opulence', he was referring to the multitude of slaves in the households of European slave-owners who apparently considered it a matter of dignity to have four times the required number of domestics.[57] He may as well have been talking about any of the Caribbean colonies during slavery. The number of domestics varied according to types of establishments and households, but there was a general tendency for slave-owners to have more servants than they needed. On the estates of rich sugar planters in Guadeloupe, domestics accounted for as much as 15 per cent of the slave force. In general, Guadeloupean planters also had a reputation for having many domestics, as most were not absentee planters[58] as was the case in Saint-Domingue. Also, slave-owners living in the towns usually had large numbers of domestics. Did they entertain more than other slave-owners? Perhaps they did.

Domestic slaves, male and female, performed a variety of tasks from as early as seven or eight years of age. This category of slaves included cooks, most of whom were males, servants, washerwomen and laundresses. But seamstresses, nurses, midwives and doctresses were domestics as well. For the most part, their work was lighter than that of field slaves and their life style was envied by the former. Of the domestics, cooks have received more attention than most, partly because they performed such a vital function. Indeed, the French placed a high premium on cooks, whose estimated value was higher than that of most other slaves, the median price in Guadeloupe being 2,600 livres in the period 1770—89. On 27 May 1783 M.L. Delagrange sold the slave cook Céladon for a record 8,000 livres. Another male cook, Gilles, owned by the merchant and militiaman E. Druault, was estimated at 4,500 livres in 1785.[59]

Scholarly interest in cooks must also be due to the fact that food was a powerful weapon in the hands of the slaves. No case illustrates this point more than that of the 55-year-old slave woman Magdeleine, head cook and surgeon on the plantation Caroline in French Guiana owned by Brémond and Favard. Around 1831, the owners incensed Magdeleine by replacing her son-in-law, the slave Mirtil, with Quenessou, a Frenchman, in the position of manager which he had occupied for many years. Through the skilful use of poison, Magdeleine made sure that neither Quenessou nor Rimal, another Frenchman who assumed the position after the former fell seriously ill, could occupy the post.[60] Thus control of the pharmacy and the kitchen put Magdeleine in a strategic position and her actions dramatise the relation between work and resistance.

Slave women, not men, cooked for the slave gangs and slave children who were left in their care while their mothers worked in the fields. The slaves called these women 'mama',[61] a designation Gautier believes is an African custom whereby men who were far from home and did not traditionally cook adopted a new mother who did the cooking for them.[62]

'Mamas' also did much of the preparatory work such as pounding manioc and transporting water. In Saint-Domingue, a group of women who pounded grain and did other domestic chores were persuaded by another group of women to become maroons in 1769.[63] As the flight of such a group would have undoubtedly dealt a severe blow to the plantation, the women may have been targeted because of the work they did. This case demonstrates that the allocation of tasks determined patterns of resistance among women.

Unlike cooks, most servants were women, both on the plantations and in private dwellings in urban centres. These were slaves who managed the household, and did the washing, using ropes, oranges and lemons for soap — as well as the cleaning and pressing. In 1785 Sr J. Vatable, militia major and merchant in Basse-Terre, had 13 slaves, among them a laundress, 2 male cooks, a woman servant and 2 washerwomen in 1785.[64] But servants also worked in commercial establishments. In 1779, L.F. Lemercier sold his sugar estate at Pérou in Abymes (Guadeloupe) for 450,000 livres and bought a large dwelling at Morne-à-L'Eau which he furnished with luxurious items such as porcelain, crystals, gilded mirrors, a cuckoo clock from Paris, ivory, marble and silverware. He established an inn and by 1782 he had 18 slaves[65] who had to polish the silver and clean the mirrors.

Though their presence was a sign of prestige, there were relatively few seamstresses among domestics, except in wealthy households.[66] Some were sent to France by their masters and creole wives to apprentice for several years. Upon their return, they made and repaired their mistresses' clothes and those of the slaves from cloth distributed by planters on Christmas Eve. They also altered ready-made clothes given to slaves.[67] Sewing for the slaves was probably a major part of the seamstress's job. Indeed, in 1778, Stanislas Foäche instructed his overseer, Paris, to keep the seamstress occupied sewing the yearly issue of clothing for the slaves. Foäche normally gave seamstresses the cloth in bulk, as it was easy to purchase. To avoid abuse, he recommended that Paris record the amount of cloth issued as some, considered *'mauvais sujets'* (bad numbers), sold some of it to buy liquor.[68]

There were also slave-owners who put young women to work as apprentices with the prospect of exploiting their labour. In a letter to his mother dated 6 August 1786, Raymund de Beaumont, who had arrived in Saint-Domingue in 1774 to seek work as a refiner and make a fortune, bought young slaves both as domestics and as an investment. To alleviate the economic hardships he faced, he told his mother that he had bought a boy and girl (10–11 years) whom he made into a valet and an apprentice seamstress. Of the girl he wrote, 'She shows great promise of becoming a first class seamstress, but she possesses every imaginable fault, among them stealing and a tendency towards *marronage*. de Beaumont found the going tough in Saint-Domingue, as salaries were low, irregularly paid and night work frequent. He was reduced to wearing his father's old clothing after the latter, a planter in Léogane, died. The fact that he purchased the slaves in spite of what he regarded as exorbitant prices, 2,500–2,700 livres, suggests that he considered the investment economically sound. Certainly, as slavery was coming to a close, a considerable number of women slaves between the ages of 17 and 24 were seamstresses, including several of 218 slaves freed by a royal ordinance in 1847.[69]

Women slave-owners often made hucksters out of female slaves who retailed items such as charcoal, fruits and vegetables. In the 1840s one such slave-owner in Saint-Pierre (Martinique) bought bulk goods and sent one of her women slaves to towns and villages to market them. According to Rouvellat de Cussac, 'This old woman had several such women slaves engaged in a profitable enterprise.' The severity of the punishment administered to slave women who did not live up to their mistresses' expectations may mean that the revenue which retail operations generated was important to them. Referring to the slave-owner above, de Cussac observed that it was 'hell for the slave who buys too dear or credits goods' as her 'old mistress would whip her with the *rigoise*,'[70] the thick thong of cowhide. Indeed, the notorious brothers, Charles and Octave Jahan, of Martinique inflicted a vicious beating on the pregnant woman slave Rosette after she returned late from Saint-Pierre where she had been sent to sell charcoal.[71] As this was the second such beating in a matter of days, it is possible that Rosette consciously chose to defy her masters' wishes, a form of resistance which the relative independence of her work likely made possible. Certainly, the tone of the spirited testimony she gave in court against them points in this direction.

The other forms of domestic labour mentioned above relate to health care. In this area of work, nurses and midwives were central, as most plantations could only afford to engage a doctor periodically and in emergencies. Thus slaves looked after most of their own health care needs with the help of doctresses. That nine of them turned up in Vanony-Frisch's sample of Guadeloupean slaves[72] is certainly revealing, as not much attention has been paid to slave women and medicine.

Nurses staffed the plantation hospital or 'sickhouse' which Stanislas Foäche viewed as the most essential building.[73] Labat gave the nursing position to well-behaved and intelligent slave women who looked after the slaves diligently, made the hospital beds and permitted entry only to those authorised by the surgeon.[74] This position was seen as a sign of upward mobility on the Fleuriau plantation in Saint-Domingue. It was highly sought after but usually given to an older slave woman who had spent her formative years in the fields.[75] Overall, age was an important criterion. On the Breda plantation, the hospital nurse was 51 years old.[76]

Caring for sick slaves involved making tea, syrups and herbal remedies prescribed by the surgeons. Nurses also prepared special meals, paid regular visits to slaves convalescing in their own huts and ensured that they complied with the doctor's orders to exercise or return to work.[77] Nurses were women with authority. They treated simple cases of illness which saved the doctor time and the plantation money; they applied bandages and reported to the surgeon or planter the condition of the sick and the nightly events at the hospital. Slave women, in Foäche's words, were far more adept at diagnosing and treating the sick than male slaves. The importance he placed on good nurses is evident from the following comments:

> A good nurse is a precious subject. She must also be intelligent as she must be able to distinguish between the early, advanced and late stages of fevers, and communicate them to the surgeon who cannot always monitor the sick. She must know how to dress wounds and use bandages in a multi-purpose way. She must be strong enough to resist the indiscreet demands of the sick and prevent their relatives and friends from bringing them things which may do them harm. If she performs her duties enthusiastically, treat her as well as you do the slave driver of the first gang. Next to him, she is the most useful slave on the plantation. If the plantation is large, give her a young, intelligent woman slave to assist and be trained by her. This is essential as the loss of a nurse can be devastating. The midwife can also assist the nurse when she is not busy.[78]

The multi-dimensional nature of domestic labour is brought out in Foäche's notes. The midwife, usually an older, prized slave woman who had put in a lifetime of service in the field gangs, and whose main duty was delivering babies, was expected to contribute to other spheres of domestic labour. This contribution was not always in the line of health care. Foäche instructed his overseer to have the cook or midwife on the Jean-Rabel estate learn how to make bread. Also, the nurse on the estate was once a cook and baker and 'like all intelligent people, she has succeeded in all the positions she has held. Fortunately, she is not old.'[79]

Given the high rates of infant mortality on slave plantations, the work of midwives was seen as crucial to the growth of the slave population. Masters believed that a good midwife could ensure more live births; that a hostile one was a danger to the expansion of the slave force. The instructions which Foäche gave to his manager in 1775 reveal both the barbarity to which women who could not produce a live child were subjected and the role of the midwife. For a live birth, Foäche ordered that the midwife be given 15 livres and the woman who delivered the baby, cloth. If the child died at birth, both women were to be whipped and the one who lost the child placed in iron collars until she became pregnant again.[80] But fear of such reprisals did not result in higher birth rates.

The foregoing case demonstrates that although domestic slaves received many perks such as money, better accommodation and larger allotments of rations, there were also drawbacks. The biggest drawback was instability. This was the case even among those who had served two generations in the same household. Such domestics were more likely to be sold when plantations changed hands and when planters left the colonies to return to France. The change was often so traumatic that it led them to become maroons.[81] Also, some female domestics had to remain single as a result of their ties to the master's household. The Jesuit priest Mongin, who lived in Martinique in the seventeenth century, also noted that some French slave-owners refused to consent to the marriage of their female slaves so as not to be deprived of their services, especially child care at night.[82] Clearly, all slaves were trapped by their condition, irrespective of the occupational categories and class distinctions to which they gave rise.

Conclusion

It is clear that gender was virtually obliterated under slavery since women, for the most part, were required to do the same work as men, in addition to work considered as women's work. Most slave women spent their lives in the fields, but others engaged in a range of domestic tasks which included not only household chores, but health care, retailing and sewing. Women performed a greater variety of tasks than men, and did proportionately more hard labour. Some aspects of women's work also put them at greater risk of infirmity and death than men, even in the case of gender-specific labour such as midwifery.

The psychological consequences of labouring in hazardous conditions or under threat of death may never be revealed, nor the social implications of a situation in which slave women did most of the hard work and men the whipping. But there are areas of women's labour which require more attention. Slave women who engaged in commerce and petty trading on their owners' behalf present good possibilities for future research. Also, there is hardly a mention of seamstresses in French historiography on slavery. Slave-owners expected many women domestics to fulfil a multiplicity of functions which makes the study of labour complex and challenging. As scholars rise to these challenges, we are certain to achieve a greater understanding of the social condition of slave women in Caribbean society.

Endnotes

1. Jean-Baptiste (Père) Du Tertre, *Histoire générale des Antilles habitées par les Français*, 4 vols., 1671 reprint (Fort-de-France: Editions des horizons Caraïbe, 1973).
2. Lucien Abénon, *La Guadeloupe de 1671 à 1759*, 2 vols. (Paris: L'Harmattan, 1987), 1, p. 7.
3. M. Moreau de Saint-Méry, *Lois et Constitutions des Colonies Françaises de l'Amérique Sous le Vent, de 1550 à 1785*, 6 vols (Paris, 1785—90); Lucien Petraud, *L'Esclavage aux Antilles Françaises Avant 1789* (Paris: Hachette, 1897).
4. Jean-Baptiste (Père) Labat, *Nouveau Voyage Aux Isles de l'Amérique*, 6 vols. (Paris, 1722).
5. Gordon K. Lewis, *Main Currents in Caribbean Thought* (Baltimore: The Johns Hopkins University Press, 1983), p. 66.
6. See for example Gabriel Debien, *Les Esclaves aux Antilles Françaises, XVIIe-XVIIIe siècle* (Basse-Terre: Société d'histoire de la Guadeloupe, 1974); Antoine Gisler, *L'esclavage aux Antilles Françaises (XVIIe-XIXe siècle* (Paris, Karthala, 1981); Gaston-Martin, *Histoire de l'esclavage Dans les Colonies Françaises* (Paris: Presses Universitaires de France, 1948).
7. Arlette Gautier, *Les Soeurs de Solitude: la Condition Féminine Dans l'esclavage aux Antilles du XVIIe au XIXe Siècle* (Paris: Editions Caribéennes, 1985).
8. See Gautier, *Les Soeurs de Solitude*; Barbara Bush, *Slave Women in Caribbean Society, 1650—1838* (Bloomington: Indiana University Press, 1990); Hilary Beckles, *Natural Rebels* (New Brunswick: Rutgers University Press, 1989); Marietta Morrissey, *Slave Women in the New World* (Lawrence: University of Kansas Press, 1989).
9. See N. Deerr, *A History of Sugar*, 2 vols (London: Chapman and Hull, 1949—50).
10. Labat, *Nouveau voyage*, 4, p. 110.
11. Rose Price, 'Pledges on Colonial Slavery, to Candidates for Seats in Parliament, Rightly Considered', cited in M. Craton and J. Walvin, *A Jamaican Plantation: The History of Worthy Park* (Toronto: University of Toronto Press, 1970), p. 191.
12. B. Higman, *Slave Population and Economy in Jamaica, 1807—1834* (Cambridge: Cambridge University Press, 1976), p. 1.
13. Labat, *Nouveau voyage*, 1, p. xxvii.
14. Justin Girod-Chantrans, *Voyage d'un Suisse dans différentes colonies d'Amérique*, 1785 reprint (Paris: Tallandier, 1980) p. 142.
15. Girod-Chantrans, *Voyage*, p. 139.
16. *Ibid, Voyage* p. 131.
17. Debien, *Les esclaves*, p. 135.
18. *Ibid*, pp. 137—38.
19. *Ibid*, p. 136.
20. M. Poyen de Saint-Marie, *De l'exploitation des Sucreries ou Conseil d'un Vieux Planteur aux Jeunes Agriculteurs des Colonies* (Basse-Terre: Imprimerie de la République, 1792) p. 14.
21. Debien, *Les esclaves*, p. 138; Bernard Moitt, 'Behind the Sugar Fortunes: Women, Labour and the Development of Caribbean Plantations during

Slavery', in S. Chilungu and S. Niang, (eds.) *African Continuities* (Toronto: Terebi Publications, 1989) p. 412.

22. Jacques Cauna, *Au temps des Isles à Sucre* (Paris: Khartala, 1978), p. 114.
23. Gabriel Debien, 'Sucrerie Breda de la Plaine du Nord (1785)', *Notes d'histoire Coloniale* # 100 (1966), p. 36.
24. Archives D'Outre-Mer (AD-M), Guadeloupe 107 (749), Bulletin des lois # 1432.
25. AD-M, Guadeloupe 107 (749), Bulletin des lois.
26. Michael Craton, *Searching for the Invisible Man* (Cambridge, MA: Harvard University Press, 1978) p. 146.
27. Hilary Beckles, *Afro-Caribbean Women and Resistance to Slavery in Barbados* (London: Karnak House, 1988), p. 17.
28. André Lacharière, *De l'affranchissement des esclaves dans les colonies Françaises* (Paris: Eugène Renduel, 1836), p. 107.
29. Victor Schoelcher, *Des colonies françaises: abolition immédiate de l'esclavage* (Basse-Terre: Société d'histoire de la Guadeloupe, 1976) pp. 23—24.
30. Debien, *Les Esclaves*, p. 158.
31. Debien, 'Comptes, profits, esclaves et travaux de deux sucreries à Saint-Domingue (1774—1798)', *Notes d'histoire coloniale*, # 6, p. 22.
32. Debien, *Les Esclaves*, p. 161.
33. Debien, 'Comptes', p. 21.
34. Labat, *Nouveau Voyage*, 3, p. 175.
35. *Ibid*, III, p. 432.
36. *Ibid*, p. 210; Gautier, *Les Soeurs de Solitude*, p. 200.
37. Richard Dunn, *Sugar and Slaves*, (New York: Norton, 1973) p. 194.
38. Christian Schnakenbourg, *Histoire de l'industrie Sucrière en Guadeloupe aux XIXe et XXe siècles* (Paris: L'Harmattan, 1980), I, p. 36.
39. Schnakenbourg, *Histoire*, I, pp. 41—45.
40. Labat, *Nouveau Voyage*, 4, pp. 202—03.
41. *Ibid*, pp. 202—03.
42. *Ibid*, p. 432.
43. *Ibid*, p. 206.
44. *Ibid*, p. 208.
45. Jean-Baptiste Rouvellat de Cussac, *Situation des Esclaves des Colonies Françaises* (Paris, 1845), p. 43.
46. Labat, *Nouveau Voyage*, 3, p. 209.
47. Craton, *Searching*, p. 203; M. Lewis, *Journal of a West India Proprietor* (London: John Murray, 1834), p. 86.
48. Gautier, *Les Soeurs de Solitude*, pp. 200—201.
49. Debien, 'Sucrerie', p. 36.
50. See Debien, 'Destinée d'esclaves à la Martinique', *Bulletin de L'institut Français d'Afrique Noire*, 26, série B (1964), p. 41.
51. Labat, *Nouveau Voyage*, 3, p. 420.
52. Rum accounted for 10—33 per cent of plantation revenues, according to Stein. See Richard Stein, *The French Sugar Business in the Eighteenth Century* (Baton Rouge: Louisiana State University Press, 1988), p. 72.
53. Labat, *Nouveau Voyage*, 3, pp. 415—20.
54. *Ibid*, p. 442. See also, Debien, *Les Esclaves*, p. 184; Anne-Marie Bruleaux *et al.*, *Deux siècles d'esclavage en Guyane Française* (Paris: L'Harmattan, 1986), p. 36.
55. Labat, *Nouveau Voyage*, 3, pp. 419—20.

56. Pierre de Vassière, *Saint-Domingue (1629—1789)* (Paris: Perrin, 1909), p. 168.
57. Moreau de Saint-Méry, *Description de la partie française de l'isle Saint-Domingue*, 3 tomes (Paris: Société d'histoire des colonies françaises, 1958), I, p. 33.
58. Nicole Vanony-Frisch, *Les Esclaves de la Guadeloupe à la fin de l'ancien Régime D'après les Sources Notariales (1770-1789)*, extract *from Bulletin de la Société de la Guadeloupe*, Nos. 63—64 (1985), p. 89.
59. Frisch, *Les Esclaves*, p. 92.
60. A D-M, Guyane 129 P2 (11), 14 July 1831.
61. Labat, *Nouveau Voyage*, 4, 457; Gautier, *Les Soeurs de Solitude*, p. 204.
62. Gautier, *Les Soeurs de Solitude*, p. 204.
63. Jean Fouchard, *Les Marrons de la liberté* (Paris: Editions de l'école, 1972) p. 289.
64. Vanony-Frisch, *Les Esclaves*, p. 89.
65. *Ibid, Les Esclaves*, p. 79.
66. *Ibid, Les Esclaves*, p. 94.
67. Debein, *Les Esclaves*, p. 90.
68. *Ibid*, p. 93; Gabriel Debien, *Plantations et esclaves à Saint-Domingue* (Dakar: Publication de la section d'histoire, 1962), p. 123.
69. A D-M, Guadeloupe 107 (749).
70. De Cussac, *Situation*, p. 44.
71. *Gazette des Tribunaux*, 4 February 1846, in AD-M, Martinique 33, 286.
72. Vanony-Frisch, *Les Esclaves*, p. 89.
73. Debien, *Les Esclaves*, p. 331; Debien, *Plantations*, p. 126.
74. Labat, *Nouveau voyage*, 4, p. 190.
75. Cauna, *Au temps des isles*, p. 112.
76. Debien, 'Sucrerie', p. 36.
77. Poyen de Saint-Marie, *De l'exploitation*, pp. 49—50.
78. Debien, *Les Esclaves*, p. 330.
79. *Ibid*, p. 92.
80. *Ibid*, pp. 129—30.
81. *Ibid, p. 93*.
82. Mongin, *Bibliothèque de Carcassonne*, VII, pp. 93—94, cited in Gautier, *Les Soeurs de Solitude*, p. 205.

10.

Street Vendors, Pedlars, Shop-Owners and Domestics:

Some Aspects of Women's Economic Roles in Nineteenth-Century San Juan, Puerto Rico (1820–1870)

Félix V. Matos-Rodríguez

Introduction

In this article, I will try to show the active participation and importance of women in the lower sectors of retail, in domestic work, and in the food selling and entertainment establishments and how plantation history has traditionally disregarded economic participation by women in the nineteenth century. In an urban context, the services provided by these women, the majority of them poor and coloured, played a crucial role in the city's economic life. Domestic work, food preparation and small retailing were important components of San Juan's 'service' economy. I also want to explore the repeated attempts by the state to regulate the economic activities of women, particularly those connected with what we would call today the informal sector. Women had to fight the efforts by local authorities to control various aspects related to their work and lives: prices, mobility, gatherings, housing, sexuality and family. Another topic I want to discuss is the heterogeneity found among economic sectors — like domestic work — traditionally associated with women. Not all domestic work was the same, and there were some important differences in the status, remuneration and quality of life associated with some domestic employment. Both the solidarities and the differences among working women need to be studied if their lives are to be truly understood from a historical perspective.

The article will begin with a general introduction to San Juan's economy between 1780 and 1870. Once the city's economic setting is provided, I will continue to document and discuss the different levels of economic participation by poor and coloured women in San Juan. I will also show the repeated attempts by local authorities to control the women involved in domestic chores and in the informal economy.

Heterogeneity of San Juan's Economy: 1780–1870

For most of San Juan's pre-nineteenth-century history, the city had been little less than a strong military outpost guarding the entrance to the Spanish empire in the Americas. The city served as the military headquarters of an island which did not figure prominently in the Spanish crown's 'economic grand design' until the late eighteenth century. Near the close of the eighteenth century, sugar prices and demand in Europe and the United states were on the rise. Some of the traditional Caribbean sugar suppliers were experiencing structural economic problems which prevented them from satisfying this growing demand. These market trends continued through the first decades of the nineteenth century. San Juan and its hinterland figured prominently in Puerto Rico's initial experience in the production of raw sugar for the world market. The port of San Juan was easily accessible by road and sea, from the fertile valleys of the neighbouring municipalities of Loiza, Trujillo, Guaynabo, Bayamón, Cangrejos, Río Piedras, Toa Alta and Toa Baja. Land became available in these areas as a result of the government's struggle against the cattle ranchers, *hato* owners, who had dominated the regional economy.[1] Once the *hatos* were dismantled, investors from San Juan were ready to exploit the agricultural resources of the city's hinterland.

San Juan's economy not only benefited from the profits of the early expansion of the sugar trade, but it also became an important distribution centre for slaves. Although a considerable number of freed blacks, peasants and former convicts lived within the city's hinterland, more labour was needed to operate the sugar *haciendas*. *Haciendas* needed the disciplined, controlled and steady labour that could only be guaranteed by slavery. As a result, the number of slaves entering San Juan increased dramatically from the late eighteenth century onwards.[2] Later in the nineteenth century, when sugar production moved to the south and west, the flow of slaves followed the expansion of the new sugar *haciendas*.

San Juan's merchants controlled a significant volume of Puerto Rico's slave imports, at least until the late 1830s.[3] Even as the north-eastern region fell behind Ponce, Guayama and Mayaguez in terms of sugar production output, San Jan remained an important location in the slave import market. The commercial contacts established since the late eighteenth century and the continued importance of San Juan's port made it impossible for city merchants to remain active in the slave trade, even when sugar production moved to other areas in Puerto Rico. Around mid-century, San Juan began exporting slaves, not only to the other municipalities in the island, but also to places like Cuba, where sugar *hacendados* were willing to pay top prices for slaves.

During the eighteenth and nineteenth centuries, San Juan's economy was further stimulated by the military's efforts to finish the protective wall around the city and to upgrade the city's existing military installations. During the eighteenth century the fear of an invasion by competing European powers had led Spain to invest considerable financial resources in securing the military invulnerability of San Juan. Most of the money employed in the city's military construction came from New Spain's silver supplies. The construction boom attracted labourers and artisans to the city, although a considerable amount of the construction work was done by penal labour transported from the Peninsula.[4] The increased presence of labourers, artisans, prisoners and military personnel in the city translated into more economic opportunity for women. The expansion in economic activity, with its related demographic growth, increased the demand for domestic services: cooking, washing, cleaning and sewing.

Although there are no direct data about the eighteenth-century experiences of *sanjuaneras* involved in domestic work, the census data indicate the growing presence of women, particularly women of colour, in the city. Most of the city's population during the late eighteenth century were women. Considering the expanding economic opportunities available to women were limited to certain occupations, it is safe to assume that many of the women in the city (especially women of colour) were involved in some kind of domestic work. The city provided an economic outlet for women who could easily find employment in the difficult chores of the domestic economy. The same significant movement of women to central urban areas, attracted by the expansion in domestic employment, has been documented in other Latin American cities in the nineteenth century, like Buenos Aires and Mexico City.[5]

San Juan's hinterland produced many of the foodstuffs consumed in the city. San Juan had very little in terms of actual agricultural production, cattle raising, fishing or manufacturing. The city's dependence on the world outside its walls for food and supplies had been one of the city's characteristics since the seventeenth century.[6] The *estancias* in Loiza, Trujillo, Río Piedras, Guaynabo, Bayamón, Toa Baja and Alta, Palo Seco, Cataño and Cangrejos, all produced goods for the residents behind the city's walls. Iñigo Abbad mentions that free people of colour cultivated yams, yucca, beans and rice in Cangrejos and Hato Rey to sell in San Juan's markets.[7] Charcoal and wood were also brought from the extramural *barrios*. Women were active in carrying and selling many of the goods produced in the extramural *barrios* into the city's streets and markets. Sometimes, buyers from the city ventured into the hinterland or into the extramural *barrios* in order to purchase foodstuffs. These *rebendones* (re-sellers), some of them women, brought the foodstuffs into the city and sold them at a lower price than retailers. This practice was condemned by San Juan's merchants and by the city council throughout the century.[8] The areas of Puerta de Tierra, Cangrejos and La Marina also had communities of fishermen who practised their trade in San Juan's bay and in its nearby rivers and mangroves.[9] Cattle also came from San Juan's hinterland.

San Juan benefited and suffered from the nineteenth-century economic cycles that Puerto Rico's export-oriented agriculture experienced. San Juan's economic life was also influenced by the changes in the Spanish and the United States economies (especially in New England and New York). During the 1820s, for example, fiscal problems in Spain affected San Juan's resident colonial and military bureaucracies. The emerging trend of depreciating agricultural prices, particularly sugar, which started around 1835, continued to haunt Puerto Rican producers until the late 1860s.[10] The intermittent boom and bust cycles associated with agricultural export production affected the merchants in San Juan, particularly in the period between 1840 and 1870. These were not easy decades for *sanjuaneros(as)*.

Particularly difficult for San Juan's residents was the period between 1840 and 1868. The 1840s was a rough decade for most Puerto Rican *hacendados* and merchants. Throughout this decade, severe droughts affected agricultural output, a shortage (and concomitant price increase) of slave labour provoked panic, and sugar prices experienced record lows. The effects of these agricultural problems were immediately felt in urban areas. Vagrancy, petty crime and water supplies often occupied the discussions of San Juan's *cabildo*. Between the late 1840s and the early 1850s municipal employees started to demand salary increases to fight escalating cost-of-living increases.[11] During the 1850s San Juan's economy was crippled by more droughts, a recession and the cholera epidemic. The 1860s did not prove to be a better decade, as the colony's structural economic problems continued. The period between 1867 and 1868, as a result of an international financial crisis, proved to be catastrophic for the city. The *época de la yuca*, as the period was called, was also combined in San Juan with the occurrence of a strong hurricane and a series of earthquakes and tremors.[12] The city's economy was in serious need of rebuilding at the close of the 1860s.

Notwithstanding all the ills which plagued San Juan's economy in the period between 1820 and 1870, the city did manage to maintain a sizeable level of economic activity.[13] San Juan's economic life was dominated during that period by commerce (especially re-exporting goods to Spain), construction, real estate and feeding and housing the state and military bureaucracies. All these activities, plus the continuous efforts by the Spanish authorities to centralise political and economic power in San Juan, maintained the city's economy during most of the mid- and late-nineteenth century.

Very little is known about San Juan's nineteenth-century class and social structure. Part of the difficulty comes from the lack of detailed studies about the city's nineteenth-century economy. More than one author has argued that it is impossible to know, at this stage, anything certain about San Juan's social and economic stratification.[14] Yet my research of the city's economic life, combined with the Latin American urban literature and studies of other Puerto Rican urban centres like Ponce and Arecibo can provide a preliminary outline of San Juan's class and social structure.[15]

There was clearly an upper class in San Juan through most of the nineteenth century. Merchants and sugar planters occupied the highest economic strata in the city's socio-economic structure.[16] High-ranking members of the colonial and ecclesiastical government were also part of the upper class and usually were owners or co-owners of *haciendas* and warehouses. Most of the members of San Juan's upper class were white. Spaniards held almost all the key military, civilian and religious positions in the city; they were also dominant among the merchant group. Creoles and other immigrants from St Thomas, the United states and France made up the rest of the planter and merchant class.

The city then had a small middle group of storekeepers (*pulperos* and *bodegueros*), shop owners and retailers (bakers, tailors and pastry makers), master artisans, professionals (lawyers, scribes, civil servants, doctors, teachers), and lower-level bureaucrats and military personnel. This middle group, which was traditionally very small in most Latin American colonial cities, was particularly small in nineteenth-century San Juan due to the city's small size and relative lack of economic development. The city's middle sectors, as well as the lower strata, were all divided by a hierarchy of occupational status and ethnic and racial classifications.[17] Finally, San Juan's lower class was composed of artisans, domestics, street peddlers (*quincalleros*, *rebendones*), food retailers (*fonderos*, *mondogueras*), unskilled labourers, *jornaleros*, and slaves. Race, ethnicity and *condicción* all played a crucial role in determining one's position in San Juan's class and social structure.

Women's Economic Roles in Nineteenth-Century San Juan

In another study, I have shown that women participated in the upper and middle tiers of commercial activity in the city.[18] There was also a lower level of retail activity in San Juan which included street vendors, peddlers, food sellers and small shop-owners. *Sanjuaneras* were very much a part of this kind of economic activity, which required little capital and addressed the needs of the lower stratum of the society's population. It was also the kind of economic activity which was not always censored by the watchful eyes of the *cabildo* and the colonial governor. I want to focus the present discussion on the women engaged in this type of economic activity and on those engaged in remunerated domestic work.

The data from the 1846 census indicate that *sanjuaneras* were engaged in a variety of small retailing trades. The San Francisco *barrio* included three women among the *fonderos(as)*: Juana Asabud, Antonia Chupani and Catalina Munero. *Fondas* were eating and drinking businesses and the San Juan data indicate that many of the women who ran *fondas* were widows. Juana Asabud was a 50-year-old white woman who had migrated from Costa Firme. Since Asabud rented the room where she lived, it is not clear whether she owned a *fonda*, or just operated one. Doñ Antonia Chupani, on the other hand, seems to have owned her *fonda*. Chupani was a 34-year-old widow from Spain. She received help from two of her daughters and from two female slaves in running her establishment. Another *fondera* was Catalina Munero, a 70-year-old *parda* widow. Munero, a native from Santo Domingo, apparently ran her *fonda* with the help of her five grandchildren, with whom she also lived. Curiously enough, Munero and her family were next-door neighbours to one of San Juan's most important merchants and slave traders, Don Casimiro Capetillo.

In the Santa Bárbara *barrio*, both Gertrudis Tanco, a 34-year-old black widow, and Juana de los Santos, a 26-year-old black single woman, were listed as *ventorilleras*. In the same *barrio*, Ana Gabriel, a 35-year-old single black slave, and Carmen Dorado, a 60-year-old African-born black widow were also *rebendonas* (re-sellers). Margarita Santiago worked as *panadera* along with several slaves in Don Pedro Cami's bakery.

The Santo Domingo *barrio* also had numerous cases of women listed in small retailing. Maria Cambien and Maria de las Angustias Morales made candy and sweets (*dulcera*). Listed as *vendedoras* were Ana Maria Guzman, Guadalupe Rijos, Emilia Cristina, Rafaela and Josefa. It also seems that the majority of the women who sold food or produce on the city's streets were either single, single mothers or widows. Some of the single women had children to take care of, as was the case of street vendor Ana María Guzmán. Guzmán was a 40-year-old black single head of household who had four young children to provide for. Guzmán was from Curazao. Some of the other street vendors seemed to be young single women trying to make ends meet for themselves. Rafaela, for example, was a street vendor who lived in a large household as an *agregada*. She was 40 years old, single and black. Another *agregada*, Emilia Cristina, was another 40-year-old single street vendor. Cristina was *parda*. The fact that four of these women were black and the other *parda* (brown) means that these women were probably street vendors and not established retailers.

Women seemed to have been well-represented among the very small grocery shop-owners. As the data from the 1846 censuses show, many women operated *quincallerías*, *ventorillos* and other small establishments. These stores required even less of a capital outlet than *pulperías*. The *ventorillos* probably sold low-quality spirits, fruits and vegetables coming from San Juan's neighbouring municipalities.

Women's presence was also strongly felt in businesses that sold prepared or cooked food. The predominance of women as cooks probably translated into more control and participation in running food retail establishments. Since in nineteenth-century San Juan most of the cooking was done at home, the businesses selling prepared food catered to very particular customers: travellers, soldiers and sailors, among others. Prepared food was also sold in locales oriented towards relaxation, entertainment or overnight lodging. In other Caribbean societies, like Jamaica, lodging houses and inns were usually owned and/or operated by women.[21] These food, entertainment and lodging businesses were not looked upon as respectable establishments by the church, the government and the *gente decente*. Tourism was not a developed industry at the time. A majority of the distinguished visitors, who were probably in San Juan for business, had probably arranged to stay with a respectable family or with a business associate.[22] So most eating, entertainment and lodging establishments had a bad reputation among the city's elite. This bad reputation came perhaps through the combination of the domestic orientation of these establishments, the inferior economic status of the women and the general immorality the elite associated with women of colour. Yet women in the food and entertainment business never failed to receive the patronage of artisans, peons and other construction workers.

Mondonguerías were another example of food-selling establishments usually run by women. *Mondongo* (tripe) is a kind of stew prepared with the intestines and other inner parts of cows. In San Juan, the *mondongueras*, women who prepared *mondongo*, were, for the most part, women of colour. Many of them were the wives or partners of butchers, most of whom lived near or in the Santa Bárbara *barrio*. The slaughterhouse was located outside the city wall just east of the La Perla garrison.[23] The town council had designated an area contiguous to the slaughterhouse for the *mondongueras* to conduct their sales.[24] Other *mondongueras* sold their product in their homes or in small roadhouses outside the city walls. Before the slaughterhouse moved outside the city wall, it was located on east San Sebastian street (Santa Bárbara *barrio*). The street section next to the old slaughterhouse was commonly referred to as the 'street of the *mondongueras*.'[25]

Spanish authorities were always suspicious of *mondongueras* because they were frequently blacks, mulattoes, *libertos* and other 'questionable characters'. One of San Juan's *alcaldes* accused Dominga Muriel and Justa Santana of selling *mondongo*.[26] The *alcalde* argued that their shops were not sanctioned by city authorities, and that by staying open until late at night their shops provided a potential meeting place for runaway slaves and other delinquents. In another incident, the Spanish authorities told Maria Concepción that if she continued to sell *mondongo* near the road leading to Puerta de Tierra, she would be punished. Her punishment was to force her to become a servant (*sirvienta*).[27] Since Spanish authorities feared that racial and anti-colonial conspiracies might be brewed within these *mondonguerías*, strict vigilance was kept over them. Yet regardless of the harassment by the authorities, *mondonguerías* remained a popular establishment among city residents, especially among blacks, mulattoes and *pardos*.

An even more modest operation was selling food and other items on the city's streets. The city of San Juan was full of such street vendors, something about which merchants and transporters always complained to the Spanish authorities. Many women who had other forms of employment, such as domestic service, still had to sell food on the city streets or door-to-door to supplement their income. Slaves and recent *libertos* were apparently very active as street vendors. In San Juan, as in other Latin American cities, the small income generated by these activities allowed many urban slaves to purchase their freedom.[28] Angela Fernández was one such slave. She was a servant for Doña Francisca Gómez and she sold food on the city streets on a part-time basis.[29] Another slave women raised 350 pesos not to manumit herself, but her son.[30] Her owner was petty enough to make the slave woman pay the 2 pesos that the notary charged for the bill of sale.

Aside from the busy rhythm of street merchants, storekeepers, peddlers and artisans, San Juan's economy was highly dependent on a variety of domestic services, most of them offered by women. Domestic service included all the activities which kept a household running: cleaning, repairing and making clothes, cooking meals, washing and attending infants and elderly people. Many women performed these tasks as part of their unremunerated roles as housewives or daughters, while others performed these services for a fee in the open market (while still being responsible for their domestic family obligations), domestic slaves, of course, formed another sort of domestic service because, for the most part, they were not paid for their services.

One of the largest groups of remunerated female domestics in San Juan were seamstresses. A significant number of women in San Juan were *modistas* (couturiers), weavers, dressmakers and seamstresses. Women ran shops related to all aspects of clothing and dressmaking. A North American traveller in San Juan, for example, was surprised to find the widow of a South American diplomat running a hat store.[31] Another woman, Antonia Rodriquez, owned a *cordonería* (string shop) in 1854.[32] Rodriquez was also part-owner of a *pulpería*.

The number of women who worked designing, sewing or repairing clothes was very high in San Juan. Of course, the census data only enumerate women who did this for a fee and do not include the hundreds of women who sewed as part of their household responsibilities. In 1846 there were almost as many seamstresses as there were servants or laundresses in San Juan (see Table 1). The census made some distinctions between *modistas* (couturiers) and *costureras* (seamstresses), but the number of *modistas* reported was minimal. Seamstresses thus made most of the clothing for the city's residents. There was high demand for this service in a city that housed the governmental, religious and military bureaucracies. Military uniforms, priests' garments and slaves' outfits probably provided a steady demand of work for a considerable number of women.

Seamstresses in San Juan seem to have come from sectors that had a higher class, racial and economic status than other women in occupations such as laundresses, domestics, and cooks, for example. As Table 2 indicates, nearly all of the 432 seamstresses identified in the 1846 census were free women. This contrasts heavily with the number of free women who were either cooks or servants. Only laundresses had a higher percentage of free women among their ranks, but their figure is still 20 per cent lower than the figure for seamstresses (see Table 2). Table 3 shows the racial composition of women in San Juan whose occupations were related to dressmaking (like seamstresses) or to domestic work (like laundresses and servants) (see Table 3). Most of these 'working women'[33] were women of colour. Four out of every five working women in San Juan in 1846 were women of colour; closer to half of them were black.

Another indication that seamstresses were economically and socially better off than other *sanjuaneras* in domestic occupations is provided by home ownership patterns. Seamstresses were among the most likely of all working women to own their own homes (see Table 4). Laundresses also ranked high among working women in terms of house ownership. Any other working women, besides seamstresses and laundresses, were very unlikely to come close to owning, or even renting, a house or a room. Data for seamstresses lagged behind data for laundresses on room renting. Clearly, house ownership and room renting were particularly difficult for working women like cooks and servants, who probably lived with the family they worked for. Also, it seems that both seamstresses

Table 1. Female domestics in San Juan by *barrio*, 1846*

	Santo Domingo	Santa Bárbara	San Francisco	Total
Laundress	148	135	72	355
Cook	34	5	45	84
Servant	n.a.	182	267	449
Mondonguera	4	3	n.a.	7
Ironer	n.a.	n.a.	1	1
Seamstress**	104	230	108	442
Other***	1	n.a.	n.a.	1
Total	291	555	493	1339

Source: AGPR, Censos San Juan 1846.
* No data available for Barrio Fortaleza or San Juan
** Includes 'falderas' or skirt-makers
*** Refers to a 'cam(a)' which I have not been able to identify.

Table 2. Female domestics by legal status and *barrio*, San Juan, 1846*

	Santo Domingo		Santa Bárbara		San Francisco		Total	
	Free	Slave	Free	Slave	Free	Slave	Free	Slave
Laundress	123	25	97	38	44	29	264	92
Cook	4	23	1	4	3	43	7	70
Mondonguera	4	3	-	-	-	-	4	3
Servant	n	n	35	147	19	270	54	417
Seamstress**	96	8	228	2	108	n	432	10
Ironer	-	-	-	-	1	-	1	-

Source: AGPR, Censos San Juan, 1846.
* Does not include the Barrio Fortaleza or San Juan
** Includes 'falderas' or skirt-makers

Table 3. Female domestics in San Juan by race and *barrio*, 1846*

	Santo Domingo	Santa Bárbara	San Francisco	Total
White	72	117	62	251
Black	75	216	271	562
Mulatto	66	218	n.a.	284
Parda	78	n.a.	160	238
Total	291	551	493	1335

Source: AGPR, Censos San Juan 1846.
* Does not include the Barrio Fortaleza or San Juan.

Table 4. Ownership of houses by San Juan's female domestics, 1846

	Owner	Not owner	Rents room	Total
Washer	13	343	96	452
Cook	0	86	9	95
Mondonguera	1	6	1	8
Servant	-	472	-	472
Seamstress*	16	426	78	520
Other**	-	2	-	2
Totals	30	1335	184	1549

Source: AGPR, Censos San Juan, 1846.
* Does not include the Barrio Fortaleza or San Juan
** 'Falderas' or skirt-makers were included along with the seamstresses. Under the other are ironer and 'cam(a)' which I have not been able to identify.

and laundresses probably received better wages than servants and cooks. The higher propensity of domestics to be slaves (when compared with laundresses or seamstresses) probably meant that these domestics could not be living, for the most part, independently. The number of seamstresses and laundresses who owned their houses or rented their own room also gives us a rough idea of the number of working women who were either living alone, widowed, or a single parent.[34] Around 18 per cent of all seamstresses and 24 per cent of the laundresses potentially lived alone, as single mothers, widows or spinsters.

Another of the most common forms of domestic employment for women was to be a laundress (see Table 1). Laundresses could be full-time help at an elite family's house or at a state, church or military institution. Other women provided their washing services for several clients. These women usually gathered their clients' clothes and took them elsewhere to wash them. Since washing was a physically demanding chore, many slaves were given this task. At least a third of San Juan's laundresses were slaves (see Table 2). Some slaves washed clothes for the person or the family who owned them. Others sold their washing services to other persons other than their owners as a source of extra income. *Cabildo* officials usually complained about the liberty these slaves had and recommended that the owners put an end to this 'self-renting' practice.[35]

Washing was no easy chore in a city which lacked accessible supplies of potable or fresh water. In many towns and villages in Puerto Rico, women could wash their clothes in the nearest river. San Juan, the tiny islet, had no such nearby rivers. In Havana, a similar fresh-water supply problem had been solved by 1835, at least partially, through the construction of an aqueduct.[36] But *sanjuaneros* did not possess the financial resources to imitate the Cuban solution. San Juan's residents were forced to rely on three springs from which to obtain the city's water needs and from small wells located in several plazas.[37] One spring was located near the Condado area, next to where the Puente de San Antonio was located. This spring's water volume and quality was among the best available to the city's residents. Another spring was located close to the Puntilla area, but the water there was not too healthy and it was abandoned in the late sixteenth century. Finally, the inlet of Miraflores had a spring which provided excellent water.

Most of the laundresses took their bundles of clothes to the wells inside the city or to the small fountain in the Condado spring. Others carried water to their houses (or collected water in an *algibe*) in order to do their job. In both cases, the job entailed walking a considerable distance and carrying a heavy load of either water or clothes. The wells and fountains became centres of women's gatherings.[38] Many laundresses must have spent hours chatting among themselves as they performed their jobs. They probably brought their children along to help with the wash and to keep them under parental surveillance. The tasks of drying the clothes and ironing them concluded what was a labour-intensive and physically demanding job.

The constant occupation of important public spaces caused laundresses to have repeated frictions with city authorities. It is fair to say that laundresses made colonial officials uneasy. First, many of San Juan's laundresses were women of colour. This immediately made them vulnerable to suspicion, surveillance and control. The predominance of people of colour in San Juan's population, up until mid-century, exacerbated tensions in a colony perpetually in fear of a slave or mulatto uprising. The authorities looked upon the gatherings of laundresses as perfect breeding grounds for seditious activity. Also, these gatherings were predominantly female-oriented and that must have increased the uneasiness of the male officials in charge of surveillance and order.

Both church and crown officials complained about the lack of decorum and order which often reigned in the city's wells and fountains. As the city grew more conscious of the latest European trends in the use of public spaces and plazas, the spectacle of laundresses there became very objectionable. Late in the century, city officials actually drafted plans for the construction of a huge fountain and washing place (*lavadero*) outside the walls.[39] This *lavadero* would have been located in the Puerta de Tierra *barrio*, where the unruly behaviour of the laundresses would prove less of an eyesore to the Spanish officials and to the city's elite. Disguised under the façade of urban development, hygiene and progress, the move to push out the poor and coloured women who washed the city people's clothes was really a defensive move by an elite and a metropolis afraid of the dislocations caused by the unpredictable world of post-abolition. The *lavadero* in Puerta de Tierra never materialised due to lack of funding.

The laundresses' threat to the colonial establishment was not just potential but real. Laundresses had organised on several occasions to demand proper working conditions. The laundresses from the Hospital de la Caridad once complained and went on strike because there was not enough water in the hospital's cistern to supply their needs.[40] They wanted the town council to allow them access to the cisterns in Ballajá. No water, for the laundresses, translated into no work and no pay. Another example of the tensions created by the laundresses' gatherings was the dispute between the laundresses and the Cangrejos *alcalde*. The *alcalde* instructed the women to leave the premises of the Condado fountain because they were making too much noise and because they were trespassing on private property.[41] After an angry exchange, which the *alcalde* believed could have only taken place with dishonourable women, the women replied that the *alcalde* had no jurisdiction over those grounds. The laundresses argued that the *alcalde* unjustly removed them from the fountain and took their grievance to the governor. The navy chief defended the laundresses by stating that the navy had jurisdiction over coastal areas like the Condado region, and that they had no problem with the presence of the laundresses at the fountain. The *alcalde's* letter to the governor survived the historical record, but the latter's reply did not. The city's laundresses clearly seemed to be a group that was not going to allow anyone to push them around easily.

These accounts of defiance, solidarity and collective organisation by laundresses should not obscure the tremendous vulnerability which these women experienced in their daily lives. As women who, for the most part, performed their work in public areas, the guarantees awarded to respectable women, those protected by remaining indoors or 'private', did not apply.[42] Laundresses and other women who were forced to work outside their homes were open prey for any kind of abuse: verbal, physical or sexual. Not only were these women vulnerable to attack, but they had few resources available in order to re-vindicate themselves after such incidents. The civil courts' records documented the 'reasonable doubt' which men (or other women) could throw upon a woman just because the nature of her business required her to be outside her house, enter clients' homes, or pass through the city streets unescorted. In a civil suit, Pasqual García, a soldier, dismissed any connection between having entered the grounds of Juana de Dios González's house and the possibility of them dating, by arguing that since it was a well-known fact that González's mother was a laundress, it was obvious to assume that he entered their house just to pick up his laundry.[43] Usually a man's entrance into a single woman's house would at least hint at the possibility of courtship or seduction. But this was not the case with 'public' women like laundresses González and her mother. The public persona of these women made them vulnerable both in the public realm and within their private homes. Their venturing into the public wiped away most of the protection 'home' awarded women. The patriarchal system placed laundresses and other domestic working women in double subordination: economic, limiting them to jobs destined to generate a low income; and social, making them fair game for physical and sexual denigration.

Some slaves and domestics also served as nannies, wet-nurses and midwives. Most of these jobs were, in a way, an extension of the domestic realm of women's lives. Although most midwives were not certified by the city, they operated under the watchful eye of the Spanish authorities. Many domestics also provided nursing services which probably entailed mostly company and surveillance, and attending to patients' basic necessities. There was a need for similar kinds of nursing services, as the case of young María de Jesús demonstrates. She was a mulatto woman who had been left to the care of the navy's Contador. When she contracted the *mal de bubas*, a type of venereal disease, she was shuffled back and forth between the Casa de Beneficencia and the Hospital de la Caridad. Finally, since her disease was considered contagious, the Casa's director decided to have her moved to an isolated house where she could recover. María was taken to the house of 'one of those women who takes care of people with venereal disease'.[44] Unfortunately, these other types of 'nurses' seldom appear listed in censuses and in other kinds of traditional documentation.

There were some women who held occupations traditionally associated with male artisan trades. The 1846 census, for example, listed two women who worked as carpenters, one who worked as a shoemaker and another as a bricklayer. These women probably worked with their husbands or partners. Other women worked as cigar-makers. Although cigar-making is usually considered a male artisan trade, in both Puerto Rico and Cuba there were plenty of women working alongside the men in cigar shops.[45] The shops were very sexually segregated as women usually handled and prepared the tobacco fillers and wrappers so that the man could actually do the cigar rolling. In San Juan, for example, Doña Josefa Más is listed as a *fumacera* in 1846.[46] Her father, Don Ramón Más, was also a *fumacero*. María Belén Fauco was a young *parda* woman listed as *fumacera*. She was also the daughter of another *fumacero*, Claudio Fauco.

Conclusion

This article has shown that women were active participants in several important areas of San Juan's economy. If there is a feeling of surprise at the level of economic participation by women in nineteenth-century San Juan, it is probably more a reflection of myths and misconceptions than of any close scrutiny of the historical record. Previous studies have always focused on the exceptional nature of women's activities in the past, and had I wanted to emphasise that aspect, there were plenty of exceptions in nineteenth-century San Juan, like the widows of Gonzalez and Ferrer who owned and operated a printing press/bookstore and a binding shop.[47] Yet this article aimed to show the continuous, quotidian, crucial participation of poor and coloured *sanjuaneras* in the city's economic life. This participation was not uncontested, however. As I have demonstrated, poor and coloured *sanjuaneras*, in carrying out their economic activities, fought intrusive local authorities. The state consistently tried to control and regulate the activities of women engaged in domestic work and in the service and informal sectors of San Juan's economy. I have also shown how women, in many cases, successfully by-passed the hurdles imposed by local authorities.

Domestic work has always been associated with women, even though few have attempted to study it seriously. I have shown the different kinds of paid domestic service in which *sanjuaneras* were involved: washing, ironing, cooking, cleaning and sewing. In San Juan, most of the domestic women were women of colour. Of the non-commercial occupations held by women, seamstresses seemed to have had a higher level of economic and social status. Laundresses, due to the nature of their job and to the city's water supplies, had a higher opportunity than any other group of working women to meet in a common area — wells and fountains — to work and share. I also showed that laundresses, when their interests were on the line, did stand up against Spanish authorities. Poor and coloured women were also active in small food and entertainment establishments, such as taverns and *mondonguerías*. These establishments were looked upon with suspicion and scorn by the city's elite. Many poor women also traveled the uneven and muddy streets of San Juan, selling food or drinks door-to-door.

It is hoped that this study will help in the continuing efforts to incorporate the work and experiences of women — particularly poor and coloured ones — into the mainstream of Puerto Rican and Caribbean economic and social history.

Endnotes

1. Fernando Picó, 'Nociones de Ordén y Desordén en la Perifería de San Juan, 1765—1830', *Revista de Historia*, 1, #2 (1985), p. 50, and Adam Szaszdi, 'Credit Without Banking in Early Nineteenth-Century Puerto Rico', *The Americas*, 19, #2 (1962), pp. 160—61.
2. Picó, 'Nociones de ordén', pp. 48—49.
3. See Birgit Sonesson, 'Puerto Rico's Commerce, 1835—1865: From Regional to Worldwide Market Relations', PhD. Dissertation (New York University, 1985), pp. 47—48, and Arturo Morales-Carrión, *Auge y Decadencia de la Trata Negrera*

en Puerto Rico (1820—1860) (San Juan: Instituto de Cultura Puertorriqueña, 1978), pp. 33—45.

4. Ruth Picke, 'Penal Servitude in the Spanish Empire: Presidio Labor in the 18th Century', *Hispanic American Historical Review* (hereafter, HAHR), 58, #1 (1978), pp. 21—40.

5. Silvia M. Arrom, *Las Mujeres de la Ciudad de Mexico, 1790-1857*, (Mexico: Siglo XXI, 1988), pp. 196—200. Also, Elizabeth Kuznesof, 'A History of Domestic Service in Spanish America, 1492—1980', in Elsa M. Chaney and Mary Garcia Castro (eds), *Muchachas No More: Household Workers in Latin America and the Caribbean* (Philadelphia: Temple University Press, 1989), pp. 24—26.

6. Fernando Picó, *Historia General de Puerto Rico* (Río Piedras: Ediciones Huracán, 2nd edn, 1986), p. 52.

7. Iñigo Abbad y Lassiera, *Historia Geográfica, Civil y Natural de la Isla de San Juan* (Río Piedras: Editorial Universitaria, 3rd edn, 1979), p. 107.

8. See, for example, the complaint on AGPR, Fondo Municipal San Juan (hereafter, FMSJ), Actas del Cabildo, 1829, 14 September 1829, 83f—84v. On 1836 the *cabildo* imposed a 10 pesos fine to anyone caught in this type of activity. See *Ibid*, 1836, 25 May 1836, 51f—v. In 1846, faced with more complaints, the *cabildo* reissued the 10 pesos fine. See, *Ibid.*, 1846, 30 March 1846, 88f—v.

9. See Gilberto Aponte, *San Mateo de Cangrejos: Comunidad Cimarrona en Puerto Rico* (San Juan: Comité Historias de los Pueblos, 1958), pp. 17—18.

10. Francisco Scarano, *Sugar and Slavery in Puerto Rico: The Plantation Economy of Ponce, 1800—1850* (Madison: University of Wisconsin Press, 1984), p. 14, and Laird Bergad, *Coffee and the Growth of Agrarian Capitalism in 19th-Century Puerto Rico* (Princeton: Princeton University Press, 1983), pp. 68—73.

11. See AGPR, FMSJ, Actas Cabildo, C 17, 21 October 1846, 291v—f, and 2 December 1846, 329f; also *Ibid.*, C 21, 10 March 1856, 40f—v and 27 March 1856, 47f—v. In his memoirs Governor Norzagaray comments on the demands of public employees for salary increases. See his 'Diario del Gobernador Norzagaray', *Anales de Investigación Histórica*, 6, #1 (1979), pp. 72—73.

12. The reference is from Federico Asenjo, a *sanjuanero*. Yuca is a bitter and rough tuber which was an important part of the average Puerto Rican's diet. Asenjo believed the combination of an economic crisis, hurricanes and earthquakes, 'had produced the most complete disturbance to the economic life of this city and of this entire Island'. See his *Las Fiestas de San Juan* (San Juan: Editorial El Coquí [1868], 1973), pp. 43—46.

13. Anibal Sepúlveda, *San Juan: Historia Ilustrada de su Desarollo Urbano, 1508—1989*, (San Juan: Carimar, 1989), pp. 171—81.

14. See Jay Kinsbruner, 'Caste and Capitalism in the Caribbean: Residential Patterns and House Ownership among Free People of Colour in San Juan, PR 1823—1846', HAHR, 70, #3 (1990), pp. 434—35.

15. An excellent synthesis of the literature on class and social structure in urban colonial Latin America can be found in Susan Socolow's, Introduction in Louisa S. Hoberman and Susan Socolow (eds), *Cities and Society in Colonial Latin America* (Albuquerque: University of New Mexico Press, 1986), pp. 3—18. On Puerto Rico's case, see Angel Quintero Rivera, *Conflictos de Clase y Política en Puerto Rico* (Río Piedras: Ediciones Huracán, 3rd edn, 1981), pp. 117—26 and James Dietz, *Economic History of Puerto Rico* (Princeton: Princeton University

Press, 1986), pp. 57—61. On Ponce's merchants, see Scarano, *Sugar and Slavery*, pp. 79—99 and pp. 144—60, and Ivette Pérez Vega, 'Las Sociedades Mercantiles en Ponce, 1817—1825', *Anales de Investigación Histórica*, VI, No. 2 (July—December 1979), pp. 52—112. On San Juan's merchants, see Sonesson, 'Puerto Rico's Commerce', pp. 48—66 and 292—433; Carmen Campos Esteve, 'La Política del Comercio: Los Comericantes de San Juan, 1837—1844' (masters thesis, University of Puerto Rico, Río Piedras, Department of History, 1987), and Nilsa M. Ortíz, 'Las Sociedades Mercantiles en San Juan, 1870—1880', *Anales de Investigación Histórica*, I, #3 (October—December 1974), pp. 74—104.

16. Dietz, *Economic History*, pp. 57—58 and Socolow, Introduction, pp. 8—9.

17. Socolow, Introduction, p. 9. Kinsbruner argues that 'social status was still determined by race' in nineteenth-century San Juan and that it was a caste system which prevented the formation of a class system. See his 'Caste and Capitalism', pp. 434—38.

18. See Chapter 4 of my dissertation, 'The Urban Women of San Juan: Economy and Society in Nineteenth-Century San Juan, Puerto Rico (1820—70), (PhD Dissertation, Columbia University, 1994 [expected]).

19. The information on the three *fonderas* comes from AGPR, Censos San Juan, Barrio San Francisco, 1846.

20. The data for Guzmán and the other street vendors come from AGPR, Censos San Juan, Barrio Santo Domingo, 1846, 27f.

21. Many of the women were women of colour. See Paulette Kerr, 'Jamaican Female Lodging House Keepers in the Nineteenth Century', *The Jamaican Historical Review*, XVII (1993), pp. 7—17.

22. Edward B. Emerson travelled to San Juan in 1831. He initially stayed in a *posada* (guest house or inn) where the sleeping accommodations were, in his opinion, very poor. Emerson landed a job with the US consul Sidney Mason and moved to his boss's house. See 'Diario de Edward Bliss Emerson, (San Juan, 1831—32', *Historia y Sociedad*, 4 (1991), pp. 168—69 and pp. 174—81.

23. On the slaughterhouse's location, see Sepúlveda, *San Juan: Historia Ilustrada*, p. 292.

24. AGPR, FMSJ, Actas de Cabildo, 15 November 1843, pp. 231f.

25. 'La Calle del Mondongo', Alejandro Tapia y Rivera recalled. See his *Mis Memorias o Puerto Rico Como lo Encontre y Como lo Dejo* (Río Piedras, Edil., 3rd Edn, 1979), p. 51.

26. AGPR, Fondo Gobernadores Españoles en Puerto Rico (hereafter FGEPR), Policia, C 163.

27. *Ibid.*

28. See the brief but suggestive piece by Mary Karasch, 'Suppliers, Sellers, Servants and Slaves', in Hoberman and Socolow, *Cities and Societies*, pp. 267—69.

29. AGPR, FMSJ, Juicios Verbales, L-49E (P.I.V.), E-67, 10 October 1860.

30. See Frank Otto Gatell, 'Puerto Rico in the 1830s: The Journal of Edward Bliss Emerson', *The Americas*, 16, No. 1 (July 1959), p. 69.

31. There is no indication as to whether she was involved in hat-making herself or whether she was just selling the hats. See 'Diario de Edward Bliss', Emerson, *op. cit.*, p. 177 (see note 22).

32. Jay Kinsbruner, 'The Pulperos of Caracas and San Juan during the First Half of the 19th Century', *LARR*, 13, #1 (1978), p. 72.

33. I will use the term 'working women' to refer to women whose occupations were listed on the 1846 census and worked on either domestic or dressmaking activities. Almost all the women for whom occupations were listed in the 1846 census were either domestics or dressmakers. The number of women listed as teachers, merchants, artisans, shopowners, etc, was very small. The Spanish census takers, of course, did not consider any non-contractual household as a valid occupation or trade.
34. This assumption is based on the census criteria for head of family status. Usually, home owners or room renters were designated heads of families in the census.
35. AGPR, FMSJ, Actas Cabildo, 21 June 1836, 63v—64f.
36. Levi Marrero, *Cuba: Economía y Sociedad* (Madrid: Playor, 1988), 14, pp. 151—56.
37. See Adolfo de Hostos, *Historia de San Juan: Ciudad Murada* (San Juan: Instituto de Cultura Puertorriqueña, 1965), pp. 477—79.
38. For an interesting account of the social conditions experienced by later nineteenth-century laundresses in Río de Janeiro, see Sandra Graham, *House and Street: The Domestic World of Servants and Masters in 19th-Century Río de Janeiro* (Cambridge: Cambridge University Press, 1988), pp. 40—45, and 52—53.
39. The 1878 proposal is found in AGPR, FOP, Obras Municipales, L62-LL, E-15, C-326.
40. The incident is mentioned in various documents. See AGPR, FMSJ, Actas de Cabildo, 4 May 1842, 88v and 30 June 1842, 122f. Another reference is found in AGPR, FOP, Edificios Públicos, San Juan, L-119, C-693.
41. See AGPR, FOP, Obras municipales, L-62LL, E-13, C-236, 14 July 1857.
42. See Graham, *House and Street*, pp. 17—18, 31—36, 40—45.
43. AGPR, FMSJ, L-73E, E-3, 22 December 1922.
44. The case of María de Jesús can be followed in AGPR, FGEPR, Beneficiencia, C-2, 19 August 1845 through 6 October 1845. The reference to the nurse reads, '*una de las mujeres que se dedican a cuidar bubas'*.
45. On women and the nineteenth-century Cuban cigar industry, see Olga Cabrera, 'Cuba y la Primera Experiencia de Incorporación Fabril de la Mujer: La Obrera Tabaquera', *Revista de Indias*, XLIX, No. 185 (1989), pp. 227—33.
46. AGPR, Censos San Juan, Barrio San Francisco, 1846, 72f (Más) and 90f (Fauco).
47. The *cabildo* records did not register their complete names. See AGPR, FMSJ, Actas Cabildo, 31 August 1868, 395f (Gonzalez) and 1 September 1868, 396v (Ferrer).

Engendering History

SECTION FOUR

Women in the

Post-Slavery Period

11.

Victims or Strategists?
Female lodging-house keepers in Jamaica

Paulette A. Kerr

The question of commercial provision for accommodation for visitors to Jamaica was addressed on an official level in the 1880s with the impending International Exhibition which Jamaica hosted in 1891. It was believed at the time that there would not be enough places offering acceptable services to visitors.

It was probably overlooked by the Jamaican officials that before the 1880s, Jamaica boasted a number of lodging houses, inns and taverns which supplied the varying needs of visitors and local inland travellers for accommodation, food, drink and other services.

It has already been established by writers like Lucille Mathurin[1] and Sheena Boa[2] that the main providers of hospitality in these houses, which were strategically located all over the island, were coloured and black women. These women were referred to as 'a despised race and a despised sex' who, according to Boa, were victims of a white male-dominated society. They suffered the injustices meted out to people of their colour and in addition were victimised as women.

They were placed in a position of subservience to white males as their mistresses and treated scornfully by other women. They were ostracised by black men, coloured men, black women and white women.

Hilary Beckles,[3] in his work on slave women in Barbados, contends that the keeping of lodging houses in Bridgetown was inextricably linked within what he calls the mistress/prostitute cycle, that is, most women involved in the hospitality trade were involved either as mistresses of white men who gave financial support for the establishment of the business or were themselves prostitutes within these houses. Some might have played double roles too. In essence, he says that these women, whether as owners or workers, were held in a sexual bind to white men who created the situation to further their own gain. He also states that it was extremely difficult for these women to break out of the cycle.

There is little concrete evidence to suggest that prostitution was institutionalised in lodging houses in Jamaica. But it is true that many lodging-house keepers were established by their white lovers and their businesses maintained by the support of white men who also formed the bulk of their clientele and for whom they provided sexual favours among other services. Most of these women were bound in informal liaisons or concubinage with white men.

Gad Heuman thinks that concubinage in Jamaica was a system engineered by the white male to continue the social inferiority of women, especially coloured women.[4] He argues that the sexual exploitation of these women was institutionalised in these relationships. Were these women allowed to become lodging-house keepers to maintain the *status quo* by keeping them tied to a traditional sexist role of providing sexual favours for men? Since white men had been involved in the hospitality trade for decades, was the rise of women in the trade manoeuvred by these men? Were these women in fact victims of male-dominated society?

A number of writers, including Aleric Josephs, contend, however, that the keeping of lodging-houses and taverns was one of the few means of economic and possibly social independence for women during and after slavery.[5] Boa also argues that from a position of being victimised, lodging-house keepers, like other coloured women, liberated themselves by using whatever resources were available to them.

Might we therefore argue like Errol Miller that the marginalisation and victimisation of women by men is simply a step away from women liberating themselves?[6] And if, as Miller says, this liberation is the unintended outcome of male conflict, did white men block the entrance of other males into the occupation of lodging-house keepers, thereby opening the way for females? What then were the historical situations which gave rise to this occupation becoming a stronghold for coloured females? Further, how did these women emerge from the relationships which they formed with their male clients? Were they in fact 'liberated'?

This article will address a number of these questions by tracing the rise of the female lodging-house keeper and showing that from a position relegated to her by dominant males where her opportunities were limited, she emerged with a number of avenues for social and economic success. She strategised rather than gave into her circumstances.

Although the focus of the article is not essentially ethnicity or colour, it is difficult to separate gender from colour when dealing with this particular occupation in nineteenth-century Jamaica, as the majority of these women were in fact coloured or of mixed race.

As with other works on gender, the discussion on these women's relations with their clients as well as their business ventures is limited because of the researchers' almost total dependence on the diaries and books of male visitors, newspapers and official documents like censuses, annual reports and inventories. The data do not express the actual views and feelings of these women.

Throughout the paper the term 'lodging house' will be used interchangeably with the term 'inn' and sometimes 'tavern'. This in no way negates the distinctions which can be made between the various institutions. It is usually agreed that an inn is a larger establishment offering drink, food and lodging, while taverns are usually restricted to the selling of wine, ale and other spirits. In Jamaica, although these differences existed, there was an overlap in services and functions. The term 'lodging house' will be used as it was the term most frequently used in the official sources and since the term 'lodging-house keeper' was a recognised occupation during the nineteenth century, while no reference was made to an 'innkeeper'.

Strength in numbers

Trelawny Wentworth who travelled throughout the West Indies in the 1830s observed that: 'All the taverns we had visited in the Antilles were conducted by a miss somebody which seemed to indicate that the office strictly appertained to the sagacity and intelligence of the fair sex; and experience confirmed us in this deduction.'[7]

John Waller in his travels noted that all the taverns in Barbados were kept by women.[8] In Havana, Cuba, Robert Baird made mention of 'boarding houses such as Madame d'Almy's or Miss Chambers, both of which were excellent.'[9]

In Jamaica the references to female lodging-house keepers were quite numerous. Matthew Lewis in 1817 was cared for by female hostesses in all the places where he stayed while travelling from St James to St Thomas-in-the-East. 'Miss Hatley', 'Miss Cole' and the famous 'Judy James' are just a few of the women who cared for him.[10] It was to Charlotte Beckford's lodging house that Lady Nugent sent her guests in 1802.[11] Robert Madden, writing in 1834, mentioned 'such establishments as Miss Hannah Lewis, Miss Winter and the innumerable brown misses, who board [and] lodge'.[12] Kitty Paisley, Judith Pines, Mary Fisher and Mary Anderson were some of the women to whom Benjamin Scott Moncrieffe paid tidy sums for lodgings.[13] Thomas Davies, Special Magistrate, used the services of women like Elizabeth Lawrence, Georgiana Tyndale and Martha Sylvester during his stay in Jamaica.[14]

Table 1. Lodging houses and lodging house keepers, Kingston, 1878

Place	Operator	Address
Barkley Hall	Mrs H. Gardner	64 Harbour Street
Blake, Harriet		45 Orange Street
Clarendon House	Susan Foderingham	23 East Street
Corinaldi, Emma		93 King Street
Farebrother, Jane		83 King Street
Fiddes House	Mrs E. B. Lillie	95 East Street
Grampian House	Jane Lamont	87 Barry Street
New Blundell Hall	Luisa Grant	7 East Street
Gosford Lodge	Mary Dewa	1 Highholborn Street, 70 King Street
Manchester House	Annette McFarlane	95 Water Lane
McDowell, Ann		5 East Street
Nosworthy, Margaret		38 Parade
Parade Villa	Sarah Hopgood	58 Harbour Street
Portland House	Mrs Dias	43 West Street
Rogers, Mrs Maria		3 Hanover Street
Shaw, Henriet		33 Duke Street
Stewart, Jane		54 Hanover Street
St Thomas House	Susan Burton	

Source: The Jamaica Directory 1878, p. 18.

The Jamaican census of 1844 gives the total number of lodging-house keepers as 157. Of these 88 were female, 26 male, and the rest were not defined in terms of sex.[15] In 9 of the 16 parishes there was no record of a male-operated lodging house. In Kingston the ratio of females to males was almost 2:1. The census of 1861 is very defective in its breakdown of occupations by sex. However, other sources for the second half of the century all suggest that there was a significantly high proportion of women in the trade. In fact, as Table 1 shows, in 1878 all lodging houses in Kingston were operated by women.

Contemporary newspaper advertisements confirmed the travellers' reports of women as the leading providers of accommodation and food all over the island. These advertisements directly or indirectly point to women in these establishments. In Falmouth in 1854,

> *Mrs Davies begs to announce that she has taken that airy and commodious dwelling in Cornwall Street lately tenanted by the Rev. W. Thornburn where she will be happy to receive lodgers.*[16]

And,

the undermentioned begs leave respectfully to inform the friends and patrons of her late sister, Miss Elizabeth Green that she has taken possession of the House near the sea-side where she will be glad to receive LODGERS and BOARDERS on moderate terms and promises that every attendance will be given. Catherine Green.[17]

It was believed that to stray from a female-operated lodging house was unwise. Trelawny Wentworth went to the extent of advising other travellers to avoid staying in taverns operated by men because 'there is nothing attractive about it; your necessities need anticipating, your appetite requires stimulants and coaxing and there is that instinctive eloquence in the female voice and especially in the fine drawn wheedling of a mulatto hostess.'[18]

Anthony Trollope thought there was something mysterious about the phenomenon of female owners:

There is a mystery about hotels in the British West Indies. They are always kept by fat middle-aged coloured ladies who have no husbands. I never found an exception except at Berbice . . . these ladies are generally called Miss so-and-so . . . I only mention this. I cannot solve the riddle, but it did strike me as singular that the profession should always be in the hands of these ladies and that they should never get husbands.[19]

Historical roots

It is not clear when free coloured and black women began operating taverns and lodging houses on a wide scale in Jamaica. Tavern and innkeeping in the seventeenth century was strictly the domain of men. Of 44 tavern keepers and victuallers in seventeenth-century Port Royal, only 2 were women,[20] possibly white women. However, as the role of taverns changed to provide the services of inns and lodging houses rather than liquor exclusively, references to female-operated taverns became more frequent. By the start of the nineteenth century several freed women were operating taverns and female lodging-house keepers outnumbered males. It might be that women created this occupation by expanding the services of taverns to include all the domestic services associated with the nineteenth-century lodging house.

With the development of the plantation system it seems that lodging-house keeping moved out of the hands of whites. This is not strange, as many other occupations did the same. As whites moved up socially to better-paid, more prestigious occupations involving less manual work, blacks and coloureds took over occupations such as those of millwrights, coppersmiths, coach-makers and masons. It is likely that tavern-keeping became a less prestigious occupation for whites in the later seventeenth century. What is strange about tavern- and lodging-house keeping is that the occupation moved into the hands of coloured females rather than coloured males.

Certainly in all towns females outnumbered males, and, according to Gad Heuman, the free coloured woman was the fastest growing part of the population. Yet according to the 1844 census females outnumbered males only in the occupation of lodging-house keeper.

There are a number of possible explanations for this peculiarity of the West Indies during the period, that is, the high percentage of women in the hospitality trade.

In examining Montpelier estate during the early nineteenth century, Higman found that the major determinants of the 'weight' of labour given to a slave were colour, sex and age.[21] Therefore coloured female slaves made up almost all of those who were domestics or washerwomen, since these jobs were seen as 'light work'. Furthermore some of the skills involved in operating lodging houses in the nineteenth century were primarily though not exclusively part of women's work during slavery. These skills included laundering and baking. The hospitality trade was therefore a logical occupation to follow.

In explaining the predominance of women in this business there arises the question of whether their willingness to provide sexual favours gave them any advantage over males in setting up these houses. Certainly women stood a better chance of receiving capital outlay from their white lovers. Most of the women who established lodging houses were in fact housekeepers or mistresses of whites.

The stark reality too was that the options for occupations open to coloured females during the period were quite limited. They had been 'trained' for little else, while coloured and black men had a variety of options open to them, such as craftsmen, tradesmen, artisans and mechanics.

There is the possibility, however, that although historical precedents had been set for women to move into this occupation, white men may have deliberately closed the doors to coloured men and made it easier for women to become lodging-house keepers. How does one explain that, throughout the nineteenth century, reference to male owners of lodging houses revealed a white-dominated group? There were no coloured male lodging-house keepers who were given contracts to operate by the white authorities. In one parish, St David, between 1801 and 1813, Mary Hatley, a coloured woman, was the only licensed tavern keeper. Liquor licences were granted by white men as magistrates or as members of the vestry.[22] They therefore had the power to decide who was allowed in the group.

Coloured men might have been seen as economic competitors to white men in the hospitality industry, and white men would hardly miss the political implications of assisting coloured men to enrich themselves.

Beckles thinks that white men understood gender implications and used this knowledge to their own advantage. Were coloured men deliberately kept out of this group or did white men feel that opening the trade to women would maintain the *status quo*? Heuman says that white males were uncertain whether coloured males would prove a threat to their continued supremacy.[23] They therefore chose to support females who did not appear to pose a threat. Probably white men felt that by allowing women in the trade their sexual wishes would be met and the women would be kept in 'bondage' to them since they had assisted them financially. What followed was exactly what Errol Miller refers to as the empowering of women resulting from the marginalisation of men by men.

What needs explanation is why more white women did not enter the occupation, or why they did not take it over from white men who had moved up into the ranks of overseers or book-keepers. There was a scarcity of white women during the plantation era. The few upper-class English women who did come to the West Indies came as wives and daughters of estate owners and in a few instances were owners themselves. There is record, however, of some working-class English women holding domestic positions in white households. Many of the women who attended to governors' wives were white, and affluent women often brought maids with them from England. And there were, of course, poor white creole women. These groups could have provided more than the very few white female lodging-house keepers who did emerge.

Part of the explanation might be that coloured women were able to amass larger fortunes than white women to go into business. Many white women were indeed 'passed over' by white men and favours sought from coloured women. For example, Charlotte Beckford in Spanish Town was a free mulatto who had two sons by George Ffrench, Crown Solicitor and later Clerk of the Council. Her lodging house was also known as 'Miss Ffrench's' lodging house although there is no record of a marriage between her and George Ffrench.[24] Additionally, because of their training in domestic chores coloured women did not find the work involved in keeping a tavern or inn below their dignity. White working-class women might have done so, and perhaps did not wish to offer these services commercially.

Furthermore, businesses became female-dominated, as once coloured women established themselves in this business, there was a tendency to involve other female family members. If a business was profitable, it made sense to prepare a daughter or sister, or some other close relative, to take it over. Anthony Trollope was cared for by Mary Seacole's sister at Blundell Hall and Mary Seacole herself learned the trade from her mother who operated a lodging house on the same site as Blundell Hall.[25] Catherine Green of Falmouth took over the business on the death of her sister Rebecca Green in 1851.[26]

Strategists - as business women

If the historical situation made it easier for women to enter this occupation, what was their role in liberating themselves from being victims? Are we to believe with Errol Miller that their 'liberation' was simply the unintended outcome of male conflict[27] and that there was no planning on their part? The evidence suggests that these women did plan especially for economic independence. The female lodging-house keeper was indeed a strategist.

First, not all these women were given taverns or lodging houses. Most of them turned dwelling houses given to them into shops, hospitals and lodging houses. They turned their 'wealth' into more wealth. Second, in the establishment of these houses, they chose strategic locations, that is, land routes and in the main seaport towns of Falmouth, Montego Bay, Port Antonio and Black River. They sought out the places where there were no planters' residences and only the houses of a few merchants. They met the demand for lodging and food from a wide cross-section of travellers and became indispensable.

Many of the women who operated these establishments became 'women of considerable wealth in both houses and slaves'.[28] Some of the visitors to the lodging houses did not fail to comment on the flurry of servants and slaves attending their tables and rooms.

The records confirm that tavern- and lodging-house keepers made fairly decent incomes when compared with other occupations. In fact, their annual income was quite comparable with other workers in the nineteenth century. The figure proposed by Eisner[29] of £1 per week is therefore quite unrealistic when one considers the range of services which were offered by these places and the cost of these services. In fact, it is quite likely that most lodging-house keepers under-reported their incomes

A number of lodging-house keepers could swell their coffers by providing a multitude of services in addition to those of food, drink, accommodation, laundering and probably prostitution, whether overtly or disguised. These additional services included being nurse or 'doctress'. Mary Seacole and other so-called doctresses operated within the context of the lodging house and catered mainly to seamen and soldiers who were often sorely in need of medical care. The white and coloured transient community depended on these public houses.

Many lodging-house keepers also catered to the vestry by providing their quarterly dinners and other refreshments. In St Ann, Catherine Paisley catered to the vestry from 1807 to 1833, being paid £10 for each diner.[30] In addition, these women organised dances and balls for members of the white community. These dances were largely attended by coloured females with white men admitted.

Table 2. Annual incomes attached to various occupations in Jamaica, 1847.

Occupation	Income, £	Occupation	Income, £
Minister of religion	400	Storekeepers	300
Schoolmasters	70	Retailers	100
Planting	-	Clerks	120
Bankers	500	Master tradesmen	150
Public servants	500	Journeymen	50
Professional persons	500	Tavern keepers	300
Surveyors	300	Lodging house keepers	150
Artists	150	Master mariners	80
1,000 persons (unclassified)	50	Miners	70
Pilots	70		

Source: G. Scotland, A letter addressed to the public of Jamaica on the political and financial state of the colony. Jamaica, 1847, cited in Douglas Hall, Free Jamaica 1838—1865: An Economic History (London: Caribbean Unviersities Press, 1969), p. 228.

These owners of lodging houses also wisely diversified their businesses, often using incomes derived from lodging houses. In 1878 a considerable percentage of lodging-house keepers were shopkeepers and owners of bakeries. Mary McPherson of Porus owned a bakery as well as a lodging house in Porus. She also owned a lodging house in Old Harbour. Mrs Magnus of Golden Spring, Emily Lyons of Annotto Bay and Maria Eastwood of Porus are a few lodging-house keepers who operated bakeries.[31] Elizabeth Sutton, who owned a lodging house on East Street and who died in the early part of the century, had amassed a large fortune. An inventory of her estate when she died revealed that it was worth £2,821 in 1803. She left 14 slaves worth over £1,200 each. Her five-bedroom house was fully furnished and there were many rooms in another building which she owned.[32]

Another coloured lodging-house keeper, Susanah French of Kingston, left an estate worth £3,219. In addition to the five-bedroom fully furnished house which she operated as a lodging house, she also owned a three-bedroom house in Hannah Town. She had 34 slaves to her credit.[33]

The famous Ann Fraser of Laughlands Tavern in St Ann, which, according to Philip Wright, was 'frequented by gentlemen of the legal profession journeying to and from the Cornwall Assizes in Montego Bay',[34] amassed personal property worth £5,838. Her furniture and goods alone were worth £2,213. Among her 37 slaves were four carpenters, one mason, ten field hands, cooks and a house washer.[35]

In 'opening up' her lodging house the lodging-house keeper ensured that she would maintain a fairly comfortable existence. The lodging house of the nineteenth century, was at times post office, sales room, community bill-board room, hospital, court house for trials of petty offences or court martials, and a kind of community centre where favoured people from the private sector and from government met for business.

Relationships

It is extremely difficult to determine the kinds of relationships which existed between female proprietors and their customers, who were mainly male. Part of the difficulty in reconstructing these relationships is due to the almost total dependence on sources which do not give an insight into the feelings of these women. With the exception of Mary Seacole, nothing is heard directly from the women.

The nature of these relationships might result from the different and varied tasks which were carried out in these establishments. Some services required a more businesslike approach, while for others the owners had to assume the role of friend and confidante. The types of relationships might also hinge on the kinds of customers; the lodging-house keeper adapted to suit her clients. As one-sided as the report of visitors might be, they do give some insight into the ways the female owners strategised for their own good.

Strategists - in relationships with customers

There were two basic types of customers of these taverns and inns: guests who lodged in the establishments for varying periods; and non-guests, who paid for various services without lodging in the establishments. Often semi-permanent guests were the relatively poor, single white and coloured clerks who were boarders for long periods. These men had their meals provided and their laundry done.[36]

A great number of people passed through the doors of these lodging houses and taverns. There must have been also hundreds (possibly thousands) of sailors, military and naval officers who stopped for lodgings, food and drink and even medical care, and who left little evidence of their presence in the records. The main seaport towns of Kingston, Montego Bay and Falmouth experienced droves of visitors intransit.[37] Towns such as Moneague saw travellers daily as they moved from Spanish Town to the North coast and vice versa.

Planters, merchants, jury men, suitors, government officials and businessmen who stopped for a night or for a meal or a drink;[38] visitors who found no planter's residence nor overseer's house to shelter in or who simply had no letter of introduction to any one of importance; all contributed to the clientele of these establishments.

There were many overseas visitors to lodging houses. Among those who recorded their impressions were James Anthony Froude (historian and writer), Anthony Trollope (novelist), Richard R. Madden (stipendiary magistrate), Joseph Sturge and Thomas Harvey (humanitarians), Benjamin Scott Moncrieffe (attorney, planter and horse-owner) and Lady Maria Nugent (wife of the governor).

All classes made use of inns and taverns. There were people who belonged to the upper class, for example, planters, merchants, government officials and some important visitors from abroad; middle-class people including lower-middle-class persons, for example, navy officers and white and coloured clerks; people of working-class origins, for example, sailors and seamen.

As non-guest customers, there were upper-middle-class planters and merchants attending balls, a few middle-class coloured women, businessmen using rooms, government officials ordering dinners, people attending balls, election victors celebrating their triumphs.

If the clientele was varied in its class composition, it was far less so in its racial and gender components. Overwhelmingly, the customers were white males, with some coloured males, apparently more coloured females (as non-guests), and a sprinkling of blacks. Anthony Trollope noticed one black man, in the Wellington Inn in Spanish Town, talking politics.[39] White women as guests or non-guest customers were rather few. The record of women's use of these establishments might, however, be very incomplete.

Black people were rarely guests; black working-class people, for example higglers and cartmen, travelling across the island and in need of shelter for a night had to make other arrangements, perhaps taking shelter in 'negro yards'.[40] Most likely there was a colour restriction in most of these taverns and inns; since the clientele was predominantly white, it would have been bad for business to have any but selected members of other races as guests. As institutions, the inns and taverns were typical of their times: they preferred white customers, allowed some selected coloured customers and mostly kept away black people, even those who might have been able to pay. However, inns and taverns presumably were of different standards and those at the lower end of the scale might have had little or no colour restrictions. Surely some blacks must have stopped at humble taverns and inns for a drink.

From all indications, certain lodging houses attracted a specific clientele.[41] There was an inn which received the patronage of legal personnel on their way to country assizes. Lady Nugent, wife of Governor Nugent, and her guests made use of some inns. Certainly she would never visit a second-rate inn; nor would she send her guests to a lodging house which attracted the lower classes. Charles Day, a visitor to Barbados writing in the 1840s, said that visitors to some inns were 'usually shopmen, tradesmen and generally of the most inferior classes.

The females are not very reputable and the low Irish visitors, . . . the habitues of the house are very offensive in their habits and conduct. Altogether it is a very unfit place for any gentleman.' [42]

Mary Seacole's house, like others, attracted ailing seamen and army personnel because of its nursing services. Most of the lodging houses in major seaport towns like Falmouth, Montego Bay and especially Kingston, were frequented by numerous sailors in transit. Some of these places attracted disreputable females as well, who certainly gave favours in return for money.

There remains the question of possible sexual relations between customers and owners of lodging houses and taverns. It has been established that in Barbados taverns and lodging houses were notorious for prostitution.[43] Travellers complained about this aspect of the business in Barbados. In Jamaica no such direct accusation has been noted in the books or diaries of travellers, even when they were men of known morality like Sturge and Harvey. Brothels existed in Jamaica and most were operated by free black women;[44] there is little indication, however, that houses of prostitution operated under the guise of lodging houses. But this does not rule out paid-for sexual services within these establishments. It would be remarkable if, for example, sailors and seamen, after months at sea, visited inns and taverns without expectations of sexual intercourse. And it would be foolish to believe that these lodging-house keepers did not capitalise on the gains which could be accrued to them by offering sexual favours at a price.

The many glowing tributes paid to these female owners by gentlemen from abroad may have had something to do with sexual services or, at least, emotional stimulation beyond the bounds of unimpeachable business. This might be what Trelawny Wentworth meant when he spoke of necessities needing 'anticipating' and 'appetites' requiring coaxing or stimulants.[45] At the same time, some allowance should be made for the growth of Christian morality and education in the community over time. A change in the morality of coloured owners might have been expected in the later nineteenth century, unlike during the era of slavery when the influence of Christian missionary activity and schools was minimal.

It seems, therefore, that there were sexual contacts between some owners of lodging houses and their customers. Certainly this would have been on a scaled down, very selective basis. It is also likely that many owners did have very amiable non-sexual relationships, but might have offered prostitutes in their establishments. Certainly those women who organised special balls for whites offered what Boa calls 'a more transitory form of prostitution',[46] where the coloured women moved from house to house. And there were owners who might have been 'madames', the 'fat, middle-aged' type referred to by Trollope who had permanent female employees offering sexual favours.

How independent were those owners of the white men who not only were their main customers, but might also have been instrumental in getting their business off the ground? One view is that they had the upper hand in their relationships with their male customers and were not subservient to them. This might be what Trelawny Wentworth, a visitor, had in mind when he wrote of a lodging-house keeper that 'her amiable familiarity places you upon a footing of equality in a moment, which seldom fails to give assurance that obligation on both sides is reduced.'[47] Possibly Cynric Williams' inquisitive landlady was the sort who smartly gathered more information from customers than the amount she provided. The services offered were important, and white men might even have come to see them as indispensable. In addition to bed, board and liquor, the lodging house was also, at times, a sort of community centre carrying out a number of functions.[48] Hence the female proprietors might have gained a place in the white establishment and in the hearts of white men which gave them some 'power' over the relationship. Their 'power' might even have sprung from their apparent weakness. They were, after all, not in the fight for political and social rights, and therefore did not offer a threat to white dominance of the society.

On the other hand, there were reports of lodging-house keepers whose sole aim was to please the customers, not to assert their own personality, like Monk Lewis' Judy James who 'did everything with such good will and cordiality no quick answers, no mutterings.'[49] It would have been interesting to hear directly from the female coloured owners about their customers, instead of always hearing what the customers said about the owners. Perhaps the women owners flattered their customers and hence gained a large reputation for caring and loyalty. As Boa noted, coloured inn keepers turned a blind eye to the indiscretions of their clients.[50] Their aim was to earn a living and a good one and in their dealings with their clients they planned the type of relationship which would ensue. They appeared to be subservient, but they were silent victors, strategising their next move on unsuspecting white males.

This article has tried to take a new approach to lodging-house keepers who formed part of a larger group of nineteenth-century coloured Jamaican women who were despised and victimised because of their race and their colour. They were rejected by coloured men, hated by black women and scorned by white women. As coloured women, their opportunities were severely limited and they were kept in check by white males. The analysis seems to suggest that the main area of their victimisation was their subservient and seemingly dependent relationship on white males for whom they were mistresses, lovers and prostitutes and who attempted to keep them in that bind by 'allowing' them to enter the occupation of lodging-house keeper. They would be kept in the traditional sexist role of domestic and more importantly giver of sexual favours, thereby maintaining the *status quo* which concubinage had entrenched. These women were allowed only because they would remain in the domestic sphere and not in the public arena. They were therefore marginalised.

What resulted from this was indeed an empowering of these women, as Errol Miller suggests would have happened. However, contrary to Miller's views, this empowering was mainly the result of planning on the women's part. These women used what would have been negative, that is, their victimisation and marginalisation, for good. They turned their weakness into strength by exploiting the white man's need for them. Their lodging houses became places 'flocked to' mainly by white males who sought them for sexual favours and more. They diversified their services so that they not only increased their incomes but eventually became women of importance.

These women demonstrated advanced business strategies in deciding on the location of their lodging houses in the busy port towns and on the established interior routes. They expanded their services so that the lodging house became a kind of community centre. They ensured that the services offered were in high demand and would ensure high remuneration. Some, therefore, did not stop short of offering prostitutes, since they would bring increased income. Their customers found them amiable because they decided to be amiable to maintain their business. They set the tone for the relationships which they enjoyed with their clients. They gained a reputation for caring and loyalty and had the upper hand in the relationships.

The lodging-house keeper of the nineteenth century chose to be a strategist rather than a victim of her situation. From a position of male victimisation and marginalisation she emerged independent and powerful, mainly by her own planning.

Endnotes

*Sections of this paper were previously published as 'Female lodging-house keepers in the nineteenth century'. *Jamaican Historical Review*, XVIII (1993), pp. 7—17. Reprinted by permission of the Editor of the *Jamaican Historical Review*.

1. Lucille Mathurin, 'A historical study of women in Jamaica from 1655 to 1844', PhD. thesis (University of the West Indies, 1974), p. 415.
2. Sheena Boa, 'Freed women's economic contribution to Jamaica 1760—1834', seminar paper (Dept. of History, University of the West Indies, 1985), p. 2.
3. Hilary Beckles, *Natural Rebels: A Social History of Enslaved Black Women in Barbados*. (London: Zed Books, 1989), pp. 144, 150.
4. Gad Heuman, *Between Black and White: Race and Politics and the Free Coloured in Jamaica* (Connecticut: Greenwood Press, 1981), p. 9.
5. Aleric Josephs, 'Mary Seacole', *Jamaican Historical Review*, XVII (1991), p. 50.

6. Errol Miller, *Men at Risk* (Kingston: Jamaica Publishing House, 1991), pp. 204—05.
7. Trelawny Wentworth, *The West India Sketchbook* (London: Whittaker and Co., 1959), p. 308.
8. John A. Waller, *A Voyage in the West Indies Containing Observations Made During a Residence in Barbados* (London: Sir Richard Phillips and Co., 1820), p. 6.
9. Robert Baird, *Impressions and Experiences of the West Indies and North America in 1849* (Edinburgh: William Blackwood and Sons, 1850), p. 221.
10. Matthew (Monk) G. Lewis, *Journal of a West Indian Proprietor* (London: George Routledge and Sons, 1929), pp. 302, 135, 313.
11. Phillip Wright (ed.), *Lady Nugent's Journal of Her Residence in Jamaica from 1801—1805*, revised edn, (Kingston: Institute of Jamaica, 1966), p. 168.
12. Robert Madden, A Twelve Month's Residence in the West Indies During the Transition From Slavery to Apprenticeship (London: James Cochrane and Co., 1835), p. 199.
13. Journal of Benjamin Scott Moncrieffe (A/S No. 26, Grand Court, Jamaica Archives).
14. Diary of Thomas Davies, Special Magistrate for St Mary, 1837, and St James 1834 (Jamaica Archives, Private file 4/47).
15. The Jamaican Census of 1844 and 1861, a new edition derived from the manuscript and printed schedules in the Jamaica Archives, edited and with an introduction by B.W. Higman (Social History Project, Department of History, University of the West Indies, 1980).
16. Falmouth Post, 21 July 1854.
17. *Ibid*. 21 January 1854.
18. Wentworth, p. 308.
19. Anthony Trollope, The West Indies and the Spanish Main (London: Chapman and Hall, 1867), p. 195.
20. Michael Pawson and David Buisseret, *Port Royal, Jamaica* (Oxford: Clarendon Press, 1975), appendix 12.
21. B.W. Higman, *Slave Population and Economy in Jamaica 1807—1834*, (New York: Cambridge University Press, 1976), p. 72.
22. Boa, 'Freed women's economic contribution', p. 3.
23. Heuman, p. 11.
24. Lady Nugent's Journal, p. 287.
25. Trollope, p. 23.
26. *Falmouth Post*, 25 February 1851.
27. Miller, p. 204.
28. Waller, p. 6.
29. Gisela Eisner, *Jamaica 1830—1930: A Study in Economic Growth* (Connecticut: Greenwood Press, 1961), p. 35.
30. Sheena Boa, 'Free Black and Coloured Women in a Whiteman's Slave Society', MPhil. thesis, (University of the West Indies, 1988), pp. 84, 85.
31. This information is derived from various sections relating to specific towns and parishes in the *Jamaica Directory 1878*.
32. Inventory of Elizabeth Sutton (1 B113 Vol. 100, Jamaica Archives).
33. Inventory of Susanah French, (Vol. 132, Jamaica Archives).
34. Philip Wright, *Exploring Jamaica* (London: Deutsch, 1969), p. 66.
35. Inventory of Ann Fraser, (Vol. 127, Jamaica Archives).

36. Boa, 'Free black and coloured women,' p. 77.
37. *Ibid.*, p. 76.
38. *Ibid.*, p. 78.
39. Trollope, p. 23.
40. *Report on the Commission into the Conditions of Juveniles in Jamaica 1879*, p. 166, quoted in Erna Brodber, *A Study of Yards in the City of Kingston* (ISER, University of the West Indies, 1975), p. 7.
41. Joseph Sturge and Thomas Harvey, *The West Indies in 1837* (London: Frank Cass and Co., 1968), p. 1.
42. Charles Day, *Five Years Residence in the West Indies* (London: Colburn and Co., 1852), p. 62.
43. Charles Day (pp. 62—63) mentioned about six establishments in Barbados where prostitution was carried on. John Waller said that the houses were houses of debauchery where there were 'a number of young women of colour always being procurable for the purpose of prostitution' (p. 6). Hilary Beckles reported that 'the more developed institutional aspects of prostitution were centred in the taverns, bars and inns' (p. 144).
44. B.M. Senior, *Jamaica As It Was, As It Is and As It May Be* (New York: Negro University Press, 1969), p. 122.
45. Wentworth, p. 308.
46. Boa, 'Free black and coloured women', p. 100.
47. Wentworth, p. 309.
48. The author's MA thesis, 'Lodging houses in Jamaica, 1800—1881', (University of the West Indies, 1992), gives details on the various functions ranging from post office and court house for trials of petty offences to a place for weddings and christenings, as well as hospital.
49. Lewis, p. 63.
50. Boa, 'Free black and coloured women', p. 234.

12.

Women, Land Transactions and Peasant Development in Jamaica, 1866–1900

Veront M. Satchell

The contribution of women to the socio-economic development of the Caribbean has only fairly recently attracted scholarly attention.[1] This is surprising, for during slavery almost half of the slave labour force comprised women while among the freed population a significant number of women owned large landholdings. Consequently women formed a significant group in the development of the plantations, and with emancipation their contributions were by no means diminished. Women continued to own large landed estates and those who were newly freed began acquiring holdings, thus joining the ranks of landed proprietors of their sex as landholders. Women also continued to provide labour on the plantations. It would appear, however, that the predominantly male biases within society have precluded earlier focus on this important group.

This article examines the role of women in the development of the peasantry in Jamaica during the late nineteenth century by presenting an analysis of transactions in land undertaken by women as conveyors and conveyees, during the period 1866 to 1900. It is argued that during this period the plantation economy, which up to then was experiencing steady decline, underwent structural changes which enabled it to regain its dominance over the economy and consequently its increasing control over land. This resurgence of the plantation system and its stranglehold on land seriously restrained the development of the peasantry during this period. The large landholders were reluctant to subdivide and transfer their holdings, preferring to sell them intact. As a result, the acquisition of small areas of good arable and accessible land became increasingly difficult as land became scarcer and dearer. The development of the peasantry during this period, therefore, depended more and more on land transfers made by other groups in society. Women constituted one of the most important of these groups in peasant development during this period.

In the context of this analysis, women are discussed as a homogeneous group. No attention will be paid to categories which divide them, such as race, colour, ethnicity and social class or occupation. The land conveyance deeds of the late nineteenth century, which provide the primary data for this analysis, do not give explicit information on sex, race and colour; these have to be extrapolated from other data such as occupation and social status. While this can be easily done for men it is not so easily done for women, as the deeds tend to be biased towards men. Thus less attention is paid to details concerning women. Whereas in transactions concerning men the deeds generally state clearly their occupation or status, for women the deeds normally state only their marital status such as, 'widow', 'spinster' and 'single woman', and in some instances simply, 'gentlewoman'. These designations do not provide much on which to base a detailed analysis. This is a serious limitation, since it precludes a full analysis of these variables. It is being assumed in this article that women who were trading in large landholdings, including whole properties (estates, pens, plantations), were of the upper- and middle-class plantocratic group, while those acquiring small rural holdings were of the labouring and peasant classes. However, they are not discussed under these status groupings but rather under the category 'women'. All other status groupings are exclusively male.

Land is defined in law as a form of property and property as 'a bundle of rights.'[2] Property means one's own and is classified as being of two kinds, real and personal. Real property is concerned with land and is termed realty, while personal property is anything else capable of being owned and is termed personalty.[3] The ownership of landed property is usually exhibited in the form of a title, deed or grant.[4] A title implies claims of ownership. A deed is a written document containing details of transfer, and a grant denotes public (government, crown) transfer of land to private citizens. A legal transfer of land, therefore, requires that a deed or title be issued. There are several ways in which one may gain interest/control or tenure of land. Tenure simply means the manner in which land is held.[5] These include, fee simple absolute possession, that is freehold tenure; leasehold, trusteeship, and rental.[6] The most secure of these is freehold, which approximates total ownership, while the least secure is rental.[7] Rental is not deemed a transfer since a renter is allowed to settle the holding on a very short-term basis, normally on a month-to-month arrangement.

The doctrine of English land law, from which evolved Jamaican land law, developed out of feudalism, with its strong paternalistic base and male biases.[8] The feudal influence, however, is not very evident in the Jamaican land laws partly because of the date of settlement of the island by the English; and English laws did not automatically become operative in Jamaica without modification.[9] Shortly after the pacification and settlement, the island was granted an independent legislature with powers equal to those of the British Houses of Commons and Lords. Consequently it had the power to repeal and alter both the statute and common laws of England and had the right to enact its own local laws.[10] No English statute relating to land, therefore, applied to Jamaica unless under specific circumstances. Notwith- standing, statutes concerning land operating in England were adapted locally to meet local conditions. As soon as a real property law was passed in England it found a counterpart in the Jamaican legislature.[11]

In 1655, at the time of the British conquest of the island, all land became vested in the state. In an effort to encourage settlement, Oliver Cromwell, Lord Protector of England, proclaimed that all would-be settlers would be granted land by letters patent at the rate of 12 acres for each male over 12 years old and 10 acres for females and males under 12 years.[12] In 1662, the gender specification in total area of land to be granted was removed with the enactment that land should be granted at the rate of 30 acres for each would-be settler over 12 years old irrespective of sex.[13] Thus there was no gender discrimination in terms of land distribution. Males and females came into possession of landholdings locally. Large land grants of 500—2,000 acres were commonly made and both sexes benefited.[14]

With the development of the sugar industry during the late seventeenth century, land became concentrated in the hands of fewer holders as the small landholders, unable to take advantage of the sugar boom, readily sold out to large planters.[15] Again both sexes were well represented as large landed proprietors.[16] However, there was one discriminatory restriction affecting women as landholders. Under Law 43 of 1663, married women were precluded from owning property. Thus women who had come into possession of property prior to marriage, at time of marriage had to have such property vested in their husbands as trustees. Thus the married woman lost her property right. This law remained in force until 1870 when it was partially repealed.[17] In 1882 the 1663 law was totally annulled with the passing of an amendment of the Married Women's Property Rights Act of 1870. Under this amendment women, at time of marriage, could retain their real as well as personal properties. The Act further gave them the sole right to any property they acquired while married.[18] Thus after 1882 married women could participate freely in the local land market as both conveyors and conveyees.

During slavery large plantations placed under sugar cane and later livestock and coffee, all worked by blacks transported from Africa as slaves, and their descendants, typified the landscape. Sugar and its by-products rum and molasses, coffee and the minor staples (pimento, indigo, ginger), were produced primarily for export. Thus from the earliest years of English settlement production was geared towards export markets. The major exceptions were the rearing of livestock on pens, the existence of small maroon settlements in the interior, and the growing of provisions and the rearing of small livestock by the slaves for local consumption. Pens provided the draught animals for the plantations and estates and, to a limited extent, beef for local consumption, while slaves' provisions found a ready market locally.

Upon emancipation a trend towards a wider distribution of landowners developed in the island and with it changes in the pattern of production. Ex-slaves, of both sexes began to gain access to land as freeholders through purchases and gifts, as leaseholders or as renters.[19] Consequently, by the mid-nineteenth century an Afro-Jamaican peasantry had developed alongside large plantations. In this way in post-slavery Jamaica all classes and sexes came in possession of land, which indicates that there existed a very vibrant land market in the island.[20]

The total area of land transferred, however, reflected the general economic conditions of the island over the period. Thus a brief examination of the island's economy will place land transactions in clearer perspective.

Plantation and peasant economies during the late nineteenth century

The plantation system declined rapidly after the abolition of slavery to around the 1880s. The freeing of the slaves and their general exodus from the estates; external economic conditions, especially competition from other cane sugar-producing countries and European bounty-fed beet sugar; and a continued lowering of sugar prices on the world sugar market all adversely affected the local production of sugar, which was the mainstay of the plantation economy.[21] The area under sugar cane cultivation, for example, declined from 47,469 acres in 1869 to 26,121 acres in 1900.[22] It was reported by the Collector General in 1869 that 'there was little effort among sugar planters to extend the cultivation of the sugar cane in any systematic or extensive scale.'[23] The number of estates in production fell from 664 in 1832 to 312 in 1867. By 1900 the total had further declined to 122.[24] Output as expected with this general decline also fell significantly, from 1,053,000 cwt in 1838 to 600,000 cwt in 1862. In 1900 the total output for the year had fallen to 295,000 cwt. Sugar's contribution to output also reflected this general decline. In 1870 sugar accounted for 44.6 per cent of the island's total output; in 1900 its contribution was a mere 10.8 per cent.[25]

The sugar industry was indeed in a period of serious recession. Planters had to seek alternatives. There were four main options open to them: first, to abandon sugar cane cultivation and place their estates under new and more remunerative crops or products; secondly, to rationalise and restructure their estates to make them more productive; thirdly, to sell to others who had the capital to make these estates productive; and finally to abandon their estates altogether. Many of the traditional planters, especially those in the north-eastern section of the island, opted for this last alternative. Consequently the land comprising sugar estates had, by 1900, shrunk from the north-eastern to the western and south central parishes of the island where geographical conditions favoured their profitable production.[26]

Plantation coffee suffered a similar fate to that of sugar. In 1838 there were 465 coffee estates; by 1853 this number had declined to 60. In 1900 there were only 39.[27] Coffee production, unlike sugar, however, did not suffer decline; rather it showed an increase. This increased production was due primarily to peasants' production of this crop.

Bananas, which subsequently became a plantation crop, were produced almost entirely by small peasant farmers up to the 1880s; in 1879 there was only one banana plantation in the island. By 1880s, however, large-scale banana production had begun.[28] Initially this was not undertaken by the traditional planters but by a new breed of agrarian capitalists comprising merchants and professionals and corporately-owned agricultural enterprises. These new entrepreneurs, recognising the profits to be gained from large-scale banana production, began purchasing abandoned sugar estates in the eastern and northeastern end of the island for large-scale cultivation of this crop. Thus in 1900 191 former sugar estates were returned as banana plantations and over 20,923 acres of their total area were under cultivation.[29] With the fading hopes of a resuscitation of the sugar industry, a few of the traditional sugar planters also began turning their attention to banana cultivation.

The rapid growth of the banana industry and its importance to the island's export economy between 1880 and 1900 is illustrated by the value of bananas to total exports. In 1867 bananas accounted for 0.01 per cent of total exports; in 1880 the value had increased incrementally to 1.95 per cent, and by 1900 bananas accounted for 35 per cent.[30] Indeed, this high rate of production signalled the entry of the large landholders into banana production.

The involvement of plantation owners in large-scale banana production proved disastrous for the peasantry, which was now engaged in an unequal competition with large-scale producers for markets and good arable lands. The peasants found it increasingly difficult to market their bananas, as the chief banana merchant, Lorenzo Dow Baker, had himself become a major producer and had shifted his attention to marketing crops of large-scale producers. As banana production expanded, land became scarce and dear and the peasants found it difficult to buy smallholdings to expand their cultivation. Many found themselves in a position of having to rent smallholdings on extremely tenuous terms in order to cultivate this most important and valuable crop.[31]

Between 1880 and 1900, therefore, there was a revival of the plantation sector, marked by a rationalisation of the sugar industry, with sugar being produced only in areas in which it could be profitably undertaken, and the emergence of bananas as the most valuable plantation crop.

The development of the peasant sector, however, depended on the availability of land and hence it was greatly affected by the changing fortunes of the plantations during this period. In contrast to the decline in the plantations between the 1840s and 1880s, the peasantry experienced significant growth. Peasants provided food for local consumption as well as the traditional staples, primarily coffee and the minor crops, such as ginger and bananas, for the export markets. Production of ground provisions increased from 27 per cent of total agricultural output in 1832 to 55 per cent in 1890. This total, however, fell to 50 per cent by 1900. Between 1870 and 1900 the value of ground provisions had increased from £1.6 million to £3.1 million.[32] The importance of the peasantry to the Jamaican economy was highlighted in 1878 by the governor. He reported in that year that the island was less dependent on food imports than its Caribbean counterparts. Using the value of food imports as an index, he noted that food imports into Jamaica amounted to £1.23 per head of population per year; in British Guiana this amounted to £3.68, in Barbados £3.57 and in Trinidad £4.52. Between 1875 and 1882 the value of food imports declined from £1.3 per head to £0.9 per head.[33] The continued reduction in the food import bill indicates clearly that the island was becoming more and more self-sufficient in food. Apart from finding a ready market for its local ground provisions, the peasantry began exporting sizeable portions to Central America as a means of satisfying the needs of thousands of Jamaican emigrants for their native foods. In 1874 the value of this export was £577, and in 1887 £16,000. With the closure of the canal works in Panama and the subsequent return of Jamaicans, exports declined to £6 in 1895.[34]

The peasants, as noted above, were not concentrating totally on ground provisions. They were also producing export crops. They were the principal exporters of bananas up to the 1870s, and of coffee. They produced over two-thirds of the total coffee exported from the island, which stood at an average of 81,000 cwt per year between 1866 and 1900.

Of the 25,902 acres returned as being under coffee in 1900, peasant coffee cultivations occupied 22,344 acres.[35] The peasantry increased its share in total exports from 10.4 per cent to 39.4 per cent between 1850 and 1890. After this period, however, its share in total exports showed no significant growth.

The apparent stagnation in peasants' exports and the decline in their share in total agricultural output suggest that the peasantry began experiencing interruptions in development after the 1880s. The area under peasant production and the peasants' continued activities in the government savings banks, established in 1870, reinforce this view. Peasant cultivation declined from a total area of 92,716 acres in 1890 to 85,747 acres in 1900.[36] Governor Sir Henry Blake reported in 1894 and again in 1897 on this apparent stagnation in peasant farming. He noted that between these years the area under ground provisions had increased by a mere 0.5 per cent, an average which was much lower than previous years.[37] In fact the decline between 1890 and 1900 was 7.8 per cent. The number of depositors in the government savings banks increased from 2,359 in 1870 to 32,860 in 1900. Depositors in the under £5 group accounted for over 65 per cent of the total. During the period 1890—1900, however, there were violent fluctuations in bank transactions involving the small accounts. In 1897—1901 alone, 5,947 accounts were closed, the highest for the period 1870—1900.[38]

After the 1880s, therefore, the peasantry entered a period of stagnation both in terms of its participation in the export trade and in its expansion locally. The resurgence of the plantations around the same time, and with it an intensification of the peasants' struggle for good arable and accessible land thwarted the realisation of the full potential of the peasantry. It is against this background of the conflict between peasant and plantation over land that the role of women in land transactions, and its implications for the development of the peasantry, will be examined.

Women in land transactions

Between 1866 and 1900 a total of 12,258 land transactions involving the transfer of 2,529,065 acres of land were completed and sealed in Jamaica (Table 1). This total area approximates 93 per cent of the total area of the island. Thus an average of 2.7 per cent of the island's land mass was transferred annually. Obviously this total includes recurring transfer, but nevertheless it gives an indication of the activity in the island's land market during the late nineteenth century. All classes and both sexes participated and women were well represented. Of the over 12,000 transactions women were involved in 495 or 4.0 per cent (Table 2). In comparison, peasants or small settlers[39] were involved in 3,000 or 25.3 per cent, planters[40] in 16.6 per cent, and merchants and professionals in 9.7 per cent and 6.2 per cent respectively. The large number of transactions involving peasants and planters, the two most important agrarian groups, suggests that there was active trading between these groups. Over 27 per cent of the transactions were made by individuals whose status is unknown (Table 2). Quite likely these included women, since the names of persons do not always clearly indicate their sex. During the period under discussion 10.3 per cent of all transfers were made by women (Tables 2, 3). In comparison, peasants' transfers accounted for 15 per cent, planters' 17 per cent and unknown 38.4 per cent. Tradesmen transferred 3.6 per cent, while institutions accounted for 1.5 per cent. East Indians were involved in a mere 0.5 per cent, the least for any group over the period. Thus women were among the top three groups of conveyors. Women's transfers ranged from a low of 5.7 per cent in the 1860s to a high of 12.4 per cent during the 1880s. During the 1870 and 1890s women's transfers accounted for 11.9 per cent and 11.2 per cent respectively. Thus during the period between 1870 and 1900 women's transfers represented nearly 12 per cent of total transfers. Women were indeed actively disposing of landholdings. It should be noted that whereas planters' transfers declined from 23.1 per cent in 1770 to 12.8 per cent in 1890s a 10.3 percentage point decline over the entire period, women's transfers remained almost constant, while those of peasants increased by 9.5 percentage points (Table 3).

Women disposed of 225,699 acres or 8.9 per cent of the total area transferred over the period (Tables 1, 3). In comparison peasants transferred 231,887 acres or 9.2 per cent. Planters' transfers, however, totalled 593,634 acres or 23.5 per cent, while merchants and professionals transferred 12.3 per cent and 13.2 per cent respectively. Planters were understandably the chief conveyors; in fact professionals, merchants and planters were the chief transferrers of land. They were the holders, owners, or trustees of large holdings in the island. Since they held control over the mass of the land it seems natural to see them disposing of most of it. A closer examination reveals, however, that the total area transferred by planters between 1870s and the 1890s declined by nearly one-half. Whereas in the 1870s planters disposed of over 250,000 acres, in the 1890s they disposed of a little over 130,000 acres. In fact the area disposed of by planters, merchants and professionals declined significantly between 1880 and 1890. The large landholders were disposing of fewer acres of land. Indeed during the earlier period with the general decline in the sugar/plantation economy and the continued abandonment of cultivation, planters who had no capital to improve their estates took advantage of the government's legislation and sold or transferred them to other more aggressive agrarian capitalists who had the capital to invest in order to make them productive. By the 1880s, therefore, the greater part of these large estates were already transferred. This explains the apparent decline in the area of land sold and number of transfers made by these large landowners. In comparison, the area of land disposed of by

Table 1. Status of conveyors by percentge of acres transferred, Jamaica, 1866–1900

Period	1866–69	1870–79	1880–89	1890–1900	Total	Per cent
Peasants	2,390.4	38,159.9	59,159.9	132,177.7	231,877.9	9.2
Planters	36,243.4	253,010.2	167,085.9	137,294.4	593,633.9	23.5
Merchants	13,726.5	95,328.6	128,343.9	74,386.2	311,785.2	12.3
Professionals	11,643.4	87,217.8	126,480.3	109,506.3	334,847.8	13.2
Tradesmen	1,681.9	3,919.4	6,730.4	8,141.3	20,473.0	0.8
Institutions	66.9	567.1	12,367.7	26,150.4	39,152.1	1.5
East Indians	610.1	423.7	3,359.2	4,349.0	0.2	-
Women	4,152.5	51,373.6	83,667.5	86,505.8	225,699.4	8.9
Unknown	129,411.7	218,136.0	225,193.5	194,452.2	767,193.4	30.3
Total	199,316.5	748,322.7	809,452.8	771,973.6	2,529,065.6	100

Source: Compiled from the Land Conveyance Deeds (1866–1900), Island Record Office

Table 2. Numbers of transactions by status, Jamaica, 1866–1900

Period	1866–69	1870–79	1880–89	1890–1900	Total	Per cent
Peasants	217	896	930	1,057	3,100	25.3
Planters	217	704	570	541	2,032	16.6
Merchants	85	295	379	433	1,192	9.7
Professionals	40	121	232	364	757	6.2
Tradesmen	30	158	180	199	567	4.6
Institutions	2	53	121	271	447	3.6
East Indians	3	40	103	92	238	1.9
Women	8	161	153	172	495	4.0
Unknown	307	883	1,113	1,128	3,431	27.6
Total	909	3,311	3,781	4,257	12,258	100

Source: Compiled from the Land Conveyance Deeds (1866–1900), Island Record Office

Table 3. Status of Conveyors by percentage of transfers, Jamaica, 1866–1900

Period	1866–69	1870–79	1880–89	1890–1900	Average 1866–1900
Peasants	5.7	13.8	18.4	23.3	15.3
Planters	13.9	23.1	18.0	12.8	17.0
Merchants	8.2	6.7	7.4	7.2	7.4
Professionals	3.2	6.2	6.8	7.8	6.0
Tradesmen	1.9	4.2	3.6	4.6	3.6
Institutions	0.1	0.2	1.8	3.9	1.5
East Indians	-	0.3	0.8	0.8	0.5
Women	5.7	11.9	12.4	11.2	10.3
Unknown	61.3	33.4	30.8	28.2	38.4
Total	100	100	100	100	

Source: Compiled from the Land Conveyance Deeds (1866–1900), Island Record Office

peasants and women increased. In the 1870s peasants disposed of 38,159 acres, and in the 1890s they disposed of 130,000 acres, an amount almost equal to that disposed of by planters. Women, while disposing of 52,000 acres in the 1870s, during the 1880s and 1890s transferred over 80,000 acres. In fact during the 1890s all groups ith the exception of the large landholders — planters, merchants and professionals — were disposing of a greater proportion of land than in former years. This period coincided with the revival of the plantation sector and with it a scarcity of land. The expansion of the peasantry during this period depended on the subdivision of holdings held either by themselves, by women or by other small landholders. It should be remembered, however, that women also held large properties; they too were planters. But in so far as they were transferring large portions of land in a relatively large number of transactions, at a time when land was becoming scarce, it can be concluded that they were transferring to the small peasant farmers. An examination of the sizes and types of holdings confirms this view.

Women relinquished holdings of all sizes (Table 4). In the category of 0–4 acres, women disposed of 959 acres. They transferred 2,685 acres within the 5–19 acres group, 3,690 acres in the 20–49 acres group, 6,228 in the 50–99 acres group, 37,778 acres within the 100–499 acres group, 48,893 acres in the 500–999 acres group and 125,463 acres within the over 1,000 acres group. Over 55 per cent of the total acreage that women transferred were in the over 1,000 acres group. In comparison, a mere 3.3 per cent of the total area transferred by women was in the less than 50 acres category, the sizes normally used by the peasantry. Women as large landed proprietors were disposing of large properties. In relative terms, women's 3.3 per cent of transfers in the less than 50 acres groupings was much better than those of planters, merchants and professionals in these same groupings. Planters' transfers accounted for 2 per cent of this total; merchants', 1.5 per cent and professionals', 1.2 per cent. Thus a larger proportion of women's transfers went to peasants.

In Jamaica the types of holdings transferred may be placed in four categories: parts of estates, plantations and pens; whole properties (estates, pens and plantations); part of larger runs; and fragmented holdings. The transfer of parts of estates, pens or plantations was of two types, original and secondary. Since planters, merchants and professionals were the principal owners of whole properties, it follows that they were the ones who would normally make original subdivisions. Transfers of parts of whole properties made by these groups are regarded as original transfers. Secondary transfers are those made by other status groups. The assumption is that they never owned large estates, hence for them to be transferring this type of holding meant that they had previously acquired them as primary transfers.

Larger runs are regarded as holdings that were either never original parts of whole properties, or parts of whole properties that had been

Table 4. Status of Conveyors by size of holdings transferred, Jamaica, 1866–1900

Size Holdings (Acres)	0-4	5-19	20-49	50-99	100-499	500-999	1000+	Total
Peasants	1,847.9	4,629.4	6,532.2	7,109.3	39,310.2	31,155.7	141,303.2	231,887.9
Planters	1,084.1	4,404.9	6,572.6	8,691.9	79,756.0	112,713.3	380,408.1	593,630.9
Merchants	375.7	1,606.9	2,561.8	3,273.5	36,196.4	61,514.9	106,256.0	311,785.2
Professionals	316.7	1,200.8	2,669.4	4,162.4	35,930.6	57,703.5	232,864.4	334,847.8
Tradesmen	479.6	1,008.0	1,244.3	870.0	4,783.3	5,020.3	7,067.5	20,473.0
Institutions	101.8	616.7	1,063.8	2,100.5	8,119.4	9,369.7	17,780.5	39,152.4
East Indians	65.7	127.7	124.0	108.4	-	1,836.5	2,131.1	4,393.4
Women	959.6	2,685.7	3,690.3	6,228.9	37,778.8	48,893.1	125,463.0	225,699.4
Unknown	2,532.6	7,993.7	9,784.8	13,138.3	107,888.8	170,230.9	455,624.3	767,193.4
Total	7,763.5	24,273.5	34,243.3	45,683.5	349,764.0	498,438.6	1,568,899.2	2,529,065.6

Source: Compiled from the Land Conveyance Deeds (1866–1900), Island Record Office, Jamaica

Table 5. Type of holdings transferred as a percentage of total transfers made by women

Period	Parts of estates or pens	Whole properties	Part of larger run	Fragmented holdings	Total
1866–69	85.4	2.4	12.7	-	100
1870–79	75.6	22.4	2.0	0.1	100
1880–89	67.9	27.3	3.9	0.9	100
1890–1900	69.6	21.2	7.0	2.1	100
Average	74.6	18.3	6.4	0.8	100

Source: Compiled from the Land Conveyance Deeds (1866–1900), Island Record Office, Jamaica

transferred but had lost all connections with the original larger holding. Larger runs are usually associated with smallholdings rather than large estates, pens or plantations. The transfer of larger runs, therefore, means the subdivided parts of larger holdings other than estates, pens and plantations and gives an indication of the level of subdivision of land to peasant farmers. Fragmented holdings refer to one transaction involving two or more smallholdings.

Nearly 75 per cent of women's transfers were parts of estates, pens or plantations. Whole properties accounted for 18.3 per cent, parts of larger runs 6.4 per cent and fragmented holdings 0.8 per cent (Table 5). Women also owned large estates; thus they were making both original and secondary transfers of this type of holding. The total, therefore, includes both original and secondary transfers. It is difficult at this time, however, to distinguish between original and secondary transfers of parts of estates, pens and plantations made by women.

The transfer of parts of estates, pens and plantations and those of larger runs made by women presents interesting features. Between the 1860s and 1880s the transfer of parts of estates, pens and plantations declined. During the 1890s, however, it increased. The transfer of larger runs made by women decreased dramatically from 12.9 per cent in the 1860s to 2.0 per cent in the 1870s. However, after this date transfers began to increase.

The sharpest increase was between the 1880s and the 1890s when transfers of this type of holdings grew from 3.9 to 7.0 per cent, nearly a twofold increase (Table 5). The continued subdivision of these smallholdings and the continued reduction of holdings being sold by planters, merchants and professionals, after the 1880s, are indicative of a scarcity of the landholdings necessary to facilitate the spatial expansion of the peasantry.

Indeed the chief clients for women's transfers were the peasant class (Table 6). This class took 21.7 per cent of women's transfers, ranging from 43.3 per cent in the 1860s to 13.5 during the 1880s. The general tendency, therefore, over this period was towards a decline of the proportion of land acquired by the peasants from women. However, during the 1890s the tendency was towards an increase. During this latter period, the expansion of the peasant class apparently became more and more dependent on women landholders, especially those owning smallholdings, as well as on other small landholders, including the peasants themselves.

Of the 2,529,065 acres transferred between 1866 and 1900, women obtained 70,872 acres or 2.8 per cent of the total (Table 7). Compared with 397,106 acres or 15.7 per cent conveyed to small settlers/peasants, 790,229 acres or 31.2 per cent were obtained by planters, 391,939 acres or 15.5 per cent by merchants, 221,918 acres or 8.8 per cent by professionals. Tradesmen obtained a mere 27,362 acres or 1.1 per cent, while East Indians acquired 12,661 acres or 0.5 per cent. Institutions (churches, schools, building societies, etc) obtained 34,058 acres and persons of unknown status and sex obtained 582,917 acres or 23 per cent. Planters were indeed acquiring the greater portion of the land being transferred. Whereas in the proportion of area of land transferred, women were among the top three groups of conveyors, as conveyees they were among the bottom four.

Of the total recipients of land women accounted for 4.5 per cent (Table 8). This total contrasts greatly with their 10.3 per cent as conveyors. Indeed at no time during the period of study did women's acquisition of land exceed the 4 per cent bracket. During the 1866–69 period, 199,316 acres were transferred. Women were involved in 4.9 per cent of these transactions (Table 9). They obtained 3 per cent of the total area transferred. In comparison planters and peasants accounted for 48 per cent of these transactions, each involving 24 per cent. Planters, however, obtained 46.5 per cent of total transfers and peasants got 15.2 per cent. During the 1870s women were again involved in 4.9 per cent of total transactions as recipients, obtaining 20,864 acres or 2.7 per cent of the total 748,322 acres transferred. Thus while they were involved in a similar proportion of transactions as in the 1860s, they received a smaller proportion of the total transferred. Planters and peasants again were the principal conveyees. Planters accounted for 21 per cent of transactions

Table 6. Status of recipients by percentage of women's land transfers, Jamaica, 1866–1900

Period	1966–69	1870–79	1880–89	1890–1900	Average
Peasants	43.3	14.4	13.5	13.7	21.7
Planters	13.3	17.4	11.9	8.0	12.7
Merchants	3.3	9.2	6.8	9.3	7.2
Professionals	6.7	2.4	4.6	4.8	4.6
Tradesmen	-	2.8	3.3	3.8	2.5
Institutions	-	4.0	7.0	11.9	5.7
East Indians	-	0.9	4.1	3.5	2.1
Women	6.7	2.8	2.6	3.2	3.8
Unknown	26.7	46.2	46.2	41.2	40.2
Total	100	100	100	100	100

Source: Compiled from the Land Conveyance Deeds (1866–1900), Island Record Office, Jamaica

Table 7. Status of conveyees by size of holdings transferred, Jamaica, 1866–1900

Holding Size (Acres)	0-4	5-19	20-49	50-99	100-499	500-999	1000+	Total	Per cent
Peasants	2,389.8	7,779.8	10,459.7	11,790.6	69,558.5	91,456.1	203,671.4	397,106.2	15.7
Planters	864.7	2,867.6	5,568.1	8,704.0	96,630.6	158,663.9	516,930.2	790,229.1	31.2
Merchants	657.8	1,982.2	3,082.9	4,788.9	40,558.2	74,367.1	266,502.2	391,939.3	15.5
Professionals	475.6	1,505.7	2,292.6	3,754.7	27,666.2	35,450.4	150,791.7	221,918.9	8.8
Tradesmen	612.2	1,318.5	1,711.5	1,873.5	7,359.0	6,158.0	8,329.8	27,362.5	1.1
Institutions	450.2	390.2	755.6	608.1	4,469.8	5,123.4	22,261.6	34,058.9	1.3
East Indians	379.7	234.1	181.8	395.7	1,463.0	6,032.3	3,975.2	12,661.8	0.5
Women	461.0	945.7	1,161.0	2,244.9	14,046.0	18,780.9	33,231.8	70,872.2	2.8
Unknown	1,490.3	7,249.3	9,029.7	11,522.7	88,012.4	102,406.4	353,206.4	582,917.2	23.0
Total	7,763.5	24,273.5	34,243.3	45,683.5	349,764.0	498,438.6	1,568,899.2	2,529,065.6	100

Source: Compiled from the Land Conveyance Deeds (1866–1900), Island Record Office, Jamaica

Table 8. Status conveyees by percentage of Jamaica, 1866–1900

Period	1866–69	1870–79	1880–89	1890–1900	Average
Peasants	24.0	27.1	24.6	24.8	25.2
Planters	24.0	21.3	15.1	12.7.	18.3
Merchants	9.4	8.9	10.0	10.2	9.6
Professionals	4.4	3.7	6.1	8.6	5.7
Tradesmen	3.3	4.8	4.7	4.6	4.3
Institutions	0.2	1.6	3.2	6.4	2.9
East Indians	0.3	1.2	2.7	2.2	1.6
Women	4.9	4.9	4.0	4.1	4.5
Unknown	29.6	26.6	29.5	26.5	28.0
Total	100	100	100	100	100

Source: Compiled from the Land Conveyance Deeds (1866–1900), Island Record Office, Jamaica

Table 9. Status of conveyees by acres transferred, Jamaica, 1866–1900

Period	1866–69	1870–79	1880–89	1890–1900	Total	Per cent
Peasants	17,399.4	113,484.7	128,416.6	137,805.5	397,106.2	15.7
Planters	92,647.1	305,420.7	218,755.3	173,406.0	790,229.1	31.2
Merchants	40,104.1	117,835.7	136,181.3	97,818.2	391,939.3	15.5
Professionals	6,543.1	26,538.4	62,544.2	126,293.2	221,918.9	8.8
Tradesmen	1,479.0	5,222.3	6,423.8	14,236.9	27,362.0	1.0
Institutions	1.4	2,419.4	4,541.0	27,097.1	34,058.9	1.3
East Indians	129.6	1,795.2	5,406.7	5,330.3	12,661.8	0.5
Women	6,517.4	20,864.1	19,243.8	24,606.9	70,872.2	2.8
Unknown	34,855.4	154,742.2	227,940.1	165,379.5	582,917.2	23.0
Total	199,316.5	748,322.7	809,452.8	771,973.6	2,529,065.6	100

Source: Compiled from the Land Conveyance Deeds (1866–1900), Island Record Office

Table 10. Net gain or loss in acres recorded by each status group in land transactions, Jamaica, 1866–1900

Status	1866–69	1870–79	1880–89	1890–1900	Average
Peasants	15,009.9	75,324.8	69,256.7	5,627.8	165,218.3
Planters	56,403.7	52,410.5	51,669.4	36,111.6	196,595.2
Professionals	-5,100.3	-60,679.4	-63,936.1	16,786.9	-112,929.9
Merchants	26,377.6	22,507.1	7,837.4	23,432.0	80,154.1
Tradesmen	-202.9	1,302.9	-306.6	6,095.6	6,889.0
Institutions	-65.5	1,852.3	-7,826.7	946.7	-5,093.2
East Indians	129.6	1,185.1	4,983.0	1,971.1	8,268.8
Women	2,004.9	-30,509.5	-64,423.7	-61,898.9	-154,827.2
Unknown	-94,556.3	-63,393.8	2,746.6	-29,072.7	-184,276.2

Source: Compiled from the Land Conveyance Deeds (1866–1900), Island Record Office, Jamaica

Table 11. Size of holdings by total area transferred and received by women

Size holding (acres)	Acres transferred	Acres received	Acres lost
0-4	951	461	499
5-19	2,686	945	1,800
20-49	3,690	1,161	2,500
50-99	6,229	2,245	4,000
100-499	37,779	14,040	23,000
500-999	48,893	18,780	40,000
1000+	125,463	33,231	90,000

Source: Compiled from the Land Conveyance Deeds (1866–1900), Island Record Office, Jamaica

Table 12. Type of holdings transferred as a percentage of total transferred by women, Jamaica, 1866–1900

Period	Parts of estates or Pens	Whole properties	Part of larger run	Fragmented Holdings	Total
1866–69	72.7	24.2	3.0	-	100
1870–79	71.6	24.3	4.1	-	100
1880–89	68.7	25.9	5.4	-	100
1890-1900	78.0	16.2	4.6	1.2	100
Average	72.8	22.7	4.3	0.3	100

Source: Compiled from the Land Conveyance Deeds (1866–1900), Island Record Office, Jamaica

and small settlers 27 per cent. Peasants gained a greater proportion over the previous period. Planters received 40.8 per cent and small settlers got 15.2 per cent of the total area transferred.

During the 1880s, 809,452 acres were transferred, an area significantly larger than the two previous periods. 4.0 per cent of the recipients were women, a 0.9 per cent reduction on the 1870s. Of this total area transferred, women received 19,243 acres or 2.3 per cent, a reduction on the previous period.

In the 1890s, of the total number of recipients, women accounted for 4.1 per cent, peasants 24.8 per cent and planters 12.7 per cent. In this period 771,973 acres were transferred and women obtained 24,606 acres, the largest proportion women received during the entire period (Tables 8, 9).

Women acquired much less land than they transferred (Tables 1, 10, 11). Though transferring 225,699 acres, they obtained 70,872 acres, an overall loss of 154,827 acres or a twofold loss. Indeed the only period in which women received more land than they transferred was in the 1860s, when they gained 2,000 acres more than they transferred. In subsequent years they obtained net losses. In the 1870s they transferred 30,500 acres more than they received, in the 1880s, 64,400 acres and in the 1890s, 61,000 acres. Women were, indeed, facilitating the growth and expansion of other land-owning classes in the society.

Sizes of holdings transferred ranged from up to 4 acres to over 1,000 acres. Like transfers, women acquired all sizes of landholdings (Tables 11, 12). Women's losses in receipts over transfers were evident in all the size categories of holdings conveyed (Table 9). Women's acquisition of holdings of less than 50 acres (peasant-size holdings) accounted for 3.6 per cent of the total area transferred to them, almost equal to the 3.3 per cent they transferred in this size grouping.

Nearly 73 per cent of holdings transferred to women were parts of estates, pens or plantations. It can be assumed that these were both original and secondary transfers. The transfer of parts of large runs accounted for 4.3 per cent of women's acquisitions. Thus these smallholdings accounted for 77 per cent of all holdings acquired by women. The large proportion of these types of smallholdings transferred to women indicates that women were obtaining land as small peasant farmers. They were numerically expanding the ranks of peasantry in the Jamaican society.

As in the case of transfers women acquired holdings from all classes in the society. Peasants, planters, merchants, professionals, tradesmen, East Indians all traded in land with women. In contrast to the large proportion of transfers made by women to peasants, women obtained little land from this group (Table 13). In fact only 4 per cent of peasants' transfers went to women. And this is understandable. The peasants were in the process of

Table 13. Status of conveyors by percentage of total transfers made to women, Jamaica, 1866–1900

Period	1866–69	1870–79	1880–89	1890–1900	Average
Peasants	-	6.6	5.1	4.2	4.0
Planters	10.4	6.9	4.4	4.4	6.5
Merchants	12.8	6.4	5.4	4.2	7.5
Professionals	10.0	4.8	2.9	2.5	5.0
Tradesmen	8.3	10.1	12.0	4.0	8.6
Institutions	-	-	12.5	3.2	3.9
East Indians	-	-	-	8.3	2.1
Women	6.7	6.4	5.0	6.6	6.2
Unknown	-	2.8	2.6	3.2	2.2

Source: Compiled from the Land Conveyance Deeds, 1866–1900, Island Record Office, Jamaica

consolidating their position as landholders, (and this is understandable), they were acquiring rather than disposing of land. Land was of tremendous socio-economic importance to them and so it would have been improvident of them to dispose of a commodity so important to their economic well-being. Consequently during the 1860s women obtained no holdings from peasants. In the 1870s they took 6.6 per cent of peasants' transactions, in the 1880s 5.1 per cent and in the 1890s 4.2 per cent. Women were getting a diminishing proportion of peasants' transfers.

The bulk of the land, as noted earlier, was owned by planters, so it would be expected that they would be the principal conveyors. Women did a thriving business with planters as conveyors and conveyees, but the main sources from which women obtained land were not planters as would be expected but, rather, tradesmen and merchants. Interestingly, the bulk of women's holdings during the 1890s came from East Indians. Prior to this period they obtained no land from this source. It is difficult to explain this sudden surge in East Indians' transfers to women during this period. Planters' transfers to women accounted for only 6.5 per cent of that groups' total transfers, ranging from 10.4 per cent in the 1860s to 4.4 per cent in the 1890s. In fact the trend was towards a decline between the 1860s and 1890s. The proportion of planters' transfers to women was not significantly greater than the 6.2 per cent involving women themselves. Women were acquiring a large proportion of their holdings from among themselves and from small landholders.

Conclusions

Between 1643 and 1882 married women were precluded from holding real property in their own right. Despite this imposition women were well represented in land transactions as conveyors and conveyees. The amendment of the law in 1882 enabling married women to own property did not, however, cause any significant increase in the number of transactions involving women. This apparently reflects the general shortage of land in the island during this period as a consequence of the resuscitation of the plantation sector of the economy.

Women were involved in 495 of the total 12,258 rural land transactions made in Jamaica between 1866 and 1900. They transferred and obtained land from persons of all groups in the island and they were involved in transactions involving all sizes and types of holdings. However, while transferring 225,699 acres they received only 70,872 acres, a net loss of 155,000 acres. In other words for every 1 acre that women gained they lost 2.2 acres. Such wide-scale transfer of landholdings seems improvident in an agrarian society where land indicates socio-economic power and prestige. It would seem natural to expect that individuals would either be acquiring as much of it as possible, retaining what they already had or both, but it would not be expected to see individuals disposing of land and at such a high rate as women were doing. This indeed had serious implications for the socio-economic development of women in the society. It is difficult to explain the reasons for women's decision to dispose of so large a proportion of so important a commodity as land during this period. But in so far as they disposed of a much larger proportion of all size holdings than they received suggests that women were undergoing economic pressure during this period forcing them to transfer holdings to others. This conclusion seems much clearer from their transfer of large holdings which may be assumed to be whole plantations or estates. The disposal of these holdings held by women planters seems to reflect the general economic difficulties which beset the traditional planter class and prevented them from taking advantage of the new wave of economic activities in the plantation sector. Many of the traditional planters, of whom a large proportion resided abroad, were either too indebted, or simply lacked the capital necessary to invest in their estates. Thus they were forced to sell to the new breed of agrarian capitalists who were actively involved in the developments in the plantation sector. Disposing of these properties, however, indicated n erosion of the economic and social power and prestige these women held in the society. But how is the loss of smaller size holdings to be accounted for? This period under review corresponded to that period in the island's history when poor economic conditions forced a mass migration of the lower-class male population to labour overseas. During the absence of these men many women assumed the position of head of households. It is assumed that those who held holdings were retaining them for economic purposes while those who had none would be using the remittances sent home from abroad to acquire land. However, in so far as women were disposing of their smallholdings at a much faster rate than they were receiving them, strongly suggests that women were experiencing real economic hardships at this time and were forced to concentrate on other economic activities rather than land for their subsistence. There is clear evidence that the revival of the plantation economy made it difficult for the independent small landholders to survive economically in the island.

The major recipients of women's transfers, however, were the peasants. Thus they played a significant role in facilitating the development of this sector of the economy by enabling it to obtain land. Their contribution became even more important during the latter part of the period when land became scarce as a consequence of the resurgence of the plantation sector. Women themselves received smallholdings of up to 50 acres, which implies that they too were becoming peasant farmers. Their acquisition of smallholdings, however, was far less than their transfers. Hence their entry into the peasantry was less significant than their facilitating others to become peasant farmers. Undoubtedly, women played a significant role in the growth and development of the peasantry during the late nineteenth century. Their position as a significant group of independent landholders in the island, however, was definitely on the decline.

Endnotes

1. See, for example, Hilary Beckles, *Natural Rebels: A Social History of Enslaved Black Women in Barbados* (New Brunswick: Rutgers University Press, 1989); Barbara Bush, *Slave Women In Caribbean Society 1650—1838* (Kingston: Heinemann 1992); Patricia Mohammed and Catherine Shepherd (eds), *Gender In Caribbean Development* (Kingston: University of the West Indies and Women and Development Studies Project, 1988); Nesha Haniff, *Blaze A Fire: Significant Contributions of Caribbean Women* (Toronto: Sister Vision, 1988); Janet Momsen, *Women and Change in the Caribbean* (London: James Currey, 1993) and Blanca Silvestrini, *Women and Resistance: Herstory in Contemporary Caribbean History* (Kingston: University of the West Indies, Department of History, 1991).
2. Alvin Bertrand, 'Land Tenure: Definition and Conceptual Frame of Reference', in Alvin Bertrand and Floyd Corty (eds), *Rural Land Tenure in the United States, A Socio-Economic Approach to Problems and Trends* (Baton Rouge: Louisiana State University Press, 1962), p. 7.
3. Paul Barber, *Land Law Note Book* (London: Butterworth, 1969), pp. 1, 4; Ernest

Dowson and V.L.O Sheppard, *Land Registration* (London: Her Majesty's Stationery Office, 1951), p. 9; Victor Grant, 'Jamaican Land law', MA Dissertation, University of London, 1948), pp. 11, 61.

4. Dowson and Sheppard, *Land Registration*, pp. 11, 16, 97—45.
5. Barber, *Land Law Note Book*, pp. 4—5.
6. *Ibid.*, pp. 4—5; Dowson and Sheppard, *Land Registration*, p. 9; and Grant, 'Jamaican Land Law', p. 6.
7. Barber, *Land Law Note Book*, p. 9; Bertrand and Corty, *Rural Land Tenure*, p. 188.
8. Barber, *Land Law Note Book*, p. 4; Dowson and Sheppard, *Land Registration*, p. 9; Grant, 'Jamaican Land Law', pp. 4—6.
9. Grant, 'Jamaican Land Law', p. 1.
10. Bryan Edwards, *The History Civil and Commercial of the British Colonies in the West Indies* (London, 1793), pp. 273—74.
11. Grant, 'Jamaican Land Law', p. 1.
12. 'Proclamation of Oliver, Lord Proprietor . . . October 10, 1655 . . .', *Calendar of State Papers. Colonial Series, America and the West Indies, (1675—1677)*, p. 98; William Claypole, 'Land Settlement and Agricultural Development in the Liguanea Plain, 1655 to 1700', MA Dissertation, (University of the West Indies, Jamaica, 1970), p. 34.
13. *Calendar of State Papers (1675—1677)*, p. 101.
14. Claypole, 'Land Settlement', pp. 40, 42; Grant, 'Jamaican Land Law', p. 6.
15. Claypole, 'Land Settlement', p. 90.
16. See for example the names of owners given in the Accounts Produce (Spanish Town, Jamaica: Island Record Office).
17. The Married Women's Property Law, 1870.
18. See Amendment to The Married Women's Property Rights Law, 1870 and 1882.
19. Up until 1882, married women were exempted from owning land in their own right; Veront Satchell, 'From Plots to Plantations. Land Transactions in Jamaica, 1866—1900' (Kingston: Institute of Social and Economic Research, 1990), pp. 37—39.
20. The extent to which the enslaved population gained access to land, however, greatly depended on the attitude of the landowners and the government to the growth of an independent peasantry, which in turn determined the extent to which large properties were subdivided and sold to the black population.
21. Satchell, 'From Plots to Plantations', pp. 39, 40, 42.
22. *Ibid.*, p. 38.
23. *Jamaica Departmental Reports* (1889), p. 10.
24. Satchell, 'From Plots to Plantations', pp. 42—44.
25. *Ibid.*, pp. 40—42.
26. *Ibid.*, p. 44.
25. *Ibid.*, p. 46—47.
28. *Ibid.*, pp. 48—49.
29. *Ibid.*, p. 49.
30. *Ibid.*, p. 49.
31. *Ibid.*, p. 49.
32. *Ibid.*, p. 53.
33. *Jamaica Departmental Report* (1882—83), p. 19; *Jamaica Departmental Report* (1887), p. 13; *Handbook of Jamaica* (1884—85), p. 386.

34. *Bluebook of Jamaica* (1891), p. 202; (1896—97), p. 201.

35. Satchell, From Plots to Plantations, p. 45.

36. *Ibid.*, p. 52.

37. *Jamaica Departmental Report* (1894—95), p. ix; (1897—98), p. x.

38. Report on the 'Government Savings Banks', *Jamaica Departmental Report* (1899—1900), p. ix; Satchell, From Plots to Plantations, p. 55.

39. The term 'peasants' is used interchangeably with 'small settlers' in this article.

40. The term 'planters' refers to owners of large landholdings. These include owners of sugar estates, owners of coffee and other plantations and owners of livestock pens.

13.

Gender, Migration and Settlement:

The Indentureship and Post-indentureship Experience of Indian Females in Jamaica 1845–1943

Verene A. Shepherd

Ethnic diversity and Caribbean women's history

The biracial and multiracial character of Caribbean populations, and thus the longstanding recognition by Caribbean historians that there is no common historical experience of women in the region, has led to a considerable outpouring of scholarship which has taken into account differences based on class, caste, colour, race, ethnicity and occupation. Admittedly, there is still some imbalance in the research, with, understandably, more focus placed on the experiences of African-Caribbean women than on other groups of women. Nevertheless, there has been a commendable number of historical works on women belonging to other groups and this has altered the epistemological foundations of historical knowledge of the region. For example, since the 1970s, scholars have increasingly applied their research efforts to detailing the history of immigrant, specifically Indian, women in the Caribbean. The research on Indo-Jamaican women has, predictably, lagged behind the research on Indo-Trinidadian and Indo-Guyanese women; for compared with Guyana and Trinidad with their large populations of Indians, Jamaica imported just over 37,000 Indians in the post-slavery period. Only about one-third of the total imported comprised females.

Explaining the historiographic pattern

The comparative neglect of the historical experiences of Indian women in Jamaica was influenced by the perception that Indian females were marginal to the larger historical experience of the island and that their numbers were too small to have had any significant impact on the economy or the society. There was also the belief that they functioned largely in the private, domestic sphere, under the control of Indian men in the patriarchal Indian family system; that they were subsumed to their male counterparts in the economic and social spheres and did not merit separate treatment in the historiography. This article will attempt to correct some of the traditional perceptions by detailing the economic activities of Indo-Jamaican women during and after their period of contract labour. It will show that Indian women in Jamaica, the majority of whom laboured on large sugar and banana plantations, contributed to the continuation of the capitalistic plantation system after the abolition of slavery, and were not at all peripheral to developments in the post-slavery period.

Gender and the female Indian experience

The central objective of the article, though, is to demonstrate the ways in which gender considerations conditioned the Indian female experience of migration, indentureship and settlement in the host society. As a result the analysis places the perception of gender at the centre of the female Indian's experience. Admittedly, race and class have traditionally superseded gender as the principal organising forces in the immigrant experience. The dominance of race and class traditionally made gender peripheral to an understanding of power, dominance and change among the immigrant communities. But gender must be taken into consideration in any analysis of the differential experiences of male and female immigrants. Class and race conflicts were not the only forms of social struggles in colonial society; nor were they the only source of philosophy and ideology. Gender conflict, in which masculinity was held to be superior to femininity, was an important site of struggle in post-slavery Jamaica. It was, overall, an important guide to the shaping of social and economic policy and social consciousness. Western intellectual tradition did not regard femininity as an authentic source of philosophy and ideology. According to this tradition, as Clinton Hutton points out, some authors maintained that 'man is more gifted by nature with powers of reasonable discretion than woman.'[1]

The ways in which the immigrant Indian female's experience was shaped by gender considerations can best be examined within the context of the attitude of Jamaican landholders towards the importation and use of female labourers in the post-slavery period, the impact on the system of recruitment of planters' perceptions of the role of women in the labour force, the resultant sexual disparity in Asian migration schemes, the eventual stipulation by Britain of a 40:100 ratio of females to males, the failure of recruiters' efforts to meet this stipulated ratio, and the economic and social implications of the continued sexual disparity. Gender considerations were also central to government policy with respect to certain Indian cultural practices, such as marriage; and it is clear that the Indian female experience of education, employment and land accumulation in the post-1930s period was directly linked to gender rather than to race and class.

The immigration of Indian women commenced in 1845 and ended in 1916, though indentureship continued until 1921. Their importation did not signify a novel migration wave; for since the seventeenth century the international deployment of capital had been paralleled by an international movement of labour. This phenomenon continued through the age of industrial capitalism and the advent of advanced capitalism and involved several racial and ethnic groups.

Indians were the most numerically significant of the groups of immigrants imported into post-slavery Jamaica. Between 1845, when the first ship, *Blundell*, arrived, and 1916 when the last ship *Dewa* arrived, just over 37,000 Indians were imported. Most, a total of 23,333, were imported in the period 1845-80.[2] They were shipped from Calcutta and Madras up to 1898, and from Calcutta only thereafter.

Attitudes to female labour in post-slavery Jamaica

It is vital to reconstruct the ideological landscape of mid-nineteenth-century Jamaica and contrast it with the period of slavery in order to understand better the ways in which planters' attitudes to female labour shaped the processes of recruitment and emigration. Slave society had been characterised by the economic, social and political dominance of white metropolitan males, who enjoyed unparalled power and prestige. It was a society in which race and class were mutually reinforcing. It was a society marked by the virtual absence of working-class white women and one in which black women were not accorded the 'gentler' characteristics of elite and middle-class white women or even of freed women of colour. The sugar plantation was the dominant economic unit and its labour force consisted primarily of enslaved black people, with black women comprising the majority of field workers. The gender division of labour was thus weakly instituted in the Caribbean, except in higher-status occupations which displayed a tendency to be dominated by black or coloured men. In slave society, Europeans saw no incompatibility between slaves being female and work units in the field; enslaved women departed from the usual characteristics of the gender and merited no special consideration.

An ideological shift occurred, however, in the post-slavery period. As Clinton Hutton has pointed out, in this period the notion was that only 'barbaric men' made their women work.[3] Europeans' patriarchal sexism, and its influence by Victorian ideals, according to which men were to function in the public area of wage work outside the home while women were to inhabit the sphere of uncompensated labour in the home, now caused male labour to be regarded as the motive force of 'civilisation'. Women's involvement in wage labour outside the home was viewed as involvement in men's domain and therefore as a way of perpetuating 'savagery'.[4] The 'male as breadwinner' ideology was also shaped by missionary efforts to recreate gender roles within the nuclear family system according to biblical principles. The missionaries believed in the 'civilising' influence of the idealised nuclear family and preached against the negative impact of the 'chaotic' and 'disorganised' black family. In their efforts to reconstruct 'civilised' society in the post-slavery period and rescue former slaves from 'descending into barbarism' (particularly in the face of their tendency to desert the civilised sphere of the plantation), planters and missionaries tried to send black women home to reconstruct the black family. Western forms of household organisation began to be encouraged along with the institution of a greater gender division of labour. Men were thus encouraged to take up their 'proper station in life' as provider. Predictably, in keeping with their belief in the sexual division of labour, proprietors gave men preference over women for jobs. By the time of the arrival of Indians in 1845, then, an attempt was being made to adhere to a 'proper gender order' in the division of labour. This development, combined with many black women's desire to shun plantation labour in preference for work at home and in the family economy, caused the Jamaican labour force to become increasingly male-dominated by the end of the nineteenth century. This trend was indicated by the censuses, although these official records tended to under-represent the extent of female presence in the labour force. They counted only women who worked outside the home for wages; and took no account of those who worked part-time at home and part-time on the plantations. The censuses show that between 1921 and 1943 the entire female labour force declined from 219,000 to 163,000. In agriculture, the main area of female employment at the time of emancipation, the female labour force declined from 125,000 in 1921 to 45,000 by 1943. The percentage decline between 1911 and 1943 was from 59.6 per cent to 34 per cent. In the same period, male employment in agriculture was rising numerically and proportionately. Male dominance in emigration schemes later led to an increase of women in the labour force; but this trend was reversed again after the upheavals of the 1930s.

It was this tendency in the mid-nineteenth century to dichotomise work and family, public and private, which determined the landholders' attitude to the recruitment of Indian women. It is clear that they initially regarded the importation of women as uneconomical. In the first place, planters did not regard Indian women as capable agricultural workers. They believed that Indian men worked more efficiently and productively. Their view, as expressed by the Acting Protector of Immigrants, was that, 'indentured women as a rule are not nearly the equals of the men as agricultural labourers', and in the early twentieth century, when steps were being made to increase the numbers of women shipped, they objected to being obliged to pay to import women who were, in their words, 'not as good' as male agricultural workers.[5] Second, unlike during slavery when black women had the potential to reproduce the labour force, the progeny of Indian females could not automatically be pressed into indentureship; so Indian women were not highly valued for their reproductive capacity. Indian children could only be indentured at age 16, though in practice many were used in the fields from age 6 or so, receiving wages of from 3—6 pence per day. But this was only with their parents' consent. Furthermore, proprietors were obliged to provide rations for immigrants' children, whether such children had been imported from India or born in the colony. In some cases, they also had to stand the cost of hiring nurses and establishing creches to look after immigrants' young children.[6] Third, landholders were not too concerned initially about the social life of the immigrants; so the sexual disparity and its implications for the stability of family life did not preoccupy them. Indeed, the requirement to provide immigrants with return passages at the end of their contracts made it less critical to be concerned about the construction of the Indian family and the impact of a shortage of women.

The sexual disparity in Indian immigration to Jamaica

Planters maintained a sex-specific importation policy which favoured men; and recruiters in India naturally obeyed the instructions of the Jamaican planters. Records up to 1882 even show that recruiters were paid less for each potential female emigrant recruited at a rate of 6 annas per head for females and 8 annas for males.[7] On the *Blundell* of 1845 women comprised just 11 per cent of the total of 261; though if the number of girls under age 10 are added to this figure, the percentage increases to 15 per cent. On the *Hyderabad* in 1846, women made up 12 per cent of the total shipment of 319 with total females comprising 15 per cent, like on the *Blundell*. On the *Success* in 1847 women comprised 10 per cent of the shipment of 223 adults.[8]

Jamaican planters relented and adjusted the ratio only in the face of governmental pressure to conform to a 40:100 female-male ratio for immigrants over age 10. But they did not go as far as to support a suggestion by the 1913 investigating team of Chimman Lal and James McNeil of a further increase in the ratio to 50:100 regardless of the age of the female immigrants. This was despite the support given to this suggestion by the delegates appointed to consider the future of indentureship after the end of the First World War, when certain difficulties in importing labourers were anticipated. They recommended that: 'Wherever it is possible to find a sufficient number of females willing to emigrate, this ratio [of 40:100] should be increased [to the level suggested by Lal and McNeil].'[9]

Planters were also forced to agree to an increase in the importation of women because of the economic imperative of encouraging the settlement of Indians rather than their expensive repatriation. Indeed, by the end of the nineteenth century, planters had successfully influenced changes in immigration policy as it related to the length of contract, repatriation and the period of industrial residence. By that time, contracts had been lengthened to 5 years, the period of industrial residence extended to 10 years, after which repatriation could be accessed; and the immigrants were being required to pay a portion of the cost of their return passages. These changes were influenced by the economic downturn after 1884 evidenced, for example, by an increase in the cost of production on estates. The period also saw an increase in the cost of immigrants' passages from India. The landholders' wish now was for immigration to represent a form of colonisation, and for time-expired Indians to remain in the region.

Consequently, more women were being imported by the late nineteenth and early twentieth century. On the *Chetah* of 1880, there were 112 females (30 per cent) and 256 males. Females comprised 31 per cent of the total number shipped on the *Hereford* of 1885 and 30 per cent on the *Volga* of 1893—94. Of the 2,130 imported on the *Moy*, *Erne* and *Belgravia* in 1891, females totalled 689 or 32 per cent. On the *Belgravia*, which imported 1,050 in all, females numbered 360 compared with 690 males.[10] On some shipments in the nineteenth century, the proportion of women landed in Jamaica even exceeded the stipulated female-male ratio of 40:100. For example, in the 1876 shipment the female-male ratio was 46:100 and it was 43:100 in 1877—78. Between 1905 and 1916, the percentage of women on each ship which arrived ranged from 22 per cent to 30 per cent.[1]

Single women, married women or families?

Recruiters were not only encouraged to recruit more women, but more women 'of a respectable class', preferably as part of families. This meant excluding single, unaccompanied women. This was because there had developed a notion in India that single women were pressed into prostitution in the colonies. Some visitors to Jamaica even seemed to have shared this belief. One H. Roberts, a noted opponent of immigration, claimed in 1847 that 'the utter disproportion of females in each locality tends greatly to the increase of vice and immorality.'[12] Chimman Lal and James McNeil later agreed on this view of the existence of prostitution, though they disputed that it was widespread. According to their report: 'Of the unmarried women, a few live as prostitutes whether nominally under the protection of a man or not. The majority remain with the man with whom they form an irregular union.'[13]

They also seemed to believe that the women were constantly tempted into 'abnormal' sexual behaviour by single men with money, 'But they [the women] are open to temptation as on all estates there are single men who have more money than they need to spend on themselves alone.'[14]

The Acting Protector of Immigrants in Jamaica also claimed that prostitution was prevalent among the Indian women in the island; so while agreeing that more women should be recruited, he warned that these should be of a 'better class'. According to him, 'It is no use increasing the proportion of women if they are to be picked up off the streets. They will only lead to further trouble as these women go from man to man and are ceaseless cause of jealousy and quarrels.'[15] It was in an attempt to induce women of a 'better class' to emigrate that landholders tried to reduce the period of indenture for women to three years. They believed that a shorter indenture and the promise of domestic life thereafter would be an attractive inducement for the women and for their husbands. But the women had a different agenda and the men could not support their wives on their low wages.

Family emigration was supposed to help to solve the 'problem' of the emigration of too many single women. Before the early twentieth century, family emigration had been discouraged on the grounds that this necessitated the importation of a large number of children who would increase the risk of epidemics, raise the mortality rate and delay the sailing of ships. This last matter was a perennial cause of concern, judging from the correspondence of the Protector of Emigrants in Calcutta. He produced statistics to show how much delay could be caused by any unusual illnesses (see Table 1).

The fact that only children aged 16 years could be indentured and that in many cases women would not emigrate without their children, had also been a deterrent. Towards the end of the indenture period, the view was that 'the emigration of whole families will be encouraged.'[16] While children of all ages were allowed to emigrate with their families by the early twentieth century, a preference was expressed for the recruitment of girls.

Still, the numbers of boys and male infants shipped continued to exceed the numbers of girls and female infants. This was revealed in the

Table 1. Period for which emigrants were detained at the depot prior to embarkation, 1875

	Days' detention at the depot		
Country	Maximum	Minimum	Average
Mauritius	43	3	23
Jamaica	89	2	29
Demerara (due to outbreak of ulcers)	121	2	17
St Vincent	24	6	12
Natal (due to outbreak of syphillis)	96	1	20
Trinidad (due to illness of a woman's child)	147	1	19
Guadeloupe	65	11	19

Source: India Office Library, London, L/24/1208. Report of J. G. Grant, Protector of Emigrants, Calcutta, 15 November 1875

sample survey of ships arriving in Jamaica between 1845 and 1916, which showed 508 boys and 333 girls being imported.

There was, predictably some opposition to the emigration of families, on financial grounds. G. Grindle of the Colonial Office, in response to the recommendation of the Indian Government officials, Chimman Lal and James McNeil, stated that: 'The encouragement of the emigration of whole families, which in itself is a desirable feature of the scheme, will make the proportion of passages to working emigrants higher than under the existing system, especially as women will be under no obligation to work [once in the colonies].'[17]

Despite the wishes of the planters, the majority of Indian women emigrated, not as part of a family, but as single, independent women, uninfluenced by the mid-nineteenth-century Victorian ideology of the 'proper gender order'. On the ship *Indus* which arrived in the island in 1905, for example, only 29 per cent of the women were noted as married and accompanied by spouses; 71 per cent were recorded as single or unattached. On the *Indus* of 1906, 33 per cent of the women were married and 66 per cent were single or unattached. The single women still predominated on this shipment despite the slightly improved proportion of married females. Single Indian females continued to outnumber the married in the post-indentureship period. In the census of 1891, 2,851 out of 4,467 Indian women were recorded as single. Similarly the 1911 census showed 4,467 single Indian women, 2,479 married and 454 widowed. Forty-three women did not state their marital status. This pattern was replicated in the 1921 census when the single Indian females numbered 5,020 out of a total female Indian population of 8,407. But by 1943, there was an increase in the proportion of married to single Indian women and the percentage of married men was lower than the percentage of married women. In the same year, 46.5 per cent of Indian males were recorded as having been ever married, compared to 55.4 per cent of Indian females. The Jamaican percentages were lower than those for Guyana, where a significant 73.7 per cent of Indian women were said to have been 'ever married'.[18]

It should be stressed though, that there was inaccuracy in census reporting of the marital status of Indians in the Caribbean, as not all of their marriages were registered according to the legal requirements of the region. At all ages in all colonies, except Trinidad and Tobago, the Afro-Caribbean population showed the lowest proportion of people ever married. Mixed groups showed only a slightly higher proportion; but the highest proportion was recorded among Europeans.[19]

The rationale for increasing the numbers of women was clearly not connected with their economic importance. The stated reason was that only by increasing the number of women in the immigrant population could the pool of potential wives and lovers for Asian men be increased and Asian men be induced to settle in the region. Another reason was the effort to save the colonies the cost of time-expired Indians' repatriation. This was expressed in a despatch from Lord Harris, a mid-nineteenth-century Governor of Trinidad, and typified the attitude of Caribbean planters. According to Harris,

> it is to be regretted that the colony should be required to find them return passages. But I could not recommend that this condition be withdrawn or that a longer period should be fixed for their residence here, unless it was distinctly understood that a much larger proportion of women than have as yet arrived should accompany them.[20]

Planters were also concerned about the tensions which developed among Indian men over scarce Indian women, and the violence against Indian women which resulted; for Indian men were not alleviating the scarcity of female Indian partners by cohabiting with African-Jamaican women. There were frequent reports from men that Indian women were displaying a great degree of sexual freedom and independence. They reportedly changed partners frequently and some cohabited with men but refused to marry them. This behaviour resulted in wife murder and wounding. Chimman Lal and James McNeil expressed the view that 'perhaps the best guarantee against infidelity to regular or irregular unions is the birth of children.'[21] But the birth rate among indentured women remained low for the entire period of indentureship.[22]

In 1913, the Acting Protector of Immigrants in Jamaica supported an increase in the numbers of females shipped to the island as a remedy for the growing incidence of abusive behaviour towards Indian women. In a letter to the Colonial Secretary he reiterated that:

increasing the proportion of women would most likely reduce the number of cases of wounding and murder on account of jealousy, and be an excellent arrangement from the male immigrants' point of view as there would not be such a dearth of East Indian women as there is now on a good many estates.[23]

Despite the attempts to increase the numbers of women in the island, the female Indian population in Jamaica was outnumbered by the Indian male population for all of the period of indentureship and most of the post-indentureship years, as is indicated by Table 2, which is based on the population censuses. The 1861 census did not detail the sex ratio of Indians in most of the parishes. The only parishes returning a male/female breakdown were St John (8 males and 1 female) and St Ann (48 males and 17 females). From the censuses with detailed parish data on the sex ratio, it is clear that up to 1943, the last year in which detailed data on Indians in the island were given, Indian women were still less than 50 per cent of the total Indian population, though their proportion had improved from 31.5 per cent in 1871 to 49 per cent in 1943. In 1943, Jamaica had 937 males for every 1,000 females. The male deficit was especially marked in the urban sections of the island. Men outnumbered women among Asians in all British Caribbean territories except Grenada and the northern Leeward Islands, a reflection of male predominance in migration schemes from 1838 to 1917.[24]

This imbalance was also noted up to 1946, evening out only by 1960. On an island-wide level, there was an excess of females over males in 1943 and 1946; but the reverse was the case among the Indian population. The censuses for 1960, 1970 and 1982, in fact, showed a 1:1 male-female ratio.

Table 2. The Indian population in Jamaica: males and females, 1871–1921

Census year	Male	Female	Total	% of Females
1871	5,339	2,454	7,793	31.5
1881	6,941	4,075	11,016	37.0
1891	6,338	4,467	10,805	41.3
1911	9,928	7,452	17,380	43.0
1921	10,203	8,407	18,610	45.2

Source: Jamaican Censuses, 1871—1921

Economic roles of Indian females: the indentureship period

Even though the intention behind increased female immigration was to increase the pool of potential wives in the island, Indian women did not play a primarily domestic role in the nineteenth and early twentieth centuries. They were important as agricultural labourers on various properties in the island. Most females available for emigration were single women who had to be recruited as indentured workers just like their male counterparts. One of the consistent features of colonial and Imperial organisation of migrant labour, the indenture or contract system, provided a means of retaining labour in the short and medium term and an institutional framework to facilitate the further movement of labour in the post-slavery period. At the inception of labour migration, contracts were only for one year, with renewal being optional. The period of contract for men and women was later extended to three years. By 1870, immigrants were serving five-year contracts with repatriation due only after a further five years of continuous residence in the island.

It is difficult to penetrate the polemic on the gender differences in the working condition of immigrants, specifically the extent to which they were subjected to sex-typing of jobs and gender discrimination in wages for equal work; for the sources tended to document the experiences of female immigrants only when it came to issues relating to fertility, the sexual disparity in migration schemes and male-female social relations.

From the limited data available, it is clear that female Indians were subjected only to a limited form of the sex-typing of jobs according to which women were confined to service industries and men to agricultural field or factory positions. This sex-typing of jobs under capitalism was one of the forms of the sexual division of labour which European colonisers attempted to reproduce in the Caribbean. It was traditionally created by the interaction in capitalist society of family and public economic life. But as Indian women could not be confined to the private sphere as wives of indentured men, and as there were insufficient openings for domestic servants in the scaled-down households of the post-slavery period, landholders were forced to use them in the fields. The proprietors still maintained a gender division of labour in non-field occupations. Thus, while Indian women were confined to field labour and domestic service much as enslaved women had been, they were not given the factory jobs or the skilled artisan positions which were deemed suitable only for men.

Indentured women also had a narrower range of jobs on the sugar estates and banana plantations which were the principal employers of their services; and they were subject to discrimination in wages. They came to Jamaica during the operation of a system where men began to be paid more than women in spite of the experience during slavery that women survived the plantation experience better than their male counterparts. The contracts signed in the nineteenth century indicate that women were paid 9d (pence) a day of nine hours and men 1s (shilling) for the same number of hours, though not always for the same types of tasks. But the acceptance of a differential rate of pay seemed to have been part of the patriarchal thinking of the period; for the wage differential was imbedded in the indenture contract even before any jobs were allocated. In any event, the existence of a wage differential was predicated on the assumption that women's work was not as valuable as men's. The arrangement by which men were paid more than women was in place up to 1909. The Protector of Immigrants, Charles Doorly, informed Governor Sydney Olivier in that year that: 'During the first three months of their residence in Jamaica, immigrants are paid a daily wage of men 1/- and women 9d. (a day of 9 hours); 2/6d per week deducted for rations in the first three months.'[25]

At the end of three months, theoretically, immigrants could ask to go on task work at rates of pay approved by the Protector; but in any event, it was stipulated that the rates for task work should allow immigrants to earn at least the minimum rates of 1s for men and 9d for women. In many cases, the tasks given to female workers were less remunerative than tasks given to men. The only exception was heading bananas, which paid 4—5s per 100 bunches to both men and women. It is not clear from the sources whether men carried fewer or more bunches of bananas on their heads from the fields to the railway or wharf.

On banana plantations, which by the early twentieth century were the principal employers of female immigrants, the most remunerative tasks, apart from heading bananas, were forking, trenching, ploughing, lining, circling and cutting. Trenching paid 2-3s per day and forking 2s an acre; but not all of these tasks were made available to women. Some men could earn up to 10s per week from some of these tasks. Picking cocoa, a job that females did, paid 2d for every 100 pods picked.[26] On sugar estates, as long as African-Jamaicans were available, they were given the more remunerative tasks. Less remunerative tasks were given to Indian men and the least remunerative to Indian women.

But there is not much evidence that even where task work was chosen female immigrants increased their wages significantly. For example, a report on wage rates in 1919 showed that women earned an average of 6s 11¼d per week while men earned an average of 9s 10½d. In 1920, men earned an average of 12s and women 8s 6d per week. The Protector, from time to time, identified outstanding immigrants who earned above this average. Three women — Dulri, Inderi and Jaipali — all earned above 12s per week in 1920; but in every case, the wages of the outstanding male workers identified exceeded those of the outstanding women at 16—18s per week.[27] In addition to earning lower wages, the annual expenditure for female workers was said to have been higher than for male workers. At a conservative estimate based on rough statistics supplied by Chimman Lal and James McNeil, it would seem that the annual expenditure for females was 76 per cent of annual wages compared with 57 per cent for males.[28]

Women with very young children experienced further problems which affected the number of hours they worked and the wages they received. Where neither nurses nor creches were provided, indentured women often had to carry their young children to the fields. This handicapped them in their jobs and could affect their productivity. This was the complaint of women on some of the estates visited by the Acting Protector of Immigrants in 1913. He stated that: 'Recently when I visited a certain estate the indentured women complained to me that it was impossible for them to do a good day's work if they had to take their children to the fields and look after them there.'[29]After appealing to the manager on behalf of these women, a nurse was employed to look after the children and relieve their mothers.

On another estate where similar complaints were made by the female workers, the manager agreed to build a creche and employ a nurse to care for the children of immigrant women while they worked. The Acting Protector expressed his wish that: 'All employers of a large number of indentured immigrants ought to be willing to do something of the kind as a great deal more of the time of the women who have children would be available for work.'[30] But not many estates adopted this practice, as they did not place much value on women's work in any case.

It was only when the continuation of the system of indenture seemed threatened in the early twentieth century that some improvements in the conditions of female indentured servants were suggested.Just as the situation of enslaved women featured prominently in the emancipatory rhetoric of the 1820s and 1830s, and just as the improvement of their conditions was enshrined in the amelioration proposals to stem the tide of anti-slavery resistance, so gender considerations were critical in the debate over the system of Indian labour which was to replace indentureship.

The discussions over the system of labour to replace Indian indentureship surfaced in the years after the First World War. It was suggested that the emigrants' agreement should be in the form of a civil contract rather than an indentured contract and that the term of contract should be reduced to three years. But the conditions of servitude for females were put at the centre of the debate. Suggestions were now made for women labourers with three children under five years to be exempted from the liability to work, subject to the approval of the Protector of Immigrants. It was also proposed that:

> any woman labourer may receive an exemption from work for any particular period either by agreement between the employer and the woman and subject to the approval of the Protector of Immigrants or on the Certificate of the Immigration Department. During advanced pregnancy and after childbirth, a woman may be exempted from work for a period not exceeding six months. Immediate steps should be taken to require the issue of free rations to pregnant and nursing women for a period not less than six months.[31]

The inducements to be held out to male labourers, though, were linked to efforts to improve their economic welfare. No such considerations were given to female labourers. It was suggested, for example, that any new scheme of Indian labour after the end of the First World War must include provisions to make land available to male labourers. Thus a recommendation was that all possible steps should be taken to require employers to provide small garden plots of one-tenth of an acre of land for each male labourer and facilities for labourers keeping cows. A larger acreage, one-third of an acre, should be given to male labourers who were more industrious than the rest. This land was to be given after the first six months of labour in the island.[32]

The post-indentureship period

The post-indentureship experience of Indian women demonstrated areas in which gender clearly impeded their upward social mobility. After indenture, the majority of ex-indentured Indian women settled in Jamaica, pursuing a variety of occupations in the rural and urban sectors of the island. This was despite the fact that their legal entitlement to repatriation was not abolished until 1930; though completely free return passages were abolished by 1910. Admittedly, the portion of the return passage which women were required to pay was lower than the portion paid by men; but even this portion was often more than they could afford. While men paid half of the cost of their return passages, women paid a third. Wives, dependent children and the ill and disabled were repatriated free. The high cost of repatriation, combined with the women's own choice and their spouses' in some cases, resulted in the majority of them settling in Jamaica.

The end of immigration and indentureship and the increasing settlement of Indians in the island resulted in the increase of Indo-Jamaicans in the population. By the time of the abolition of indentureship in 1921, the majority of Indian females had been born in Jamaica. In 1911, 4,663 Indian women had been born in Jamaica and 2,750 had been born in India. The 1921 census recorded 5,087 Indian females born in Jamaica compared with 2,531 who had been born in India. A minority were born elsewhere. Not surprisingly, this declining number of Indian-born females was reflected in the age composition of the female population: Indian-born females were within the older age groups, Jamaican-born within the younger age groups. In all the censuses, the majority of Indian women were in the 20—50 age group. In 1891, for example, of a total female Indian population of 4,467, only 835 were over 40 years old.

The post-indentureship experience of women was shaped by many factors: the unavailability of remunerative employment opportunities outside the plantation, the racism evident in society towards people from other countries, the low standard of education of the female Indian population, the negative attitude of employers towards female labourers, rural-urban migration, male out-migration, the return of migrants in the 1930s depression and the opportunities for employment in the period after the 1938 labour struggles. Not all of these factors were gender-specific. Some affected men just as much as women, conditioned as they were by factors of race, class and culture, rather than to gender. But the educational level of women and their employment opportunities in the period after the 1880s were clearly linked to gender-specific factors and will be discussed in more detail.

It is clear that few Indian women in Jamaica received much formal education up to 1943 and that the educational system, combined with Indian customs, sought to keep them in a subordinate position in the society. It is no surprise then that the majority of Indian women were recorded in the censuses as illiterate. The 1891 census showed that only 110 girls were going to school, but attendance among Indian boys was only slightly better at 126. In that year, 956 Indian boys and 953 girls of school age were not attending school. The situation had not improved dramatically by 1943. According to the 1943 census, people from the British Isles had the highest literacy rate in Jamaica at 98.7 per cent, while Indians and their descendants had the lowest, at 51.4 per cent. Of the literate Indian population, 95.5 per cent were educated up to the elementary-school level, with only 2.8 per cent attaining secondary education. This was still above the all-island level, where 94.6 per cent were educated at the elementary-school level. The figure was 98 per cent for literate blacks.

The high level of illiteracy among female Indians was linked to cultural factors affecting the schooling of both boys and girls, the implications of the sexual disparity and the differing attitudes of Indian parents towards schooling for boys and girls. For most of the nineteenth century the Indian population clamoured for the establishment and maintenance of special Indian schools to prevent ethnic mixing and changes in their religions and customs. Such special schools were only allowed for a brief period in the early twentieth century before being closed by the government on the grounds that the Indian population should mix with other races in the government schools, or establish and fund their own schools. As the Indo-Jamaican population could not afford to maintain their own schools, and as they settled and changed their attitude to the host society, racial mixing in schools occurred.[33]

But even when girls went to school, the type of education which they received often served to confine them to female occupations. The education system introduced into the Caribbean in the post-slavery period was based on that of nineteenth-century Victorian England. It alienated people from their culture and environment and prepared them to serve a developing British capitalist society. Inevitably, the sexism and sex stereotypes which were part of the British system were transmitted to the Caribbean. The image of the male as head of the household and as breadwinner with economic responsibility for the family, and of the ideal woman as housewife and mother, frail and feminine, helpless and genteel, were values of a British middle class which ignored the plight of working-class women in Britain; yet they were thought right and proper for the colonial societies in the British Empire.

As organised education expanded, both boys and girls of the masses (there were some elite single sex schools) were educated in the same schools; but the stereotypes were firmly entrenched as the sexes pursued separate activities. Boys were trained to be skilled artisans and girls were trained to be domestic servants;[34] and primary education was seen as sufficient for this class. Consequently, Indian women who were not in agricultural activities were increasingly found in the service sector as domestic servants. Only those who broke out of their class position were able to occupy other ranks such as in the professional, industrial or commercial fields.

The type of education provided for girls in the orphanages and homes reinforced the sex-typing of education, as they stressed domestic science. Sada Stanley, Superintendent of Lyndale Girls' Home in Highgate, St Mary, stated quite unapologetically in 1924 that 'the women of any land may be a great determining factor in the uplift of the land . . . and no people can be truly great without true and good mothers.'[35]

But Indian women were subject to another kind of oppression with respect to their access to education; they were often kept at home to be prepared for housewifely roles while the boys were sent to school. For each year for which data are available, it is clear that more Indian boys than girls were enrolled in primary schools in Jamaica. In 1943 1,400 Indian boys were attending primary schools compared with 1,244 girls.[36] While many Jamaican children of both sexes of school age were kept out of school for economic reasons, the non-attendance of Indian girls was also linked to the sexual disparity in Asian migration schemes and the new importance attached to (scarce) Indian girls, who were betrothed at a very early age. A survey of marriage certificates for the period revealed that Indian girls were being married at ages from 10 upwards. This was despite the fact that the revised Immigration Law of 1896 had stipulated a marriage age of 13 for females and 15 for males. The government of Jamaica moved to outlaw this young age of marriage, making it illegal under the Age at Marriage Act of 1929 for Indian girls to be married unless they had attained the age of 16.[37]

Creolised Indian women abhorred this practice of early betrothal and expressed their disapproval in letters to the editor in the newspapers of the day. Writing to the Editor of the *Daily Gleaner* in 1940, Nora Bedasee, who claimed to have refused three marriage proposals, stated her disapproval of such a custom, on the basis that 'today the growth of education and culture must allocate such preternatural customs to the past.'[38]

The low rate of school attendance and the high rate of illiteracy among Indians kept the majority tied to the land as rural agricultural workers up to 1943. This means that the locational pattern in the period of indenture changed little in the post-indentureship period. This is supported by the censuses. The 1861 census detailed the distribution of the population by parish; but did not carry details on ethnic distribution as opposed to parish distribution by colour. However, the details on the native country of the inhabitants enabled an analysis of the distribution of the population from India by parish. It showed the majority living in Westmoreland, Metcalfe, Clarendon, St Mary and Vere.[39] In 1871, the census showed a slightly altered parish distribution. The total Indian population in that year was 7,793, comprising 5,335 males and 2,454 females. The majority of Indian women were settled in Clarendon, Westmoreland, St Thomas-in-the-East, St Catherine, St Mary, St James, Hanover, St Elizabeth and Portland.

In 1881 the Indian population totalled 11,016, of whom 4,075 were female. The parish distribution in order of numerical importance was: St Catherine, Westmoreland, Clarendon, St Mary, St Thomas and Portland. Similarly, in the 1891 census, Indian women numbered 4,467 or 1.6 per cent of the total population of Jamaica. The majority were to be found in Westmoreland, Clarendon, St Catherine, St Mary, St Thomas, Kingston, and Portland. From 1911 to 1943, St Mary was the leader in terms of numbers of Indian females. Indeed, a notable factor after 1891 was that the banana-producing parishes, and not the sugar-growing parishes, employed the majority of Indian labourers. On the whole, though, the censuses revealed a distribution which reflected a preponderance of Indian women in the rural areas, whether in the sugar- or banana-producing parishes. This rural bias was most marked up to 1881, and more notable among Indian women than among other female ethnic minorities. By contrast, the census of 1881 revealed that Chinese and white women were concentrated in Kingston and St Andrew.

A shift took place only after 1943 when the rural-urban migration movement was reflected in the growing numbers of Indian women in the urban centre. This trend had actually started since 1881, a reflection of the trek of ex-indentured immigrants from rural parishes, but it intensified after the 1940s. The parishes experiencing the highest drain were St Mary and Westmoreland. Up to 1946, however, the Indian population was still primarily rural. This was a trend reflective of the larger Caribbean situation. Only 9.14 per cent of the total Indian population (and 21.80 of the entire population) in the British Caribbean were to be found in the urban areas in 1946. However, it was noted that 'Jamaica with 4,052 Indians in the urban parishes appears to have a smaller rural bias among

East Indians."[40] It was pointed out in this census report that this trek to the urban core was not a reflection of a movement away from agriculture, as the majority in the urban sections of the parishes engaged in market gardening.[41]

The largest percentage of rural Indians was actually found in Trinidad and Tobago, Guyana and the Windward Islands. By contrast, other Asians were more heavily settled in the urban areas, particularly in Guyana and Jamaica. In Guyana in 1946, only just under one-third of the Chinese population was not in the urban centres.[4]

Table 3. Distribution of Indian females by parish: selected years, 1861–1960

Parish	1881	1911	1921	1960
Kingston & Port Royal	54	196	357	446
St Andrew	196	219	292	3,018
St Thomas	206	692	626	624
Portland	189	610	627	630
St Catherine	824	1,145	1,439	2,056
St Mary	659	1,865	1,856	1,652
St Ann	21	11	25	68
Clarendon	732	1,070	1,215	2,313
Manchester	34	36	30	88
St Elizabeth	139	77	102	158
Westmoreland	779	1,275	1,461	2,649
Hanover	111	108	171	126
St James	59	79	147	163
Trelawny	72	69	59	35
Total	4,075	7,452	8,467	14,026

Source: Jamaican Censuses, 1881—1960

The censuses provide the only detailed account of the occupations of the female Indian population. They show clearly that Indian women continued to be an important part of the labour force, though the extent of their participation may have been under-represented on account of the narrow definition of work. It is clear that the majority of Indian women were engaged in agricultural activities up to the mid-twentieth century, more than most other women, though not their male counterparts, except in the tobacco industry. The 1891 census revealed that over 72 per cent of the bread-earning population was engaged in agricultural or pastoral pursuits. Among the Indian population, 66 per cent (or 7,223 out of 10,805) were in agriculture (see Table 4). Many were returned in the

Table 4. Occupations of Indians in Jamaica: males and females, 1891

Occupations	Men	Women	Total
Peasant proprietor	59	3	62
Overseer	15	-	15
Agricultural labourer	3,707	2,534	6,241
Attending stock on pasture	10	-	10
General labourer	523	399	922
Attending agricultural machinery or boilers	1	-	1
Merchant/agent/dealer	10	-	10
Shopkeeper	246	151	397
Shop/sales/ clerk	39	46	85
Market gardeners	60	50	110
Indoor domestic servant	35	50	85
Washer	-	26	26
Interpreter/messenger	4	-	4

Source: Jamaica Census, 1891

census as 'indefinite and unproductive', but some of these may have included part-time workers in agriculture.

Other characteristics in these censuses are that Indian women continued to have a narrower range of occupations than their male counterparts. Indian women were confined to the lowest-paid occupations and were under-represented in the commercial and professional areas. As under indenture, there continued to be a gender division of labour in the skilled and supervisory positions even within the agricultural sector; and women were over-represented in certain jobs such as laundering, care-giving and domestic service. In the 1921 census, only one Indian woman was represented among the 144 rangers and supervisors on agricultural properties in the island. Among the peasant farmers, male Indians dominated. Of 188 Indian banana farmers returned in the 1921 census, there were only 31 females. There were 13 Indian females out of 62 Indian cane farmers; 2 out of 13 cocoa farmers; 107 out of 399 provision farmers; 40 out of 110 rice farmers, and 7 out of 30 tobacco farmers (even though more females than males worked on tobacco farms).

In 1911 as in previous censuses, the majority of Indian females worked as agricultural labourers mostly in the banana and sugar industries. On the all-island level, there were 49,116 females in agricultural labour: Indian women comprised 3,461. They also worked on livestock farms and pens and in rice cultivation. A significant proportion worked as domestic servants. On the all-island level, there were 35,701 domestic servants, of which women made up 30,316. Of 188 Indian domestic servants, 134 were women; an additional 10 Indian women worked in other domestic or personal service.

Table 5. Summary of occupations of Indians in Jamaica: males and females, 1911

Type of work	Males	Females	Main categories
Professional	35	11	Students, nurses, teachers
Domestics	91	152	Indoor house servants
Commercial	386	204	Barkeepers, peddlers, shopkeepers, store servers
Agricultural	6,649	3,373	Wage earners on plantations
Industrial	165	78	Skilled trades, e.g. milliners, washers
Indefinite/unproductive	2,602	3,273	

Source: Jamaica Census, 1911

Employment opportunities for women increased only marginally as a result of male out-migration from the 1880s. The migration wave was-dominated by African-Jamaican men and the gap created by the emigration of African-Jamaican men was increasingly filled by Indian men, with African-Jamaican and Indian women getting work where male labour was not available. The period preceding the 1938 labour rebellion, however, reversed any gains Indian women might have made as a result of male out-migration. This was because of the worldwide economic depression of the 1930s, which was accompanied by the return of male emigrants. The large-scale return of emigrants combined with the downturn in some economic sectors created a surplus labouring population and a predictable lowering of wages.[43] In the competition for scarce jobs which ensued, headmen reportedly gave preference to male workers who had returned with special skills. Headmen also evinced a tendency to employ African-Jamaican men over Indian men and Indian and African-Jamaican women.

J.D. Tyson, who visited the Caribbean in 1938–39 and investigated the causes of the economic and social position of Indians in the region, commented on the special plight of Indian women in the period leading up to the riots. He reported that a scarcity of work had existed among women on banana, coconut and sugar estates. Many women had reportedly gone for weeks without a single day's work at a time when close to 60 per cent of Indian women depended on the large estates for employment. He reported that while male Indians got two or three days' work per week, Indian women were hardly that fortunate.[44]

In the aftermath of the labour rebellion which broke out during the months of May and June 1938, protesting against the low wages, high unemployment and poor working conditions of the masses, employment opportunities for women did not increase dramatically. One reason was the continuation of the trend to locate working-class men in the agricultural labour force rather than women. The Moyne Commission, appointed to investigate the causes of the 1930s riots in the Caribbean and suggest solutions, reinforced the male breadwinner and female housewifisation ideology current after the mid-nineteenth century; for the Commission concluded that one of the reasons for the suffering of the masses was the absence of a proper family. Such a proper family could only be constructed through a system of family formation in which there was stable monogamy and in which women stayed at home and men became the breadwinners.[45] They were assisted in the perpetuation of this ideology by middle-class women's organisations such as the Jamaica Federation of Women which, in addition to opposing universal adult suffrage on the basis that literacy should be a qualification for the franchise (with all its implications for the further political marginalisation of poor women) used their class position and biases to further confine working-class women to the domestic sphere. Their training of such women concentrated heavily on housewifely skills.[46]

As men were being encouraged to work in the agricultural sector, more and more opportunities opened up to women in the industrial, commercial and professional fields. Indian women definitely increased their participation in non-agricultural fields in the period after 1938. But limited educational qualifications kept Indian women in the minority in these areas when compared with women of other ethnic groups.

The struggles over wages and working conditions in the 1930s did not result in any great improvements in the lives of female Indians. Although over 70 per cent of the female Indian population depended on wage labour, only 1,168 or 46 per cent were employed at the end of 1942; and the wages they were receiving were low. The scale of wages, while generally known for the indentured population, was hardly ever documented for the ex-indentured population. No census until 1943 provided data on comparative wage rates for men and women. This census, however, showed that in December 1942, 658 Indian women earned less than 6 shillings per week; 302 earned between 6–10 shillings; 141 earned between 10 shillings and £1 sterling, and 48 earned between £1–2 sterling.

Indian women who could not find wage work in agriculture in the late 1930s and 1940s, and who were not qualified to be in the commercial, industrial and professional fields, were not even assisted in becoming small farmers, as men were, in the aftermath of the labour rebellion. Gender discrimination was clearly observable in the allocation of land under the Government Land Settlement Scheme, the pivot of the British colonial land policy which came into being in the 1940s. Joan French argues that the Land Settlement Scheme presumed a nuclear family unit with a male as head of household to whom the land was leased or sold. A female head of household stood little chance of getting land;[47] and statistics from the census showed clearly that the majority of Indian females up to 1943 were single. This was a reversal of an earlier practice of land allocation in lieu of return passages when women who emigrated as single women were entitled to the same amount of land as their male counterparts. This equitable distribution of land in lieu of repatriation had resulted in 48 women (67 per cent of whom were single) getting 10 acres of land each in 1904; and 38 women in 1906.[48] In any case, on account of their poor economic condition, Indians as a group, and Indian women because of gender discriminatory employment and wage practices, hardly stood a chance of getting any of this land, which had to be accessed in parcels of at least 5 acres. The list of Indians applying for land under this scheme showed clearly that the majority were applying for parcels of much less than 5 acres.[49]

Table 6 summarises the main findings relating to occupations in 1943, the year of one of the most detailed census returns. It is clear that the 1891, 1911 and 1921 occupational patterns were more or less replicated in

Table 6. Distribution of Indian population by major occupational categories, 1891–1943*

Category	Year	Male	Female	Total
Professional	1891	835	1	9
	1911	28	11	46
	1921	27	10	38
	1943		17	44
Domestic or personal service	1891	66	59	125
	1911	92	152	243
	1921	252	359	611
	1943	208	576	784
Commerical	1891	313	197	510
	1911	386	204	590
	1921	333	157	490
	1943	94	66	160
Agricultural	1891	4,375	2,986	7,361
	1911	6,694	3,734	10,383
	1921	6,145	3,828	9,973
	1943	3,612	1,535	5,147
Industrial	1891	117	42	159
	1911	165	78	243
	1921	281	153	434
	1943	427	41	468
Indefinite/unproductive	1891	1,102	1,134	2,256
	1911	2,602	3,273	5,875
	1921	3,164	3,999	7,064
	1943	n.a.	n.a.	n.a.

*Additional categories appearing in the 1943 Census are: Transport & Communication: 237 M and 10F; Recreational service: 251 M and 596 F; Public service: 15 M amd 13 F; Clerical: 81 M and 38 F; General labourers doing odd jobs: 794 M and 132 F. It should be noted that the figures for 1943 represent only wage workers rather than the total Indian population.
Source: Jamaican Censuses, 1891–1943.

the 1943 census report, though there were important numerical gains in the non-agricultural areas. The sharp drop in the numbers of women in agriculture between 1921 and 1943 was related to the bias of the census return which made no provision for workers who were not full-time wage workers. The 1943 census indicated that of those women engaged as (full-time?) agricultural labourers, 56 per cent were Indians compared with 28 per cent African-Jamaican, 13 per cent 'coloureds', 1 per cent Chinese and 1 per cent Syrian. By contrast, whereas 56 per cent of Syrian women and 49 per cent of Chinese women were in the retail trade, only 12 per cent of Indian women were involved in that activity. Indian women not in agriculture worked as seamstresses, milliners, messengers and domestic servants.

It is clear that although the Indian female experience of migration, indentureship and settlement was conditioned by the colonisers' own perceptions and prejudices, and by race and class factors, gender discrimination was a visible element. The landholders' preference for male labourers, and their irrational belief in the inefficiency of female labourers, led to a sex-specific immigration policy; and the sex-typing of jobs and the accompanying wage differentials all helped to shape the Indian female experience in Jamaica. The types of occupations of female Indians in the period after the end of the system of indentureship reflected the lack of the educational standards which were necessary to propel them into higher status jobs. It also reflected the ideology of the day which sought to confine women to female-type jobs. This weak position of women in the labour market encouraged by wage differentials and the promotion of the male breadwinner ideology, the same notion of the proper gender order which missionaries tried so hard to instill into African-Jamaican women in the immediate post-slavery period was still in place up to 1943.

Endnotes

1. Quoted in C. Hutton, 'Colour for Colour: Skin for Skin: The Ideological Foundation of Post-slavery Society, 1838—65: The Jamaican Case', PhD. Dissertation, UWI, (Mona, 1993), p. 18.
2. Ships' Papers, Jamaica Archives, Spanish Town (hereafter JA).
3. Hutton, 'Colour for Colour', p. 20.
4. *Ibid.*
5. Public Record Office (London), C.O. 571/1. Acting Protector of Immigrants to the Hon. Colonial Secretary, 13 December 1913.
6. *Ibid.*
7. India Office Library (London), India Office Records, V/24/1210.
8. Ships' Papers, JA.

9. C.O. 571/4, 'Report of the Delegates Appointed by the Governments of British Guiana, Trinidad and Jamaica to Consider . . . the future Policy to be Adopted ... in regard to Immigration from India . . .' Enclosure in British Guiana Despatch No. 226, 9 August 1916.
10. Ships' Papers, JA and India Office Library.
11. Protectors of Emigrants and Immigrants Reports; Ships' Papers, 1845—1916.
12. C.O. 318/173, 'Analysis of Observations Personally Made Amongst the Coolies of Jamaica', 19 October 1847.
13. Extract from a Report by Chimman Lal and James McNeil, Jamaica_Times, 8 May 1915.
14. Ibid.
15. C.O. 571/1, Acting Protector of Immigrants to the Hon. Colonial Secretary, 13 December 1913.
16. C.O. 571/6, Comments by G. Grindle, 26 July 1917.
17. Ibid.
18. West Indian Census, 1946, p. 28.
19. Ibid., p. 27.
20. Lord Harris to Secretary of State Pakington, 8 August 1852.
21. Jamaica Times, 8 May 1915.
22. Jamaica Annual Report, 1920.
23. C.O. 571/1, Acting Protector of Immigrants to the Hon. Colonial Secretary, 13 December 1913.
24. West Indian Census, 1946, pp. 16—17.
25. JA 4/60/10A/29, Charles Doorly to Governor Olivier, 25 March 1909, Enclosure in Despatch No. 13.
26. Sanderson Committee on Emigration from India, evidence of Sir Arthur Blake, 6 May 1909.
27. Report of F.N. Isaacs, Protector of Immigrants, 1919/20.
28. V. Shepherd, 'Emancipation through Servitude?: Aspects of the Condition of Indian Women in Jamaica, 1845—1945', in H. Beckles and V. Shepherd (eds), Caribbean Freedom: Society and Economy from Emancipation to the Present (Ian Randle, Jamaica: James Currey, London, 1993), p. 246.
29. C.O. 571/1, Acting Protector of Immigrants to the Hon. Colonial Secretary, 13 December 1913.
30. Ibid.
31. C.O. 571/6, 'Note on Indian Emigration', December 1916.
32. Ibid.
33. V. Shepherd, Transients to Settler: The Experience of Indians in Jamaica, 1845—1950 (Peepal Tree Press: Warwick University, Leeds, 1994), Chapter 6.
34. Pat Ellis, 'Education and Women's Place in Caribbean Society', in P. Ellis, (ed.), Women of the Caribbean (London: Zed Books, 1986), pp. 91—100.
35. Jamaica Annual Report, 1924, p. 85.
36. JA, File 1B/9/136, Protector of Immigrants Annual Report.
37. Shepherd, Transients to Settlers, p. 212.
38. Daily Gleaner, 21 November 1940.
39. B.W. Higman, The Jamaican Censuses of 1844 and 1861, Social History Project, Department of History, Mona, 1980, pp. 31—39.
40. West Indian Census, 1946, p. 14.
41. Ibid.

42. *Ibid.*
43. J.D. Tyson, *Report on the Condition of Indians in British Guiana, Jamaica and Trinidad, 1939* (n.p., 1939), p. 33.
44. *Ibid.*
45. Joan French, 'Colonial Policy Towards Women after the 1938 Uprising: the Case of Jamaica', *Caribbean Quarterly*, 34: 3, 4 (September—December 1988), pp. 39—53.
46. *Ibid.*, pp. 50—51.
47. *Ibid.*, p. 50.
48. JA, Patent Books, 1B/11/1/42.
49. Shepherd, *Transients to Settlers*, Chapter 4.

14.

Access to Secondary Education for Girls in Barbados,1907–43:
A Preliminary Analysis

Janice Mayers

This article stems in part from research for a doctoral thesis on the wider area of education policy as a whole in Barbados. This research exposed the influence of race and class on policy, but also indicated that gender operated as a constraint on secondary education despite the commendable efforts for change initiated by some. The Swaby Commission of 1907—09, the first major local education commission of the century, for example, recognised the need to remedy the perceived deficiencies in facilities for secondary education for girls in Barbados. Over 30 years later, in assessing the provision for secondary education, the newly appointed Director of Education, Howard Hayden, pointed to the need for positive discrimination in favour of girls. This article will demonstrate that during the first half of the twentieth century there was discrimination against girls in access to public secondary education both in terms of the facilities provided, and in the means provided for taking advantage of the offering.

Education and Barbadian society in the early twentieth century

Education cannot be isolated from the wider context of the society in which it operates. Therefore, before examining some of the influences on educational provision over the period 1909–43, it will be necessary to locate education within the context of historical and structural features of Barbadian society at the turn of the century. On an island where sugar-dominated economic activity, the Barbadian planter-merchant elite-dominated social and political institutions. The colony was predominantly agricultural: 22 per cent of the population was employed in agriculture in 1911, while a mere 0.1 per cent was in professional occupations.[1] The realities of the objective conditions in the economic, social and political sphere indicated a desire by the ruling class to preserve the *status quo*. This group's concern with retaining a labour force for the plantation as well as maintaining class divisions was reflected in education as elsewhere in the society. An outline of the educational provision makes it clear that education, a potential avenue for social mobility, had been structured since the nineteenth century to maintain class divisions and to narrow opportunities for such mobility.

The mid-nineteenth century witnessed the genesis of state support for a general system of education in Barbados when, in 1846, the legislature made its first grant of £750 to the church for popular education. The desire for social control and character formation was still paramount among decision-makers. With the passage of the first Education Act in 1850, a formal structure was instituted, with an Education Committee assuming responsibility for education policy.[2] Significant development stemmed from the 1875 report of a local commission headed by Bishop Mitchinson. This commission demonstrated an awareness of the premises of, and a willingness to copy from, English practice.[3] The development of the English educational system is attributed principally to the philosophical basis of the Platonic ideal.[4] With its stress on *inherited* inequality and differing capacities for performing appropriate social functions, this philosophical source supported a stratified society and education for leadership.[5] In adapting the English system, the Barbadian system incorporated these theories, translating the inherent goals into a system designed to effect them. The Commission's recommendations for improvement in the educational system, therefore, clearly prescribed a system along class lines. While the labourer was to be the product of the elementary system, the potential thinkers, leaders and organisers were to be the middle- and upper-class beneficiaries of the secondary school system. These recommendations, which were embodied in the 1878 Act and its longstanding successor, the consolidating 1890 Act, set the tone for Barbadian education for the next century. The 1878 Act replaced the Education Committee by an executive Education Board, fixed the annual budget for education at £15,000 per year, and reconstructed the governing bodies of Harrison College and the Lodge School. These two schools were designed 'first grade' while provision was made for the establishment of 'second grade' or 'middle-class' schools, intermediate between primary and first grade.[6] By the twentieth century, when this analysis begins, the philosophy of the Swaby Commission made it explicit that the idea of popular education had been accepted as part of a system geared to producing leaders and followers and preserving the island's racial *status quo*. The distinction between elementary and secondary education was effectively made:

> *The purpose [elementary] is a school training which will end at a*
> *comparatively early age, and may produce the intelligent and industrious*
> *labourer, or form the groundwork on which may be built the technical skill*
> *required by the mechanic or artisan. The latter [secondary] is carried on to an*
> *age when manhood is approaching, and aims at fitting for their work the*
> *thinkers of the community, those who follow the learned professions, the*
> *leaders and organisers, or at least those who serve in the higher ranks of*
> *industry and commerce.*[7]

The nineteenth-century premise of the two systems so ably restated by the Swaby Commission allowed for perpetuation of the class bias. By 1909 provision for educating the bulk of the island's children was concentrated in 167 elementary schools. These schools recorded an enrolment of 26,963 in 1909 and a percentage attendance of 58.3 per cent.[8] Attendance at this level was curtailed by the persistence of child labour. There were still two categories of secondary school: first and second grade. Average attendance at first grade and second grade respectively was 307 and 302 pupils. As seen in Table 1, first-grade education was serviced by two male institutions, Harrison College and the Lodge, and by one female institution, Queen's College. One of the six second-grade schools catered exclusively to girls. The annual award of two island scholarships tenable at Codrington College and one at a British institution provided the rewards of competition for a university education. Significantly, only the first-grade boys' schools offered the curriculum for attaining entrance to this level.

Table 1. Secondary schools, by grade, 1909

First grade	Second grade
Harrison College	Combermere
Lodge School	Christ Church Foundation
Queens College*	Coleridge
	Parry
	Alleyne
	Alexandra*

*Girls' schools.

Since the government was providing the bulk of financing, educational provision was subject to the dictates of the prevailing philosophy of the decision-makers. Resources were, therefore, channelled into effecting the class-based aims of the Mitchinson Commission. Secondary education received less money overall than elementary, but more per head on fewer schools and pupils. Government expenditure on education in 1900 totalled £16,726 16s 1d. Of this sum, £11,000 was spent on 169 elementary schools with an average attendance of 13,695 each. The six second-grade schools with attendance averaging 228 received £1,091 13s 4d, while three first-grade schools with approximately 300 pupils in attendance received £2,435.[9]

Secondary education for all was not contemplated at the turn of the century. Each secondary school received a fixed grant from the government but additional revenue was generated from school fees. The imposition of fees, along with the distinctions outlined above, meant that race and class were determinants of access to secondary education, assured by their parents' ability to pay. Middle-class black children, whose parents could afford it or could make the necessary sacrifice to afford it, also benefited from secondary education.

A narrow scholarship ladder provided some access to higher-than-elementary education for those with parents in straitened circumstances. Dispensation of awards rested with the Education Board and the vestries, members of the same small group which controlled other facets of life in the colony. Highly competitive scholarships were dispensed by the board, while the vestry, with its overall charge of fostering educational opportunities for the poor, was supposed to cater more ostensibly to expressed need. The 1890 Act empowered the Board to award six exhibitions from primary to first grade of the value of £25 per year, one being awarded annually for a six-year period, with the conditions of competition to be set by the board.[10] In addition, there were 60 exhibitions of £5 per year, 20 to be awarded annually on the basis of an open, competitive examination to the second-grade schools.[11] Not more than £350 was to be spent annually for regular exhibitions at the first grade. Parents were not to be well off, and awards were to be made only to boys showing 'real merit'.[12] The vestries, meanwhile, were empowered to impose rates to raise money to support an unspecified number of exhibitions at the first and second grade for persons 'in straitened circumstances'. Various endowments supplied other exhibitions. Vestry nominees for vacancies in the first grade were to be examined according to the Board's requirements.[13] The Board then decided how to expand the ranks of the 'thinkers' by admitting the 'brightest pupils', while the vestry was limited to considering parental circumstances.

This outline reveals that potential mobility for groups other than the white elite was constrained by the available educational facilities as well as by the means of accessing them. Race and class were determining factors for access to education for both boys and girls, but gender was an added dimension for girls.

Facilities for secondary education for girls

From the nineteenth century there was an evident concern with the education of girls of the middle and upper class. The Mitchinson Report projected girls' education as an aid to boys' education, since it would provide personnel for 'maternal' teaching.[14] The report concluded that the inadequate provision for such female education necessitated government support for a good girls' school.[15] Queen's College was the first-grade institution catering to this group from 1881.[16]

At the beginning of the twentieth century, facilities for secondary education for boys outnumbered those for girls. Seven of the nine secondary schools were for boys, and two of the three first-grade schools catered to boys. The paucity of the provision for girls, even at the second-grade level, indicated that they were not intended to prepare for even the minimum outcome of secondary education envisaged by the Swaby Commission — serving in 'the higher ranks of industry and commerce'. The limited aims for the education of girls were borne out by the comments of the commission even when it seemed to be advancing the cause of girls. The commissioners made no apology for considering facilities for girls as they felt that the time was long past when elementary instruction and a few accomplishments were regarded as the apogee of education for females. However, like Mitchinson, they argued the value to the entire community of a sound education for the 'mothers of the next generation'. They recommended a second-grade school for girls in Bridgetown specially.[17] They also considered that a need existed in the Windward parishes for a provision similar to Alexandra. This recommendation was backed by the receipt of a 'numerously signed' petition from St John, St Philip and St Joseph urging establishment of such a school for those parishes and for parts of St George and Christ Church.[18]

Such action merely echoed earlier calls for justice for the female segment of the population. A 1903 proposal for a second-grade school for girls had originated with the St Philip vestry and was intended to serve St Philip and neighbouring parishes. The cost had been estimated at £350 per year and the vestry had decided to vote £60 per year towards the upkeep and to petition the Education Board for an annual grant of £100.[19] The Education Board and the vestries of Christ Church and St John cited the island's financial condition as a reason for their inability to support the venture. Like them, the St Philip vestry argued that it was constrained by financial conditions into rethinking the proposal[20] even in the face of a petition from parents and taxpayers who submitted that: 'aiding boys only is one-sided . . . and good education to a girl enables her in these days to be more likely in securing employment by which she can support herself and aid her family.'[21]

Yet the idea of improving access for girls was not lost, as the Swaby Commission's report showed, and both the vestries and the Education Board were still in sympathy with the idea of a second-grade school. At its meeting of 5 December 1910, the Education Board decided to ask the rector of St John's Parish to forward an outline scheme for a school for the Windward parishes, as recommended by Swaby. Meanwhile, the vestries of St John, St Joseph, St Philip and Christ Church would be circularised about their willingness to support such a school financially.[22] St Philip and St John were most willing to offer support.[23] After at least two properties were considered unsuitable for the site of the school, the Board promised to consider erecting a new building on a site near to the Lodge School, but by 1912 there was no further mention of official support for the cause.[24]

It was not until the 1920s that concession by the decision-makers to a demand for expanded middle-class and female education resulted in a limited expansion in the secondary system. Significantly, it was in the overtly middle-class provision, the second grade, which now boasted eight schools, by the recognition of Foundation School as second grade and by the construction of the St Michael's Girls' School. As seen in Table 2, the balance of provision still favoured the males. There were still two male institutions and one female institution at first grade but five male and three female institutions at second grade.

Table 2. Secondary schools, by grade, 1930

First grade	Second grade
Harrison College	Combermere
Lodge School	ChristChurch Foundation
Queens College*	Coleridge
	Parry
	Alleyne
	Alexandra*
	St Michael's Girls*
	ChristChurch Foundation Girls*

*Girls' schools.

The Christ Church Foundation schools had been founded as a charity for white children in the eighteenth century, and were supported by income from land left by Captain Francis Williams. The trustees were the rector and the two members of the House of Assembly for the parish. In 1905 boys and girls were being taught in one building, which catered to white and coloured pupils of two types: foundation pupils and paying day pupils. Children from the parish were awarded vestry and board exhibitions to attend Combermere School because, as the Director of Education, Howard Hayden noted, 'complexional distinction' prevented them for attending Foundation School. To counter this and bring the school into the educational system as a second grade school, an Act was passed in 1906 to amend the 1894 Act relating to these schools. Apparently the girls' school had been left out of this Act and was therefore not eligible for a government grant.[25] In 1927 the trustees petitioned the Education Board for recognition of the school as second grade and recommended an annual grant of £300.[26] In April 1928 the school was recognised as second-grade.[27] Exhibitions to Queens College were subsequently discontinued as provided by law.[28]

While the Christ Church Foundation School represented the conversion of an existing institution, the St Michael's Girls' School was born of the efforts of members of the St Michael vestry. The progressive character of this urban vestry may be partly attributed to the presence of black middle-class businessmen — as contrasted with the conservative planter interests of rural vestries. These middle-class blacks pushed class interests in an attempt to secure improved opportunities not only for their sons but also for their daughters. One such vestryman, Washington Harper, was a major force in the developing thrust for attention to female education. He criticised the existing system as selfishly educating boys and not girls, and vowed to keep reminding Barbadians of the necessity for affording women of all classes a fairer education.[29] Until the second-grade school was established, he fought consistently for exhibitions to Queens College.[30]

In constructing the school, the St Michael vestry was obviously responding to an expressed need. Vestryman Alonza Bullen received unanimous support for a resolution drawing on the 'great demand of the public for secondary education for their daughters' and calling for a public meeting to discuss the establishment of a second-grade school for girls.[31] That meeting secured resolutions favouring the establishment of the school.[32] Further signs of support were indicated when the Governor, in the Executive Committee, expressed a willingness to consider any application for assistance with such a scheme if there were evidence of a substantial measure of support from sources other than the government, since there was no known precedent for the government undertaking the entire cost of establishing a first- or second-grade school. The matter was referred to a committee appointed to consider the question of the establishment of a second-grade school for girls.[33] The committee held several meetings, appointed subcommittees to deal with the site and finance, and within three months was ready to report. Weymouth had been selected as a site, contractors' estimates for building and estimates for land had been prepared and it was recommended that the vestry seek the legislature's approval to raise a loan not exceeding £10,000 for erecting the school.

The political significance of the school was often raised by some members of the vestry. In moving the adoption of the report, Alonzo Bullen felt it necessary to record that the question of a second-grade girl's school had been raised at the hustings and he was sure that the scheme had found total favour.[34] Later in the year, C.A. Brathwaite was anxious to resolve the issue of a site since he did not want it said that the vestry of 1924 was not capable of looking after the people's wants.[35] Eventually the vestry was authorised to raise a loan under the St Michael's Girls' School Act 1924,[36] and to purchase a site for the school.[37] The school was formally opened at the Grassfield site on 7 May 1928 by Governor Robertson.[38] Washington Harper did not live to see this part of his dream materialise, as he died in 1925. Although Alonzo Bullen also died before the opening, his commitment to the school survived him. While the vestry was considering how best to provide exhibitions at the new school, it received a bequest from H.A. Bullen's estate of $2 per month for a scholarship.[39]

The conflict over curriculum at this school epitomised the continuing struggle over what properly constituted the fare for various classes. Debate surfaced in 1927 before the official opening of the school and resurfaced in 1938 during discussion of funding for increased accommodation. Recollections of the 1938 dispute over the school's syllabus revealed that the ideas of most of the board and of members of the Legislative Council apparently did not coincide with those of the Assembly.[40] The curriculum proposed by the Education Board in 1926 included domestic science and needlework.[41] While the scheme passed the Legislative Council with little comment, there was a protracted debate in the Assembly. Middle-class members of the Assembly objected strongly to topics such as laundry and housework, and support for these came from the planter-merchant elite like Dr W.B.H. Massiah, S.C. Thorne and Sir Harold Austin. Debate centred on the inclusion of Latin rather than domestic economy. H.W. Reece, who introduced the scheme, was very caustic in his remarks, suggesting the inclusion of Latin and the exclusion of those subjects intended to prepare girls to be female servants or clerks. What all agreed on was the perception of the new school as intermediate between the elementary level and Queen's College, and as fulfilling a role similar to that of Combermere for boys. Concern was expressed about the ability of the curriculum to meet the needs of the girls who would attend the school. But those advocating Latin and those in favour of domestic economy expressed a desire to provide for future mothers and wives of middle-class men. The Assembly finally agreed to the retention of domestic economy and the deletion of laundry and similar words, as all were agreed on the practical value of exposure to these subjects. What was apparent in the debate was the strong desire of some members to restrict the numbers to be exposed to education of the type offered at Queens College.[42]

The need for the St Michael second-grade facility was borne out by the rapid increase in its enrolment from 169 in 1937 to 245 in 1938, necessitating an enlargement to the school.[43] The £2,000 proposed for increased accommodation for the school was the subject of spirited exchanges in the legislative session of 1938 during the lengthy debate on the Education Loan (Amendment) Bill, which had resulted from a comprehensive building scheme put forward by the Education Board for schools of various grades. The debate is interesting as a comment on attitudes to female education, but is also important for the purposes of extrapolation to the general education scene and establishing the continuity in policy throughout the period.

J.D. Chandler of the Legislative Council voiced opinions which were obviously supported by members of that chamber. While not denying the government's right to provide all with the opportunity for a 'reasonable' education (3 Rs), he noted that Barbados had gone beyond this to secondary provision. He questioned the utility of St Michael's Girls' school to its products and the community if it extended to girls from the 'middle walks of life' an education of the higher plane offered by Queens College. To reactionary members of the Legislative Council, like S.C. Thorne and J.D. Chandler, the 'future prospects' raised by the Swaby Commission were to be narrowly prescribed for pupils of a second-grade school, especially girls. Girls from the 'middle walks of life' required not so much book learning as exposure to subjects of domestic economy, such as laundering, which would enable them to fill positions in the community. Since, in their opinion, the school was not producing brighter nurses or graduates trained in domestic economy, these legislators did not share the enthusiasm of the St Michael vestry for it.[44]

What is disturbing here is that the argument carried a mere hint of labour force concerns, but was more firmly rooted in a perception of a station in life. The board's ideals were questioned and it was suggested that if the ideal were the extension of this type of education to all primary pupils, then this would be a disservice to the community and surely a move to 'over-educate a child beyond its standard of life'. Chandler was quick to note his support for education, but this was closely defined when he declared himself 'in favour of educating each class to the extent that will be of use to them in after life'.

Chandler received support from Dr Hutson and S.C. Thorne. The latter criticised the 'general run of education' as 'unfitting the people for their proper life'. His conclusions are best stated in his own words: 'We are taking people who are practically contented and when through educating them they are no use to God or man. They are certainly no use to themselves; they merely become discontented and there must be something wrong with a system of education that does that.'[45]

The old guard, bent on avoiding education for discontent, had retreated into the safety of traditional assumptions about education's role in maintaining the social order. The discussion indicated the prejudices, particularly of class and gender, to be faced in sponsoring increased opportunity at this level.

Although second-grade provision had increased by the end of the period, the record of achievement in girls' education was not laudable and suggested the need for positive discrimination. The new Director made the point:

> *While provision is made, as on April 1st 1945, for the secondary education of 1,543 boys, similar provision is only made for 878 girls; there are 651 boys in 1st Grade schools and 316 girls. It would appear that, should any further secondary school accommodation be envisaged, the question of girls' education should receive some priority of attention.*[46]

Awards

Given the existing fee barrier and the reluctance to increase facilities, awards remained a significant avenue for those in straitened circumstances desiring access to secondary education. Girls remained at a disadvantage in this respect as compared with boys throughout the period.

Table 3 details the scholarships available for secondary education in 1937. Statistics on the percentage of exhibitioners in school enrolment indicate that just over a quarter of school enrolment was catered to by exhibitions. Of 1,403 secondary-school pupils on roll in 1937, 408 held

Table 3. Exhibitions provided at secondary schools during 1937

School	Roll	Board	Vestry	Foundation	Endowment	Total
Harrison College	270	40	10	9	39	98
Lodge School	146	0	13	11	4	28
Queens College	172	0	8	2	3	13
Combermere	301	47	33	2	5	87
Foundation Boys	84	3	19	12	0	34
Coleridge	38	3	22	0	0	25
Parry	34	5	15	0	2	22
Alleyne	31	1	6	5	5	17
St Michael's Girls	178	0	27	0	4	31
Alexandra	93	0	39	0	0	39
Foundation Girls	56	0	5	8	0	13
Total	1,403	99	198	49	62	407

Source: Report of the Education Department, 1937

exhibitions. It is noticeable that vestry awards outstripped those from other sources. As was evident at the turn of the century, girls were heavily dependent on vestry awards, since there were no government exhibitions for them. In terms of numbers benefitting, the leading second-grade, Combermere, was close behind Harrison College. Both these male institutions enjoyed more awards than the sole first-grade girls' school.

Nevertheless, the presence of progressive forces supporting improved provision for girls must be acknowledged. The St Michael vestry was in the forefront of such movements. In 1917, Washington Harper introduced a motion for at least 10 scholarships tenable at Queen's College, contending that 'the girls of the parish are in fact and in right equally entitled to due consideration in matters educational.'[47] He also took care to remind his colleagues of the weighty support of ratepayers for such a move. The vestry lent its support: with a slight amendment restricting scholarships to Queens College, the motion was passed by eight votes to two.[48]

Although the vestry had now agreed in principle to the award of ten scholarships to Queen's College,[49] there was still some opposition from a merchant, Joshua Baeza. Such opposition was not uncharacteristic of him, based as it was, on the grounds that the country was already spending too much on education and religion.[50] He was dedicated to achieving economy in parochial administration: in 1916, he had reminded his colleagues that the vestry had been elected on a platform of reform and economy, to be interpreted as substantial economy.[51] F.N.A. Chairmonte reminded him of the vestry's commitment in principle and conceded that since they were not providing the manifest need, a second-grade school for girls, they could do no better than award the scholarships. It was agreed to make them competitive, with the same age limits as for Harrison College. Baeza was the lone objector.[52] The Education Board pledged its support for the vestry's action[53] and by 1920 Harper saw his efforts rewarded by the arrival of a letter from the Education board informing the vestry of the ten exhibitions awarded on an order of merit.[54] This new development was so well received that the Churchwarden found it possible in 1923 to successfully pilot a motion for an additional 10 scholarships to Queens College.[55] The St Michael vestry was once more responding to an expressed need.

Continued emphasis on second-grade education for girls was demonstrated in the vestry's decision not to maintain more than three exhibitions at Queens College and to transfer money from vacancies arising to increase exhibitions at the St Michael's Girls' School. This application of funds was intended to increase opportunity for girls of exceptional ability who might otherwise have to leave school if their parents were unable to pay the fees for the higher forms.[56] The St Michael vestry continued to show its progressive character in acceding to the request of the governing body of St Michael's Girls School for permission to grant 10 enabling scholarships at $2 each instead of five at $4 each as then obtained. The move resulted in the governing body's successful application to the Executive Committee for an increased grant, which enabled school fees to be reduced.[57] This reduction in turn promoted access, as it resulted in a considerable increase in numbers.[58]

Not all vestries were as progressive as the St Michael vestry. The St John vestry raised the issue of exhibitions for girls early in 1941, but because of delays posed by checking the procedure used by other vestries, setting up a committee to consider the proposal by checking the legality of such an action,[59] nothing was achieved until 1943.[60] The obvious need was indicated by the response to the first vacancies: 12 applicants for the 3 vacancies, of whom 7 reached exhibition standard. The St Thomas vestry seemed unaware, until informed by the Education Board in 1932, that an exhibition for girls could be maintained legally at Queen's College.[61] In the St Philip vestry, D.S. Payne rediscovered in 1938, what petitioners had said in 1904, namely, that the time had arrived when girls as well as boys should be considered for help in obtaining better posts in the future.[62] For the first time in 1941, awards were made to second-grade, to five boys and three girls.[63]

Ameliorative action was not left to the vestries alone. The Barbados Elementary Schoolteachers' Association (BESTA) also lobbied for attention to girls' awards. In 1939, its call for increased scholarships included a plea for all awards to be opened to girls. The board responded with summary statistics on available awards and a promise of action. The statistics confirmed the picture of discrimination against girls: of 408 scholarships, boys held 312 and girls 96; 127 of the boys and 71 of the girls were vestry scholars. In addition, St Michael's Girls' School was now benefiting from an additional 30 scholarships established in the previous year. The board, however, conceded that it awarded no scholarships directly to girls and promised to recommend that its scholarships be opened to girls.[64] Two years later, BESTA was issuing a reminder to the board, and by the end of the period under review, action was still pending on the amendment of the Act necessary to allow girls to compete for awards tenable at first-grade schools.[65]

General Considerations

In Barbados the shortcomings of educational provision for girls should be examined against the background of a persistent excess of females over males in the total island population (see Table 4). As in Trinidad, the balance of educational provision in favour of males may be partly explained by perceptions of the relative value to the society of educating the two groups.[66] The attitude towards the education of girls must also be viewed as part of existing attitudes to women in general and their participation in society. As a regional problem, the low status of women was discussed at length in the Moyne Commission Report. Among the indicators of the status of women were the absence of the right to vote, limited participation in administration and a lower rate of wages than men.[67] This last discrepancy was in stark contrast to the reality that 'the woman so often is the supporter of the home'.[68] At the turn of the century, female Barbadian teachers received three-quarters of the salary of males, with the justification that men married and had families to support.[69] On the other hand, married women were 'not to be regarded as suitable persons to be teachers'; the Education board considered the wife's proper place to be her home.[70]

Table 4. Excess of females, 1921 (%)

| Age last birthday | No. of persons | % of total | | Excess of females (%) |
		Males	Females	
<15	53,843	49.4	50.6	1.2
15–19	17,909	45.2	54.8	9.6
20–24	14,757	34.8	65.2	30.4
25–29	10,168	31.9	68.1	36.2
30–39	16,944	27.7	72.8	44.6
40–49	16,617	34.2	65.8	31.6
50–59	12,786	37.8	62.2	24.4
60–69	8,839	37.4	62.6	25.2
70–79	3,774			
80–89	976			
90–99	115	31.2	68.8	27.6
100+	16			
Not stated	9			

Source: Report on the Census, 1921, Tables VII and IX.

Much of the urging for female involvement at higher levels of education originated in the Colonial Office or Commissions of Enquiry. The Swaby Commission had recommended that women serve on the board of the proposed second-grade girls' school.[71] The Marriott-Mayhew Commission of 1933 commented generally on the lack of women with educational authority and strongly recommended the appointment of women to every board of Education in the islands visited.[72]

While watchful of its international image, Britain was able to influence a decision involving two areas of intransigence for Barbados: race and gender. In response to an invitation from the Carnegie Corporation,[73] the Education board selected delegates to a course to be held at Yale University in the summer of 1934.[74] A subsequent emergency session changed the proposed presentation.[75] The shift in fact reflected Colonial Office concerns for 'coloured' and female representation. These concerns were communicated in confidential correspondence to Governor Young.[76] The president of the Education Board, H.B.G. Austin was not made aware of the imperial feelings on the matter until March, after initial selection had been made.[77] At his instigation, the board reconsidered its decision and Governor Young was able to inform H. Beckett that one 'coloured', C.T. Phillips, was among the first three representatives and another, L.T. Gay, was first of the reserves. The official reply signed by Beckett advised of the desire to increase the small proportion of female nominees and suggested that Miss L. Brown replace either Carter or Phillips. Further, if Carter was white, Phillips should be sent.[78] This obviously complicated matters and necessitated an emergency meeting at which the Board's decision allowed the Secretary of State's wishes to prevail.[79] Mayhew recorded 2 women and 6 blacks among the 20 delegates for education from the British West Indies.[80]

This is not to create the impression that women did nothing to improve the lot of their gender. The official record reveals some instances of female protest. Three examples over the period will suffice. In 1921 a female assistant teacher appealed to the Board for a salary increase on the grounds of her length of service. The Board rejected her application on the basis of inadequate funds, the fact that the regulations would not permit it and the customary rationalisation that male responsibility required that they be paid more.[81] In 1943 Miss C. Johnson's application to remain in the service after her pending marriage was granted because of the exceptional circumstances of the expected difficulty of replacing her.[82] The Women's Welfare League petitioned the board for representation of women on the Education board and other bodies concerned with education of women.[83] Although appointment to the Education Board met with considerable resistance from the island's decision-makers, the board admitted that its suggested amendment to the Education Act, to allow women to sit on the Queens College governing body was a response to this petition.[84] The first woman to act on the Education Board was Lucy Brown, Headmistress of the St Michael's Girls' School.[85] Although many of these efforts by women were unsuccessful, their existence and informal conversations suggest some possibilities for further research through oral history to gain information on the possible role of women who might have been involved behind the scenes in action to improve access for girls.

The apparent dominance of men's names in the story of the struggle to remove some of the deficiencies in provision for girls is understandable.

As Margot Badran remarks in her discussion of feminism in Egypt, 'the pivot of women's oppression is understood to be patriarchal hegemony which contains and restrains women'.[86] In the Barbadian context, the social and political realities conferred superior political power to males and especially males from the upper and middle classes. Women were not given the franchise until 1943. Therefore on issues which needed to be fought in the political arena, men were enabled to appear as facilitators, since the rising black middle-class politicians like Washington Harper in the 1920s and those who came to prominence in the 1930s, accessed the locus of power before females did.

Male perceptions of female behaviour also need to be scrutinised. For example, C.F. Broomes of BESTA, speaking before the Moyne Commission offered this rationalisation of the absence of women from the deputation 'The women in Barbados are very slow to speak in public. They are very slow to take on public offices'.

This statement was made against the background of an admitted majority of women among the membership of BESTA. However, Broomes evaded the question whether women had been invited to participate in the delegation.[87] Contact with many female teachers of that time reveals them as forceful and articulate. These considerations lead one to question the validity of Broomes' assessment and suggest that, as elsewhere in education, women were deliberately denied the opportunity to attain leadership positions. Instances such as this indicate that the testimony of women is needed to make more perceptible the constraints imposed by gender.

Endnotes

1. Report on the Census 1911, p. 24.
2. J.E. Reece *et al.*, 'The System of Education in Barbados', Great BritainBboard of Education, *Special Reports on Educational Subjects*, Vol. 12 (London: Dawson, 1968), pp. 44—45.
3. Report of the Education Commission, 1875 (hereafter Mitchinson Report). See for example Preface, p. 7.
4. This position is adopted by several writers who discuss the Platonic/Aristotelian models in the Western European context. See for example, Brian Holmes, *Problems in Education: A Comparative Approach* (London: Routledge, 1965) p. 223; Vernon Mallinson, *The Western European Idea in Education* (1980; Oxford: Pergamon, 1981), p. 16.
5. Holmes, *Comparative Education: Some Considerations of Method* (London: Allen, 1981), p. 124. See his discussion of Plato's 'just' society, pp. 135—39.
6. Reece, 'The System of Education', p. 45.
7. Report of the Education Commission 1907—09 (hereafter Swaby Report), p. 2.
8. Report of the Elementary Schools, 1909.
9. Report of the Education Board, 1900.

10. Sec. 21. The version of the Act used here is that as amended by the Act of 1897 and included in Reece, 'The System of Education', Appx. B.
11. Sec. 32, of the Education Act.
12. Sec. 39 of the Education Act.
13. Secs. 33, 43, 49 of the Education Act.
14. Mitchinson Report, p. 15.
15. *Ibid.*, p. 26.
16. Reece, 'The System of Education', p. 57.
17. Swaby Report, pp. 17—18.
18. *Ibid.*, p. 21.
19. Figures were stated in a letter from St Philip vestry to Christ Church Vestry, Christ Church Vestry Minutes [CCVM], 23 November 1903.
20. Some members revealed that they were having second thoughts about being able to raise the money. St Philip Vestry Minutes [SPHVM], 17 February 1904.
21. SPHVM, 6 April 1904.
22. Minutes of the Education Board, 5 December 1910.
23. Education Board, 1 May 1911.
24. Education Board, 22 May, 21 August 1911.
25. For a fuller account of the foundation schools see Howard Hayden's statement to the Christ Church vestry on which this outline is based. CCVM, 22 November 1945. Hayden had been specially invited by the vestry to discuss the proposal to repeal the Act of 1906 , in order to include the Foundation Schools in the new Schemes prepared for secondary schools.
26. Education Board, 28 November 1927.
27. The Chairman reported that he had been informed of this by the Education board CCVM, 4 April 1928.
28. CCVM, 10 December 1928. Subsection 2 of Section 34 of the Education Act provided for parochial exhibitions to be maintained at Queens College until a second grade for girls was established in connection with a parish.
29. St Michael vestry Minutes [SMVM], 22 February 1917.
30. See discussion on pp. 17—18 of this article.
31. SMVM, 27 September 1923.
32. SMVM, 21 January 1924.
33. SMVM, 21 January 1924.
34. SMVM, 1 April 1924.
35. SMVM, 6 November 1924.
36. The vestry advertised for the full loan of £10,000. SMVM, 19 January. 1925.
37. SMVM, 13 November 1924. Grassfield was the site chosen in preference to Weymouth. SMVM, 19 November 1924.
38. SMVM, 1928—29. The initial page records the opening at 10.30 a.m., noting that Bishop Bentley blessed the building 'just as the clock struck 11 o'clock'.
39. SMVM, 23 February 1928. Bullen had been a churchwarden of the St Michael vestry. His will stipulated that the money was to be used for no other purpose than the scholarship. The first award was made on 24 October 1929.
40. The Assembly had rejected domestic science in favour of Latin, as far as Thorne recalled.
41. Education Board, 5 July 1926.
42. *House Debates*, 4 October 1927.
43. Education Board, 23 January 1939.

44. *Legislative Council Debates* 16 August 1938.
45. *Legislative Council Debates* 16 August 1938.
46. Howard Hayden, *The Provision for Secondary Education in Barbados*, (Bridgetown, 1945) p. 5.
47. He actually gave notice of the motion at the meeting of 22 February, but the motion was dealt with on 8 March 1917.
48. SMVM, 8 March 1917.
49. The resolution had asked for the vestry to seek an amendment to the Education Act.
50. SMVM, 13 September 1917.
51. SMVM, 25 March 1916.
52. SMVM, 13 September 1917.
53. By letter of 12 October 1917, SMVM, 1 November 1917. See also SMVM 13 December 1917 promising support for the private bill necessary to carry into effect the vestry resolution.
54. SMVM, 25 November 1920.
55. 8 February 1923.
56. SMVM, 13 July 1932; 21 September 1933.
57. SMVM, 3 May 1937.
58. *Legislative Council Debates*, 16 August 1938.
59. St John Vestry Minutes [SJVM], 13 January, 26 March, 15 April 1941; 20 April, 1 July, 20 July 1942; 19 April 1943.
60. SJVM, 22 September 1943.
61. The Secretary of the Board referred to them in subsection 2 of Sec. 34 of the Act. St Thomas Vestry Minutes [STVM], 19 September 1932.
62. SPHVM, 6 April 1904; 15 September 1938.
63. SPHVM, 17 July 1941.
64. Education Board, 17 April, 15 May 1939.
65. Education Board, 20 January, 17 May 1943.
66. See, for example, Joyce Cole, *Official Ideology and the Education of Women in the English-speaking Caribbean, 1834—1945*, with special reference to Barbados, in J. Massiah (ed.), *Women and Education*, (ISER, University of the West Indies, 1982), p. 3, and Carl Campbell, 'Good Wives and Mothers: A Preliminary Survey of Women and Education in Trinidad, 1834—1981', Social History Workshop, November 1985, Women and Society, Seminar, No. 2 (Department of History, UWI, Mona), p. 1.
67. Great Britain, Colonial Office, *Report of the West India Royal Commission* (hereafter Moyne) (London, HMSO, 1945), pp. 217—20.
68. Moyne, p. 220.
69. Rules and Regulations for Public Elementary Schools, 1898, Rule 21.
70. Rules and Regulations, Rule 1c.
71. Swaby Report, p. 18.
72. *Report of a Commission appointed to consider problems of secondary and primary education in Trinidad, Barbados, the Leeward and Windward Islands. Proposals of the Commission relating to Barbados* (London, HMSO, 1933), p. 109.
73. Education Board, 15 January 1934.
74. The selection was the subject of much discussion and voting. Education Board, 19 February 1934.
75. Education Board, 9 April 1934.

76. Confidential correspondence, Beckett to Young, of 14 December 1933 and Beckett to Young, of 23 March 1934 in reply to Telegram No. 31, Young to Beckett of 13 March 1934; Confidential correspondence about selection of candidates for Yale Education Course, GH /4/62 BDA.
77. See his letter of 9 March 1934 thanking the Governor for showing him the confidential letter, GH/4/62 BDA.
78. No. 30081/34 of 23 March 1934 in reply to Telegram No. 31 of 13 March 1934, GH /4/62 BDA.
79. Fortuitously, theBboard was already present in their capacity as members of the Governing Body of Queens College and Combermere, Education Board, 9 April 1934.
80. In his notes on the Yale seminar, CO 318/414/15.
81. Education Board, 10 June 1921.
82. Education Board, 21 June 1943.
83. Education Board, 14 March 1927.
84. Education Board, 10 August 1925; 21 September 1925.
85. *Barbados Teachers Quarterly Magazine*, 1, 1 (1932), p. 12.
86. Margot Badran, 'The Origins of Feminism in Egypt', in Arina Angerman *et al.* (eds), *Current Issues in Women's History* (London: Routledge, 1989), p. 156.
87. *West Indies Royal Commission. Proceedings of Investigations in Barbados* (Bridgetown: Advocate, 1939), Eleventh Day. Evidence in the booklet was reproduced from the newspaper the Barbados Advocate.

SECTION 5

Women, Protest
and
Political Movement

15.

'Females of Abandoned Character?'

Women and Protest in Jamaica, 1838—65*

Swithin Wilmot

Woodville Marshall's illuminating study of post-slavery protest emphasised the importance of viewing the ex-slaves as 'historical agents, with clear perceptions of their world and striving to preserve or re-shape it.' This approach has been developed in other studies of protest in the post-slavery period in Dominica, Tobago and Trinidad. They underline the involvement of women in street demonstrations and labour protests.[1] This article expands the area of discussion to Jamaica, where women featured in various protests between 1838 and 1865, the period between full emancipation and the Morant Bay rebellion. None of these protests were exclusive to women, but it is hoped that this focus on them will deepen the understanding of the role of women in Jamaican history as they struggled as part of a disadvantaged people in a society emerging from slavery.[2]

Plantation strikes

The withdrawal of women from regular field labour was one of the first issues to sour labour relations in Jamaica in the first months after full freedom. Raymond Smith has suggested that this development, which was also common in other post-slavery societies in the Americas, could either have represented the freedmen's assertion of patriarchal control over women, or could have reflected the freedwomen's own interest in domesticity.[3] In the case of Jamaica, the freed people were certainly exhorted by the missionaries to pursue a 'proper gender order in which men worked for money and women stayed at home', thereby establishing a 'new marital economy modelled on that of the English middle class'.[4] However, very few of the women could afford the luxury of retreating to the home sphere. Instead, their focus on activities beyond the confines of labouring on the plantations formed an important part of various strategies that freed people developed to provide for their families. Thus, whenever possible, the women established autonomy of work from the plantations and focused more effort on the cultivation and marketing of provisions. As later happened in the American South and in Cuba, the freed women in Jamaica organised their labour as part of a broader strategy to maximise earnings, thereby contributing to the needs of the family economy.[5] Indeed, this focus reflected the concern for the reconstruction and consolidation of the black family which female apprentices had demonstrated before 1838 when they were the chief ones pursuing manumission.[6]

However, this drive for greater autonomy among the freed women presented serious problems for their former masters and potential employers who were determined to continue the command over labour that slavery had guaranteed them. The planters were abundantly aware that 'by the eve of emancipation, not only were the majority of Jamaican black women labourers in the field, but the majority of Jamaican labourers in the field were black women'.[7] Therefore, confronted by the women's determination not to be tied down to the rigid demands of regular work on the plantations, the planters, in the first three months of full freedom, initiated a series of labour recruitment strategies, many of which were aimed at coercing women to perform estate work, especially during crop time.

This struggle between the planters and the freed women is underlined by the data available for the Plantain Garden River District in coastal St Thomas-in-the-East, one of the most fertile areas of the island, where the sugar industry dominated in the immediate post-slavery period.[8] Golden Grove was one of the largest sugar estates in this area of Jamaica. On the property resided 279 effective agricultural workers, of which 137 were women. Up to 12 October 1838, only 19 of the women had resumed work on the estate whereas only 5 of the 142 men had withdrawn their services. While the men had responded to attractive offers for job work, most of the women had 'declared they are not again to work in the field', that is, the canefield, as they were busy in the provision grounds which belonged to the estate. As the crop time in December 1838 approached, the attorney, Thomas McCornock, who was also the Custos for the parish, imposed new rents per head for the cottages and the provision grounds, which were aimed at redirecting the women's labour to the estate. Moreover, he gave notice that the customary access to the provision grounds would cease on 31 December 1839, unless the estate specifically agreed to allotments. Clearly, he was reclaiming land which had provided the women with sustenance and which enabled them to refuse to perform estate labour. And, as if to emphasise his intentions, he promised that 'none will be ejected who work well and behave properly.'[9]

Moreover, within a week of the imposition of the new rents, McCornock adopted other methods to compel the women to work. He insisted that three hogsheads of sugar had to be made each day during the crop, a target which could only be attained if the women worked for five days in the week. When this level of production was not met, he suspended operations on the estate and during this period the rents for the cottages and the grounds were doubled. Finally, he warned his labourers/tenants that 'although many have behaved very ill, I do not wish to eject one from the estate, but all must either do the work required of them or leave immediately.'[10]

Although these bullying tactics were adopted in November and December 1838, regular labour did not commence until late January 1839, when McCornock offered more conciliatory terms which the women agreed to accept. He exempted mothers of 'young children' and women with large families from field work though they still had to meet the rents for the provision grounds. Clearly, McCornock had been forced to recognise the women's determination to devote more of their time to their homes and children. Other women were informed that they 'must work or there will only remain the painful alternative of ejecting them as their houses . . . must be given to others, who must be employed to take off the crop'.[11] In this instance, some of the women at Golden Grove had successfully insisted on more flexible terms for their continued access to the provision grounds and residence in the estate cottages, while others had to submit to more regular labour on the estate if they wanted to keep their cottages.

Similarly in the parish of Hanover, the issue of compulsory work for women strained labour relations. Like McCornock, planters in the parish had initially manipulated rents to coerce work from 'married women' who had chosen to devote more attention to their family instead of estate work. The labourers refused such terms and in some cases struck. Labour relations only improved in the parish after workers and employers negotiated contracts which stipulated, among other things, that 'married women' were 'not required to labour unless they are so disposed to labour'.[12]

Both St Thomas in-the-East and Hanover were parishes which had profitable provision grounds and this enabled the women to exercise some degree of autonomy from the plantation. Trelawny, another important sugar parish, did not have good provision grounds and the majority of women would have had no permanent alternative to plantation labour in the first year of freedom.[13] Nevertheless, they still exercised their options to choose between employers who offered more attractive wages and general working conditions. For instance, Green Park sugar estate, 3 miles south of Falmouth, had attached to it 404 freed people, of which 204 were women. While the data do not specify how many of these women were effective agricultural workers, it is clear that the vast majority of workers who resided on Green Park had refused to labour there because of the comparatively inferior wages offered in 1838. Even when the attorney increased his offer to match those of his neighbours, the ex-slaves refused to work there because the attorney insisted on using the old slave practice of shell-blowing and sending drivers to the fields. Thus, up to October 1838, only 35 of the 404 former apprentices worked on Green Park. Tilston was another large sugar property in Trelawny. In the three months after full freedom only 40 of the 800 acres in sugar and pastures had been cleaned. Tilston had 356 resident agricultural workers, of which 206 were women. But, only 26 of the total labour force had regularly worked on the estate during that period. Significantly, even before the end of the Apprenticeship, the workers had made it abundantly clear that they would not labour under the direction of the overseer and faithful to their warnings, they sought employment on other properties.[14] Thus, the women workers on Green Park and Tilston, who never had the option of withdrawing from plantation labour, certainly exercised the newly acquired freedom of movement to offer their labour to employers who were discerning enough not to insist on managers and methods which affronted the ex-slaves' dignity and status as free labourers.

In the parish of St George, in the mountainous coffee districts, the conflicts over rent and wages in the immediate post-emancipation period eventually led to violent confrontations. As the disputes simmered, some of the former slave owners attempted to coerce labour by resorting to well-established practices of assaulting the workers. For example, on the Mahoe coffee property, where 15 men and 11 women comprised the workforce, Henry Mason, the proprietor, 'cursed and abused' his workers and 'ordered them out of his yard' when they protested to him about his rent exactions.[15] Eveline Williams was one of the Mahoe workers. She refused to accept Mason's terms, even after some of her colleagues either finally agreed or offered their labour elsewhere. Confronted by Williams' determined objections to the deductions from her wages for rents, Mason resorted to physical force to discipline her and beat her with a staff until it broke.[16] Other women also had to bear the burden of the rent demands in St George. Elizabeth, the wife of William Jenkins, an aged cripple, managed to support herself and her husband from the provision lands belonging to Orange Vale, another coffee property. She was an elderly woman and 'afflicted with pain' but was confronted by demands for rent when she refused to offer her labour to that property.[17] Sally Mead, a resident worker on Lovely Grove, another coffee property, shared a cottage with her daughter, Theresa, and her young son, John Louis. She and her children also worked a provision ground on the property. That they were faced with three separate rental charges for the same house and ground was typical of the coercion applied in the parish. Seraphine, the common-law wife of another worker on Lovely Grove, was also assessed for rent of the house and ground she shared with her partner. He complained ironically that 'free is no good to we, if we must pay all we work for' in rent.[18] Moreover, the oppressive rent exactions were also applied to other women who combined work as domestics with the cultivation of provisions. For example, there was Madeline, a 'washerwoman', who worked for Dr Rapkey, the proprietor of Lovely Grove. She resided in one cottage with her common-law husband and her four children, three daughters and a son. Two of her daughters, Nano and Tonson, were sufficiently mature to work their own provision grounds, though they shared the same residence with their mother. Thus it was not unreasonable to charge them separate rent for the three provision grounds. However, it was patently unjust to impose six individual rentals for the one cottage.[19]

These sorts of rent exactions explain the protracted labour unrest in St George and led to the violent confrontation on the Spring Hill coffee plantation in July 1839. The workers on Spring Hill became increasingly antagonistic to the whole issue of rent once it was apparent that the proprietor only manipulated it to punish residents who either dared to work elsewhere for more attractive wages or relied primarily on their provision grounds to eke out a livelihood, for instance, in the case of the women and children who were charged separate rents for residing in the cottages.[20] The owner eventually appealed to the stipendiary magistrate to intervene in the dispute. But the residents on Spring Hill were resolute and refused to pay the rents demanded, even after the stipendiary magistrate had managed to get the owner to scale down his initial demands.[21] Faced by this determined resistance to rent and the stipendiary magistrates' inability to effect some compromise, the proprietor took the issue to the courts. However, this only antagonised the Spring Hill people since the lower courts, which met in the parish capital at Buff Bay, were notorious for the exclusion of black artisans from the juries in preference to whites, who were as often drunk as they were sober.[22] Therefore, when the courts upheld the claims for rents against the Spring Hill residents, they violently resisted the parish constables who tried to levy on their goods. On the second attempt, the stipendiary magistrates accompanied the constables, but they were violently resisted. As the Governor reported, 'the magistrates were not only received with violent language, but were pelted with stones by some of the most turbulent of the party, amongst whom . . . the women were the most conspicuous.'[23] The levies could only be effected and the leaders of the protest arrested when the military was sent to Spring Hill to support the local civil authorities. Among those arrested was a woman who had hit the stipendiary magistrate with a stone.[24]

Popular protests

Furthermore, in the immediate post-slavery period, issues that affected the broader community of labourers also attracted very impressive female responses. Twice in August 1838, men and women workers in Trelawny threatened violent retribution when they believed that the planters planned to kill the Baptist ministers who had tried to negotiate wages and general working conditions for their congregations. The first threat of a confrontation took place on 4 August 1838, when a rumour spread that William Knibb was to be hanged in effigy in front of his chapel in Falmouth. His followers mistakenly believed that a real hanging was to take place and they assembled with 'cutlasses' and 'sticks' to defend Knibb. They dispersed only after Knibb assured them that his life was not in danger.[25] Two weeks later, on 19 August, the situation again became volatile when Thomas Ward, Knibb's assistant, fell from his horse on his way to Sunday service at Waldensia Chapel, 8 miles from Falmouth. He managed to make his way on foot to Southfield Pen, the residence of Adam Christie, the Inspector of Police, who provided Ward with breakfast and a bed to rest. Soon over 200 labourers, who were distrustful of Christie's hospitality, gathered at Southfield and chanted, 'Bring Massa Ward down, he shan't remain here to be poisoned.' Moreover, they also threatened another policeman, William Smith, whom Christie had asked to escort Ward to Waldensia. As Smith and Ward journeyed to the chapel, labourers with 'large sticks and machetes', led by a woman from Chester estate, and including 'old women who had bludgeons in their hands', warned the policeman: 'If anything happens to Massa Ward, we will murder you and drown you afterwards in the river like a dog.'[26]

While Ward travelled south of Falmouth to Waldensia, news of his accident had spread to the properties to the east of Falmouth, as far as Duncans and the Baptist chapel at Refuge, a distance of nearly 5 miles. As the word of the accident spread, the rumours became more extreme and some people believed that Knibb had been ambushed and killed near Christie's residence.[27] Crowds of labourers from the estates poured on to the roads toward Falmouth armed with 'sticks', 'clubs' and 'machetes'. Their intentions are summarised by the words of Sarah and two other women, one of whom came from Spring Estate: 'Before night Falmouth should be in ashes; and those houses which Vermont had put up should fall about his head, for now was the time the negroes and the buckras should wrestle; that buckra and mulattoes should swim in their own blood.'[28] It is significant that these three women mentioned Thomas

Vermont, who was a coloured wharfinger and magistrate. Having purchased Union Wharf in Falmouth in 1837, he fully refurbished the area. It was these new buildings that the women were threatening to destroy. Moreover, he was a determined opponent of Knibb's and was commonly believed to have first threatened to hang Knibb in effigy in early August.[29] Clearly, white planters and their coloured allies were to suffer for Knibb's reported murder. Fortunately, Edmund Lyon, a stipendiary magistrate, who had gained the confidence of the labourers in the parish because of his outstanding reputation for fair administration of the law and his partnership with Knibb in negotiating contracts for some of the workers, met the crowds at the Congo Bridge before they entered Falmouth. After helping to calm them, he agreed to permit some of the leaders to travel into the town where they saw for themselves that Knibb was unharmed and conducting his usual Sunday service.[30]

The women in the crowds, who had rushed to protect Ward and later threatened revenge for Knibb's rumoured killing in August 1838, were rural labourers spread over the estates to the south and east of Falmouth. Twenty months later, in May 1840, the women in the town of Falmouth were also among the blacks who clashed with civil and military authorities. The incident was precipitated when the Falmouth police apprehended 16 African indentured servants, 9 males and 7 females, who had absconded from New Galloway estate in Westmoreland and were visiting the Baptist residence. The African immigrants had made their way to Falmouth because Mohammad, one of their shipmates, resided there while the Baptist missionaries were training him for missionary work in Africa. Apparently, Mohammad was romantically linked with one of the female indentured servants and had visited her previously at New Galloway. He may either have encouraged them to come to Falmouth or he was the only person they felt they could turn to since they had complained of bad treatment at New Galloway and were determined not to return there.[31] Thus, when the police tried to escort the Africans, they refused to cooperate and a crowd of men and women blocked the path of the police. The crowd grew increasingly belligerent when the police roughed up one of the African women, who sat on the street and refused to move. Under instructions from the magistrates, the police picked her up and 'pitched' her into the cart. Such aggression on the part of the police angered the crowd of 'mostly black people', who warned that 'they would not stand there peaceably and see such things, and would not allow a woman to be threatened in that manner'. They further accused the police and magistrates of racial bias, since other European servants who had absconded had never been so treated, while the Africans were being forcibly removed 'because they were poor blacks'.[32] Clearly, issues of class, gender and race were of great concern to the urban blacks who protested against the police's handling of the African indentured servants. Foremost among the protesters was Mary Clarke, a domestic employed by the Baptist Missionary. A policeman described her behaviour as follows:

> She abused the Police frequently and we were obliged to put her back. She always retreated with reluctance, and came back again . . . to get among the Africans. Mary Clarke was conspicuous from first to last . . . She damned the police and asked what right they had to interfere with people in the street.[33]

The magistrates sent for the soldiers at the barracks in Falmouth and read the Riot Act so as to clear the streets so that the Africans could be removed. Even so, this was accomplished with some difficulty as the soldiers were stoned by people, prominent among whom were Letitia Edwards and Frances Jones. Along with Mary Clarke, they and six men were sentenced to three months in prison for rioting against the police and soldiers.[34]

Three months after this incident women in Falmouth again protested against the administration of justice in the courts in Falmouth. The event that drew their attention was the trial of a white captain of a Halifax brig for an assault on the coloured cook on the vessel. When the captain was acquitted, all the popular notions about the partiality of justice were confirmed and he was jostled and assaulted as he made his way to the wharf. He was rescued by the police and magistrates but not before he had received 'several blows from the loose women of the town, one of whom struck him severely on the neck with a dried coconut'.[35] One cannot be sure of the characterisation of these so called 'females of abandoned character', for it is possible that they were so described because they demonstrated scant respect for the men in authority who administered the law in what they considered a blatantly partisan fashion. Indeed, as David Trotman has demonstrated for Trinidad, authorities in the nineteenth century were quick to characterise the behaviour of lower-class women in such terms when they did not reflect the Victorian notions of 'sobriety, decorum and respectability'.[36]

As the women among the urban poor in Falmouth stood up against the activities of the magistrates, so too did the women in Kingston. In 1840 and 1841 they participated in riots against the mayor's unilateral orders to suppress John Canoe, which was one of the popular festivals that provided entertainment during Christmas celebrations. The mayor's actions clashed with the people's determination to safeguard those African-derived cultural practices that had provided them with important self-expression during slavery. However, the mayor wanted to put an end to the John Canoe festival precisely because of its 'barbarous' African linkages. In his view, the 'wild' dancing and the 'noisy' drumming had to be curtailed if the former slaves were to acquire new habits of 'civilisation' and decorum.[37] The Kingston blacks resented this interference and readily grasped the cultural and racial bias that underpinned the mayor's actions. They complained that the 'white people' were allowed to indulge in horse racing, while the blacks were not permitted to pursue their pleasures.[38] Given the wide gap between the people's and the Mayor's interpretation of culture, when the police seized drums and arrested the revellers, they attacked the police and the magistrates. John Nethersole, one of the senior magistrates, described the attack as follows: 'I saw many stones thrown and glass bottles. They flew about me like hail . . . I saw women with stones tied up in their petticoats. They supplied the mob with them and threw them themselves.' Three other observers stated that the women 'seemed to the most violent' and stood their ground and threatened 'blood for blood and to lick down the police.'[39]

Women and politics

Like elsewhere in the Americas in the nineteenth century, Jamaican women were barred from formal participation in the politics of their society because of their gender. In keeping with the patriarchal notion that only men were suited for politics and the women's place was at home, the women were not perceived as being 'public actors' and thereby were 'banished from contemporary politics and from history'.[40] Yet any balanced discussion of politics in the immediate post-slavery period in Jamaica must take into account the extent to which women never accepted that legal marginalisation. Even though women were voteless, as indeed were the majority of men who did not qualify for the property franchise, women's issues were among the concerns of the male politicians who courted the support of the black community. In addition, women were very active in political protests that involved the mass of the people, most of whom were disfranchised by high property qualifications, or as in the case of women, by gender as well.

Certainly, women's issues attracted the attention of the new breed of black, coloured and Jewish politicians who challenged the white mercantile and planter hegemony. For instance, the 'liberals' in the Kingston Common Council criticised police attempts to remove women street vendors whose selling affected the business of shopkeepers.[41] Moreover, the acute shortage of medical care in rural areas was an issue used by blacks to mobilise votes among their class. Thus George Clarke, a black carpenter and political activist, was critical of the health services in the parish of St David because a woman had died in childbirth without being able to get care.[42] In Trelawny, Daniel Nathan, a coloured solicitor, was equally critical of the local vestry which refused to take strong action against the doctor with responsibility for public health who had refused to render medical assistance to Catherine Stanley on the grounds that she was a 'pregnant prostitute'.[43] Finally, William Kelly Smith, a black political activist in Kingston and St Andrew, publicly complained against officials who solicited sexual favours from women in lieu of taxes which they were finding it difficult to pay.[44] In this way, election campaigns did not neglect issues which affected women, as the politicians hoped to win men's votes by appealing to their wives, mothers and sisters.

In some instances, election results determined crucial benefits for women. For example, the 1849 election in the parish of Port Royal was hotly contested by James Taylor, the coloured incumbent, who supported the Governor's firm stance against the retrenchment policies of the planters, and James Porteous, a Kingston merchant with coffee properties in the Port Royal mountains. The contest was very close and even though Taylor kept his seat, the commodore of the naval dockyard at Port Royal, who used all his influence to direct the votes of the shipwrights and others employed there to Taylor's benefit, barred a female provision seller from the area because her son had voted for Porteous,[46] showing how female non-voters were not exempt from political victimisation, always a reality in the days of open voting. On the other hand, there were instances when women benefited from linkages with political groupings. Mrs Absalom was favoured for political patronage when she was appointed pound keeper for the Manning Town area of St Mary. Apparently, she had close connections with the politicians, led by Alexander Lindo, who was the Custos of the parish and a merchant at Port Maria. However, she only held the post for one year because political ascendancy in the parish shifted temporarily to another grouping led by William Silvera, a coloured tinsmith at Port Maria.[46]

Although ordinary women labourers would not have been as personally affected by the outcome of elections as Mrs Absalom had been, they were active in election campaigns. One such was the by-election in St David in 1851. Both the planters and the coloureds worked hard to fill the vacancy and both wooed the black voters, who were mobilised by Andrew Bogle, a blacksmith, and Samuel Clarke, a carpenter. Nonetheless, the planters managed to entice Joseph Brown, a black carpenter, to cast his vote for their candidate and he narrowly won the seat by one vote. However, a crowd of men and women, who had gathered for the election, voiced their disappointment at the result because they were convinced that the returning officer, who was also an employee of the victorious candidate, had manipulated the poll against the unsuccessful coloured candidate. When the police were called up and arrived with bayonets attached to their guns, a woman was heard to comment, 'You come here to stick us, we will not allow it'.[47] This was no idle boast as the Governor reported: 'Fifty of the police and the Custos, magistrates and principal persons of the parish were put to flight by a negro mob carrying cudgels, and who, women as well as men, hurled a shower of stones without the least regard to consequences.'[48]

Two women, Juliana Rogers and Ann Warren, were among those who were later convicted for participating in the election riot in St David.

While Juliana Rogers had come to the poll with Andrew Bogle, who, because of his frail health, had to be brought on a stretcher to cast his vote, Ann Warren had formed part of the group led by Samuel Clarke who monitored the voting. Clearly, both women had been involved in the mobilisation campaign and were provoked to violence, given the circumstances of the defeat.[49]

The mayoral election in Kingston in 1853 also provoked a riot which featured women. The two candidates were Edward Jordon, the leader of the coloured political faction, and Philip Lawrence, a Jewish merchant. Both men had been political allies for years, but each aspired to be the first of their respective social group to become the Mayor of the island's chief commercial centre. Given their ambitions, their supporters manipulated the latent hostility between the Jews and the coloureds in Kingston and the canvass was marked by increasing bitterness and recrimination. Charles Price, a black Assemblyman, had initially offered to support Jordon for the post. However, when Jordon hesitated to contest the election, Price was wooed by the Jews into supporting Lawrence instead. Eventually Jordon announced his candidacy and Price, insisting that he had given his word and could not retract it, refused to switch his support to Jordon. Few of the coloureds accepted Price's explanation and they accused him of taking bribes from the Lawrence faction. When Jordon lost by one vote, some of his supporters, blacks and coloureds, assaulted Price as he tried to make his way home. So intense was the hostility that Price had to take shelter in various business places and private homes as the crowd pursued him relentlessly through the streets of Kingston. Four women were among the seven persons who were later found guilty for riot and assault of Price. Two, Jane Curtis and Margaret Wilkins Sutherland, had been seen in King Street 'with bottles, broken and firing them'. A third, Phoebe Francis, who had 'beat Price' and thrown stones at him on Duke Street, had complained that Price was 'ungrateful' as Jordon had helped Price to 'get political offices'. So conspicuous were the women in the post-election fracas, that the judge commented that it was 'a pity to see females mixing up with elections, but yet such is the case, and [in] every riot women are sure to be included'.[50] Clearly, for the women of St David and Kingston, elections were no mere social outing. Although they had no vote, they certainly had clear perceptions of whose victory would benefit their class.

Furthermore, it is against this background of perceived self-interest that women's involvement in protests against taxation in the 1840s and 1850s can be appreciated. As the estates declined under the pressures of free labour and free trade, the Assembly and the local vestries increasingly sought to shift the incidence of taxation away from the larger landholders by increasing the tax burden of the black peasantry.[51] When efforts were made to collect taxes or to levy on goods for non-payment, the peasantry resisted violently. One such case occurred in St Mary in 1848 when Richard Rigg, the coloured deputy collector of taxes, attempted to forcibly seize goods at Goshen and he and the two police constables and other assistants were stoutly resisted. As he reported, 'men, women and children lined the road on both sides and attempted to lick us off our horses with sticks'.[52] In the following year, the market women, the so called 'mountain negroes' of St Dorothy and St John, twice protested against the increased fees imposed by the vestry for the use of the Old Harbour Market. In the first instance, on Saturday, 24 March 1849, the women rushed into the market and occupied it and the stipendiary magistrate and the police were assaulted when they entered the market and attempted to collect the fees. On the following Saturday, the authorities were better prepared. A cordon of police was placed round the market and only vendors who paid the fees could enter. Those who refused to pay harassed those who did and disorder erupted when the police tried to arrest one of the leaders from the previous week's protest. The market women hurled 'stones and sticks' at the police and only the reading of the Riot Act and the arrival of armed police calmed the situation.[53] In 1855 women in Falmouth were again active in the popular resistance to levies carried out on old residents who could not pay the water tax. Four of the eleven persons indicted for that riot were women and so volatile was the situation that extra police had to be brought in from other parts of Trelawny and from a neighbouring parish to execute the warrants.[54] Clearly, the black women in post-slavery Jamaica refused to accept the back seat that the political system had assigned to their gender.

Morant Bay

Therefore, as we seek to redefine and broaden the understanding of the politics of the 'masses' in post-slavery Jamaica, the participation of women in crucial political movements needs to be highlighted and the sources re-examined. For example, the Morant Bay rebellion has been the protest most discussed in this period. Yet the women's participation in the rebellion has received very little attention in the accounts of that pivotal event in the island's history, even when the writers have been fairly sympathetic to the cause of the rebels. So there are frequent references to 'Bogle and his men', and when the women are recognised, they are often consigned to the ignoble position of being among the 'hooligans', who were on the fringe of the crowd who stoned the volunteers before they fired on the 'mob'.[55] Yet, as will be demonstrated below, the general invisibility of women in the historiography of the Morant Bay rebellion does not reflect an absence of information about them. Rather, their omission from the accounts reveals the extent to which such information was considered irrelevant to the concerns of 'history' and underlines 'the connection between past history and current historical practice'.[56]

Although there is no evidence that women occupied any of the formal positions as 'Captain' in Bogle's 'regiments', or indeed participated in the drilling that preceded the march on Morant Bay, women were part of Paul Bogle's organisational network in the Blue Mountain Valley area of St Thomas-in-the East. A month before the rebellion, Bogle had unsuccessfully tried to expand his followers to include the village of Wilmington, which was a stronghold of the Church of England. Interestingly, it was an unnamed woman who had attempted to arrange a place there for the 'Baptist meetings', only to be blocked by the local constable who was a strong adherent of the Church of England.[57] This suggests that the woman may have had some influence in Bogle's organisation, as well as in the Wilmington community, to have been entrusted with such an important task. Moreover, once the confrontation had taken place in the square at Morant Bay, women were among those directing the attack on the men who had taken refuge in the court house and in the adjoining buildings. Three women, Rosanna Finlayson, Caroline Grant and Sarah Johnson, stood out in this regard. Finlayson was described as giving orders to her 'own people' while a policeman referred to Grant as being 'a queen of the rebels'. She and Sarah Johnson, when they encountered men who had fled from the parade after the firing of shots by the volunteers, ordered them to return to the scene of the fighting.[58] Indeed, Caroline Grant was involved even before the main confrontation in the square since she was among the people who raided the police station for 'guns, bayonets and swords', and then marched to the courthouse.[59] Sarah Johnson too was visible at important junctures before the confrontation at Morant Bay. She was among the people in Paul Bogle's Yard at Stony Gut when the police went there on the day before the rebellion to serve warrants on Bogle. She was also a part of the crowd led by Bogle, 'marching like soldiers', who paused at Spring Garden on the way to Morant Bay in the early afternoon on 11 October. Sarah Johnson's intentions were quite clear as she made her way with the men to Morant Bay, for, as Alexander Bothwell, a policeman, later testified, she proclaimed at Spring Garden that 'every mulatto was to be killed as well as the white man'.[60] Other women also identified very closely with Bogle's activities and perceived themselves as being part of his movement. Joseph Williams, a black volunteer, who had fled the parade, experienced this in a very direct manner. As he ran away, he was held and beaten by Elizabeth Taylor, who was a member of the 'Bogle society'. As she assaulted Williams she questioned him as follows: 'Don't your mother is black, why did you join the volunteers? Why didn't you come up the Mountain and join us?' Another woman, Ann Thompson, was among the people who raided the various stores in Morant Bay for gunpowder and cutlasses once the confrontation had begun.[61] Clearly, none of these women were marginal to the events at Morant Bay on 11 October 1865.

Moreover, some of the data suggest that other women may have had their own grievances in addition to the general ones relating to land, low wages on the estates and oppressive and partial administration of the law. For instance, Elizabeth Faulkner, who lived at Church Corner, a mile from Morant Bay, wanted to kill John Bonner Barret, a black shopkeeper in Morant Bay, because of his dishonest business practices. Mary Ward and other women who urged the killing of Charles Price, a black contractor and former assemblyman, were labourers who had worked for Price and had not been remunerated. They were quoted as saying, 'We work for him on the road and he not pay us, and we burn bricks for the Church at Morant Bay and he not pay us.'[62] These women were grasping the opportunity to settle personal scores that had very little to do with the men and women who set out from Stony Gut and the other communities of the Blue Mountain Valley to confront the authorities in Morant Bay.

The impressive participation of women in the protests discussed in this article is not an attempt to exaggerate the female influence in the patriarchal society that characterised Jamaica in the post-slavery period. Nor should it be considered as part of a search for alternative heroines. Rather it is hoped that the discussion here will rescue women from the derogatory manner in which male adversaries viewed those who refused to confine themselves to domestic matters and to conduct themselves in ways consistent with Victorian notions of decorum. Thus, far from being 'vagrants of the lowest description' or 'harlots and vagabonds',[63] the women discussed above were an integral part of the struggle of the freed people in Jamaica to construct a society that reflected their new status as free citizens. Even though patriarchy ruled supreme, the Jamaican freed women resisted their banishment from the public sphere and played an important part in the politics of the black community, thereby maintaining the tradition that they had established in slave society as 'persistent rebels'.[64]

Endnotes

*An earlier version of this article was presented as a paper at the 19th Annual Conference of the Association of Caribbean Historians held in Martinique in 1987.

1. Woodville Marshall, "'Vox Populi': The St Vincent Riots and Disturbances of 1862', in B. Higman (ed.), *Trade, Government and Society in Caribbean History, 1700—1900* (Kingston, 1983), p. 85; Russell E. Chace, Jr, 'Protest in Post-emancipation Dominica: The 'Guerre Nègre' of 1844', *Journal of Caribbean History*, Vol. 23, No. 2, (1989), pp. 121—22; David Trotman, 'Women and Crime in Late Nineteenth Century Trinidad', and Bridget Brereton, 'Post-Emancipation Protest in the Caribbean: The 'Belmanna Riots' in Tobago,' in *Caribbean Quarterly*, Vol. 30, Nos. 3 and 4 (1983), pp. 60—72 and 110—23.

2. For a pioneering work on post-emancipation protest in Jamaica see Lorna Simmonds, 'The Spirit of Disaffection: Civil Disturbances in Jamaica, 1838—65', unpublished MA thesis, University of Waterloo, 1982. While the involvement of women is mentioned (p. 12), the point is not developed in the thesis.

3. Raymond Smith, 'Race, Class and Gender in the Transition to Freedom', in Frank McGlynn and Seymour Drescher (eds), *The Meaning of Freedom* (Pittsburgh: University of Pittsburgh Press, 1992), pp. 267—68.

4. Catherine Hall, 'White Visions, Black Lives: The Free Villages of Jamaica', *History Workshop Journal*, Vol. 36, (Autumn 1993), pp. 108—14.

5. Woodville Marshall, "We be wise to many more tings': Blacks' Hopes and Expectations of Emancipation', in H. Beckles and V. Shepherd (eds), *Caribbean Freedom* (Kingston: Ian Randle Publishers, 1993), p. 17; Rebecca Scott, *Slave Emancipation in Cuba* (Princeton: Princeton University Press, 1985), pp. 242—44; Jacqueline Jones, *Labor of Love, Labor of Sorrow* (New York: Basic Books, 1985), pp. 44—46 and 58—61.

6. Verene Shepherd, 'The Effects of The Abolition of Slavery on Jamaican ·Livestock Farms (Pens)', *Slavery And Abolition*, Vol. 10, No. 2, (1989), p. 193; Woodville Marshall, 'Apprenticeship and Labour Relations in Four Windward Islands', in David Richardson (ed.), *Abolition And Its Aftermath* (London: Frank Cass and Co., 1985), p. 213.

7. Lucille Mathurin, 'Reluctant Matriarchs', *Savacou*, 13 (1977), p. 4.

8. B.W. Higman, *Slave Population and Economy in Jamaica, 1807—1834* (Cambridge: Cambridge University Press, 1976), p. 18.

9. C.O. 137/234, Smith to Glenelg, No. 189, 1 November 1838, reports of Stipendiary Magistrates David Ewart and Richard Chamberlaine; C.O. 137/242, Smith to Glenelg, No. 41, 6 February 1839, report of Stipendiary Magistrate Richard Chamberlaine.

10. *Ibid.*

11. C.O. 137/243, Smith to Normanby, No. 99, 11 May 1839, enclosure 1.

12. C.O. 137/230, Smith to Glenelg, No. 218, 25 December 1838, report of Stipendiary Magistrate James Harris; C.O. 137/237, Smith to Glenelg, No. 53, 25 February 1839, report of Stipendiary Magistrate James Cocking.

13. Douglas Hall, *Free Jamaica*, (London: Caribbean Universities Press, 1969), pp. 50 and 173.

14. C.O. 137/230, Smith to Glenelg, No. 189, November 1838, report of Stipendiary Magistrates Edmund Lyon and James Kelly.

15. *Ibid.*, report of Stipendiary Magistrate Edward Fishbourne.

16. C.O. 137/241, Smith to Glenelg, No. 8, 5 January 1839, report of Stipendiary Magistrate Edward Fishbourne.

17. C.O. 137/242, Smith to Glenelg, No. 74, 6 April 1839, report of Stipendiary Magistrates Fishbourne and Hewitt.

18. *Ibid.*

19. *Ibid.*

20. *Ibid.*

21. *Morning Journal*, 1 July 1839.

22. C.O. 137/239, Smith to Normanby, No. 160, 16 August 1839, report of Stipendiary Magistrate Edward Fishbourne.

23. C.O. 137/239, Smith to Normanby, No. 136, 17 July 1839.

24. *Ibid.*, C.O. 137/230, Smith to Glenelg, No. 189, 1 November 1838, report of Stipendiary Magistrate Fishbourne.
25. *Falmouth Post*, 8 August 1838.
26. *Falmouth Post*, 22 August 1838.
27. *Ibid.*
28. C.O. 137/229, Smith to Glenelg, No. 167, 7 September 1838, enclosures. No doubt, Sarah's words were refined for official purposes.
29. Falmouth Post, 8 August 1838; *Baptist Herald*, 10 June 1840.
30. C.O. 137/229, Smith to Glenelg, No. 167, 7 September 1838, enclosures.
31. C.O. 137/250, Metcalfe to Russell, No. 123, 13 November 1840; *Falmouth Post*, 27 May and 10 June 1840.
32. *Falmouth Post*, 3 and 10 June 1840.
33. *Ibid.*, 3 September 1840.
34. C.O. 137/250, Metcalfe to Russell, No. 140, 11 December 1840.
35. *Morning Journal*, 2 October 1840; *Falmouth Post*, 3 October 1840.
36. Trotman, 'Women and Crime in late Nineteenth Century Trinidad', p. 71.
37. C.O. 137/255, Metcalfe to Russell, No. 212, 30 April 1841; Marshall, "We be wise to many more Tings': Blacks' Hopes and Expectations of Emancipation', p. 16.
38. C.O. 137/264, Elgin to Stanley, No. 59, 16 December 1842, enclosures.
39. *Ibid.*
40. Joan Wallach Scott, 'The Problem of Invisibility' in S. Jay Kleinberg (ed.), *Retrieving Women's History* (Berg/UNESCO, 1992), pp. 22—23.
41. *Morning Journal*, 28 February 1843.
42. *Morning Journal*, 5 September 1854.
43. *Falmouth Post*, 18 August 1854.
44. *Daily Advertiser*, 10 October 1855.
45. *Falmouth Post*, 19 and 24 August 1849.
46. *Morning Journal*, 12 May 1854; *Daily Advertiser*, 8 February 1855.
47. *Colonial Standard*, 29 January 1851.
48. C.O. 137/309, Charles Grey to Earl Grey, No. 17, 27 February 1851.
49. *Falmouth Post*, 4 May 1852.
50. *Falmouth Post*, 10 August 1853.
51. C.O. 137/297, Charles Grey to Earl Grey, No. 78, 19 September 1848; *Falmouth Post*, 29 August 1848.
52. C.O. 137/299, Charles Grey to Earl Grey, No. 91, 20 October 1848, enclosures.
53. *Colonial Standard*, 4 April 1849.
54. *Falmouth Post*, 13 November 1855.
55. For two examples of references to 'Bogle and his men', see Mavis Campbell, *The Dynamics of Change in a Slave Society: A Sociopolitical History of the Free Coloreds of Jamaica, 1800—1865* (Rutherford, NJ: Fairleigh Dickinson University Press, 1976), p. 336, and Don Robotham, *'The Notorious Riot: The Socio-Economic and Political Bases of Paul Bogle's Revolt* (Kingston: Institute of Social and Economic Research, 1981), p. 89. For two examples of the women as stonethrowers and 'on the side of the main body of the crowd', see Sydney Olivier, *The Myth of Governor Eyre* (London 1933), pp. 214—21, and Thomas Holt, *The Problem of Freedom* (Baltimore: Johns Hopkins University Press, 1992), pp. 459—60. For a work which includes a gender perspective in a discussion of the Morant Bay rebellion, see Clinton Hutton, "Colour for Colour': The

Ideological Foundation of Post-Slavery Society, 1838—1865, the Jamaican Case', unpublished PhD. thesis, University of the West Indies, 1993.
56. Joan Wallach Scott, *Gender and the Politics of History* (New York: Columbia University Press, 1988), p. 31.
57. P.P. 1866 [3682] XXX, Papers laid before the Commission by Governor Eyre (hereafter Papers), 82.
58. Papers, p. 356.
59. Papers, p. 355.
60. Papers, pp. 354—55.
61. Papers, pp. 419 and 449—50. The emphasis is mine.
62. Papers, p. 369.
63. *Falmouth Post*, 29 December 1841; *Morning Journal*, 21 January 1848.
64. Hilary McD. Beckles, *Natural Rebels: A Social History of Enslaved Black Women in Barbados* (New Brunswick, NJ: Rutgers University Press, 1989), p. 152.

16.

Social and Political Motherhood of Cuba:

Mariana Grajales Cuello

Jean Stubbs

Es Santiago de Cuba!	This is Santiago de Cuba!
No os asombréis de nada!	Nothing should amaze you!
Los ojos de las madres están secos	The eyes of mothers are dry
como ríos sin agua!	like rivers without water!
Están secos los ojos de todas las mujeres!	All of the women
Son fuentes por la cólera agostadas	are dry-eyed for the anger
que están oyendo el grito	they are hearing in the cry
heroico de Mariana:	of heroism from Mariana:
'Fuera. Fuera de aquí!	'Out. Out of here!
No aguanto lágrimas!'	I'll have no tears!'

Manuel Navarro Luna, quoted in Nydia Sarabia, *Historia de una Familia Mambisa: Mariana Grajales: Madre de Cuba,* Havana: Instituto del Libro, 1975.

In 1957 the Mayor of Havana, Justo Luis Pozo del Puerto, officially declared Doña Mariana Grajales de Maceo the 'Mother of Cuba'. The occasion was recorded in a small book by Aída Rodríguez Sarabia entitled *Mariana Grajales: Madre de Cuba.* In it were reproduced the solemn words pronounced by Pozo, describing Mariana Grajales as the 'symbol of abnegation and patriotism', declaring a municipal government decision taken 'in posthumous recognition of her virtues and tireless devotion to the Liberty of Cuba.'[1]

It was agreed that the second Sunday in May should be the day to pay public tribute to such a clear-thinking Cuban mother, and that all municipalities should be encouraged to follow suit and have a Mother's Corner (Rincón de las Madres) with her bust; 14–21 June was declared Maceo Week (Semana Maceísta). It was thereby hoped that the homeland (*patria*, more literally fatherland) be periodically 'replenished' with 'the exemplary teachings' of 'the life doctrine and action of this exceptional woman and the offspring she gave to the Liberty of Cuba'.[2]

Mariana Grajales was the Santiago de Cuba-born mother of 13 children, of whom 9 lost their lives in Cuba's independence struggles. The most famous were Antonio and José Maceo, generals in the Liberation Army. The military standing of Antonio Maceo in the nineteenth-century Cuban revolution has been likened to that of Toussaint L'Ouverture in the eighteenth-century Haitian revolution.[3] Mariana herself has acquired legendary proportions akin to Nanny of Jamaica, and all the Maceos have gone down in Cuban history as the 'heroic tribe' of a valiant, self-sacrificing mother.

It was the importance of the mother figure that was eulogised by José Manuel Cortina in Sarabia's 1957 volume. In 1913, Cortina had tabled a motion to the Cuban House of Representatives for a law to found Home Economics Schools (Escuelas del Hogar) and Professional Schools for Women (Escuelas Profesionales de la Mujer). In a speech on 10 January 1927 to the Senate on educational reforms, Cortina had declared:

> No one who has studied the psychology of pedagogy can but be aware of the powerful influence of the home on the character and sentiments of a child, such that some physiologists consider the influence of the mother to be a secondary inherited physiological trait and esteem it to be so fundamental as to be on a par with blood and ancestral influences. To prepare the mother, therefore, endowing her with the adequate tools for a fitting education, is to work directly in the urgent task of reforming the Cuban character: it is to take the very weapons of Nature working in collaboration to improve our race.
>
> The 'Escuelas del Hogar' will shape the mother-type; and thereby, each and every one of them, through their actions over their children, will multiply the effects of their influence, producing true centres of social transformation.[4]

Aída Rodríguez Sarabia, the author entrusted with writing the panegyric of Grajales, commented: 'We are sure that when Cortina spoke these words, Mariana was in his thoughts, so brilliantly expressed, a guide, an example of what women of our country are capable.'[5] His was, she claimed, a 'Marianista message'.[6] In his preamble to Rodríguez's book, Cortina himself wrote:

> Mariana Grajales was an exceptional case of powerful character and energy, who has no parallel in the history of Cuba and the world . . . Mariana Grajales felt so deeply the enslavement of her country and her people, that what might

> *be called a mystic reaction enveloped her conscience, with such an indomitable*
> *spirit of rebellion, that, when she became a mother, she became the creator of*
> *epic heroes . . . Mariana Grajales was like a taut bow, forged of steel, firing*
> *warriors like spears of death against Spanish rule and against all forms of*
> *slavery and humiliation of mankind.*[7]

Neither Pozo nor Cortina made any mention of Grajales' colour. While pencil drawings depicted shaded figures, there is only one written reference slipped in near the end by Rodríguez to this new Cornelia, who had now come to earth in the flesh of a Cuban mulatto woman.[8] In the context of Cuba in the 1950s, this was not altogether surprising, and mirrored the 'whitening' element present in the treatment of her sons as national heroes. This could not have contrasted more with nineteenth-century vitriolic against the 'black Maceos', coming especially from Spanish loyalists, but also from among the rebel camps in Cuba.

More interesting still, for the purposes of this article, is the way in which the 1950s' image of Mariana evolved from home manager to patriot matron-saint. The latter was undoubtedly bolstered by both the fascistic regime of President Fulgencio Batista, himself interestingly enough light brown, and Vatican Marianism. It is argued here that this was but one version of the myth of Mariana; and yet one in which there are elements that are still pervasive today.

Symptomatically, there has been little written on Mariana in her own right: in addition to the 1957 eulogy, there is a lengthy study, excellently researched, by Nydia Sarabia entitled *Historia de una Familia Mambisa: Mariana Grajales* (1975), and a short, popularised monograph by Matilde Danger and Delfina Rodríguez, *Mariana Grajales* (1977). There was also an earlier study by Longinos Alonso Castillo, *Mariana Grajales, Vuida de Maceo: Labor Patriótica* (1942). There is only one biography of the lesser hero, *El General José* by Abelardo Padrón (1973), but by contrast the historiography on Antonio Maceo is far too voluminous to itemise here.[9]

While with the exception of Alonso Castillo the three biographers of Mariana have been female, the biographers of Antonio and José have all been male. Most, but not all, have been white. Much of the historical evidence on Mariana originates from male, often white male, sources and is arguably filtered through corresponding perceptions of woman and mother. The studies by Padrón and Sarabia are exceptions in that they use oral history, culling stories and testimony from a broad range of contemporary informants, including related female descendants.

What follows is taken from all these studies, and includes extensive quotes from several of them, in an attempt to trace the construction of the mother myth of Mariana, and its variations over time. Always centering on a motherhood that is heroically self-abnegating, the myth has oscillated between Catholic and secular. It has been accompanied by political interpretations that range from the liberal patriotic to the revolutionary. Where race has been a factor, the emphasis has been strikingly secular, and integrationist rather than separatist. Without new primary research, it is impossible to distinguish myth from reality, but it is possible to suggest an alternative Afro-Cuban myth. The Afro-Cuban myth, however, is one in which the centrality of gender as signifier in the form of the mother figure functions quite differently.

A legend in the making

In the early 1890s José Martí was the newly emerging leader of Cuba's struggle for independence from Spain. He was proving to be highly successful in building support for his Cuban Revolutionary Party, actively seeking civilian and military alliances among his own exile community in the United States, other kindred communities in the region and the island itself.

Antonio Maceo, who had displayed great military prowess in the liberation army in the earlier 1868—78 war fought against Spain, was among those Martí courted. Maceo had been in exile since the end of the first war, when he and his family were deported to Kingston, Jamaica. He had spent the better part of the intervening years in and out of Jamaica, travelling the region — Haiti, the Dominican Republic, Honduras and Costa Rica, as well as Louisiana and Key West in the United States — mustering support for renewed struggle.

Mariana Grajales Cuello was the mother of Antonio Maceo. She and her whole family had joined the 1868—78 insurrection and she herself, then in her 60s, spent the entire 10 years running hospitals and provision grounds in Antonio's base camps. With her second husband Marcos Maceo (father of 9 of her children, including Antonio) and her son Justo (by her former marriage to Fructuoso Regueiferos) dead, and Antonio mortally wounded, legend has it she tended him back to health, but not before driving other women out for crying (hence the poem above) and sending a younger son off to fight in his place. Sent into exile in 1878, she remained in Kingston for the next 15 years, until her death in November 1893, aged 85.

One month later, in December 1893, José Martí published a first posthumous tribute to Mariana, having visited her while in Kingston the previous year. He wrote:

> *He [Antonio] is his mother's son, more than his father's, and it is a great misfortune to owe one's body to one who is weak or useless, to whom one cannot owe one's soul; but Maceo was fortunate, because he was born of a lion and lioness. He is losing his mother, the glorious old lady is dying in indifferent foreign parts, and yet still has a girl's hands to caress one who speaks to her of her country . . . She lifts her wrinkled head, wearing her*

headwrap like a crown. And knowingly, she kisses the hand. At the bedside of her sick grandson, a slip of a man, the old lady speaks ardently of her sons' battles, the terror and the joy, of what was and will again be. Huddled in a hole in the ground, she spent mortal hours while sabre and machete crossed pommel. She saw her son, covered in blood, and with only ten men, disband two hundred. And she serves with her own hands and accompanies to the door all those who in Cuba's name go to see her.[10]

In a second tribute a month later, he asked:

What, if not the unity of the Cuban soul, forged in the war, explains the unanimous and respectful tenderness, and the accents of indubitable emotion and gratitude with which so many have given accounts of the death of Mariana Grajales, the mother of our Maceos? What was there in this woman, what epic poem and mystery was there in this humble woman, what sanctity and devotion was there in her mother's bosom, what decorum and grandeur was there in her simple life, that when one writes about her it is from the depths of the soul with the gentleness of a son, and with the deepest affection?[11]

Maceo himself wrote in response to Martí:

Only three times in my anguished life as a Cuban revolutionary have I suffered such strong and tempestuous emotions of pain and sadness as I have just had with her death in a foreign land. Ah! How terrible were these three things! My father, the Treaty of Zanjón, and my mother . . . The third cause of my sorrow you yourself came to know, when she could barely make herself heard, speaking of Cuba Libre [Free Cuba], as she would say, of the Revolution, with the tenderness of her soul and the natural charm that comes of so much blood shed generously and that binds us to our political duty . . .[12]

Several months after, Martí wrote to Maceo:

You are indispensable for Cuba. To me you are, and I say it sincerely, one of the most complete, magnificent, strong, and useful men of Cuba. You are so great, Maceo. I must say that I feel such a deep and intimate affection for you that, believe it or not, it is as though I were conceived in the same womb with you. Doesn't María love me like a brother? Didn't your mother caress me as she would her own son? Didn't she publicly call me her son? Rest assured that while I have a hand in the matter you will be fully recognised.[13]

The unity of Martí and Maceo was cemented, if short-lived: both were to die in battle, Martí in 1895, within days of landing in eastern Cuba, and Maceo in 1896, ambushed in the west. However, the myth of Mariana, matron-creator and mother-patriot, was in the making and would live on.

The son's mother

The substantive biographical sketch of Mariana's personal and family life can be traced back to a 1930 lecture to the National Academy of Arts and Letters by Eusebio Hernández, a former aide-de-camp of Antonio Maceo. The story was to be repeated, with its details, angles and emphasis changed over time. This was due in part to new information coming to light, in part to prevailing attitudes and concerns at the time of writing. One can start with Hernández's view of the upright family in 1930:

> *Through their labours, their good conduct, their fine honesty and the rectitude of their principles, Mariana and Marcos acquired good friends . . . The organisation of that model home was complete: the father ran the farm, the mother the home . . . the mother would allow no member of the family to enter the house after ten at night; would tolerate no dubious friendships . . . A family with sound conjugal relations and economic independence, with good friends among both rich and poor, worthy of the respect of workers in their service.*[14]

There was at the time, of course, a curfew in place, whereby coloured folk had to be off the streets by 10:00 pm. Mariana's formative years saw the rapid expansion of sugar and slavery, a growing fear of the black on the part of the white plantocracy and a relative erosion of the position of free people of colour. However, Mariana was born into the demographically and economically strong free coloured stratum in eastern Cuba, the only one, it might be said, in which women outnumbered men, since the settler white and slave populations were more predominantly male. Her parents had a small farm, and both Regueiferos and Maceo were of the small farming and merchant class. Mariana and Marcos consolidated three farm properties and a town house in Santiago de Cuba, and were well-connected among the white and free brown middle propertied classes in the more racially fluid Santiago society.

There are signs that Mariana played an active role in consolidating the family business. And yet the 1940s biographies of Antonio all bolstered the image of the mother in the stable home:

> *Everything about the home prospered: the children, the patrimony, the moral and material values, the domestic peace, and the sense of being useful, a sense of responsibility and of duty . . . Mariana Grajales is man's glory, as Saint Paul would want the wife to be. She is the magnificent mother, educator of her children . . . Marcos Maceo and Mariana Grajales have a relationship that is complete and edifying. Their children see in their conduct a vivid and lasting example of worthy sacrifice, fecund abnegation, reciprocal esteem, and consider it both sound and binding to follow in their footsteps.*[15]

Mariana, it was argued by some, acquired liberal ideas from her

Dominican and Haitian parents, but was deeply religious, and inculcated these views in her own family. Some denied the religion and upheld the vision of her freemasonry. For others she was a defender of her race: 'a daughter who would inherit the upright character of her parents and the broad understanding of their social convictions, placing love and justice above narrow race privilege'.[16] She had such strength and vision of life that it was easy for men with such women: 'Maceo had the good fortune of a mother who instinctively guided him to be of solid principles and sound character . . . A good mother is worth one hundred teachers . . . sublime mother of sublime sons.'[17]

She had to sacrifice everything: the family properties were confiscated and a death warrant was put out for her bandit sons. The warrior mother then became a legend. In Barajagua, when Antonio was taken for dead, María nursed him, José stood watch and:

> there also was his adored mother, Mariana Grajales, standing by his side, watching his rebirth . . . She was in attendance for the 'resurrection' and the pained glory of her motherhood gave him renewed strength and vigour . . . With him [Antonio] over the Cuban countryside went the caravan of men with the heroic and tireless Mariana y María . . . they are the backbone of the Cuban insurrection, keeping up the men's spirit . . . [along with] the caravans of other women returning to the cities squalid, almost naked and moribund, widowed some, orphans at the breast, dry from hunger and sickness, who have seen dry-eyed the corpses of their husbands and children ... Mariana and María were not the only ones. There also, magnificent and anonymous, were creole women.[18]

Patron saint mother

By the 1950s, the image of Mariana the mother patriot and matron-saint far superseded any other:

> Other mothers, blinded by the purest of love, cannot see in all its magnitude the common need to cast out of the Island the vile despot. Others, forgivably inconsequential, censure the son dreaming of magnificence and glory and draw him to the calm and peaceful fold of the home. Not her. She launched them to the dignity of battle. What's more, she went after them and, on the very battlefield, she tended their wounds and was their inspiration in hours of pain.[19]

The image was elaborated by quoting from the Liberation Army General, Enrique Loynaz del Castillo:

> María Cabrales de Maceo is an honourable model of the Cuban woman. She appeared in the encampment among the hurrahs of those valiant Orientales. They knew her virtues from the time when she was a child, and her virtues were even more admired than her impeccable beauty. With her companions she

conquered the wild and difficult mountains, and none was more agile in
climbing to the summit, nor more solicitous in caring for the sick. Only
Mariana Grajales, the mother of the Maceos — who can only be compared to
Cornelia of the Gracchi — only she could match her as a majestic character in
the grand epic . . . Mariana was a superior being . . . Whereas other mothers
try to protect their offspring out of love, she not only sent them off to battle
but also went with them.[20]

These attributes found their grounding in her parents José and Teresa's
home, described as one of 'exemplary moral grandeur, sound civic
principles, and human integrity beyond compare':

Of that union of a good man and woman, with a sense of responsibility and
rectitude in life and ideas grounded in freedom and a moral and ethical
integrity, without hate or prejudice, because they were above the slavery and
hatred prevailing, their eyes set on the skies or on the highest Turquino Peak;
of that sound union — I repeat — on the 26th of June 1808, was born the
Cuban star that would later shine for ever in the red triangle of our flag:
Mariana Grajales Coello [sic] . . . From birth, Mariana was a blessing to her
noble parents . . . The house was always happy because she was so good and
loving . . . she helped her mother to keep the home going . . . She never
received any formal education. And yet, this woman who would later be the
incomparable matron-creator of freedom fighters, was endowed by God with
amazingly clear judgement, penetrating intuition and a sense of moral
guidance.[21]

Mariana was pregnant with Antonio at the time of the 1844 Escalera
conspiracy, in the aftermath of which the brown poet Plácido was shot. A
year later, she would receive a copy of Plácido's *Plegaria a Dios*, which she
would recite at night, and:

While she breathed she would be a force contrary to slavery alongside the
suffering . . . and so it seemed that the life growing in her womb applauded the
mother's heroic decision and moved with such strength as for her to lose her
balance. Sweet, tender Mariana would say with gentle strokes: Be calm, my
revolutionary, you've yet to see the light. And Marcos prayed God for a
liberator for Cuba.[22]

It is said that Mariana rocked baby Antonio to sleep with a slave lullaby
and was the sole force behind her family: 'she and she alone laid and
affirmed the groundings of their character, the foundations of their
personality'.[23] Mariana was, for her children:

temple, altar, divinity and religion . . . The influence of mothers like her is so
great and so deep, the cord binding them to their children is so strong and
resistant, that in the life of the child, she is everything; without her, there is
nothing. That is why, in the life of her children, Mariana was the first and last
religion, because she enveloped and absorbed them from her womb to the tomb,

filling their whole existence with her exemplary life, her sound habits, her dogmas, her rituals, her prayers, her admonitions, and even her predilections and tastes were to them like emanations from a priestess. She was a beacon amidst the darkness and incomprehension of those days. Such that in the sad and woeful night of any of the heroes of her flesh none ever heard a lament or sorry complaint from the lips of those lions. The suffering were only heard to say: 'Mother! Mother of mine!'[24]

Mariana's crowning moment of glory in 1868 is recounted in a truly apocryphal light:

At that moment three stars fall from the sky onto the white collar of Mariana's dress. God has invested her with the rank of general! Possessed of this divine sign, she accepts the responsibility of this great investiture and acts accordingly: she calls her troops, who are her own, and in the silence of this crucial moment for the Fatherland, General Mariana gives the order . . . clasping the crucifix, her spirit . . . spoke to her only of the calvary of Jesus in his immortal struggle for equality on earth, of the glorious maternity of the Virgin Mary . . .[25]

Revolutionary mother

The more radical and race-conscious interpretations of Antonio Maceo in the 1950s and especially since the 1959 Revolution were concerned primarily with rescuing the revolutionary image of the brown hero, and contributed little new on the hero's mother.[26] When an award-winning study in 1966 by Raúl Aparicio did look more to the man behind the hero, and the mother behind the man, the mother image was little changed. Aparicio started out lamenting significant gaps in the information:

The most disconcerting gap I found in studying the home life which, in association with the political and social life in which he was immersed, shaped the personality of Antonio Maceo: it was precisely when I anxiously sought the psychological key to his personality, especially regarding his childhood. There is no direct information. In the current state of psychology no serious biography can fail to examine those first important ten years . . . I have had to work that part of his life through the sole intuition of retrospective events of his adult life and that of his family, especially the conduct of Antonio as a young fighter.[27]

After this proviso, the study then goes on to give the reader the portrait of Maceo the man moulded especially by Mariana: 'Mariana's work in the home bore fruit. The seeds were sown of what would become his character traits.'[28] She knew how to run a good home:

Of necessity, when she was left widowed after the death of Regueyferos [sic], Mariana had to develop a strength of character. For three years, she had to bring up her four children, in keeping with the standards set by their parents, as well-mannered and well-turned out children. There would be no grubbing around in tatters. She would not be weak and tolerate that, precisely because they were not white. Mariana did not want her children to be criticised either for their behaviour or their apparel. When she had her nine children by Marcos, she was ready for the task, the exhausting task of a home with many offsprings. She made of this battalion — even more so than with those of her first marriage — children who were an example of respect. She was more experienced in child-rearing and knew how to impose discipline. Everything about her inclined to order about the house. Order, cleanliness, especially personal cleanliness, and dressing as decently as possible. That was how she always was, right up until her death . . . . When hit by extreme poverty, whatever she was wearing might be old but spotless . . . . That was her iron character.[29]

Mariana Grajales bore Marcos nine children between 1845 and 1860, one pregnancy often following on after another: three years was the most between the ages of any two children. She had her last child when she was 52. Her physical strength was, reportedly, matched by a strength of character which not even the war and exile would destroy, and which she passed on to her family. Both Antonio and José apparently stuttered as children, and are said to have overcome this thanks to Mariana's firmness. In conclusion:

Those childhood years of Antonio were decisive . . . in shaping his character, because scarcely had he left Mariana's fold when he went up into the hills to war . . . . And he was the one to set the high moral note in the war, who most stood out, aside from his valour and heroism, for his courteous behaviour . . . for his concern for the men under his command to be not only disciplined but also the best turned out . . . and for the pulchritude of his own dress; for the absence of vulgarity in his speech . . . . None of that he learnt in the hills; it came from the mothering of his home.[30]

A decade later, the first full-length biography of Mariana by Nydia Sarabia would build on Mariana's strength of character. A more down-to-earth picture began to emerge, with Mariana as a key revolutionary influence. The family values, Sarabia argued, of patriotic awareness, revolutionary stance, and the iron will to fight for freedom, came from Mariana. Fernando Figueredo, who knew her at the time of the war, described her when past 55, robust, middling to small build, tense, quick-moving, determined, in contrast to the character of her husband.[31] She was the first to prepare her family for war:

Mariana Grajales knows from experience that the Spaniards will be back to harass them in Majaguabo and took the Spartan decision to return to the hills with the rest of her children. She gathered their belongings and took them all to Piloto, to the insurrectional camp. She's no young woman, she's almost an

old lady, for she's sixty, but she's strong and can still withstand life exposed to
the elements, to the rain, the cold, the storm and even cholera. Farm life has
hardened her character.[32]

Sarabia recounts how Mariana was the midwife for María Cabrales who arrived in the camp with her small daughter and about to give birth. The son died after only seven days, and a few months later the daughter died also, due to lack of food and medicine. From then on the women moved camp constantly. They crossed the mountains, rivers and forest on foot. They were regularly on the move, time and circumstance permitting, behind the troops with their sons and brothers. They were near to tend the wounded, and procured them food and clothing.[33]

The picture replicated by Maltilde Danger and Delfina Rodríguez was of a marriage based on 'understanding, virtue and moral rectitude'; a home achieved by Mariana with 'mutual respect and consideration, where the seeds of freedom and solidarity found fertile ground'. The revolutionary character of Mariana was forged out of knowledge which she passed on to her family of the Escalera Conspiracy, the death of Plácido and others; and her destiny was with the rebel forces with whom she would share their misery and grief in adversity, their joy in triumph; would suffer sickness in her own flesh or that of her children, would spur on the fighters and cure their wounds.[34]

Lover, wife and mother

The overwhelming portrait one has of Mariana is, without doubt, one of a mother and wife of moral rectitude. There are, however, some rare hints of Mariana the young lover. Rafael Marquina, who won the 1943 Bacardi prize for his biography of Antonio, opened the narration as testimonial fiction of a love affair:

Teresa Coello [sic] looked down the street. Curving her wrinkled right hand
over her eyebrows, she shaded her eyes from the sun . . . . A half smile softened
her lips as her young widowed daughter came into sight round the corner,
serene yet animated. She was on her way to her mother's home and looked
resplendent from afar. Mariana and her mother embraced as they came close,
and the dialogue was one of comforting confidentiality.[35]

On the shoulders of the young widow, according to all in her prime, lay the fate of her family and future life:

And she told her mother, that morning, the city bathed in tropical sun, of her
love with Marcos Maceo, the Santiago-based Venezuelan merchant, according
to all, a man of excellent qualities, a man of order, respect and honour . . .
Teresa Coello[sic], the discreet mother, was approving of her daughter's
decision, in the conviction that her father too would give his consent . . . their

> *own fortunes had not been so prosperous as to pass over the happy event of*
> *seeing their daughter married with a well-to-do man of noble condition . . .*
> *José Grajales, on hearing of it, as Teresa imagined, saw to drawing his*
> *daughter's relations to an advantageous end. And in 1843 in Santiago de*
> *Cuba, Mariana Grajales and Marcos Maceo entered into free union . . .*[36]

In another account that same year, a young and ardent Mariana gradually gives in to her new love, asking herself why should she not join destiny with the emigré who has seduced her. Love had notched another victory, and Mariana, convinced and in love, cast aside all hesitation and decided to embark on a new phase of her life accepting fully the demands of her assiduous suitor, the dual condition of lover and mother.[37]

There is another reference to the love story a few years later, but one ending in marriage:

> *Mariana Grajales, daughter of Cuba, arrives on the scene at the right time.*
> *Marcos has seen her passing by. He is captivated by the strength of her*
> *personality from first sight. As the days go by, contemplating her youthful,*
> *fresh beauty, perceiving behind the smile the sadness of premature widowhood*
> *which left her with the responsibility of four sons, he is moved to emotion.*
> *Marcos is in love. Mariana feels alive again . . . Mariana is a good woman.*
> *She lives devoted to her husband, her children and her home.*[38]

Although it is not mentioned in the matron-saint versions of Mariana, and has been played down in all but the more recent studies, it is the case that Mariana went to live in free union with Marcos Maceo in 1843. He was at the time with Amparo Tellez, who left for Bayamo and took with her their six children (including one by the name of Antonio who was to die a lieutenant-colonel in the first war). Mariana and Marcos did not marry until 1851, after Amparo died, but there are versions of the story that claim Marcos and Amparo had never been together in legal matrimony. After their marriage Mariana and Marcos legalised all their children, who had been baptised and originally entered as the 'natural children' of Mariana in the baptismal register for coloureds at the local parish church.

The general assumption made about free browns in her time is that they sought such legality, and this would certainly tally with Mariana's latter-day image of virtue and respectability. However, there is no way of knowing what importance Mariana herself attached to legal marriage, beyond certain obvious points. The marriage certificate states that Marcos was born in Santiago de Cuba, which was not actually true. This was, however, the decade of a clamp-down on free browns, following conspiracies and revolts involving both free browns and blacks, and in the build-up to the major 1844 Escalera conspiracy. One measure was not to allow in foreign-born coloureds. Mariana and Marcos must clearly have used their connections among Santiago society, not least their son

Antonio's white lawyer godfather, to arrange the papers. The marriage did, therefore, serve a legal convenience.

There is little evidence about Mariana's attitude on such matters from the lives and loves of her family. Mariana herself was clearly close and devoted to Antonio's wife María. Documentation and testimonial accounts and Antonio's correspondence during his war and emigré years testify to his loyal relationship with María (and her continued involvement in the struggle) but also to liaisons with other women. Hernández was the first to allude to this:

> Maceo's detractors have accused him of being a gambler and a Don Juan.
> From early 1880 to 1887, the great man and I lived in close intimacy, and
> during that time I never heard him mention any kind of game, and as for
> women, I won't say he was a misogynist, but he was attentive and reserved
> with the ladies.[39]

Other accounts are less equivocal:

> In Jamaica, the love flame was kindled in his heart: the man who would
> surrender to no force, succumbed to the charms of a beautiful woman. He
> would have no children by María, and Maceo, like all who loved glory, wanted
> a son who would bear his name. And he surrendered to the devotion of an
> idyll, that was like an oasis amidst the concerns of his life. A son was the fruit
> of that union which would help sweeten the sorrows of his life of relentless
> struggle . . . . In the future he would look out for his son's education, but
> fearful of censure and out of respect for his good wife, he would not display his
> effusive temperament to the beloved son.[40]

The lady in question was a white woman by the name of Amelia Marryat and when she bore him a son in Kingston in 1881, it is said that the financially embarrassed Maceo had to sell many of his personal possessions to bear the extra expenses. Antonio appears to have handled the affair with 'la madamita seductora' with discretion and tact: 'Dr Hernández was the doctor who attended them both, and, at times, must have had to cure souls, calming and aiding two persons equally loved and respected who were facing the hard reality of an adverse fate.'[41] It is unclear whether the affair continued and what became of the boy, but there are references in letters to provision for his early education. In Mariana's view:

> The renewed trips and absence of Antonio in Central America were worrying.
> María had been very ill and doña Mariana loved her like a daughter, but she
> also knew of María's embarrassment, because she knew that Antonio had a
> son out of wedlock with Amelia Marryat, whom he had known years back . . .
> María hadn't been able to have any more children . . . . It was doña Mariana
> who asked Antonio not to neglect the child.[42]

There is said to have been an earlier liaison in Puerto Plata, in the Dominican Republic, with María Filomena Martínez, part Indian, part black and part Spanish. Maceo frequented her so much that she became known as 'La Generala'. On the basis of stories such as these, it was declared: 'While Maceo never liked tobacco and detested alcoholic drinks, he definitely loved women. They were attracted to him — women of all colours and nationalities — and Maceo reciprocated their attention.[43]

Significantly, the story of the lesser hero José is the most revealing, and sheds new insights into the Maceo family's lives and loves. José was reputed to be both temperamental and passionate. Five of the women in his life are known; and four of his known children were born in the last 16 months of his life. Patrocinia Rizo Nescolarde was his first woman, a Spanish and Indian mestizo (*blanca-trigueña*), who was 14 when pregnant with their son Elizardo. In fact a Maceo sister and brother were involved with a Rizos sister and brother: Baldomera with Magín and José with Patrocinia. Cecilia López, the mother of Manuel Romero López who later married Dominga Maceo, is said to have been José's woman in exile and imprisonment in Spain.

In Nicoya, Costa Rica, in 1894, the then 40-year-old José married 22-year-old Jamaica-born Elena González y Nuñez. Descendants say it was Antonio who salvaged Elena's honour with a wedding, and tell the story of how in Costa Rica a photographer refused to take their photo because José was a black man and Elena a white woman. By then, three Maceo brothers were with three González sisters: Emilia with Tomás, Manuela with Marcos and José with Elena.

In 1895 Elena sailed for Jamaica, pregnant with their future son José. She was to never again see her husband, who went back to fight in Cuba. Although he wrote letters to Elena saying how much he missed her and how only Martí could have lured him from his love nest, he soon had two children with Teresa Pérez Nicot, of Baracoa, 'a dark-skinned black, but with good hair' (*negra, de tez oscura, pero de pelo bueno*). Also, in Ramón de las Yaguas, he had a 14-year-old lover Agripina Barroso Lazo, known as 'La Negra' who was Indian-black, dark-skinned, with straight hair, a fine nose and mouth; she rode horseback with him, wearing a big hat, and an aide transported their baby son José, born when she was 15, in a barrel.[44]

Afro-Cuban icon

Antonio had his wayward moments; José revelled in his women and seemingly they too in him. Yet the narrative about Mariana leans towards moral rectitude, with only a hint of ardent love. Only in the accounts of José by Abelardo Padrón and of Mariana by Nydia Sarabia, incorporating invaluable oral tradition gathered in the remote eastern regions of Cuba, does one get a more complete story including the outside families — the Téllez, Regueiferos, Cabrales, Romeros, Rizos, Marryats and Bustamantes.

As anthropologist Sydney Mintz reminds us, it is:

> *immensely important to maintain an insistence on the socio-political*
> *significance of the tyranny of everyday life . . . . Throughout history, the*
> *massive struggles of whole peoples to discover and claim their own destiny*
> *have been waged against a background in which love, hate, personal loyalty . .*
> *. and the ordinary pleasures of experience continue to make irrevocable claims*
> *upon the human spirit . . . . The animal and spiritual needs of all human*
> *beings demand satisfaction, no matter what the convulsions of history.*[45]

With this in mind, and noting how a particular ideology of reproduction has been used to legitimise the vision of Mariana the mother, it is possible to suggest that race might be key to a rethinking of Mariana's mother image. Cuba, like all the Caribbean, evolved historically as a heavily hybrid society in terms of ethnicity, race and class. What determined these was a complex code of sexuality and reproduction. Mintz himself classified Caribbean societies and cultures according to differing patterns of sexual relationships in the context of white male power and the relative scarcity of women, except for among intermediate ethno-genetic groupings, particularly in the Hispanic colonies — Cuba was a case in point.

Conjugal patterns and civil codes accompanying the changing status and identity of intermediate racial groupings in nineteenth-century Cuba were studied by anthropologist Verena Martínez-Alier.[46] She traced how, as theories of class superiority invoked racial superiority, and social identity thereby became equated with genetic identity, upper-class men needed to control the sexuality of the women of their class through marriage and the women's consequent seclusion. While the dominant ideological form, this concept of woman and marriage did not pertain to society as a whole, and yet became pervasively accepted as if it did. What has commonly come to be referred to as the *'casa'/'calle'* (women in the home/man on the street) paradigm, was in fact historically contained along race and class lines.

It can be argued from a gender perspective, if not from a class or race perspective, that elite white women had much less manoeuvrability and space than their free brown and black sisters. They were, quite literally, confined to the home space. Interestingly, elite white women in the first independence war went down in history for demanding equality in the new republic, equating their condition with that of the slave (*la mujer esclava*). While little is known about their brown and black sisters, how they acted and how they thought, the brown woman in particular became a multiple icon: sensual in the form of tempter and seductress,[47] but also morally strong, nurturing the promise of the future and freedom.

It is the contention of this analysis, that in Afro-Cuban cosmology there can be no separate and discrete reading of that multiple icon, and it is in this reading that Mariana can be situated. It is an indictment of the written historiography to date that there has been no serious attempt to approach Mariana, or indeed any of the Maceos, as Afro-Cuban in not only political but also cultural terms. (This is discussed elsewhere in the context of establishing the centrality of Cuban free browns, and especially free brown women, to the shaping of nineteenth-century incipient national culture and nationhood).[48]

Here attention will simply be drawn to how, when considering brown society in nineteenth-century Cuba, as in other parts of the Americas, one has to grapple with the real and the ideal of personal and community relations, influenced but by no means controlled by white racial assumptions. Faced with the emasculation of slavery and racism, the gender ideals of the middle brown stratum have been centred on the woman charged with fertility and respectability, with raising the next generation for the good of the race, teaching the value of hard work, responsibility, strength and self-reliance;[49] teaching sons the value of manhood and daughters respect for their men, without flaunting their sexuality. However, it would be an oversimplification to assume that women and men accepted the ideals. While not wishing to negate the fact that those ideals resonate in the accounts of Mariana, it may be the case that this has more to do with the assumptions of the tellers than the substance of what there is to tell.

Let us, for a moment, project a hypothetical Afro-Cuban interpretation of her story and enlist in our aid the recent debate in Afro-Cuban historical anthropology and art history. In Cuba, it has been suggested, ethno-genetic processes allowed for a strong cultural transfer and reconstituted cultures, rather than the syncretism implicit in transculturation, much less acculturation or deculturation. There were nineteenth-century Afro-Cuban institutions such as 'cabildos' (which functioned as mutual aid societies) and belief systems such as Santería, Abakuá or Vodún, all of which evolved mechanisms of transmission across ethnic barriers by broadening their ethnic base. Afro-Cuban Santería was the most prevalent, and like Haitian Vodún and Brazilian Candonblé, was not assimilated by, but rather consciously used European Catholicism. Saints functioned as intentional masks, and up until today the greater the immersion, the less relevant the Catholicism and the greater the African-derived elements.[50]

The symbols of Catholicism, such as church baptism and marriage, and carrying a crucifix, were required and indeed accepted in Santería, but not necessarily imbued with Catholic meaning. There may well have been a similar overlap between masonic lodges and Afro-Cuban 'cabildos'.[51] Vodún priests might have been masons; women 'comme il faut', members of Vodún temples.

The people of the Los Hoyos neighborhood in Santiago de Cuba, where the Haitians and their *tumbas* were strong and where the Grajales-Maceo's house stood, have reclaimed for their carnival *tumba* today the names of their past revolutionary leaders Maceo Bandera-Moncada.[52] Oriente in the first quarter of the nineteenth century was the most important centre of maroon settlements in all Cuba, and their culture is said to be French-Haitian-African. 'Los Brujos de Limón' of Los Hoyos originated there and, according to one story, the Maceo brothers were members of the original Tumba Francesa Lafayette. Some say Maceo located rebel troops by the sound of the cata drum; others that he operated on the basis of a sworn oath of silence.[53]

Mariana herself was of course Cuban-Dominican-Haitian. The descriptions of her headwrap suggest that this was African-style. Her healing powers and her knowledge of herbs and other plants were proverbial. Her son Antonio courted near death and she nursed him back to health on more occasions than would seem humanly possible. Whether or not she was one of those women 'comme il faut' who were members of Vodún temples, we may never know. She and Antonio have, however, been appropriated within a broader Afro-Cuban cosmology.

Central to Santería is the worship of orishas or 'santos' of Yoruba descent, each essentially a unique manifestation of ache, the power to make things happen, a key to futurity and self-realisation in Yoruba terms.[54] Among the most widely worshipped are Yemaya, orisha of the seas; Oshun, orisha of fresh water, love and giving; and Ogún, orisha of iron.

Yemaya is represented by round fans, crowns and earthenware vessels filled with water from the river or sea, rounded stones and sand. The fan is an emblem of the cool command of spirits and power and protection against evil. Earth is the ultimate arbiter of life, and Yemaya is particularly close to earth. The fused image of Yemaya and the Virgin Mary share the qualities of love, faith and purity. Yemaya is the quintessential mother, not charged specifically with the art of conception; for that she is complemented by the sensual Oshun. Also, while the female mothering aspect is Yemaya, the male aspect is the powerful and often feared Olokun. In all Yoruba orisha, there is a male-female dichotomy, in this case Yemaya/Olokun is both nurturer and warrior, care-giver and protector, self-protected in turn by a balancing force.

Ogún is the god of war and iron, and lives on the battlefield and on the cutting edge of iron, addressing the forest with a sharpened machete. He is the warrior, for whom the fused image would be the Catholic Saint James on horseback. Ogún is polite, well-behaved and considerate, with a deep sense of justice and tremendous potential for physical action. He has an ability to work tirelessly, and his work is never done; his pleasures are taken intensely and quickly.

There can be no doubt that Mariana is Yemaya and Antonio is Ogún. However, this would be a West Cuban appropriation of the myth, since that is where Santería has been strongest. In East Cuba, we would need to look more to Vodún, which has Papa Ogún but replaces Yemaya with the sea goddess Avrekete/Aizan-Velekete[55] and the strong queens of *cabildo* and *tumba* culture.

The intricacies of race and gender politics in twentieth-century Cuba are beyond our scope here. However, in the post-colonial transition to modern state, an attempt was made to drive Afro-Cuban cultures and belief systems back to the margins. There was also extreme ambivalence over issues such as divorce, adultery and the rights of illegitimate children. Patriarchs and feminists alike, mainly white and elite, were preoccupied with the need for family stability and civic responsibility. This was the context for the suppression of normatively deviating detail and the 1950s exaltation of Mariana to matron-creator and mother-patriot, elements of which were carried over into the post-1959 revolution.[56]

Mariana is remembered today because she was faithful to Cuba and independence. Her motherhood was not only that of the protective, nurturing mother. Hers was the motherhood of total and selfless dedication to a cause, sacrificing home, husband and children to war and making it good. She could become a strong revolutionary icon, because she symbolised Afro-Cuban resistance. In Afro-Cuban cultures and belief systems, women can lead and commune with the orishas to redress imbalance through ritual and action. A mother exhorting her prodigy to go to war, to kill and to die is within the power and right of a strong woman.

It is significant that this is how Cubans have chosen to interpret the meaning of Mariana's life. They could have interpreted it otherwise, but instead they have recognised and celebrated the resistance of the defiant and heroic mother-leader. What in other cultures and belief systems, both in Cuba and elsewhere, might be considered improper and abusive, was heralded as a virtue. She epitomised the good woman for whom virginity was ultimately less important than self-sufficiency and loyalty to causes beyond her own image and those of husband, father or son.

In the context of revolution and the overt resurgence of Afro-Cuban cultures and belief systems, especially of late, it is perhaps time for the spirit power of Mariana to emerge more strongly into the Afro-Cuban light.

Endnotes

This article was written for the centenary of the death of Mariana Grajales Cuello, and is dedicated to her memory, in the hope that it will stimulate further research on her, and other women like her, in Cuban history. It is also in memory of Nissa Torrents, whose untimely death in October 1992 deprived us of a kindred soul and scholar.

I am indebted to the University of North London for giving me a sabbatical in the autumn 1994 semester and to the Centers for Latin American Studies and

African Studies at the University of Florida, Gainesville, for having me as a Rockefeller Scholar during the semester, enabling me to undertake my research and writing. I would like to thank Richard Phillips, Latin American and Caribbean librarian at the University of Florida, for his help in locating bibliographical material; Pedro Pérez Sarduy, Barry Chevannes, Helen Safa, Olabiyi Yai, David Geggus, Nina Menéndez and Ofelia Schutte for our many stimulating discussions; and Louis Pérez and Lynne Stoner for their thoughtful comments on an earlier draft.

1. Aída Rodríguez Sarabia, *Mariana Grajales: Madre de Cuba* (Havana: Impresora Modelo, 1957), p. 5.
2. *Ibid.*, p. 5.
3. Gonzalo de Quesada in *The War in Cuba*. See also Arthur Schomburg 'General Antonio Maceo', *The Crisis*, 38 (May 1931).
4. Rodríguez Sarabia, *Mariana Grajales*, p. 8. This was presumably influenced by the American home economics movement which had started at the turn of the century, striving for both 'scientific motherhood' and 'scientific home management' — the 'educate a woman and you educate a nation' approach. It would seem to have predated the movement spreading to the British Caribbean, during the Second World War, outlined in Rhoda Reddock, 'Feminism and Feminist Thought' in Patricia Mohammed and Catherine Shepherd (eds), *Gender in Caribbean Development*, (Kingston, Jamaica: University of the West Indies, 1988).
5. Rodríguez Sarabia, *Mariana Grajales*, p. 18.
6. *Ibid.*
7. *Ibid*, pp. 11—13.
8. *Ibid*, p. 38.
9. The sources are listed and discussed in some detail in Jean Stubbs, 'Mariana Grajales Cuello: Revolutionary Free Brown of Cuba'; in Barry Gaspar and Gad Heuman (eds), *Brown Power in the Caribbean* (Duke University Press, forthcoming).
10. José Martí, 'Mariana Grajales de Maceo', *Patria*, 12 December 1893, in *Antonio Maceo, Ideología Política, Cartas y Otros Documentos*, Vol. I (Havana: Sociedad Cubana de Estudios Históricos y Internacionales, 1950), pp. 427—28. See also Julián Martínez Castells (ed.), *Antonio Maceo, Documentos para su Vida*, (Havana: Publicaciones del Archivo Nacional de Cuba, 1945).
11. José Martí, 'La Madre de los Maceo', *Patria*, 6 January 1984, in *Antonio Maceo, Documentos*, p. 429.
12. Antonio Maceo, 'A José Martí', in *Antonio Maceo, Documentos*, p. 411.
13. Quoted in Gonzalo Cabrales (ed.), *Epístolario de Héroes, Cartas y Documentos Históricos* (Havana: Imprenta El Siglo XX, 1922), pp. 30—31.
14. Eusebio Hernández, *Maceo: Dos Conferencias Históricas (1913 & 1930)* (Havana: Instituto del Libro, 1968), pp. 33—35.
15. Emeterio S. Santovenia, *Raíz y Altura de Antonio Maceo* (Havana: Editorial Trópico, 1943), pp. 18—21.
16. Fermín Peraza Sarausa, *Infancia Ejemplar en la Vida Heróica de Antonio Maceo* (Havana: Editorial Lex), p. 41.
17. Leopoldo Horrego Estuch, *Maceo, Héroe y Carácter* (2nd extended edn.) (Havana: Editorial Luz-Hilo, 1944), pp. 17—18.

18. Octavio R. Costa, *Antonio Maceo, el Héroe* (Havana: Imp. El Siglo XX, 1947), pp. 86—90.
19. L. Griñan Peralta, *Maceo: Análisis Carácterológico* (Havana: Editorial Sánchez, 1953), p. 19.
20. *Ibid*, p. 19—20.
21. Rodríguez Sarabia, *Mariana Grajales*, pp. 19—20.
22. *Ibid*, p. 28.
23. *Ibid*.
24. *Ibid*, pp. 30—31.
25. *Ibid*, p. 30.
26. The work of José Luciano Franco stands out in this respect: *Antonio Maceo, Apuntes para una Historia de su Vida* (1951—57), 3 Vols. (Havana: (Ciencias Sociales, 1975); *Ruta de Antonio Maceo en el Caribe* (Havana: Oficina del Historiador de la Ciudad, 1961); *La Vida Heroica y Ejemplar de Antonio Maceo*, (Havana, 1963). Philip Foner, *Antonio Maceo: The "Bronze Titan" of Cuba's Struggle for Independence* (New York and London: Monthly Review Press, 1977), is based largely on Franco. See also José Luciano Franco 'Mariana and Maceo' in Pedro Pérez Sarduy and Jean Stubbs (eds), *AFROCUBA: An Anthology of Cuban Writing on Race, Politics and Culture* (Melbourne, New York and London: Ocean Press, Center for Cuban Studies and Latin American Bureau, 1993).
27. Raúl Aparicio, *Hombradía de Maceo* (Havana: UNEAC, 1967), pp. 13—14.
28. *Ibid*, p. 17.
29. *Ibid*, p. 22.
30. *Ibid*, p. 25.
31. Nydia Sarabia, *Historia de una Familia Mambisa: Mariana Grajales*, (Havana: Editorial Orbe, 1975), p. 79.
32. *Ibid*, p. 81.
33. *Ibid*, p. 83.
34. Matilde Danger and Delfina Rodríguez, *Mariana Grajales* (Santiago de Cuba: Editorial Oriente, 1977), pp. 3,4,8.
35. Marquina, *Antonio Maceo, Heroe Eponimo* (Havana: Editorial Lex, 1943), p. 9.
36. *Ibid*, pp. 10—11.
37. G. Rodríguez Morejón, *Maceo Heroe y Cuadillo* (Havana: Imprenta Fernández y Cía, 1943), p. 7.
38. Costa, *Antonio Maceo*, p. 10.
39. Hernández, *Maceo*, p. 34.
40. Horrego Estuch, *Maceo*, p. 103.
41. Franco, *Antonio Maceo*, p. 64.
42. Sarabia, *Historia*, p. 127.
43. Franco, quoted in Foner, *Antonio Maceo*, p. 143.
44. The stories are told in much greater detail in Abelardo Padrón Valdés, *El General José: Apuntes Biográficos*, (Havana: Instituto del Libro, 1973).
45. Sidney Mintz, *Caribbean Transformations* (Baltimore: Johns Hopkins University Press, 1974).
46. Verena Martínez-Alier, *Marriage, Class and Colour in Nineteenth-Century Cuba*, (Oxford: Cambridge University Press, 1974), and Verena Stolcke, 'Women's Labours: The Naturalisation of Social Inequality and Women's Subordination', in Kate Young *et al.*, (eds), *Of Marriage and the Market* (London: Routledge, Kegan and Paul, 1984).

47. This imagery is best developed in the great nineteenth-century Cuban literary classic Cirilo Villaverde, *Cecilia Valdés or Angel's Hill* (1st edn.; 1879), (New York: Vantage Press, 1962). Cecilia is the beautiful, sensual woman, 'all sex and no brain, vain from head to toe . . . who can be humble or haughty, scornful or seductive . . . born to be loved'. See Reynaldo González, *Contradanzas y Látigazos*, (Havana: Letras Cubanas, 1983); and 'A White Problem: Interpreting Cecilia Valdés' in Pérez Sarduy and Stubbs 1993, *AFROCUBA, op. cit.* It is interesting to note that the film of Cecilia made by Humberto Solás was not well-received in Cuba, among other things because it left out any suggestion of incest: in the book Cecilia and her wealthy young white lover Leonardo were, unbeknown to them, half-sister and brother. The film did, however, give Cecilia a brain and a cause: she used her intermediary status for the good of the abolition and independence struggle.

48. Stubbs, 'Mariana Grajales Cuello', *op. cit.*, (forthcoming).

49. It is important to note that these are qualities that have also been central to the Africanist-feminist approach to black woman cross-culturally. See Rosalyn Terborg-Penn, 'Black Women in Resistance: A Cross-Cultural Perspective' in Gary Y. Okihiro (ed.), *In Resistance*, (Amherst: University of Massachusetts Press, 1986).

50. An excellent overview of the debate can be found in Stephan Palmié, 'Ethnogenetic Processes and Cultural Transfer in Caribbean Slave Populations', in Wolfgang Binder (ed), *Slavery in the Americas* (Wurzburg: Konighauser und Neumann, 1993). On the most recent phase of reconstituted culture, viz Cuban Santería in the United States, see Stephan Palmié, 'Afro-Cuban Religion in Exile: Santería in South Florida', *Journal of Caribbean Studies*, Vol. 5, No. 3, (1986) and 'Against Syncretism: Africanising and Cubanising Discourses in North American Orisa-Worship' in Richard Fardon (ed.), *Counterworks: Managing Diverse Knowledge*, (London: Routledge, forthcoming). See also Raúl Canizares, *Walking the Night: The Afro-Cuban World of Santería* (Rochester, Vermont: Destiny Books, 1993); David H. Brown, 'Garden in the Machine: Afro-Cuban Sacred Art and Performance in Urban New Jersey and New York' (PhD. thesis, Yale University, 1989); George Edward Brandon, 'The Dead Sell Memories: An Anthropological Study of Santería in New York City', (PhD. thesis, Rutgers University, 1983). For Haitian Vodún, see Karen McCarthy Brown, *Mama Lola: A Vodou Priestess in Brooklyn* (Berkeley: University of California Press, 1991).

51. Philip Howard, 'The Spanish Colonial Government's Responses to the Pan-Nationalist Agenda of the Afro-Cuban Mutual Aid Societies, 1868-1895', *Revista/ Review Interamericana*, Vol. 22:1—2, (1992).

52. Judith Bettelheim, 'Carnival in Santiago de Cuba' and 'La Tumba Francesa and Tajona of Santiago de Cuba', in Judith Bettelheim (ed.), *Cuban Festivals: An Anthology with Glossaries*, (New York: Garland, 1993).

53. James O'Kelly, *The Mambí-Land or Adventures of a Herald Correspondent in Cuba* (Philadelphia: J.B. Lippincott & Co, 1874). O'Kelly's unique account of the 'other Cuba', Cuba Libre or the Mambi-Land of the insurrectional forces during the 1868—78 war vividly describes the fugitive patriots and their families, whom he affirms were overwhelmingly coloured, in the depths of the woods of eastern Cuba. His descriptions range from the simplicity yet gentle

elegance of their settlements to their brotherhood of 'El Silencio' and Vodún ceremonies.

54. Robert Farris-Thompson, *Flash of the Spirit* (New York: Vintage Books, 1984), p. xv.
55. *Ibid.*
56. This is developed in K. Lynn Stoner, *From the House to the Streets: The Cuban Woman's Movement for Legal Reform, 1898—1940* (Durham and London: Duke University Press, 1991).

17.

Women of the Masses:

Daphne Campbell
and 'left' Politics
in Jamaica in the 1950s

Linnette Vassell

A working class voice

The aim of this exploratory article, based primarily on the oral testimony
of Daphne Campbell, is to give space to the presence of this one woman
whose experience can mirror that of the women who were involved in
organised political action in Jamaica in the 1940s and 1950s. She stands in
the tradition of women like Adina Spencer, called 'woman of the masses',
and Satira Earle, who were committed stalwarts for change on behalf of
the poorer classes.[1] This glimpse into the life of Daphne Campbell allows
for an exploration of the issues relating to working-class women's political
activism, the interests that are defined and the goals that are pursued,
particularly in the context of an anti-colonial thrust.

Issues relating to the nature of Jamaican and Caribbean feminism, its
impulses and expressions, are also raised. One of the interesting findings
of this preliminary study that needs further exploration is the evidence of

convergence on an anti-feminist position of forces of the 'right' and of the 'left' by the 1950s. Colonial ideology stressed women's 'service' and warned against the promotion of women's 'rights'; the anti-colonial Communist tendencies which had developed in Jamaica seemed to also feel that feminism would split the working-class movement; hence women's pursuit of 'rights' was restricted to the elaboration of trade union demands and did not embrace calls that questioned or sought to change power relations between men and women in society.[2]

Women's agendas and interests were being defined from both sides of the political divide and in ways that might blunt perception and hence the expression of women's interests as women. This kind of experience might well help to answer Roberta Clarke's query on how, in the Caribbean context, gender ideology and male dominance are perpetuated.[3]

Campbell's narration raises many issues (not all of which are discussed in this article), such as: the nature of the relationships between women of the working and middle classes, of working-class women and middle-class men in the political process, and the extent to which the difficulties of working-class women overcoming economic and social disadvantage might determine how and on what terms they come to participate in political movements for change. Some of these matters can be explored in works that look more broadly at other women who, like Campbell, participated in the radical politics of the late 1940s and 1950s.

Daphne Rose Campbell was born in Endeavour, Mile Gully, Manchester on 19 August 1925. She was one of the two daughters of Sarah Eliza Fleming, house-wife, and George Harold Campbell, an electrician. She, however, has ten other brothers and sisters on both her mother's and father's side.[4] Although her parents never lived together, she and her sister were supported by their father who lived and worked in Kingston.

Early organisational experience

Campbell first attended Endeavour Primary School, then went to Middlesex Primary School to age 16 after she had gone at age ten to live with her grand-uncle in Christiana. According to her, 'as there was not much going' [in Christiana], she came to Kingston in 1942 to live and 'help' a family which had lived previously in Christiana and then resided at Little Kew Road in the Maxfield area. In the afternoons after work she attended classes which Edith Dalton-James, a noted educator, held at Half-Way-Tree school. Campbell studied English and Mathematics. She also joined the Young Women's Christian Association (YWCA), became a member of the Pathfinders Club and 'used to do cooking, baking, embroidery, tatting . . . camping . . . I went to Knockalva one year and I went to Fairy Hill another year'.

The organisation, she said, played an important role in young women's lives, as it 'kept young girls out of trouble for you were engaged in social activities, interacting with the other girls. . . . And the training you got from these people!' She explained that training also came from women who were volunteers with the organisation and who were good role models. She explained:

> Yes, Miss Bent and others weren't teachers at Half-Way-Tree, you know, but they were club leaders. There was Miss Carpenter, she was from Half-Way-Tree, . . . living in front of the school there; there was Miss Mavis Sutherland, she is the eye specialist; there was Winnie Moss, women like those, older women who used to assist the girls, you understand.

For Campbell, one YWCA leader stood out: 'a great girl, that Dorritt Bent'. She explained with animation about her:

> She is a great women in every way; she is well-lettered you know . . . she is not a person who go out and say the rights of women and all that, but in the fight for women she has been helpful with young girls and women on a whole, you understand, because in her field of social work she did a lot . . . a great black woman. She was always natural, for the years I know her, she never do her hair . . . she was well-groomed, pretty teeth, Dorritt Bent. Lawd man, she was really something, and she well-educated, well-clean, polished woman. When you hear Dorritt Bent speak!

Evening classes, the YWCA and the example of older women created the bridge to Daphne Campbell's wider social involvement and her move into more direct political action. In her words, 'I didn't leave the Y completely, but I was more engaged through Mrs Dalton-James. She was a member of the People's National Party (PNP) and she was engaged in politics and because we have grown up in the Half-Way-Tree school with her, we would support her.' Campbell joined a PNP group in the Delacree Road area and became a member of the Jolly Girls' Club, an offshoot of the PNP group, organised to attract young girls close to the party group and the PNP itself. The Jolly Girls was in many ways like the YWCA. The girls in the Delacree/Maxfield area did singing, dancing and sewing; they performed in plays and went on outings. In addition, Dalton-James would conduct training sessions on how to hold meetings, on personal hygiene, dieting and matters of personal conduct and development. Through her influence, Jolly Girls became affiliated with the Jamaica Youth Movement (JYM) and Campbell and a number of other Jolly Girls became involved in the work of the organisation.

The JYM had been established in 1942 following the first All-Jamaica Youth Conference, sponsored by the Central Council of Voluntary Social

Services. It was a forum for young people, mainly of the middle class. Members of the JYM came from a wide cross-section of organisations, for example, religious bodies, student groups and training colleges, schools, old students' and teachers' associations, employee groups, social services, study groups and political organisations, sports and other independent bodies.[5] This was not an organisation of 'little small people; the JYM was educated people like Hector Wynter, Pansy Hart, we had those big people there', Campbell explained.[6] Its aims were to unite youth in a common effort to build the community, to encourage the study of the country's problems, to strive for equality of opportunity, and to foster international contacts and solidarity among young people. Jolly Girls members, mainly working-class youths, would, through their association with the JYM, come into a wider network for information and action on national issues and within an anti-colonial orientation.

The elaboration of these issues was certainly influenced by the Marxist left, the most radical section of the anti-colonial movement, which was then active within the PNP. This Communist grouping was represented in the JYM by one of its most influential leaders, Richard Hart, also Secretary of the PNP Youth Commission in 1941, and an officer of the PNP itself.

The Communist and left forces in Jamaica had been organised from 1937 around Hugh Clifford Buchanan, a mason. A secret group called the Inner Circle had been formed and included barrister Hart, journalist Frank Hill, journalist and trade unionist Ken Hill, seaman and railway worker Arthur Henry, the four popularly identified as the 4Hs. They, among others, were to become prominent in the organisational development of the PNP, building party groups and support organisations, influencing the 1940 Declaration of Socialist Principles, initiating the study group movement in 1942, in short, influencing the ideological direction and growth of the party among the people.[7]

Forces both within the PNP as well as the state authorities were opposed to the work and influence of the Marxists. Ken Hill, a member of the Marxist left, vice-president of the PNP, president of the Trades Union Congress (TUC), had won the West Kingston seat for the PNP in 1949 with over 10,000 votes. Such success, indicating the ascendancy of the left in the PNP and the country, bred continued harassment and propaganda against the Marxists, and fed internal party crises which resulted in the 1952 expulsion of Ken Hill and Frank Hill, Hart and Henry from the party. Campbell herself as a young woman had become involved in the work of the PNP in Dalton-James, West St Andrew constituency, the secretary of which was Hart.[8] She therefore started her association with the Marxists in the process of PNP group-building. She attended meetings at the South Corner Group in the Waltham Park area. Even after Dalton-James lost the 1949 electoral contest to Rose Leon of the rival

Jamaica Labour Party (JLP), Campbell continued her political work in the constituency.

Between the late 1940s and the early 1950s Campbell worked as a cigar-maker at Gore's Tobacco Factory. Her wages of £6 per week she believed were reasonable, as workers at Gore's factory were among the highest paid in the industry. The postwar period had increased the demand for cigars and Gore's factory did good export business.

Her political involvement developed out of her community networks. She established a PNP group at 255A Spanish Town Road, the area in which she lived. This was the Myrie Lane group. She outlined her activities thus: 'You bring people together under the aegis of the People's National Party. You discuss political matters, made [attempts at] advancement of the community, [and] the training of people in different aspects.'

According to Campbell, more women than men joined the party groups. She explained:

> *Women were anxious to find a way out, you know that type of thing. And, they are at the base of the ladder and they want to find somewhere, they need to find somewhere to align themselves, to associate and to find a better life, because in these groups there [are] a lot of little opportunities . . . like finding jobs and that kind of thing.*

The expulsion of the Marxists from the PNP in 1952 brought the West St Andrew group into opposition with the party. A letter signed by 16 party groups, dated 21 April 1952 and addressed to V.L. Arnett, PNP secretary, advised that 'the groups in West St Andrew have decided to and hereby resign from the PNP'.[9] According to the local leaders, 'The vast majority of the people are working-class people and by turning against Ken Hill and his supporters the PNP and its leader had deserted the working class.'[10] The West St Andrew group leaders, including Campbell, who, with Claudius Biggs, signed on behalf of the Myrie Lane group, said they would continue to serve the people under the banner of the Friends of the Trade Union Congress (TUC).

Trevor Munroe, in a reassessment of the influence of the Marxists in Jamaica's political life in the 1950s, has proposed that the left was not in 1952 a marginalised group. He argues that they remained an influential force in the country's labour and political history until the latter part of the 1950s.[11] For Daphne Campbell, the expulsion of the left from the PNP in 1952 was a turning point:

> *that was when my activity in the PNP became less and I aligned myself with Ken Hill, Richard Hart [and] move to the PEO. Now Ken Hill set up a movement called Friends of the Trade Union Congress and we joined up with them. Then Mr Hart set up the PEO — the People's Educational Organisation — and it was from here that we had to read the history of the*

country because of the books provided. It was a kind of a library, you know, where you could get books and materials from abroad, a wide spectrum of books and material that you could read. The history of Marcus Garvey, Sam Sharpe, the national heroes, I knew very little about until I went into the PEO. After I went into the PEO and learned all about these things, having international experience in reading, you understand, I became acquainted with a number of organisations. At that time all over the world women were writing in the hope of finding freedom.

The PEO was formed in June 1952 with some 30 members to 'improve the knowledge and education of the Jamaican people'.[12] Its most active work was in public education, such as Campbell described, and emphasis was placed on discussion of Jamaican history including slave revolts and the maroons. Meetings featured discussions of Marxist theory, of Communism, socialism, capitalism, of regional issues, for example, developments in British Guiana, as well as the issues of colonialism and imperialism.[13] The PEO had a lending library and a bookshop.

Number one woman leftist

Campbell was not a member of the PEO's executive committee, but as a member of the finance committee was responsible for raising funds for the organisation by selling mainly the Communist and pro-Communist literature received from the socialist countries.[14] Along with Hart and Chris Lawrence, PEO Executive members, Campbell in 1952 formed part of the 'sales squad' in West St Andrew.[15] This squad, which seemed to combine sales with agitational work among the people was abandoned in 1953 in favour of a system of centralising sales in the bookstore under Lawrence.[16] Campbell was also involved with the work of the PEO's Committee on Conduct.

Campbell's most active involvement in the PEO followed on her representation of the Jamaican left movement at international conferences sponsored by the socialist and Communist movement. In 1953 she was nominated by the PEO and the JYM to represent women at a conference sponsored by the Women's International Democratic Federation (WIDF) in Copenhagen, Denmark, in early June.[17] She was also to go on to join a delegation of young Jamaicans who would attend the Fourth World Festival of Youths and Students in Bucharest, Romania.[18]

In this period of intensification of hostility to Communist and progressive forces, the Jamaica Federation of Women (JFW), the leading women's organisation in the country, expressed vehement opposition to the WIDF and to the idea of the women's congress and refused to be associated with the event.[19] Further, within the youth movement, intense conflict had also developed and in 1952 the JYM was expelled from the Council of Voluntary Social Services because of the strong influence which the 'left' exercised within the organisation. More stringent laws to prohibit the sale of and to seize Communist and progressive literature, and powers to the police to search premises for banned publications, were signs of the escalation in the anti-Communist 'drive' that had been launched by the state in the early 1950s.[20] There was also some threat to freedom to travel: passports of leftists were being seized. Campbell recalled her experience when she went to acquire her passport:

that time the Immigration Office was out at East Street . . . and then the Governor have to stamp your passport because it was colonial days . . . but me no 'fraid for anything you know, for me can face up to anything. Him tek me passport, him look inna mi face:

'You going to Denmark?'

I say, 'Yes, I am going to Denmark. I am going to visit some friends and I am going to stay with some people, some friends of ours.'

And him look pon me good and him give me. And when me tiptoe back to Duke Street, them say, 'Lawd, you get it!'

She was away for three months. This experience seemed the highlight of her life as a young woman.

I have been to Rumania, I have been to Czechoslovakia, I have been to Hungary and all those places and invited by women and seen and heard of the struggles. They still have the monuments there to show you what struggles they have been through, you understand?

I was in Rumania for nearly two months . . . I traveled up and down, everywhere with the Rumanian women. I came to Britain and stayed with the National Assembly of Women in Britain.'

At the Congress itself, Campbell said she had a high profile; she was put on the presidium. She spoke of what was happening in Jamaica, was applauded by delegates and proudly received by other blacks. She seemed to have made a good impression:

I was nice, man, the West Indian clothes and the way how my hair was done and plait up and thing, and when I got to the meeting they say, 'beautiful Jamaik'; it was an experience, you know! I say when you going out in the nights them have to turn off the lights because meself and Polly Lusan were the only two coloured girls 'round there at the time . . . Polly Lusan . . . I think she is from San Fernando and she was representing the women from Trinidad, and she and I became very friendly at the conference . . . You go to different functions . . . and they have to turn off the lights because if they ever turn on the light and them see you, them would eat you raw!

Oh! Coloured! . . . What them call you? Nigre, Negro! Everybody. If you come out on the balcony, Jesus, the crowd down there. And they would a kill you, the police have fi ring you fi get you through the crowd. . . [They want] to touch you and see you so beautiful . . . and nice. You see in the ballroom when I went downstairs, when you come down from your hotel room and come . . . to have dinner and when the Australian Amerindians see we, Jesus man, they would kill you with love. When negroes meet you in a remote area you dead with love, you know!

Festival, the organ of the JYM, published reports from Campbell on her visits to Bucharest and Romania. She described her 'very interesting and pleasant' experience, reported her interview with Radio Moscow, and stated that the women's conference was a great success.[21] She was forthright in her praise of socialism,

I go there and see education, living standard and everything was good. I find no fault with them. I have no reason because my situation here is worse than theirs, so I couldn't go there out of my bad situation where I didn't go to school properly,and go and say there is something wrong with theirs, when all their children were provided education. When you fight other nations of the world who you following? The one who enslave you. You are advocating for the one who enslave you, so the reason why them don't want us to see it is because you would be fired and wake up to know you under bondage. That's how I see it, because Britain didn't want the colonial people to see those things because if you see those things you would want to lift up and live like those people . . . . The important thing is to know, because after I go round — according to them — the Iron Curtain, and I go to Rumania, Czechoslovakia, East Germany, Hungary, and see things there, they couldn't expect me to come back here and say 'Lord, Jesus, the people round there are under bondage', and it is not true. It is not true . . . . When you see the children, when you go to the factories and see the food provided for the workers and when you are here, you going to buy one snow cone and patty. When you go to Rumania and eat the rye bread it is the most beautiful bread I ever saw. When I come back, I couldn't taste the Chineyman plastic bread; for months I couldn't eat the plastic bread. I couldn't eat the plastic soda bread . . . . When you see the creches in every factory. You have to a lef' you poor little pickney with one little old woman, when you come back the place renk, him nose raw, how me think of those things. One day me leave Robin, when me gone work, because me was very particular with me baby, mi leave her out in the days to go to work and pick her back up. When me come back home one evening, the same way me leave me baby in the morning . . . me come back and see her wet and me no carry her back to this day and nobody know why. Which brings me back to the creche.

She spoke of the workers' spas, of women driving tractors in the fields, of women in garment factories, in medicine, 'I couldn't come back here and come tell them say me go round there go see Iron Curtain.'

This was the message she gave to her organisation and the general public at a meeting held at the Mutual Cooperative Hall, Wildman Street in Kingston, to report on her tour. She said everywhere she had been, she had looked for and asked about prisons and insane asylums. She told her audience what she herself seemed to believe, that these did not exist in Romania. According to the *Jamaica Times*, she said that neither the Soviet Union nor the other Communist countries should be regarded as the 'Iron Curtain':

> *The Iron Curtain is here. All they do is feed us with a pack of lies. I now know the truth and regardless of the 'redbaiting', Jamaican women must stand up and play their part . . . I have seen Socialism in action all over Romania and it filled me with joy to see how the common people live.*[22]

She said that the Congress had outlined the rights of women and shown women that they have a great part to play in the universe. Women had been encouraged to return to their countries to fight for those rights.

Campbell, who, according to the *Jamaica Times* report, could lay claim to 'being the island's number one woman Leftist', could not dedicate herself fully to this task. She expressed regret that she could not work full-time with the PEO since here financial position did not allow her to do so. However, she continued to be active in the PEO's public campaign between late 1953 and 1954, which opposed the colonial government's programme of persecution of Communists and progressive people, and in particular the banning of literature. The organisation also rallied public support against the persecution by the British government of the People's Progressive Party and the suspension of the constitution in British Guiana in 1953. Two meetings about Guyana were attended by some 1,200 persons, according to PEO estimates.[23] Campbell was a regular speaker on the News Forum programme of the PEO, which analysed the current events. In March 1954, for example, she was responsible for a speech on Guyana; in April she was slated to speak on a panel with Lawrence, Hart and others; in May she was responsible for making a fundraising appeal; in September she and Lawrence were to speak on human rights at meetings at Fleet and Tower Street.

There is no verification that these activities were held, but they do indicate that Campbell was seen as a prominent speaker in the public agitational work of the PEO and of the People's Freedom Movement (PFM), which the left forces founded in August 1954. The PFM encompassed much of the work of the financially weak PEO and was designed to take a more direct and active role in the political process. From 1954 the PFM began to organise to influence the 1955 general elections and took part in the municipal and parish council elections in 1956.

Campbell was also active in the work of the PFM: 'I was one of the main speakers, to be very frank with you, because Rose and Ivy would speak, but I was one of the main speakers from time to time. I wasn't cowed, you know, you have people gear facing, well, I wasn't fearful'.

She identified other women who were involved as 'Ivy Harris, Brenda Campbell, May Clayton, Rebecca Williams, many more women'. Ivy Harris was identified by Campbell as one of the public speakers, and was a member of the Management Committee of the PEO. According to Campbell, she owned a dress shop.

Rebecca Williams, or Rose, another of the noted public speakers, was said to have been active in Hannah Town. A dressmaker, she sold readymade clothing and also made and sold baked goods in Kingston. She held the position of third vice president of the PFM and seemed to come into prominence as a major public speaker and delegate to international events. Sometime in 1954, for example, Williams was the delegate to the International Mothers Congress in Switzerland.[24] In October 1954 she was doing public campaigning for the PFM when she went to Hanover for a week to work in Teacher Lascelles Murray's Western Hanover constituency. It was assessed that the presence of a woman was very critical, 'because the Labour party's greatest strength was among the women'.[25] Williams, it was reported, did a good job in public meetings and other activities. She herself stressed the importance of house-to-house canvassing in the campaign.

Campbell also worked in that campaign, she recalled, 'We had a candidate in Hanover and I went down there to try and help him, Teacher Las Murray. He was a staunch PNP man but he was an advocate of the 4Hs.'

In 1956 Rose Williams became a candidate in the local government elections in the No 2 Division in Western Kingston constituency under slogans of 'Work or Unemployment Pay' and 'Freedom'. She was one of the six candidates fielded by the PFM, all of whom were unsuccessful.[26] In May 1956 she was one of the speakers at a May Day celebration sponsored by the Jamaica Federation of Trade Unions and the PFM and by June was again off to attend the First World Congress of Women Workers in Budapest, Hungary, sponsored by the World Federation of Trade Unions. She was mandated to 'expose the inhumane conditions of Jamaican women' and to represent the Jamaican Federation of Trade Unions. According to Campbell, Williams never returned to Jamaica, but stayed in England. She died there.

As for the other women, Campbell recalls that May Clayton was active among the left forces from the time she was a student nurse living in Stony Hill. Brenda Campbell, she said, was a teacher at her own preparatory school in Hannah Town. The school seemed to have been unsuccessful and in late 1954 Clayton was asked to assist with the PEO bookshop at a subsidy of 15 shillings per week. She later worked in Hart's law practice and migrated to the USA in the early 1960s.

Jamaica Women's Assembly

The many others mentioned by Campbell included Fay Moore, E. Lawrence, C. Hibbert, Ivy Bryce and Millicent Grant. Fay Moore was a member of the management committee of the PEO and at one stage was in charge of music and drama. A clerk by profession, she once worked as manager of the bookshop. According to Campbell, she lived in Allman Town and her grandmother was an avid supporter of the PNP. Ivy Bryce was elected to the PEO's finance committee in 1952 and was, according to Campbell, an office helper in Hart's office. Hibbert and Lawrence were associated with the Jamaica Women's Assembly (JWA).

The JWA had been formed by the left forces in 1953, more, it seemed, from considerations of strategy than from consultation with, or expressed interest by, the women whose interests were to be served. Campbell's exposure to the international conference was a major motivating force towards the formation of the organisation. The WIDF itself had sent correspondents to the PEO and at a September meeting it was decided that the organisation would 'deal with the woman's question led by comrade Daphne Campbell'.[27] By the October 1953 meeting of the management committee, the PEO had taken a decision to form the JWA and there was a notation that a request was to be made for the women's group to meet at the PEO's headquarters.[28]

Campbell said that the PEO saw the formation of the group as a way to build up interest among women. The aim of the JWA, she explained, was to uplift the status of women, especially working-class women, and to alert them of their rights. These rights she saw as the 'right to education, the right to a good living standard, the rights of their children to education and all that type of thing'. She added that there was concern with 'having children without [support of] fathers'.

The original executive of the JWA consisted of Daphne Campbell, president; Fay Moore, vice-president; May Clayton, secretary; E. Lawrence, assistant secretary; and Rebecca (Rose) Williams, treasurer. These were all working-class women active in the broad work of the left, including trade union struggles. Campbell said that the JWA was active in Central Kingston, West Kingston and St Andrew. It distributed and sold books among women and held regular meetings where 'women's rights and the question of employment' were discussed.

The existence of an organised group of working-class women, active in the struggles, seemed to have prompted attention to certain specific issues. The programme for a 1 May workers' rally at Regent and Beeston Street (in 1954 or 1955) at which Ivy Harris was a named speaker, included a demand for 'a minimum wage for domestic workers' as well as an increase in the minimum wage.[29] Further, a 'people's programme of the PFM which was discussed at conferences held in Green Island and Lucea in Hanover, Union and Windsor in St Elizabeth, and at Trinityville in St Thomas in 1954, contained specific demands for women workers. These were: (1) complete equality with regard to hiring, conditions of employment, payment, promotion and training; (2) the same social security benefits as for men; (3) maternity leave with full pay for at least 14 weeks, partly before and partly after confinement; and (4) the prohibition of dismissal of pregnant women or nursing mothers.[30]

These were important demands which, if implemented, would have benefited working women of all classes. Further, they addressed women's gender interests, but without speaking explicitly to women's oppression, hence their call was not justified either within the PEO, the PFM or the JWA. Campbell explained: 'We never had any gender problems, whether we should be equal with men was never discussed; we never had any problems with men. This don't mean I don't feel that women have their rights — equal pay for equal work and that women should not be a wall plaque.'

It seems that within the left movement, issues of gender and feminism were carefully avoided by a focus on working women's rights and not women's rights in general. The issue of children's maintenance by men, which was an issue of concern to working-class women (but perhaps not as much to those who had paid employment), was carefully avoided. Asked to what extent the male leadership of the PEO influenced the formation and activities of the JWA and the demands made for women, Campbell said that the women 'saw the need for these things and advocated it, but we knew that our needs wouldn't be attended to under the system that we were under, you understand. The first thing we wanted was freedom from the shackles there so that we could demand these things.'[31]

Challenges of the struggle

Campbell gave primacy to the anti-colonial struggles because she, like others of the comrades, came face to face with the force of the colonial state. For example, along with 77-year-old Catherine Myrie, she was arrested and charged at Hunts Bay police station in March 1954 for possessing prohibited literature.[32] She recalled,

The police came in about midday and it was me and Mother Vie (not actually my grandmother but she was like my grandmother. I was living with her at Spanish Town Road, 25A, where I set up the group) . . . . I saw this load of policemen drive up and get out and come in the house and they start

> *searching. They had a paper and they said they were advising me that they had come to search for banned literature . . . and they went in and started searching the press, wardrobe, this, that, whatever and they claimed they found this issue of the World Federation of Trade Union.*[33]

Campbell said she was not in the least bit fearful because she was accustomed to harassment. She recounted an incident at the airport: when she had returned to Jamaica in 1953, remarks had been made by the police that they were looking for 'Moscow gold'. This was a reference to their own viewpoint that the Jamaican Communists were being financed by Moscow. She knew that the raid of her premises and her arrest and charge were part and parcel of the usual persecution of Communists,

> *Yes, they used to dodge around. There wasn't a meeting we ever had that they were not there taking notes. They were working for the British Government, you know, that's what they were doing, and at that time . . . the police inspectors were pure white. It was all white folks, the police head was white, no black police had any senior position in the force at the time. So they used to go around and hound their own people.*

The charge against Mother Myrie was dismissed, but Campbell was found guilty, and fined £10 or two months' imprisonment. She paid the fine. The appeal filed by Hart in June 1954 was not upheld by the court.

Such persecutions did grave damage to the left movement. The JWA, for example, had to stop holding meetings at Mother Myrie's premises, because the old lady could not put up with the constant police harassment. The organisation suffered as a result. By 1955 the PEO was also in a crisis of its finances, but general harassment was a major factor in its demise.

> *Michelin and those English oppressors, Richard Hart them couldn't open them mouth that them arrest them. Remember he was arrested and charged and Ken Hill arrested and charged. What were they there for, advocating for the rights of the colonial people . . . That is the same thing the South African people are dying for. If more people in Jamaica would stand up like the South African people we would have been freed long time. Norman Manley and all those people wouldn't have to go through all them problems, and we would have been free from all those years.*

Personal economic difficulties took their toll. Although Campbell became an executive member of the PFM in 1955, she had to reduce her level of involvement because of the pressure of making a living. Since her employment at Gore's she had moved into various areas: she had worked as a sales clerk at a grain store at Heywood Street, as an office helper with a doctor, gone into the dry goods trade, tried her hand at dressmaking after doing a course at Deaconess House at Hanover Street, and finally in 1959, secured a temporary position with the Kingston and St Andrew

Corporation. This was after she rejoined the PNP towards the end of the 1950s, at a time when the 'left' was well into decline. In 1959 she had her first child. She lived for a short time with her child's father, but was not satisfied with the relationship and would not marry him, remaining single by choice, 'I wouldn't marry him because he wasn't a go-getter and from I see that I wouldn't bury down myself . . . although he was progressive.'

The father of her other two children died and so she basically faced the challenges of life as a single mother. A big challenge was when after the 1980 general elections she had to run away from her home because it was invaded by political thugs. She recalled, 'A mob came, first about four came and hold me up inside and start take things and start to say PNP this and that . . . and as that batch gone, I draw out my pickney and I leave, and as I say, is our we a save, so come.'

They captured her house and she lost all her possessions including her photographs and pictures and mementoes of her treasured experiences.

> *Eh-eh, and me go through all those struggles and face life. Some people couldn't go through them struggles, because people knew how I had things, because I work all the while and have nice things. People when they see me downtown, them cry eye water, 'Lawd Miss Daphne, how you do?', Me say 'What you a cry for 'bout things and me nah cry you know.' All some people say, 'She must be gone a mad house.' You know, me born 19 a August, look at Garvey and all those people what born August, a hell fi you batter them down you know.*

Campbell's conviction is that if she and others like herself had been more educated, 'we would have captured a lot of things'. She seemed to re-evaluate her comments and continued:

> *But when you think of it, the women today are not as active as we were. With all the advancement in education and training, they are not active more than us . . . If [it was] one for all and all for one, you would find a better society, but too much class distinction, class pride, class prejudice . . . You have colonialism in a new way.*

Endnotes

1. Ken Post, *Arise Ye Starvelings; The Jamaican Labour Rebellion of 1938 and its Aftermath* (Hague-Boston-London: Martinus Nijhoff, 1978), p. 151, 152, 171, 241, 291. See also Linnette Vassell (compiler), *Voices of Women in Jamaica 1898—1939* (Department of History, University of the West Indies, 1993) pp. 27—28.
2. Linnette Vassell, 'Voluntary Women's Associations in Jamaica: The Jamaica Federation of Women, 1944—1962', M.Phil. Thesis, University of the West Indies, Mona (1993) p. 299.

3. Roberta Clarke, 'Women's Organisations, Women's Interests', *Social and Economic Studies*, Vol. 35, No. 3 (1986) pp. 107—56.
4. Her mother later married a Mr Fleming.
5. *Youth Speaks*, the quarterly newsletter of the Jamaica Youth Movement, No. 1, (November 1942).
6. Members of the first executive committee were Rev. Walter Foster, Student Christian Movement; Georgia Gordon Somers, Central Council of Voluntary Social Services; Adele Wint, YWCA; Odel Fleming, Rover Scouts and the YWCA; Pansy Robinson (Hart), Civil Service Association; Vivian Blake, St Matthew's Church Guild; Sybil Hill, Land Settlement Association; Lester Kirkcaldy, Social Study Group; Marjorie Stewart, YWCA; Richard Hart, PNP. In 1945, Hector Wynter was Secretary of the JYM.
7. Richard Hart, *Rise and Organise, The Birth of the Workers and National Movements in Jamaica (1936—1939)* (London: Karia Press, 1989), pp. 16—20; Trevor Munroe, *The Marxist 'Left' in Jamaica 1940—1950* (Mona, Jamaica: ISER, 1978).
8. Dalton-James was the PNP candidate for the West St Andrew constituency in 1944 and 1949. She was unsuccessful on both occasions.
9. Richard Hart Papers (hereafter Hart Papers), Letter from 37 St Josephs Road, to V.L. Arnett, Secretary, PNP, dated 21 April 1952.
10. *Ibid*.
11. Trevor Munroe, *The Cold War and the Jamaican Left, 1950—1955: Reopening the Files* (Kingston, Jamaica: Kingston Publishers, 1992), pp. 99—144.
12. Hart Papers, PEO Constitution, 1952, in PEO Files.
13. See Munroe, *The Cold War*, p. 125—26.
14. The first Executive Committee was composed of Hart, chairman, first vice-chairman, C.A. McKoy; second vice-chairman, Chris Lawrence; secretary, Harry Drayton; treasurer, Hugh Buchanan; assistant secretary, Iris Officer. Other members of the Finance Committee were Daphne Mitchell, Hugh Buchanan and Ivy Bryce.
15. Hart Papers, PEO Management Committee meeting, 13 December 1952.
16. Hart Papers, PEO Management Committee Meeting, 21 February 1953.
17. The Women's International Democratic Federation (WIDF) was formed in 1945. The formation of the WIDF was influenced by the Communist and socialist bloc and was dedicated to the fight against fascism and militarism and for economic, political, social and civil rights for women. See *Women of the Whole World* No. 1 (1985) pp. 12—13.
18. Hart Papers, 'Jamaica Shall be There', *Festival*, Supplement of *Youth Arise*, July—August 1953, pp. 1, 10.
19. Vassell, 'Women's Voluntary Associations', pp. 195—97.
20. Law 53 of 1953 and Law 10 of 1954 amended the provisions of the Undesirable Publication Law of 1940.
21. Hart Papers, 'Forward to the Third World Congress of Youth — I see Bucharest', from Daphne Campbell, and 'Daphne Campbell in Romania', *Festival*, July—August 1953, pp. 3, 5, 10.
22. 'No Iron Curtain She Says', *Jamaica Times*, 12 September 1953.
23. Hart Papers, Meeting of Management Committee of the PEO, 28 November 1953.
24. Hart Papers, 'Rose Williams Goes Again to World Congress', *Freedom*, No. 15, 20 June 1956, p. 1.

25. Hart Papers, Committee meeting of the PFM, 25 October 1954. Women organised in the Jamaica Federation of Women were regarded as the main support base among women of the Jamaica Labour Party (JLP). See, Vassell, 'Women's Voluntary Associations', pp. 141—49, 173.

26. Hart Papers, *Freedom*, No. 8, 29 March 1956.

27. Hart Papers, Minutes of PEO Management Committee, 5 and 19 September 1953.

28. Hart Papers, Meeting of the Management Committee, 3 October 1953.

29. Hart Papers, 'Come One, Come All' (handbill).

30. Hart Papers, 'A People's Programme' (handbill).

31. This focus was very much in line with the then current position of the Communist movement on the 'woman question' coming out of the United States, for example. A response to the question 'What is feminism and why must it be fought against?', defined feminism as 'A bourgeois ideology which holds that *men* are the 'cause' of the oppression of women, and that the 'liberation' of women can be realised through winning legal and formal equality under capitalism. It is harmful to the working class, first, because it conceals the class basis of the oppression of women, and second, because it fosters the so-called battle of the sexes rather than the necessary working class unity of men and women in a common struggle against a common oppressor. Feminism is not to be confused with the healthy fight of women for equal rights and full participation in the struggles of the working class. According to this doctrine, 'sustained working class struggles for women's rights' and 'education of working women in the Marxist-Leninist ideology' were the 'most effective ways to combat feminism'. See Irene Epstein and Doxey A Wilkerson (eds), *Questions and Answers on the Woman Question* (New York: The Jefferson School of Social Science, 1953), p. 12.

32. 'On Reds Book Rap, Women Raided', *The Star*, 29 March 1954.

33. The notes of evidence of the case and the exhibit refer to a copy of *Caribbean News*, in which there was an article on Federation. See Hart Papers, 'In the Resident Magistrate's Court For the Parish of St Andrew Holden At Half Way Tree Before His Honour Mr C.D. Fitchett, Resident Magistrate for the Parish of St Andrew, Regina v Daphne Campbell and Catherine Myrie. Mr A. Richard Hart for Defendants'. April 22, 1954 and 21 May 1954.

SECTION SIX

Comparative

Perspectives

18.

Women and Infanticide in Nineteenth–Century rural France

Jonathan Dalby

On 24 April 1841 the dismembered and trampled body of a newborn baby was discovered in the pigsty of a farm belonging to Pierre Bonnet in the village of Cassaniouze.[1] Part of the jaw and both hands and feet had already been consumed by the pigs but according to the doctors who carried out the autopsy, the baby was neither stillborn nor premature and showed signs (bruising round the neck and a knife wound) of having been killed by violence. The suspected mother, Cécile Bouygues, 30, a distant relation of Bonnet's, was shortly indicted on charges of infanticide and sent before the departmental assize courts.

Her story was a sad and all too common one: illegitimate, she had been abandoned anonymously at birth by her mother, who reclaimed her from the hospice a few days later only in order to benefit from the wages the authorities paid to wet-nurses (*nourrices*) prepared to look after orphans. Following the death of her mother, the child was once again returned to the hospice, where against all the odds — bearing in mind the horrific rates of infant mortality in such institutions — she survived, and went to live with her aunt until the age of 12. For the next 14 years, she worked as a shepherdess, then as a day labourer (*journalière*) on different farms in the area, before illness forced her on the road to beg. In August 1840, possibly already pregnant, she returned to the hospice, from where she was expelled on 22 April 1841. Helpless and nine months pregnant, she made her way somehow to the farm of Pierre Bonnet, one of her few living relatives, and gave birth alone on the night of 23-24 April. She knew the baby was born alive, for it was crying, and fearful of Bonnet's reaction, she admitted to throwing it in the pigsty. Whether or not the baby was dead by the time it reached the pigsty is in some doubt, but three months later Bouygues was found guilty of infanticide, with extenuating circumstances, and condemned to three hours' public exposure and to forced labour for life.[2]

Bouygues was in several respects representative of those accused of infanticide in the Auvergne and indeed in the rest of France during the nineteenth century: female, unmarried, illiterate, trying to scrape together a makeshift livelihood in that marginal world of the rural proletariat. Of the 97 individuals brought to trial for infanticide before the Cantal assize courts between 1791 and 1889,[3] 87 (90 per cent) were women; of the 78 accused mothers of the victims, 64 (83 per cent) were unmarried, and of the 63 of these whose occupations were known, 48 (76 per cent) were in some form of domestic service (*domestiques, servantes, journalières*). Nor was Bouygues unusually old, for the average age of prosecuted mothers was 27.6, the youngest defendant being 18, the oldest 45.

The Bouygues prosecution, moreover, illustrates many of the characteristics common in infanticide cases: the mother had sought to keep her pregnancy secret and gave birth alone. There were no witnesses either to the birth or the crime. The body was discovered within a few hours of the birth. The doctors were able to state with some degree of certainty that the child had been born alive, on time and in good health, but they were not able to determine the cause of death. Several questions remained unanswered, but the burden of proof was a good deal more incriminating than in most prosecutions and the fact that the jury was willing to accept extenuating circumstances is evidence merely of their desire to avoid a capital sentence.[4] There is no mention in the trial dossier of the identity of the baby's father, something which perhaps even the accused did not know, and nowhere is there an explicit reference to motives for the crime, other than Bouygues' continued determination to prevent Bonnet from learning the truth. In this case, as in many others, there was indeed no particular motive. The functional explanation — that the baby was killed simply to conceal the pregnancy and birth — may be insufficient and unsatisfactory, but nevertheless constituted an important element in the logic of motivation. Add to this the circumstances of material need, loneliness and lack of family support, the traumas of a clandestine labour, fear of dishonour and of the potential obstacles to future marriage, and we are left with a plausible cocktail of motives.

Infanticide is by its very nature a gender issue, and is a phenomenon which transcends boundaries of culture and time. It was almost certainly present in Caribbean slave society — if for significantly different reasons than in Europe[5] — and intermittent press reports attest to its survival in the contemporary Caribbean. One hundred and fifty years after the Bouygues case, the Jamaica *Daily Gleaner* carried a front-page story

('MIRACULOUS SURVIVAL: week-old baby still alive after five days in pit latrine') on an attempted infanticide committed in circumstances very similar to many of our French cases:

> *According to police sources, the mother, Heather Plummer, 35, domestic servant of Blue Mountain District, gave birth to the baby boy around 4 o'clock on Sunday evening at her employers' house, while they were away from home. She then went to the latrine and threw the baby in the pit. Her employers had suspected that she was pregnant, but she kept denying it, saying the bulge in her belly was caused by someone obeahing her. Sometime after giving birth Sunday, unknown to her employers, she fell ill and her employers gave her tea and home remedy, and noticed that she looked a bit thinner, but thought nothing more of it . . .*[6]

We have here only the bare outlines of the affair: the mother, in her 30s, and presumably unmarried, was in domestic service. She had attempted to keep her pregnancy secret from her employers, had given birth alone, and had disposed of the baby very shortly afterwards. There is no speculation in the report about the motive and it is significant that the reporter should have chosen to ignore this aspect, focusing instead on what was obviously considered the more sensational angle: a 'miraculous tale of survival'. The crime itself is reduced, by implication, to the banal category of Police Information Centre bulletins on recent killings published in the *Daily Gleaner*.[7] Whatever the specific motives in this affair, however, the similarities to our French examples are evident. Whether in late twentieth-century Jamaica or nineteenth-century France, infanticide, defined in most legal codes as the murder of a *newborn* child,[8] has been almost exclusively a female crime, whose structural origins can be seen to lie in women's subordination and alienation in a patriarchal society.

This paper addresses primarily the question of motivation for infanticide in nineteenth-century Cantal, a rural *département* of the western Massif Central, formerly part of the *ancien-régime* province of Auvergne. The first section consists of a brief review of the historiographical context of infanticide, its history in Europe since classical times, and the problems associated with the prosecution of offenders. Bearing in mind the dangers of divorcing a particular crime from its general environment,[9] the second section analyses those structural conditions of French rural society which were prejudicial to the welfare of both unmarried mothers and illegitimate children and ultimately conducive, at the least, to child abandonment. In the final section, following a discussion of the options available to the pregnant, unwed mother, several commonly advanced explanations of infanticide are subjected to closer scrutiny in the light of evidence revealed in the 81 prosecutions in the Cantal assize courts between 1791 and 1889.

The historiographical context of infanticide

As one writer has recently observed,

> For us, cruelty to children is such an emotive topic that we lapse all too easily into confusion. Faced with evidence of infanticide, abandonment, murder and child labour, we are at a loss as to how to construct historical arguments adequate to their explanation. There is a genuine problem of imagination here.[10]

Twenty years ago, any study of infanticide might have been slotted conveniently into the interpretative framework provided by Philippe Ariès' pioneering *Centuries of Childhood*,[11] which was soon established as the orthodoxy on a topic then rarely broached by historians. Relying primarily on literary sources and pictorial evidence, Ariès argued that the general conditions of poverty, disease and high infant mortality rates under the *ancien régime* tended to blunt parental feelings towards their children and to discourage the investment of too much emotional capital in them. In short, he came to the conclusion that parental attitudes to the infant were characterised by indifference and neglect, and that a concept of childhood in the modern sense did not emerge before the seventeenth century at the earliest.

Such views were expanded upon, qualified, but rarely questioned by a succession of historians working on various aspects of the history of the family in the 1970s.[12] 'Good mothering is an invention of modernisation,' declared Edward Shorter. 'In traditional society, mothers viewed the development and happiness of infants younger than two with indifference'.[13] Not only infanticide itself,[14] but also baby-farming, wet-nursing, abandonment and exposure have been treated in a way which implicitly accepts the thesis of 'indifference and neglect'.[15] In 1980, indeed, a French feminist writer used the thesis as the basis for an attempt to disprove the existence of the maternal instinct.[16]

Nevertheless, successive planks of Ariès' central argument have been progressively undermined over the last few years. Le Roy Ladurie's *Montaillou* produced sufficient evidence of parental love and affection for children in a peasant society to cast doubt on the notion of generalised indifference and neglect in medieval Europe;[17] Natalie Davis distinguished a distinct youth phase of childhood in sixteenth-century France;[18] Stephen Wilson argued that parent-child relations under the *ancien régime* were different because the context was different, and that so-called evidence of indifference and neglect (swaddling, wet-nursing) could be interpreted in ways different from those of Ariès and his followers;[19] Adrian Wilson's thoughtful critique of *Centuries of Childhood* stressed Ariès' 'present-mindedness' and concluded that historians had too readily and naively embraced his interpretations as a 'ready-made solution' to their methodological problems.[20] Finally, in what is probably the most substantial work on the history of childhood since that of Ariès, Shulamith Shahar took as her central thesis 'that a concept of childhood existed in the central and late Middle Ages . . . and that parents invested both material and emotional resources in their offspring.'[21]

There is, of course, a fundamental problem of evidence here. Written sources may exist — in the form of autobiographies, correspondence and diaries — for the milieu of the educated aristocracy or middle classes, but they are predictably scarce for the peasantry. In France it was only after the Ferry reforms of the 1880s began to provide the rudiments of an education for the rural masses that peasants themselves, or former peasants, occasionally ventured into print.[22] Their testimonies on parental attitudes towards children, however, are ambivalent: evidence of indifference and neglect on the one hand, love and affection on the other.

In one of the most recent publications of this sort, Emilie Carles recalls how, at the beginning of this century, her severe concussion resulting from a fall at the age of six seems to have induced little more than a sorrowful stoicism in her otherwise loving father. In spite of her evidently dangerous condition, he refused to call the doctor.

> *It was not indifference, it was something else. Death struck roughly at children under fourteen. In most families, for every one that survived there was one who died; I've seen parents bury two in the same week and not show much emotion, especially if the little one was under five . . . That's the way it was, with peasants often showing more consideration for a cow about to calve than for their own wives and children. The torment of poverty outweighed the aching of the heart.*[23]

Perhaps, as Stephen Wilson implies, the notion of a 'pure' maternal instinct is inappropriate,[24] and the fundamental question is the degree to which it is influenced, reconfigured or overridden by cultural and community norms. In late twentieth-century western society, free for the most part from chronic food shortages and high rates of infant mortality and enjoying advanced medical and child-care facilities, such norms tend to reflect the ideal of maternal love.

In past times, however, the maternal instinct was often shaped by cultural norms, economic imperatives and religious beliefs which produced examples of child-care customs clearly harmful to the health of the infant: swaddling and wet-nursing in Europe; ritual 'neglect' of the baby under nine days old, for instance, in parts of West Africa and in the slave society of late eighteenth-century Jamaica.[25]

Viewed from a more anthropological and cross-cultural perspective, therefore, the Ariès thesis is less convincing. Moreover, it will be argued, infanticide did not amount to the murder of another human being in the eyes of the mother. Committed immediately after birth, there was not time for her to develop any maternal bond and the infant appears to have been regarded as no more than a foetus. In this respect, the legal definition of the crime notwithstanding, infanticide was for the mother simply a late abortion.

A brief history of infanticide in Europe

In classical times infanticide would appear to have been an acceptable and relatively common means of population control, applied particularly in the case of unwanted female offspring; it was only during the course of the fourth century that it became a crime under imperial Roman law.[26] The Christian church, which from the beginning had consistently condemned it as contrary to the principle of the inviolability of all human life, had much to do with this change in attitude and it is in this period that infanticide seems to have acquired the image of a crime of particular and unnatural enormity that it has retained more less to the present day. This might be explained partly by government determination to outlaw infanticide during a period of demographic crisis, but more importantly, by the church's desire to distinguish more clearly between pagan practices and Christian belief.[27]

Its real incidence during the Middle Ages is impossible to determine but the spread of foundling hospitals from the late eighth century has generally been interpreted as evidence of the church's response to a perceived increase in infanticide and exposure and of growing Christian concern for the welfare of the illegitimate child,[28] for illegitimate offspring, together with sickly or deformed babies, would appear to have constituted the majority of victims throughout the medieval and early modern periods in Europe.

Yet on the subject of procreation, as Flandrin has pointed out,[29] the teaching of the Church remained in certain aspects contradictory: on the one hand, the ideal of celibacy continued to be stressed, whilst on the other hand, at the same time, married couples were taught that it was their duty to have children. And the only solution offered by the Church to overpopulation was continence within marriage. Furthermore, it has been argued, it was the Church's very success in convincing the population of the evils of unmarried motherhood that indirectly contributed to the persistence of infanticide and abandonment of the newborn in early modern Europe.[30] In short, women in early modern Europe killed their offspring at birth because their fear of the shame and dishonour associated with unmarried motherhood outweighed all other considerations. Research on infanticide in England, Scotland, Germany and Corsica tends to support such an interpretation.[31] Certainly, the vast majority of those prosecuted were single women determined to conceal their pregnancy and the birth of their bastard children. In Nuremberg, for example, all but four of the 87 women condemned to death for infanticide between 1513 and 1777 were unmarried.[32] Rarely, after the Middle Ages,[33] does infanticide appear to have been used specifically as a method of population limitation.

It was during the sixteenth and seventeenth centuries that the prosecution, if not necessarily the real incidence, of infanticide appears to have reached a peak. Laws dealing expressly with the killing of illegitimate newborn babies were passed in Fiesole at the beginning of the sixteenth century, in the Holy Roman Empire in the 1520s, in France in 1556, in Lithuania in 1588, in England in 1624 (*An Act to Prevent the Murdering of Bastard Children*), and in Scotland in 1690.[34] This legislation had several common features, but one in particular, which is of overriding importance: the presumption of guilt of the mother in the event that an illegitimate child died at birth. To rebut the charge, the accused had to prove that the baby was stillborn, which necessitated the testimony of witnesses. But since many such births took place in secret, this was often not possible. In England, at least, the 1624 law was unique in that it reversed the fundamental legal principle of presumption of innocence. All these laws were concerned specifically with the killing of bastard offspring and all prescribed the death penalty.

Explanations for this rash of legislation vary. It has been associated with the trends towards government expansion, centralisation and judicial reform of the Renaissance monarchies; with the perceived increase in the incidence of infanticide; but above all, perhaps, with the desire of religious and lay authorities to reassert official values and established norms, whether Catholic or Protestant, during a period of profound religious upheaval. It is probably no accident that the introduction of these draconian infanticide laws coincided with the period of the 'witch craze'. Child-killing was specifically associated with witchcraft in the notorious witch-hunters' handbook of 1486, *Malleus Maleficarum*. 'Five thousand would be a conservative estimate of the number of women in France executed under the statute of 1556,' writes one historian, 'and it may well be that the great infanticide craze took as many lives as the great witch hunt.'[35]

Such figures should, however, be put into perspective. The brutally repressive policies of the sixteenth and seventeenth centuries gave way to an increasing reluctance on the part of courts and juries to convict on often flimsy evidence in cases where the death sentence was mandatory. By the eighteenth century conviction and prosecution rates were falling. In the *bailliage* of Alençon, in north-western France, for example, there were only ten prosecutions of infanticide between 1715 and 1745, out of a total of 930 criminal trials;[36] in Lorraine, between 1740 and 1790, only three out of 974.[37] Nevertheless, infanticide did not simply die out with the *ancien régime*. The nineteenth century may have witnessed a more enlightened judicial approach to the problem and a repeal of the 'terrorist' legislation of earlier years in Europe, but the continued lack of contraception and safe abortion ensured that it remained a distressingly common, even growing phenomenon. The medical practitioners of early Victorian London, for example, regarded the problem as one of epidemic proportions: one coroner even went as far as to claim that as many as 12,000 infant murders had gone unprosecuted.[38]

The prosecution of infanticide in the Cantal

In the century after 1789, 81 cases of infanticide came before the Cantal assize courts, involving 98 accused and including 13 cases in which accomplices were formally charged.[39] But it was not until the middle of the nineteenth century that the high point of prosecution was reached: only 21 cases in the 50 years between 1789 and 1839, rising to 60 between 1840 and 1889 (15 in the 1840s, 11 in the 1850s, 15 in the 1860s, 10 in the 1870s, and 9 in the 1880s). Thereafter, prosecutions fell away to 5 in the 1890s, 6 between 1900 and 1909 and 7 between 1910 and 1919.

Such an evolution appears to fit in broadly with the pattern observed for France as a whole by Vallaud and Lalou,[40] although the Cantal case does anticipate the curve of the national average by a decade or so, peaking in the 1840s—1860s rather than the 1850s—1870s. The extent to which these prosecution figures reflect the real incidence of infanticide is, of course, a moot point, for the so-called 'dark figure' — those cases which escaped detection — is impossible to estimate accurately. Besides the assize court prosecutions, there are only fragmentary references in the archives to a total of a further 48 cases of suspected infanticide: some of these did not even reach the courts, others went before the courts of summary jurisdiction (*tribunal correctionnel*) and were either dismissed or prosecuted as misdemeanours (*délits*).

For a rural department whose population remained less than 250,000 for most of the nineteenth century, the Cantal would appear to have experienced more than its fair share of infanticides. In the Hautes-Pyrénées, a comparable department in terms of population, topography and social structure, there were only 13 prosecutions for infanticide between 1830 and 1852 (22 for Cantal),[41] while in the much more heavily populated Eure-et-Loire there were 89 prosecutions between 1795 and 1859 (46 for the Cantal).[42] Infanticides as a percentage of total prosecutions in the assize courts between 1790 and 1883 represented 3.5 per cent in the Cantal, compared with only 2 per cent for the Eure-et-Loire (1795—1859) and 2.82 per cent for France as a whole (1840—59),[44] suggesting again that infanticide was rather more prevalent in the Cantal than elsewhere.

Lalou estimated that around four times as many infanticides were in practice committed as were prosecuted in the assize courts in nineteenth-century France, amounting to a rough average of 800 presumed infanticides per year between 1851 and 1900.[45] Corbin has suggested figures of one infanticide for every 583 live births in France as a whole in the period 1825—59, compared to 1 in 320 in the Haute-Vienne, 1 in 252 in the Creuse and 1 in 232 in the Corrèze, all of which departments were neighbours of the Cantal.[46] A proportion of, say, 1 in 250 in the Cantal would give us 25 infanticides per year in the mid-nineteenth century,[47] and a total of 2,500 between 1789 and 1889, over 30 times the number of assize court prosecutions. But we are descending here into the realm of simple guesswork. We can confidently state merely that our 81 prosecutions represented only a fraction of the real incidence of infanticide.

With the possible exception of abortion, infanticide was the most difficult of all crimes to prove in a court of law,[47] and cases were frequently abandoned at an early stage for want of evidence. As one public prosecutor (*procureur*) remarked in 1814, lamenting the increasing number of fruitless prosecutions, 'The public interest requires that pointless publicity — more often inclined to promote scandal than to serve any useful purpose — not be afforded this kind of affair. It is better not to prosecute at all than to do so without any real hope of conviction'.[48]

Infanticide was invariably committed clandestinely. The accused mother (and in only three cases was the mother not among the accused) inevitably did her utmost to ensure that pregnancy and birth remained secret. In the vast majority of cases, there were no witnesses at the birth. Only 13 of the accused mothers were persuaded to make a full confession, most of them in the late nineteenth century, by which time courts were far more indulgent and penalties less harsh.

In practice, a successful prosecution depended on the following by the early nineteenth century: the existence of the baby's body and its discovery sufficiently soon after death to allow for a proper autopsy; medical proof that the baby was not stillborn or premature, or both; the establishment as far as possible of the cause of death; proof that the accused mother had recently given birth, that the dead baby was in fact her child and that she was of sound mind; and finally, there had to be clear evidence of premeditation. Additional circumstantial evidence (absence of declaration of illegitimate pregnancy, *déclaration de grossesse*, in the eighteenth century, failure to make declaration of birth, lack of preparation for labour and birth, poor reputation, doubts about the fate of previous children) might be taken into account, but was rarely enough on its own to secure a conviction.

Much depended, therefore, on the rudimentary diagnostic capacities of the local doctor who, by means of a simple test, was normally able to tell whether or not a baby had been born alive: one of the baby's lungs, or a portion of a lung, was placed in a bowl of water. If it floated, it was concluded that the baby had breathed and had therefore been born alive; if it sank, that the baby had been stillborn.[49] But such a test was by no means infallible and in any case doctors were rarely able to establish cause of death with any degree of accuracy. As a result, it was only in those cases where the burden of proof was overwhelming that guilty verdicts were returned. Of the accused mothers, 35 per cent (26 out of 75 cases where the verdict was known) were acquitted.[50] Furthermore, of the 45 mothers originally accused of infanticide, 13 were ultimately convicted on lesser charges: involuntary homicide, a charge brought generally in cases where the mother was suspected of infanticide but where her intentions could not be proved (three cases);[51] *suppression*, introduced under a law of 1863, usually brought in cases where the baby was found dead and the birth kept secret, but where the cause of death was not known or could not be proven, and where a full charge of infanticide would almost certainly have been dismissed for lack of evidence (one case);[52] and the charge of having caused the death of the baby through lack of care, brought where proof of the intent to kill and of the cause of death was even less evident (nine cases).

Structural origins

As we shall see, explicit motives, beyond the functional explanation of a desire to keep pregnancy secret, are frequently not revealed in the trial dossiers. In the Bouygues case, as in most infanticide trials, the prosecution was apparently uninterested, indeed, in establishing an explicit motive: it was merely observed that the defendant was poor and unmarried and that she had concealed her pregnancy. Such was considered sufficient motivation in the eyes of the law. Yet, the killing of a newborn child was clearly not an act of gratuitous violence, nor — in most cases at least — the result of madness or temporary insanity. It had its origins in the objective structural conditions of a traditional peasant society still more characteristic of pre-industrial Europe than of the nineteenth century, in which material need, Catholic morals, rigid marriage and inheritance customs, and the law combined to impose a community intolerant of illegitimacy.

Above all, rural society was profoundly patriarchal. From birth, boys were preferred to girls. Families consistently demonstrated a preference for male offspring: sons were more productive workers and sources of income and since they did not require dowries, they were also cheaper. Too many daughters was regarded as a calamity, as numerous popular proverbs attest: 'Une fille brave fille, deux filles trop de filles, trois filles et la mère, quatre diables contre le père' (Limousin); 'Trop de vignes, trop de filles, trop de pigeons sont la ruine des maisons' (Anjou). Girls remained a burden on the household and their virtue needed constantly to be protected: 'Fille, vigne sont malaisées à garder, sans cesse quelqu'un passe qui voudrait y goûter' (Provence).[53] In nineteenth-century Cantal, such sentiments were pronounced. The following description of reactions to childbirth in a peasant household illustrates this point. The birth of a son

> *is a great event for the whole village; the neighbours flock to congratulate the happy father and to view the handsome baby boy who will be called upon to represent and perpetuate his humble dynasty; he is enveloped in fine white linen decorated with ribbons and carried in triumph to the church by a cortege of relatives and friends . . . But it is altogether different if the mother gives birth to a baby girl. Her unfortunate daughter is destined one day to become a stranger to the household . . . and to impoverish the family which will be obliged to provide her dowry; her birth is a misfortune; people hesitate to speak of it to the father, or come to present their condolences . . .*[54]

From adolescence, or earlier, girls were put to work on the farm. Once married, as Eugen Weber succinctly puts it, 'women were for breeding, and to be used as beasts of burden'.[55] At mealtimes in Cantal, 'The women serve the men and never take their place at table with them, a somewhat barbarous custom that these mountain people have no doubt inherited from their ancestors the Gauls. But the male servant always eats with his masters; he is not in a secondary position to them . . .'[56]

Such comments, of course, refer above all to the milieu of the propertied peasantry, for whom any threat to the patriarchal authority represented a threat to the patrimony. In so far as they owned little or no property, the attitude of the rural poor may have been very different. But there is little reason to suppose that the general environment by today's standards of sex discrimination was any less pervasive among the proletariat.

For all peasant girls marriage was the prime goal in life. It held out the promise of a degree of status in the community, of security in old age. And for the poor in particular, it enabled a pooling of resources and offered the opportunity to escape from a lifetime of perpetual struggle. Spinsterhood was everywhere regarded as a sign of failure.

Yet marriage was not always possible. Even in wealthy peasant households, unlucky daughters might find themselves excluded from a marriage market in which matrimonial strategies were determined above all by the needs of the family patrimony.[57] Satisfactory matches were frequently hard to come by. In this poor, overpopulated upland region, men migrated in their thousands for several months of every year to supplement their incomes in Paris and Bordeaux, or travelled round the country plying their wares. Many, particularly those travelling to Spain on business, returned only intermittently, if at all.[58] By the mid-nineteenth century, 10,000 a year — or 10—35 per cent of the total male population between the ages of 20 and 60 — were leaving the department during the winter months.[59] In 1851 the female population of the Cantal outnumbered the male by 134,000 to 119,000.[60] The marriage rate per 1,000 inhabitants was less than half the national average in the 1840s,[61] and nearly two-thirds of women in their 20s, one-third of women in their 30s, and one-quarter in their 40s were unmarried,[62] and therefore expected to remain celibate under the prevailing norms of church and community.

In practice many were condemned to what Claverie and Lamaison have described as the 'hazards of a vagabond, unstable, marginal and often violent sexuality'.[63] Such women, but most particularly those born into the rural poor, thus became the victims of a society which saw fit to exclude them from the world of respectability, to reproach them as a potential threat to conventional sexual morality while at the same time tolerating their exploitation by predatory males who regarded them as fair game. Single women in rural society, whether young servant-girls, middle-aged spinsters, or widows, were often regarded with some suspicion, even fear. They were deviant from the norm and might lead men astray and threaten the sanctity of family life. As such, they had already become the prime scapegoats in the witch-craze of the sixteenth and seventeenth centuries.[64]

But amongst all the categories of single women, it was the poor day-labourer or servant-girl who was the most vulnerable to sexual exploitation. For the eighteenth century, Olwen Hufton has described her struggle to earn a livelihood in vivid detail:[65] 10 or 15 years or more of unremitting toil on behalf of others, in an unstable labour market, in order to scratch together the savings for a dowry of sufficient size to attain the ultimate goal, marriage.

Conditions had changed little by the nineteenth century, at least in the Cantal, and it was inevitable that some of these women found the burdens of work, loneliness and community-enforced celibacy too heavy to bear. In the *ancien régime* registers of illegitimate pregnancy for the later eighteenth century,[66] we have a fairly precise picture of the prototypical unwed mother in the Haute-Auvergne (roughly equivalent to the department of Cantal created in 1790). Of the 578 women whose occupations were known (out of a total of 1,031), 487 (84 per cent) were in some form of farm or domestic service,[67] a reflection both of the high proportion of this category within the overall female population of child-bearing age,[68] but also of their particular vulnerability to seduction and abandonment by employers, fellow-workers or passing strangers. From the second half of the eighteenth century, in fact, the illegitimacy rate all over France was on the rise.[69] Certainly more pronounced in the cities and towns, it was nevertheless apparent also in the countryside of the centre and south, traditionally areas of very low illegitimacy. Accurate figures for the Haute-Auvergne are not available, but the neighbouring Basse-Auvergne registered a significant increase in the illegitimacy ratio,[70] and the Aurillac registers of illegitimate pregnancy suggest a similar trend: 69 declarations between 1765 and 1769, rising to 126 in 1775—79, and 183 in 1785—89.[71]

Whatever the explanations for this increase — as in Aix, it can have had little to do with the beginnings of industrialisation and urbanisation[72] — it does suggest that traditional community control was being subjected to a gradual process of erosion. Moreover, in the absence of more modern mechanical or pharmaceutical means, the methods of contraception available in the eighteenth and nineteenth centuries remained rudimentary and limited: the unreliable rhythm method was only beginning to be discussed as a serious option in medical circles in the mid-nineteenth century,[73] and the still rather expensive sheath or condom never spread beyond the world of the urban prostitute.[74] There remained only *coitus interruptus*, consistently condemned by the Roman Catholic church (like masturbation) as onanism, but nonetheless probably becoming the predominant method of birth control among the popular classes from the later eighteenth century.[75] By the mid-nineteenth century, at least, it would appear to have been well-known in the countryside, as demonstrated by such popular aphorisms as 'Do as the miller does: unload it at the mill gates.'[76]

But the growing number of illegitimate pregnancies from the later eighteenth century is sufficient testimony to the fact that contraception was frequently either ignored or did not work. The withdrawal method, by its very nature, put the responsibility primarily on the man, who had rather less to fear than his partner from the consequences of the act, particularly in view of the evolution of the law in this regard. Under the *ancien régime*, the pregnant, unmarried woman had at least some recourse in law against the main who had seduced her on the promise of marriage, based on the generally recognised principle of 'Qui fait l'enfant, doit le nourrir'. Henry II's edict of 1556,[77] introduced primarily in response to the perceived increase in infanticide and to protect the pregnant unwed woman from the presumption of infanticide in the event that her baby was stillborn, made the *déclaration de grossesse* in practice obligatory. The declaration, in turn, had the added purpose of discovering the identity of the father, thereby enabling the woman to bring a paternity suit.[78] This policy had the dual purpose of making some provision for impoverished women and their illegitimate offspring, and protecting the local parish from having to pay the cost of the provision by obliging the father to contribute to the upkeep of the child.

While in practice falling well short of a comprehensive system of welfare support, such a policy did demonstrate a considerable official concern for the well-being of the illegitimate child and provided the mother with some minimal legal protection against exploitation by unscrupulous seducers. However, since investigations were rarely made into the veracity of the mother's claims, the system was also inevitably open to abuse and the law of 12 brumaire Year II, followed by Article 340 of the Code Napoléon, formally prohibited all paternity suits.[79] Henceforth, the father of an illegitimate child, unless he chose voluntarily to acknowledge paternity, no longer had any legal responsibility for his offspring. As Van der Walle remarks, 'The nineteenth century avowedly aimed at protecting the family and its patrimony against the claims of spurious issue. It was generous neither to the child nor to the mother.'[80]

While such discriminatory legislation must to a degree have acted as a deterrent to female promiscuity, it was quite possibly overshadowed in practice by the spur it provided to male promiscuity and was seen by many in the early nineteenth century as primarily responsible for the continuing rise in illegitimacy rates. At the least, it withdrew what legal protection the poor unwed mother had enjoyed under the *ancien régime*, burdened her alone with the costs and responsibilities of bringing up a child, and thereby increased the likelihood of abandonment, abortion, and ultimately, infanticide.

The dilemma of the pregnant single woman

What, then were the available options in the nineteenth century for the single woman who became pregnant? Clearly, the most unsatisfactory option, but also the most unlikely in the milieu of the rural proletariat, was marriage,[81] either to her lover or to another unsuspecting or understanding suitor. For the man, the promise of marriage was certainly the most successful means of overcoming a woman's reluctance to sleep with him, particularly if he was in a position of some status in the local community. And despite evidence that pregnancy could rarely be successfully employed as a form of blackmail, the hope, at least, of marriage was probably in the mind of many consenting women. But in practice, the onset of pregnancy became, in most cases, the signal for an abrupt severing of relations, and the woman was left to fend alone as best she could.

This becomes evident when we look at the type and nature of relationship in which accused women became involved. In fact, in only 11 out of the total of 81 infanticide cases can we establish with any degree of certainty the identity of the putative father, and in six of these (including one abortion prosecution) he figures among the accused. In a further 16 cases, the suspected father was referred to vaguely, but no proof was available and he was rarely questioned. In a few instances, no doubt, this might be explained by the fact that the mother herself, because of the variety of possibilities, could not be sure who the father was.[82] But in the vast majority of cases, there was simply no reason for the authorities to take any interest in the alleged father, unless he was suspected of complicity in the crime. As we have seen, by the nineteenth century, he had no legal obligation to the girl he had seduced and had every incentive to avoid becoming embroiled in proceedings which would certainly reflect badly on his reputation. Moreover, unless specifically questioned on the subject, the accused mother rarely volunteered such information.

Nevertheless, approximately one-third of the trial dossiers provide us with some information, of very varying detail, on the nature of the relationship between the accused and her lover: in seven cases, the putative father was the woman's employer, or a member of the employer's family; in four, he was a fellow employee working in the same household; in a further 12 instances, pregnancy was the result of a chance encounter; finally, there is evidence of only four cases in which the relationship was apparently long-term, even if it fell short of qualifying as a stable consensual union.

Female servants, it is clear, were frequently seduced by their employers: at least one in four of those women who made declarations of illegitimate pregnancy in the later eighteenth century cited their employer, or a member of their employer's family as the father,[83] and several employers figure in our nineteenth-century dossiers. Antoine Baldus, a 63-year-old widower and *propriétaire* from the village of Ally, was one of the few actually to be charged with infanticide. The case reached court as a result of the death of Marie Tissandier, one of his servants, following a difficult labour in January 1846.[84] Tissandier had worked for Baldus for the past three years and it was common knowledge locally that the two lived 'en concubinage'. According to one witness, 'She liked her master . . . and he had a certain fondness for her'. She gave birth on the night of 24-25 January and died as a result of a haemorrhage two days later, by which time investigations into the disappearance of the baby had begun. Rumours were already circulating: 'They got rid of the child in the same way as we dispose of sickly lambs. We throw them on the dung heap.'

Further investigation revealed Baldus as a man of universally poor reputation. Local people rarely visited his house, according to another witness, since his 'dissolute life style' discouraged any contact. The only regular visitor was Jeanne Rilhac, a part-time midwife. On the first day of the investigation, Baldus was clearly heard to plead with Tissandier in the following terms, just before her death: 'I am in your hands. If you speak out, I am lost.' A few days later, another servant in the household miscarried, and everyone assumed that Baldus was once again the father. But the body of Tissandier's baby was never found, Jeanne Rilhac was acquitted of complicity, and Baldus himself, in spite of the circumstantial evidence against him, was sentenced only to one year's imprisonment for *suppression.*[85]

A further glimpse of the type of relationship common between master and servant was revealed in the case of criminal abortion brought against the 16-year-old Jeanne Roche, her employer Joseph-Camille Peuvergne, *propriétaire* of Leyvaux, and Jeanne Piret, an amateur abortionist, in the summer of 1847.[86] Several witnesses testified to the fact that Roche had been seduced by her employer — possibly by force — and had then been dismissed without pay when she became pregnant. The *procureur* believed Peuvergne to have been the main instigator in the affair and when questioned, the latter had given what, in the circumstances, was an indiscriminatingly ambiguous reply: 'I did not give her any such advice; other girls became pregnant in my household and I never advised them to seek an abortion.' On 16 October, a warrant of arrest was issued for Peuvergne, who shortly afterwards disappeared. A fortnight later, however, the authorities received a supporting letter of *justification* from a local *notable*, stressing the absence of proof and the fragility of the case against Peuvergne:

> Should a man of the upper class, linked to the most distinguished local
> families, be treated in such a way? Should we not, in the interests of equity,
> hesitate to stain the reputation of a man and the honour of a family simply on
> the word of a woman in whom, by virtue of her position as an interested party,
> we can have very little confidence?

All charges were shortly dropped against Peuvergne, allowing this well-connected bourgeois to escape prosecution altogether. While Jeanne Roche was ultimately acquitted, Piret was found guilty of criminal abortion and sentenced to 15 months in prison.[87]

Elise Juillard's relationship with her former master appears to have been of a more obviously mercenary kind. For two years she had worked as a servant in the household of the 78-year-old Chadefaux, with whom she had lived *en concubinage* and by whom she had had a child in April 1872. She was able to afford a house with money she had received from her employer, who evidently continued to support her once she had ceased to work for him. But in the winter of 1873—74, she became pregnant once again, this time clearly not by Chadefaux, and finally admitted to strangling her baby in August 1874 in order to hide the truth from him and to safeguard her very profitable arrangement.[88]

None of these cases reveal much trace of a relationship sufficiently enduring and caring to survive the news of pregnancy. That prosecution was the result is for the most part proof in itself of this. Pregnancy generally led to hasty termination of the relationship, occasionally to vague promises on the part of the seducer to support the child. Usually, he would deny all responsibility. Jeanne Toucheboeuf's experience is probably fairly typical.[89] She claimed that she only slept with her employer's son because he promised to marry her, and encouraged this belief by offering her regular gifts. They continued to see each other after she changed jobs but when she told him she was pregnant, he replied unsympathetically, 'If you are pregnant, that's your problem', and suggested she take an abortive potion. Her attempt to gain revenge by accusing him of complicity in infanticide failed, and no charges were brought against him.

Although it should not be overlooked that we are dealing here with a few exceptional cases of illegitimate pregnancy which ultimately led to infanticide or abortion, out of thousands which did not,[90] these examples do demonstrate the nature of the dilemma facing the pregnant woman. If she was in domestic service, she risked summary dismissal if her pregnancy was discovered. As a day-labourer, she could not hope to bring up her child without help or secure the funds to pay a wet-nurse. In both cases, unwed motherhood was incompatible with work. The most desperate women, their hopes of marriage destroyed, would ultimately be forced, at the least, into abandonment of their infant at birth or shortly after. And the rate of child abandonment rose inexorably in line with the increase in illegitimacy in the later eighteenth century: 391 infants were deposited at the gates of the Aurillac hospital in 1778–81, 544 in 1782–85, 641 in 1786–89, rising to 1,868 in 1790–93.[91] In the year 1793 alone, when 1,089 births were registered in the commune of Aurillac, 830 children were abandoned,[92] a figure no doubt swollen by the massive influx of foundlings from the surrounding countryside. Thereafter, however, in spite of the dechristianisation, conscription and economic dislocation of the revolutionary years,[93] and the introduction of *tours* (revolving cradles set into the walls of foundling hospitals, permitting anonymous abandonment) after 1811, abandonment in Aurillac levelled out at an average of 150 per year in the 1790s and the early eighteenth century. Only twice after 1795 did the figures exceed 200: in 1817 and 1824.[94] For the department as a whole, the annual number of abandonments rarely topped 250 before the closure of all *tours* in 1847.[95]

For reasons yet unexplained, this trend was not in line with the steep increases in abandonment at the national level in the early nineteenth century: 68,000 in 1809, rising to nearly double that figure in 1835.[96] The growing scale of abandonment nationally, indeed, and the enormous pressures put on the rudimentary welfare structure together with the consequent frightening increase in the mortality rate for foundlings,[97] soon led to a change in government policy. The *tours*, seen as encouraging sexual promiscuity, were first put under surveillance from around 1830 and then began to be closed in the 1840s. Since this period in the middle of the nineteenth century also witnessed an increase in exposures and in prosecution of infanticide, many contemporaries, with some reason, saw the disappearance of *tours* as one of the basic causes.

The remaining alternative (short of infanticide) for the unmarried pregnant woman who, for whatever reason, had decided that she could not bring up her child alone and could not afford the services of a wet-nurse, was abortion.[98] The simplest, cheapest and probably most widely used method involved the consumption of an infusion of herbs believed to have abortive properties: saffron, hyssop, powdered rosemary, ergot of rye, rue, savin and mugwort.[99] Other means, of very doubtful efficacy, included some form of violent exercise, lifting of heavy weights, heat treatment and bleeding with leeches. Clearly the most effective, but also the most dangerous method was through the insertion of some kind of instrument, either by the woman herself, or by an abortionist. In the contemporary circumstances of relative medical ignorance, inadequate hygiene and the consequent high risk of haemorrhage and infection, however, all such attempted abortions were potentially lethal for the mother.

As today, the attitude of the Roman Catholic church was unequivocal: the foetus possessed a soul, and abortion under any circumstances was strictly proscribed. Under the *ancien régime*, indeed, abortion was regarded as a homicide which deprived the innocent soul of baptism and eternal salvation, as a sin which could not be absolved in confession and which carried with it the penalty of excommunication. The state, likewise, treated abortion as a serious crime and it is possible that the edict of 1556 was inspired by government concern about abortion as well as infanticide. Few cases were in practice brought before the courts under the *ancien régime*, but those that were demonstrated the determination of the state to set an example to the population at large. In one of the most celebrated cases, in 1655, a midwife abortionist was hanged for inducing a miscarriage and causing the death of a court lady seduced by the Duc de Vitry.[100] In the nineteenth century, Article 317 of the Penal Code of 1810 punished 'whosoever, by aliments, potions, medicaments, violence or any other method, would provoke the miscarriage of a pregnant woman' with a term of imprisonment or forced labour.[101]

Abortion, however, to a greater extent even than infanticide, was a crime whose real incidence is impossible to determine. It was rarely discovered and only prosecuted in those cases where it led to the death of the mother, and where clear evidence against the abortionist was available. In France as a whole, over 20,000 instances were investigated between 1800 and 1914, but only 1,319 cases actually came to trial, and fewer than half the defendants were actually convicted.[102] Between the 1820s and 1850s, there was a considerable increase in prosecutions followed by an even steeper rise in the last twenty years of the century. Averaged out, there were around 30 prosecutions of criminal abortion per year in France during the nineteenth century. It is not clear, of course, to what extent the prosecution figures reflected an actual increase or simply more effective repression, but the apparent increase prompted a spate of alarmist medical tracts concerned with the low birth rate and with fears of race suicide after the traumas of defeat in the Franco-Prussian war of 1870–71. One such work, published in 1911, proposed figures of up to 400,000 abortions a year in the early twentieth century. Dupâquier, however, suggests the more modest figure of 200,000.[103] For example, at the regional level, 52 individuals were prosecuted for abortion in the

Drôme in 1856, of whom fewer than half were the mothers themselves.[104] In the Haute-Garonne, only two cases came before the courts between 1810 and 1842, five in 1842—50 and 24 between 1850 and 1880.[105]

In the Cantal, no more than nine cases were prosecuted during the whole of the nineteenth century. Why so few? Primarily because abortion was an immensely difficult crime to prove: there had to be incontrovertible proof of pregnancy and evidence of induced miscarriage, neither of which was likely to be available unless the abortion caused the death of the mother, or the discarded foetus was discovered, or the affair came to the knowledge of the authorities through an indiscretion or through the denunciation of a vengeful neighbour. Moreover, statistics suggest that whereas infanticide was a predominantly rural crime, abortion appears to have been a more characteristically urban — above all Parisian — phenomenon.[106] Nevertheless, it is clear that many more abortions took place in the Cantal than were actually prosecuted. The woman who lived alone might induce her own miscarriage in the early months of pregnancy with little fear of discovery. And those few cases of criminal abortion that reached the courts reveal that professional abortionists certainly existed, and that their services were in demand.

In the case of Jean-Baptiste Ribbe,[107] *officier de santé* of Egliseneuve d'Engraygues (Puy-de-Dôme), brought to trial in 1836 for carrying out abortions on three women, there was evidence that since 1829 he had performed at least nine other terminations for which there was insufficient proof to prosecute. He was aided and abetted by his mistress, who acted as his agent and 'procurer' in searching out potential clients. Although well-known as an abortionist and as 'a dangerous and immoral' individual, Ribbe's activities appear to have been tolerated by local public opinion until the death of one of his patients. 'My father does like all the others,' testified his son, 'only this allows doctors to earn a living.' Ribbe was probably representative of the upper end of the abortion business. The other abortionists prosecuted in the Cantal were altogether more amateur: Louise Pignol, an unemployed spinner from Massiac, who admitted to having used a pocket-knife on her client, who later died;[108] Jeanne Piret, from Saint-Beauzire (Haute-Loire), one of the accused in the Peuvergne case discussed above;[109] Marie Journiac, *journalière*, who advertised her skills in the Tourniac are and was condemned to ten years' imprisonment for attempted abortion in 1856;[110] and Anne-Marie Madelbos, an Aurillac midwife who performed an abortion on a woman who had come all the way from Burgundy to have the operation in 1858.[111]

Those young women who sought abortions were predictably from very much the same milieu as those prosecuted for infanticide in the Cantal: poor, unmarried servant-girls or rural textile workers seduced by their employers or colleagues. It is possible that as abortion became more accessible and less dangerous, so infanticide declined. This would certainly be suggested by the national crime figures: between 1861—65 and 1901—05, the total number of prosecutions of crimes against the newborn child fell from 1,833 to 1,242 (a reduction of 32 per cent),[112] while prosecution of criminal abortion increased from 1,633 to 3,046 during the same period (an increase of 86 per cent).[113] But abortion remained a predominantly urban crime and there is little hard evidence to support the view that it was becoming more widespread in the Cantal in the later nineteenth century, at least among the category of women we are discussing. One reason for this may have been cost. In those cases where payment was mentioned, the going rate appears to have been anything from 40 francs upwards: Ribbe charged 38—60 francs, but tried to extort 300 francs from one of his clients in the early 1830s; Louise Pignol charged 40 francs in 1838, Marie Journiac 60 francs in 1854 and Anne-Marie Mandelbos 105 francs in 1858. Much no doubt depended on the reputation, status and qualifications of the abortionist, but in a period when the servant-girl or day-labourer was unlikely to earn more than 100 francs per year,[114] even the cheapest operation would cost the rough equivalent of six months' wages.

The question of motivation

The structural conditions of peasant society, Catholic morality and civil law, as we have seen, were generally unfavourable to the unmarried mother in the nineteenth century, and amongst those who chose not to bring up their child themselves, most opted for exposure or abandonment. Why, then, did a small proportion of these unfortunate women decide upon the far more drastic solution of infanticide? Did the fear of shame and dishonour, regarded as the prime motive in the early modern period, continue to exercise a hold in the nineteenth century, or was it outweighed by other considerations like material need and the traumas of solitary childbirth? Such hypotheses may be tested by reference to some individual cases.

Of all those brought to trial for infanticide, it is the eight married women whose motives are most easily explicable.[115] In every case, the murdered child was the product of an adulterous relationship and in at least five the prime motive appears to have been the desire to conceal the pregnancy from the husband.[116] And husbands, in this region of seasonal migration, were frequently absent for long periods. Marie Basset's spouse was an itinerant vendor who had only been home for four months when his wife gave birth. She told the public prosecutor that she had buried the stillborn child shortly after birth in order to avoid arguments: 'I was pregnant, but not by my husband. I did not confide in him on this subject. For his part, he asked me no questions . . .'[117]

Marguerite Glénadet, a married woman of 22 living in the village of

Saint-Santin-Cantalès, was the defendant in perhaps the most clearcut case of infanticide in the whole of the nineteenth century.[118] She gave birth on the night of 3—4 October, claiming the baby was four months premature. Two days later the child died in highly suspicious circumstances: several witnesses testified to having seen the baby vomiting and to having remarked traces of white powder on its lips. The autopsy proved that the infant had in fact died of arsenic poisoning. Further investigations revealed that the baby had been born on time and healthy. According to the mayor who had ordered the initial investigation, Glénadet already had a poor reputation before marriage and had a clear motive for killing the child: to conceal the truth about her adulterous affair from her husband. The evidence against her was overwhelming and on 20 August 1844 she was found guilty and sentenced to 20 years' forced labour.[119] Even in this most sordid and clearly premeditated case of infanticide, the jury once again felt obliged to accept extenuating circumstances. This case was untypical in various respects: the defendant was married; the birth was witnessed; the baby was not killed at birth; the method of killing.

Bearing in mind the lowly occupations of the accused and the details of their existence which emerge from the investigations, it is difficult to believe that material need did not exercise a considerable influence on the mother who exposed, abandoned or killed her illegitimate offspring. Yet, poverty was put forward as a specific defence in only four cases in nineteenth- century Cantal, no doubt primarily, as Vallaud remarks, because juries were known to be unsympathetic to such explanations.[120]

Susanne Mirabel, a 36-year-old *journalière* living in Saint-Cirgues-de-Malbert, had come to Aurillac in June 1851 to look for a job, but also evidently to conceal her pregnancy. She gave birth alone on the night of 9 August and admitted to having thrown the baby into the river because she could not afford to bring it up. When asked why she did not deliver the infant to the hospice, she claimed not to know of its existence, in spite of having already served three days in prison in 1847 for *exposition*.[121] Marie Rose Tarisson, an unmarried *domestique* of 23 with one child, in similar circumstances, admitted disposing of her baby because she could not afford another.[122] Marguerite Bonnet's rather half-hearted pleading of poverty as a reason for dumping her baby in an Aurillac privy resulted in a detailed investigation by the authorities into her personal and financial situation: four or five years before, she had given birth to a baby which had died in infancy; a second child of three now lived with her parents, and a third had died the previous year at the wet-nurse's. The latter two had been born in the hospice. Why, she was asked, having earned an adequate wage for the past two years, had she not taken her latest offspring to the hospice?[123] The court was not convinced of her excuses and she was found guilty of attempted infanticide and sentenced to six years' forced labour in February 1877.[124]

A further explanation for infanticide formally proposed for the first time in the mid-nineteenth century was the trauma suffered by the woman during and immediately after childbirth. According to one influential school of medical thought, she was, by definition, ill and therefore could not be held responsible for her acts.[125] If such was a plausible argument in the case of the average married woman, it must be regarded as that much more relevant in the case of the unmarried mother who gave birth alone, without medical or family support. But, predictably — for admitting to mental disturbance implied a confession of guilt — the trial dossiers reveal only the occasional hint that the trauma of solitary childbirth was partly responsible for the mother's subsequent actions ('I killed the baby in a moment of aberration'; 'The baby died accidentally, as a result of my "nervous crisis"'; 'The devil took me over').

There remains only the argument concerning the safeguarding of honour defended by several prominent intellectuals, from Enlightenment philosophers like Beccaria and Kant to the late-nineteenth-century French criminologist Henri Joly, all sympathetic to the unmarried mother's predicament. For Beccaria, infanticide was

> the almost inevitable result of the appalling alternatives available to the unfortunate woman . . . On the one hand, disgrace, and on the other the death of a being incapable of sensing loss of life. Why would she not prefer the latter, which unburdens her of shame, to misery for herself and her child?[126]

In practice, however, very few of our trial dossiers reveal much evidence of the infanticidal mother's concern above all for her reputation and it is significant that all the following examples are from the early nineteenth century. Marie Pialoux (alleging that her baby was premature and stillborn) claimed that she failed to make a *déclaration de grossesse* and concealed her pregnancy and labour in order to 'preserve her reputation' and because she feared a beating from her brutal father.[127] Françoise Catignol admitted that 'everyone in the village regarded my behaviour as scandalous, which caused me much shame.'[128] Jeanne Borderie, a married woman whose husband had deserted her, hid the body of her allegedly stillborn baby because she feared 'scandal, and the reproaches of my family from whom I hid my pregnancy.'[129] Several other defendants mentioned similar sentiments in passing, but with no great conviction.

In the case of the 30 or more accused mothers (19 unmarried, 6 married, 5 widows) who had previously had children, the honour argument is even more difficult to sustain. These were not naive and frightened adolescents but for the most part mature women in their 30s, experienced enough to have known what they were doing and to have been fully aware of the alternatives. If honour was not a factor at the time of the first pregnancy, why should it have become so for the second or third?

Certainly, few of this group showed any signs of remorse after their arrest. The deed itself, generally committed immediately following delivery to prevent the baby crying, seems to have represented little more than a kind of late abortion, the elimination of a being for whom they could have developed no feelings of maternal attachment.

Several were of notably poor reputation. Jeanne Bonenfant, according to the local mayor, had for long, lived a 'life of debauchery. This woman is so unrestrained that she offers herself to all comers';[130] Marie Barbat, an unmarried day-labourer with three children, 'has the reputation in the commune . . . for being a loose woman.'[131] Juilly Vaury had been dismissed for 'indelicacy and misconduct' by her previous employer, who testified that 'This wretched woman debauched my 15-year-old son; I surprised her one day copulating with him . . . She even slept fully clothed so as to be always at the disposition of the men who flocked to her; she was like a bitch on heat.'[132]

If very few of the accused could be described as outright prostitutes, there is plenty of evidence of 'loose morals', 'licentious behaviour' and 'uncontrolled passions'. Such testimonies, in this *société d'interconnaissance*, in these closed village communities in which petty jealousies and rivalries abounded, should of course be treated with caution. But they do imply the existence of a marginal rural subculture whose values were no longer determined by those of the peasant elite in the later nineteenth century. In this milieu, as in rural Bavaria,[133] illegitimacy was perhaps no longer seen as such a disgrace. Even in the trial dossiers, there are enough examples of common-law relationships to suggest that attitudes towards marriage and family were changing.

Conclusions

Having dealt with the conventional hypotheses, it should perhaps be stressed that we cannot expect definitive documentary evidence of motivation in these dossiers. The responses of defendants under interrogation may well have been governed primarily by considerations of what they perceived the authorities wanted to hear or of what the courts regarded as an acceptable defence. A wholly satisfactory explanation of the specific reasons for infanticide as opposed to its structural 'causes' remains beyond our grasp, not least because the state of mind of the pregnant woman cannot easily be subjected to rational historical analysis. Concealment of pregnancy, for example, does not in itself constitute clear proof of premeditation. It might simply have been a manifestation of the woman's desire to postpone decisions, to keep her options open, to deny the truth to herself, as well as to her family and neighbours. Once the first public denial had been made, subsequent denials became a matter of pride, of self-respect. And the longer the fiction was maintained, the more fiercely it was defended. Although her colleagues had long been joking about Jeanne Malbert's 'prodigious size', she persistently denied being pregnant and continued to work in the fields until the day before she went into labour;[134] Jeanne Dufour admitted that she had put on weight but explained that this was due to having eaten too many green potatoes;[135] Marie Saurine, offered help by a suspicious neighbour, replied 'that she would rather have her head cut off than consult the doctor.'[136]

It should not indeed be assumed that the successful concealment of pregnancy was impossible, even for the closely supervised servant-girl. There are several instances in the dossiers in which all the witnesses interviewed claimed ignorance. Emilie Carles recounts the story or a recently-widowed neighbour who had become pregnant by the village Don Juan:

> *She managed to fool us all to the very end, including her 17-year-old son. She came within a hair's breadth of carrying off her plan: gave birth without anyone being the wiser and perhaps set to get rid of her newborn. Unfortunately for her, the day she went into labour, she took to her bed and could not hide the pain . . . The most extraordinary part of the story is that no one in the village noticed a thing. I myself was completely taken in and yet I got my milk from her every day . . .*[137]

Months of concealment and constantly repeated denials in many cases seem to have reduced these women to a psychological state in which they refused to admit the truth to themselves or to recognise that the object in their belly had an identity. Denial of pregnancy often led to denial of birth, which inevitably entailed the rapid disposal of the infant.[138] In such circumstances, infanticide had become not only a logical necessity, but an act of self-justification, even of emancipation, by which these despairing women sought to determine their own future.

In concluding, we might, after all, be justified in arguing that infanticide, at least in the earlier nineteenth century, was in this narrower sense a crime of honour. Deserted by the father of her baby, the pregnant woman became the focus for community disapproval and the inevitable victim of her own sexuality in a society where the bastard child and the unmarried woman continued to represent a threat both to conventional morality and the stability of property relations. By the later nineteenth century, however, as the rural exodus began to ease the pressures of overpopulation and society became more tolerant of illegitimacy, honour seems to have been of less importance. Throughout the period, poverty, particularly in the case of domestic servants who faced immediate dismissal if their pregnancy was discovered, also exercised an influence on the infanticidal mother.

Overall, infanticide was a rare offence, committed generally by only the most desperate women, in nineteenth-century Cantal. It should not be regarded as a residual manifestation of what Ariès interpreted as the absence of parental love for the infant in early modern Europe. The newborn child was till more of a foetus than a human being for the infanticidal mother. In practice, notwithstanding the terrorist character of infanticide legislation in the Reformation period, Church and state throughout Europe since the Middle Ages had implicitly accepted the status of a newborn baby as less than that of an adult or older child.[139] Moreover, one has the impression, as in the Gévaudan,[140] that murder of the newborn was not in fact regarded with any particular horror in the rural community; that it was not so much the death of the infant that governed the local response, as intolerance in the face of the mother's denial: that what the community demanded above all was a public admission of guilt. Bearing in mind the enduring peasant hostility to outside authority of all kinds,[141] it appears that local cooperation in infanticide investigations was also highly selective. 'All the neighbours are relatives of the accused,' complained one mayor in a letter to the *procurur*, 'so I have been unable to obtain the required information.'[142] The community seems often to have had a decisive voice in deciding whether or not the infanticidal mother should be delivered to the authorities.[143] Local reputation and position were the key factors here. Only those women with notably poor reputation, or beggar-women, or outsiders, were readily denounced to the authorities.[144]

Although rare, infanticide was rooted in the conditions of peasant society, a society whose values were radically different from those of the contemporary bourgeois world. And in many respects these trial dossiers are more interesting for what they reveal about the nature of that peasant society than for the light they shed on the crime of infanticide itself. From this perspective, the study of deviant behaviour can offer special insights into the daily life, language, cultural norms and social relationships of the rural masses.[145] Analysis of the atypical can enrich our understanding of the typical. And since infanticide was almost by definition a female crime, these dossiers also provide a unique source of information on the position of women within this *société d'interconnaissance*. Where else may we re-discover, in such eclectic detail, the hidden world of the peasant woman who has left so little trace in more conventional sources?

Endnotes

1. The following information comes from the trial dossier of Cécile Bouygues, *Archives Départementales du Cantal* (hereafter ADC) 38U 129 (assize court dossiers), April—August 1841.
2. ADC 35U 37 (register of sentences), 3 August 1841.
3. ADC 38U 3-281.
4. The law of 25 April 1832 permitted juries, as well as judges, to accord 'extenuating circumstances' in all cases which came before assize courts, and reflected that general trend towards liberalisation of the Napoleonic criminal law characteristic of the early nineteenth century. If extenuating circumstances

were admitted — as they were in fact in all but two infanticide cases leading to a guilty verdict after 1832 — then the court was obliged to reduce the penalty by one or two degrees. Primarily, then, this law was intended to counteract the excessive number of acquittals by juries reluctant to convict when the automatic penalty was death, and to bring about more efficient prosecution of serious crime. (See R. Lalou, 'L'infanticide devant les tribunaux français, 1825—1910', *Communications*, 44 (1986), pp. 189—90; and D. Vallaud, 'Le Crime d'infanticide et l'indulgence des Cours d'Assises en France au XIXème siècle', *Information sur les Sciences Sociales*, 22, 3, 1982, p. 479.

5. See B. Bush, *Slave Women in Caribbean Society, 1650—1838*, (London: Heinemann, 1990), pp. 137—50, on abortion and infanticide as a possible contributory factor to low fertility.

6. *The Daily Gleaner*, 16 November 1991, p. 1. The baby apparently died shortly after being admitted to Mandeville hospital, according to a report in the same newspaper, 17 November, p. 1.

7. The only other recent case of infanticide reported in the Jamaican press warranted merely a short paragraph on p. 2 of *The Daily Gleaner*, 11 February 1986.

8. In France, Article 300 of the Code Napoléon defined it as such. Not until 1835 did the *Cour de Cassation* formally announce that 'newborn' would henceforth be taken to mean within one week of birth (see Vallaud, pp. 477, 481, 493).

9. See the comments on this in A. Soman, 'Deviance and criminal justice in Western Europe, 1300—1800: an essay in structure', *Criminal Justice History*, Vol. 1, 1980, p. 23.

10. L. Jordanova, 'Children in History: Concepts of Nature and Society' in G, Scarre (ed.), *Children, Parents and Politics* (Cambridge: Cambridge University Press, 1989), p. 8.

11. *L'Enfant et la Vie Familiale sous L'Ancien Régime* (Paris: Ploy, 1960), translated into English as *Centuries of Childhood* (New York: Vintage Books, 1962).

12. See, for example, E. Shorter, *The Making of the Modern Family* (New York: Basic Books, 1975); L. Stone, *The Family, Sex and Marriage in England, 1500—1800* (abridged edn., London: Penguin, 1977); J.-L. Flandrin, 'L'attitude à l'égard du petit enfant et les conduites sexuelles dans la civilisation occidentale', *Annales de Demographie Historique* (1973), pp. 143—205; more recently, F. Lebrun, *La Vie Conjugale sous l'Ancien Régime* (Paris: Armand Colin, 1985).

13. Shorter, p. 168.

14. See, for example, Vallaud and Lalou.

15. For example, G.D. Sussman, 'The wet-nursing business in nineteenth century France', *French Historical Studies*, IX (1975—76); F. Lebrun, 'Naissances illégitimes et abandons d'enfants en Anjou au XVIIe siècle', *Annales* (juillet—août, 1972), pp. 4—5; and P.-F. Aleil, 'Enfants illégitimes et enfants abandonnes à Clermont dans la seconde moitié du XVIIIe siècle', *Cahiers d'Histoire*, (1976).

16. E. Badinter, *L'Amour en Plus* (Paris, 1980, translated as *The Myth of Motherhood: a historical view of the maternal instinct* (1981).

17. E. Le Roy Ladurie, *Montaillou: Cathars and Catholics in a French Village* (London: Penguin, 1980), Chapter 13.

18. N. Z. Davis, 'The reasons of misrule: youth groups and charivaris in sixteenth-century France', *Past and Present* (1971), p. 50.

19. S. Wilson, 'The myth of motherhood a myth: the historical view of European child-rearing', *Social History* (May 1984).

20. A. Wilson, 'The infancy of the History of Childhood: an appraisal of Philippe Ariès', *History and Theory*, XIX, 2 (1980), p. 153. For an overview of Ariès's work, see also R.T. Vann, 'The Youth of " Centuries of Childhood"', *History and Theory*, XXI (1982).

21. S. Shahar, *Childhood in the Middle Ages* (London: Routledge, 1992), p. 1.

22. Amongst the most interesting examples are P. Besson, *Un Pâtre du Cantal* (Aurillac, 1914); E. Guillaumin, *La Vie d'un Simple* (Paris: Stock , 1943); and P.-J. Helias, *Le Cheval d'Orgueil: mémoires d'un breton du pays bigouden* (Paris: Plon, 1975).

23. E. Carles, *A Wild Herb Soup: the Life of a French Countrywoman*, translated and introduced by Avril H. Goldberger (London; Gollancz, 1991), pp. 6—7.

24. S. Wilson, p. 197.

25. See Bush, pp. 146—47.

26. W.L. Langer, 'Infanticide: a historical survey', *History of Childhood Quarterly*, I (winter 1974), pp. 354—55.

27. K. Wrightson, 'Infanticide in European History', *Criminal Justice History* 3 (1982), pp. 3—4.

28. Langer, p. 356.

29. Flandrin, pp. 143—60.

30. Wrightson, p. 8: 'The crime sprang not from the persistence of norms alien to the conventional morality of Christian Europe, but rather from the fact that those norms and sanctions which upheld them made so deep an impression on the minds of pregnant women.'

31. See K. Wrightson, 'Infanticide in earlier seventeenth-century England', *Local Population Studies* (autumn 1975); R.W. Malcolmson, 'Infanticide in the eighteenth century' in J.S. Cockburn (ed.), *Crime in England, 1500—1800* (London: Methuen, 1977); R. Mitchison and L. Leneman, *Sexuality and Social Control: Scotland, 1660—1780* (Oxford: Blackwell, 1989), pp. 210—14; O. Ulbricht, 'Infanticide in eighteenth-century Germany', in R.J. Evans (ed.), *The German Underworld: Deviants and Outcasts in German History* (London: Routledge, 1988); and S. Wilson, 'Infanticide, child abandonment and female honour in nineteenth century Corsica', *Comparative Studies in Society and History*, 30 (1988).

32. Langer, p. 356.

33. On the Middle Ages, see E. Coleman, 'L'infanticide dans le Haut Moyen Age', *Annales* (mars—avril 1974); and Y.-B. Brissaud, 'L'infanticide à la fin du Moyen Age, ses motivations psychologiques et sa répression', *Revue Historique de Droit Français et Etranger* (1972).

34. R.C. Trexler, 'Infanticide in Florence: new sources and first results', *History of Childhood Quarterly*, 1 (1973), p. 114.

35. See Soman, pp. 22—23.

36. Lebrun, *La Vie Conjugale*, p. 152.

37. M.-J. Laperche-Fournel, 'Les enfants indésirables: l'infanticide en Lorraine au XVIIIe siècle', *Cahiers Lorrains*, 1 (1989), p. 26.

38. See A.R. Higginbotham, '"Sin of the Age": infanticide and illegitimacy in Victorian London', *Victorian Studies* (spring 1989), p. 319.

39. These 81 cases included three which involved the death of infants between

the ages of three months and two years, which were not, in legal terms, infanticides. I have found only four prosecutions among the trial dossiers of the *Bailliage et Présidial d'Aurillac* for the eighteenth century and none in the collections of the other royal and seigneurial jurisdictions for the Haute-Auvergne, though much of these series remains unclassified.

40. Vallaud, p. 492, and Lalou, p. 181. Both authors used the statistics in the *Compte General de l'Administration de la Justice Criminelle*, 1825—1910, in the Bibliothèque Nationale in Paris.

41. M. Tribut, 'La criminalité dans les Hautes-Pyrénées de 1830 à 1852', *Annales du Midi*, XCIII (1981), p. 423.

42. J.-C. Farcy, 'Les archives judiciaires et l'histoire rurale: L'exemple de la Beauce au dix-neuvième siècle', *Revue Historique*, 524, (octobre-décembre, 1977), p. 334.

43. *Ibid.*, p. 333.

44. Lalou, p. 181.

45. See R. Price, *A Social History of Nineteenth-Century France* (New York: Holmes and Meier, 1987), p. 73.

46. These figures are calculated on the basis of an average of 6,600 births per year in the 1840s. This would amount to the almost inconceivable ratio of 1 infanticide for every 16 illegitimate births. However, the following testimony of one defendant accused of killing her 4-month-old baby while in prison in Saint-Flour suggests that such a ratio may not have been quite so unlikely. While under interrogation by an assize court judge, Catherine Vedel claimed that one of her cell-mates had told her that, "*in my parts of the world, many were disposed of by inserting a needle into the hollow of the baby's skull. Legitimate as well as illegitimate children were killed in this way. The local doctors who were charged with investigating this matter were quite unable to determine the cause of death. Only an expert called in from outside by the authorities was finally able to discover the truth.*" (ADC 38U 141, 1846).

47. For the problem of proof, see Lalou, pp. 191—94, and Vallaud, pp. 480—82.

48. ADC 123U 15, 14 December 1814.

49. On the lung test, see Lalou, p. 193; Vallaud, p.481; M.-C. Phan, 'Les déclarations de grossesse en France (XVIe-XVIIe siècles): essai institutionnel', *Revue d'Histoire Moderne et Contemporaine*, XXII (janvier-mars 1975), p. 83; and Malcolmson, p. 200.

50. At the national level, of the 5,591 accused who came before the assize courts between 1833 and 1862, 1,998 (35.7 per cent) were acquitted. Of all *crimes* (in the French legal sense), infanticide had the greatest proportion of acquittals: 26 per cent in 1826-62, rising to 35 per cent thereafter (Vallaud, p. 480).

51. Lalou, p. 181.

52. *Ibid.*, p. 180, and Vallaud, p. 480.

53. See M. Segalen, 'Le mariage, l'amour et les femmes dans les proverbes populaires français', *Ethnologie Française*, 5 (1975) pp. 134—35.

54. M. Deribier du Châtelet, *Dictionnaire Statistique ou Histoire, Description et Statistique du Département du Cantal*, Vol. 11 (reprint, Mayenne, 1964), p. 137.

55. E. Weber, *Peasants into Frenchmen: The Modernization of Rural France 1870—1914* (London: Chatto and Windus, paperback edition, 1979), p. 175.

56. Deribier du Châtelet, p. 133.

57. For examples of the way in which matrimonial strategies were determined by the mode of transmission of property in the nearby Gévaudan (department of

Lozère), see P. Lamaison, 'Les stratégies matrimoniales dans un système complexe de parenté: Ribennes en Gévaudan (1650—1830)', *Annales* (juillet-août 1979).

58. See M. Trillat, 'L'émigration de la Haute-Auvergne en Espagne du XVIIe au XXe siècle', *Revue de la Haute-Auvergne* (1955).

59. These figures are approximate. The seasonal migration figures appear in Deribier du Châtelet, p. 139, and the percentages are calculated from the census figures of 1851 in the same source (p. 120).

60. *Ibid.*, pp. 120—21.

61. *Ibid.*, p. 121. The figures from Deribier were compared with those for France as a whole appearing in Price, p. 75.

62. *Ibid.*, pp. 120—21. The proportions for men were, respectively, 70 per cent, 25 per cent and 13 per cent.

63. See E. Claverie and P. Lamaison, *L'Impossible Mariage: Violence et Parenté en Gévaudan, XVIIe et XIXe Siècles* (Paris: Hachette, 1982), p. 219.

64. See for example, J. Klaits, *Servants of Satan: The Age of the Witch Hunt* (Bloomington, Indiana: Indiana University Press 1985), particularly Chapters 3 and 4.

65. See O. Hufton, 'Women and the family economy in eighteenth-century France', *French Historical Studies*, IX (1975); and 'Women, Work and Marriage in eighteenth century France', in R.B. Outhwaite (ed.), *Marriage and Society: Studies in the Social History of Marriage* (London: Europa, 1981). Also O. Hufton, *The Poor in Eighteenth-Century France* (Oxford: Oxford University Press, 1974), particularly Chapter 12.

66. ADC 1B 918 (*bailliage* of Aurillac, 1749—92); ADC 14B 226 (*bailliage* of Salers, 1782—91); ADC 15B 598 (*bailliage* of the Carladès, 1751—90); and ADC 16B 864 (*baronnie* of Naucaze, 1756—71).

67. By far the most numerous listed occupation in this category were *servantes* (448). The remainder were made up of *filles de chambre, cuisinières, journalières, bergères* and *gouvernantes*.

68. Domestics of all kinds represented anywhere between 2 per cent and 12 per cent of the total population in eighteenth-century rural France and the large majority of these were female: see C. Fairchilds, *Domestic Enemies: Servants and their Masters in Ancien Régime* France (Baltimore: Johns Hopkins University Press, 1984), p. 2; Malcolmson, p. 202, suggests that up to 50 per cent of unmarried women between the ages of 16 and 25 were servants in eighteenth-century England. Laslett has produced figures indicating that 27 per cent of all women in the 15—19 age group, 40 per cent in the 20—24 age group, and 15 per cent in the 25—29 age group were 'life-cycle' servants in pre-industrial England (P. Laslett, *Family Life and Illicit Love in Earlier Generations* (Cambridge: Cambridge University Press, 1977), p. 34). For servants in France, see also P. Guiral and G. Thuillier, *La Vie Quotidienne des Domestiques en France au XIXe siècle* (Paris: Hachette, 1978), p. 11.

69. See, for example, F. Lebrun, *La Vie Conjugale*, pp. 97—98; Hufton, *The Poor*, pp. 320—21; M.W. Flinn, *The European Demographic System, 1500—1820* (Baltimore: Johns Hopkins University Press, 1985), pp. 81—82.

70. A. Poitrineau, *La Vie Rurale en Basse-Auvergne au XVIIIe siècle* (Paris, 1965), pp. 59—60. See also Aleil, pp. 307—33.

71. ADC 1B 918.

72. C. Fairchilds, 'Female sexual attitudes and the rise of illegitimacy: a case study', *Journal of Interdisciplinary History*, 4 (spring 1978), p. 633.
73. See J.T. Noonan, *Contraception: A History of its Treatment by the Catholic Theologians and Canonists* (Harvard: Belknap Press/Harvard University Press, 1966), pp. 438—39.
74. On the condom, see *ibid.*, pp. 347—48; N.E. Himes, *Medical History of Contraception* (New York: Gamut Press, 1963, pp. 186—202; and Lebrun, *La Vie Conjugale*, p. 161.
75. See, for example, Lebrun, *La Vie Conjugale*, pp. 163—65.
76. 'Faire comme le meunier: décharge sa charrette à la porte du moulin', quoted in A. Maclaren, 'Abortion in France: women and the regulation of family size, 1800—1914', *French Historical Studies*, 10 (1978), p. 469.
77. On the edict of 1556, see Phan.
78. Vallaud, p. 486; see also Hufton, *The Poor*, pp. 321—24.
79. Vallaud, pp. 487—88.
80. E. Van der Walle, 'Illegitimacy in France during the nineteenth century', in P. Laslett *et al.* (eds), *Bastardy and its Comparative History* (London: Edward Arnold, 1980), p. 265.
81. In only four cases was the possibility of marriage even mentioned by the accused.
82. Félicité Figeac, for example, a 21-year-old *domestique*, mentioned three possible candidates: her employer and two friends, all of whom denied it. 'I kissed her when I got the chance,' admitted one of the friends, 'but I didn't go any further.' ADC 38U 216 (1869).
83. See note 66 above for sources.
84. ADC 38U 140.
85. ADC 35U 38 (June 1846).
86. ADC 38U 143.
87. ADC 35U 38 (November 1847).
88. ADC 38U 234. She was found guilty of infanticide and sentenced to eight years' hard labour on 14 November 1874 (ADC 35U 45).
89. ADC 38U 237 (1875).
90. The rising rate of pre-nuptial conceptions evident in the village of Ribennes, in the neighbouring Lozère (5 per cent in the early eighteenth century; 20 per cent in the early nineteenth; 40 per cent by the mid-nineteenth century) would suggest that a certain proportion of illegitimate pregnancies of even the poorest women might in fact lead to marriage (see Claverie and Lamaison, pp, 219—20).
91. ADC 2E 48—51.
92. Dr de Ribier, 'Les enfants abandonnés à Aurillac à la fin du XVIIIe siècle', *Revue de la Haute-Auvergne*, 1933, pp. 122—23.
93. On the plight of *enfants trouvés* in the 1790s see A. Forrest, *The French Revolution and the Poor* (Oxford: Blackwell, 1981), pp. 116—37.
94. ADC 2x 8681-8685.
95. ADC 2x 8686-8688; ADC x1 146.
96. Vallaud, p. 489.
97. In the Haute-Vienne, for example, 71.5 per cent of the 12,862 children abandoned between 1810 and 1842 died before the age of ten (A. Corbin, *Archaïsme et Modernité en Limousin au 19e siècle* (Paris, 1975), p. 520.

98. On abortion, the following sources were used: Flandrin, 'L'attitude à l'égard du petit enfant'; J.-L. Flandrin, 'L'avortement dans l'ancienne France (XVIe-XVIIIe siècles)', *L'Histoire*, 16 (1979), pp. 33—34; J. Gaillard, 'Le Médecin et l'avortement au XIXe siècle', *L'Histoire*, 16 (1979), pp. 35—37; A. Maclaren, 'Abortion in France: women and regulation of family size, 1800—1914', *French Historical Studies* (spring 1978), pp. 461—85; A. Fine, 'Savoirs sur le corps et procédés abortifs au XIXe siècle', *Communications*, 44 (1986), pp. 107—36; and J. Dupâquier, 'Combien d'avortements en France avant 1914?', *Communications*, 44 (1986), pp. 87—106.
99. Ergot of rye, for example, might induce miscarriage by causing haemorrhage and partial separation of the placenta. It is reportedly still used on occasion in clandestine abortions in contemporary Jamaica.
100. Flandrin, 'L'attitude à l'égard', p. 164.
101. See Fine, p. 107.
102. Dupâquier, pp. 94—95.
103. *Ibid.*, pp. 92—93.
104. Gaillard, p. 35.
105. Fine, p, 107.
106. See the statistics in Dupâquier, p. 106.
107. ADC 38U 115. The case was heard in the Cantal, on appeal from the assize courts of the Puy-de-Dôme.
108. ADC 38U 119 (1838).
109. ADC 38U 143 (1847).
110. ADC 38U 168 and ADC 35U 41.
111. Madelbos died in prison while awaiting trial and her client, Madeleine Zingerlé, was found guilty of complicity and sentenced to two years prison in November 1858 (ADC 38U 184; ADC 35U 42).
112. Lalou, p. 181.
113. Dupâquier, p. 94.
114. By way of example, in 1810, Françoise Lastane, *servante*, was hired in April for 30 francs until 1 November (ADC 38U 37). In 1852, *journalières* could expect to earn 70 centimes per day in summer and 40 centimes in winter; *domestiques* in Aurillac earned 25—40 francs a year (ADC 170M 1). By 1860, *servante* earned 60 francs a year (50 per cent of the lowest male wage on the farm, and 180 francs a year by 1895: see A. Durand, *La Vie Rurale dans les Massifs Volcaniques des Dores, du Cézallier, du Cantal et de l'Aubrac* (Aurillac, 1946). Food and lodging would normally be included for *servantes*, food only for *journalières*.
115. The real incidence of infanticide by married women is beyond even speculation since the opportunities for concealing the crime were that much greater, most particularly if the husband was involved as an accomplice.
116. In the remaining three cases the husbands were long-term absentees: one had disappeared years before; one was an inmate of the Aurillac mental asylum and the last had been a prisoner in Brest for the past six years.
117. ADC 38U 120 (1838).
118. ADC 38U 136 (1833—34).
119. ADC 35U 38.
120. Vallaud, p. 485. On the problems of juries in criminal trials, see also E. Claverie, 'De la difficulté de faire un citoyen: les 'acquittements scandaleux' du jury dans la France provinciale du début du XIXe siècle', *Etudes Rurales*, 95—96

(janvier-juin 1984); and Y. Pourcher, '"Des Assises de Grace?" Le jury de la Cour d'Assises de la Lozère au XIXe siècle', *Etudes Rurales*, 95-96 (janvier-juin 1984).

121. ADC 38U 156.
122. ADC 38U 256 (1881).
123. ADC 38U 243 (1877).
124. ADC 35U 46.
125. See Vallaud, p. 484, and Lalou, p. 194.
126. Quoted by Vallaud, p. 485.
127. ADC 38U 21 (Year VII-VIII).
128. ADC 38U 47 (1814).
129. ADC 38U 126 (1840).
130. ADC 38U 129 (1841).
131. ADC 38U 156 (1851).
132. ADC 38U 281 (1889).
133. See R. Schulte, 'Infanticide in rural Bavaria in the nineteenth century', in D. Medick and D. Sabean (eds), *Interest and Emotion: Essays on the Study of Family and Kinship* (Cambridge: Cambridge University Press, 1984), p. 84.
134. ADC 38U 129 (1841).
135. ADC 38U 126 (1840).
136. ADC 38U 30 (1809).
137. Carles, *A Wild Herb Soup*, pp. 130—31.
138. The phenomenon of denial, according to researchers into modern infanticide, who distinguish between 'neonaticide' (killing of a newborn child within 24 hours of birth) and 'filicide' (murder of an infant over one day old), plays a key role: in destroying the infant, the murdering parent kills an object whose very existence may have been effectively denied. There has been no advance preparation for either the care or the killing of the child. This absence of relatedness may account for the lack of remorse commonly encountered in the offending parent after the crime of neonaticide. See I.L. Kutash, S.B. Kutash *et al.*, *Violence: Perspectives on Murder and Aggression* (San Francisco: Jossey-Bass, 1978), p. 175.
139. See C. Damme, 'Infanticide: the worth of an infant under law', *Medical History*, 22 (1978); and K. O'Donovan, 'The medicalisation of infanticide', *Criminal Law Review* (May 1984).
140. See Claverie and Lamaison, p. 239.
141. For peasant attitudes to the law in the Auvergne, see O. Hufton, 'Les paysans et la loi en France au XVIIIe siècle', *Annales* (mai-juin 1983).
142. ADC 38U 121 (1838—39). The accused, Toinette Bronzac, was nevertheless found guilty and condemned to death *in absentia*. There is no evidence that she was ever found.
143. See Schulte, p. 98, for similar attitudes in Bavaria.
144. Of the 16 cases where the accused were reported as having a poor reputation, only four were acquitted and their sentences were notably heavier.
145. On court records as a source for rural history, see Farcy.

19.

The Status, Role and Influence of Women in the Eastern Delta States of Nigeria, 1850–1900:

Examples from New Calabar*

Waibinte E. Wariboko

New Calabar, a 'city-state' (also called a 'trading state') located about 16 miles from the mouth of a river of the same name (New Calabar River), was one of the Eastern Delta states of Southern Nigeria. The other states were Bonny, Nembe Brass, Opobo and Okrika. All of these states had initially (from about the mid-fifteenth century to the mid-nineteenth century) traded in slaves to the European countries of Portugal, Holland, Spain and Britain. From the mid-nineteenth century, however, the Eastern Delta trading states began trading in palm oil and kernels, following the effective establishment of the trade in these commodities until the 1930s. Unlike the trade in slaves, Britain and Germany (especially the former) dominated European trade to the Eastern Delta throughout the nineteenth and early twentieth centuries.

In view of the longevity and intensity of this socio-commercial contact with the Atlantic world, Nigeria's pioneer historians- Dike,[1] Jones,[2] Alagoa,[3] Afigbo,[4] Cookey,[5] Ikime,[6] Horton,[7] Anene,[8] Ajayi[9] and Ofonagoro[10] — have been attracted to the study of the Eastern Delta as a geographical and historical unit. However, virtually all of these authors, whatever their standpoints, have discussed the consequences of this Euro-African contact (seen in terms of British consular rule, transatlantic commerce and Christian missionary propaganda) for the Eastern Delta from two perspectives. They have described the economic change from the slave trade to forest-based products and the consequential political change from African independence to European colonial rule.

Apart from Horton,[11] who examined the role of women in the acculturation of domestic slaves, none of these authors examined the status, role and influence of women in the nineteenth-century transformation of the Eastern Delta. As a result, this important aspect of the evolution of the Eastern Delta states has remained a little understood and underestimated area in Niger Delta studies. In the absence of any published chronicle on the status, role and influence of women, it is tempting to say that they perhaps were helpless, exploited, downtrodden and voiceless beings dominated by their male counterparts in society.

This was, for example, Leith-Ross's distorted image of women in traditional Africa, writing that the African man perceived and treated his wife as being 'of little account, that her whole life is in his hands, that she has no will, no property, no power, no organisation, nor means of redress.'[12] I suggest that this view of female marginalisation in society is an overstatement. While attempting to show that traditional Africa was to a large extent a male-dominated society, I wish to redress the imbalances and distortions in the historiography which Leith-Ross's remark represents. This is the aim of the present article.

In order to achieve this aim, I shall investigate the status, role and influence of women as New Calabar responded to the tripartite forces of change — consular rule, transatlantic commerce and Christianity — from about 1850 to 1900. To place the issues relating to women during this period into perspective, I discuss how New Calabar perceived the female image, potentials and capacities through some of its extant myths and legends relating to the origins of communal socio-cultural and political institutions. Apart from the legends, the information for this reconstruction is derived from oral traditions and written sources, published papers on New Calabar in which scattered references are made to women. Extant written information has also been culled from files deposited in the Public Records Office, London, and the Church Missionary Society files in the Heslop Room of the University of Birmingham Library.

New Calabar's perception of the female image as seen through some surviving myths of origin relating to communal institutions

In a preliterate society, such as New Calabar, myths may provide the most convenient starting point for historical investigation. In this connection, I shall recount the myths relating to Ekineba and Owamekaso, two female mythical figures who contributed immensely to the process of state formation in New Calabar. The stories about these figures exemplify the theme of 'the woman creator of the male-dominated institution'[13] which abounds in West African literature.

Ekineba was a very beautiful woman of a certain Delta town (unnamed). She was abducted by the dancing water-spirits and taken to their homes beneath the creeks; but the mother of the water-spirits became angry because of the impolite actions of her children. As a result, these water-spirits were ordered by their mother to take Ekineba back to the land of mortal men. Before returning Ekineba, however, each dancing water-spirit taught her its own unique play and dance-steps. When Ekineba returned eventually, these dance-steps were, in turn, imparted to people. The plays Ekineba introduced became very popular and were constantly being performed. But misfortune soon struck because the young men who performed these plays were unfaithful to the only rule which they were required to keep before performance. The water-spirits, mentors of Ekineba, demanded that she be the first person to beat the drum whenever her people prepared to put out the plays. This was the golden rule that the young men violated. It is said that after the third violation of this rule, the water-spirits became implacably angry and withdrew Ekineba from men.

After Ekineba's withdrawal, the performers of these dance-steps founded the *Ekine* society and elevated Ekineba to the level of a patron-goddess. Paradoxically, the Ekine society, founded to perform and celebrate dance-steps and plays introduced by a woman, turned to imposing prohibitions on women. For example, the organisation remained exclusive to men and women were not allowed to perform masquerades. Hence, women were reduced to the peripheral role of spectators whenever masquerades were being performed by the Ekine society.

Horton[14] has argued that, unlike other West African societies, masquerade in New Calabar was not (and is still not) a male device for dominating women. Be that as it may, the denial of Ekine membership to women contributed to their marginalisation in New Calabar society. This was because women lost tremendous influence and authority in society when the *Ekine* organisation evolved into one of the pillars of traditional Kalabari society. The pre-eminence of this organisation can be perceived from the ends which it served. It was a socio-religious institution designed to solicit the assistance of water-spirits through invocations and dramatic representations of them by masquerades. It may be recalled that, prior to the advent of Christianity, New Calabar always solicited the cooperation and assistance of the water-spirits for its water-borne occupational pursuits of fishing and trading. Secondly, through the performance of these masquerades, the *Ekine* society became the main agency for the provision of recreational facilities in society. Finally, the society tended to arbitrate in all minor cases between members of society.

The point is that by not admitting women into this vital organisation, they were being reduced to the periphery in politics and socio-religious matters.

The myth about Owamekaso[15] also exemplifies the theme of 'the woman creator of a male-dominated institution.' She was a Portuguese nun who came to New Calabar after a shipwreck. It is said that she introduced New Calabar to the transatlantic trade, first in slaves and later in palm oil and kernels. The achievement of a stable socio-political order is also ascribed to Owamekaso. Upon Owamekaso's acquaintance with New Calabar, so goes the myth, she had asked to be the patron-goddess (head-goddess) of the community. But before the community accepted this she was required to first drive out a terrible creature from the town well which killed everyone who attempted to fetch water from it. When Owamekaso went to the well, she found water people in the guise of seven pythons. After very hard negotiations, the head of the monstrous creatures promised that they would all leave the well if Owamekaso would marry him. She assented and all seven pythons left the community to live peacefully.

In another related version of the Owamekaso myth, she was presented as a patron-goddess who abhorred cannibalism and human sacrifice. Upon becoming the patron-goddess, she issued injunctions against these practices. It is said that New Calabar evolved into a stable society when it proscribed these practices in compliance with Owamekaso's injunctions. Therefore, in New Calabar's mythology, Ekineba and Owamekaso represented the creative value and inventive potentials of the woman. To underline this point, it is pertinent to point out that the people of New Calabar conceive God (*Tamuno*), creator and sustainer of the world as a whole, as a female. However, the myths leave us in no doubt about men taking over what women originated in society.

In the following pages, I shall discuss the theme of female subordination to men under the subheads of: women in commerce and politics; and women in religion. I shall attempt to redress the distortion created by Leith-Ross in order to contribute to a more balanced assessment of the female role in traditional Africa before 1900. Finally, I shall also examine the initial attitude of New Calabar society to female education.

Women in commerce and politics

Although legends have ascribed the introduction of Atlantic commerce to a female creator, Owamekaso, the enterprise, from its commencement to end, was dominated by men. It may be safe to assume that the slave trade lent itself to male domination because of the inherent violence involved in the procurement and sale of slaves; but the palm oil trade was peaceful and should have facilitated the participation of male and female competitors. Regrettably, women in the trading states of the Eastern Niger Delta were eliminated as brokers or middlemen in the export palm oil trade.[16] This cannot be attributed to an inherent lack of entrepreneurial dynamism on their part. Rather, it was due to their lack of capital. There is, therefore, one very pertinent question to pose: why did women lack commercial capital when men had access to it?

Superficially, it may appear sufficient to state that the structural arrangements that were put in place for the provision of capital to prospective export merchants discriminated against women. But female non-participation may have been influenced by other considerations.

Delta middlemen in transatlantic commerce were heavily dependent on their European trading partners for credit. Known as the trust-system, a European supercargo advanced an assortment of manufactures, known as trade goods to the African partner, such as salt, textiles, mirror, guns and gunpowder, tobacco and beads.

The Eastern Delta middleman was usually the head of a trading house.[17] The house or lineage (*wari*) was the first and most basic unit of socio-economic organisation. It was made up of the man (merchant chief), his wives and children, far and near relatives, voluntary sojourners, slaves and other dependents.

Through the ablest male members of the house, the merchant chief exchanged the trade goods for primary commodities, be they slaves or agricultural products, in the hinterland of the delta. As a rule, which was upheld for most of the nineteenth century, only house heads were entitled to European supercargo credit facilities.

Because the socio-political organisation barred women from heading these trading houses, they were denied access to European credit facilities. As a result, women were precluded from the export sector and consigned to the subsistence and petty trading sectors of the economy. But this may not be the only rational explanation for female non-participation as brokers. Before the nineteenth century, long-distance trading in West Africa had been the monopoly of men. This was because, given the nature and mode of transportation (usually camels, donkeys, mules, head porterage or canoes), long-distance trade was a test of strength and endurance. There was also the risk of marauding en route. Therefore, New Calabar society, like other trading West African societies, had probably worked out a division of labour by sex to take account of the potential and real hazards associated with long-distance trading along the riverine commercial highways. The long absences from home which long-distance trading involves may not be compatible with simultaneous child-bearing and raising.

Be that as it may, the exclusion of women from the lucrative export sector meant that, unlike men, they were in a much weaker position to accumulate enough surpluses to be translated into political power. In terms of politics, therefore, women were unable to compete with men.

However, this never meant that women were docile or insensitive to political matters. On the contrary, we have evidence that women were able to influence political decisions; this was, however, indirectly accomplished through the male rulers of society, the merchant chiefs. It is possible to discern two ways by which women influenced men in traditional times. This was firstly through the food power of wives, which may be combined with their control of sexual life. Secondly, women brought influence to bear on men, and especially on house heads, through the institution of female cult servants of the tutelary deity Owamekaso and the priestesses of divinities, especially water-spirits.

In traditional society the kitchen was the exclusive province of women; that is, it was the women's office and interference from men was resisted. Through control of the kitchen, women were generally able to influence the decisions of men in domestic and political affairs. In terms of sexual control, it is said that before sexual permissiveness became commonplace in society, the woman had firm control over when to go to bed with her husband and when to have a baby. The two factors of food power and control over sexual life and procreation have always proved to be tremendous influences on men, including political rulers.

Instances abound in history to show that men went to war over disputes originating among women. According to Bishop S.A. Crowther,[18] the Church Missionary Society (CMS) representative to the Niger Delta, in 1875 New Calabar actually came close to the brink of an internal feud owing to quarrels between the wives of the two most prominent political leaders, King Princewill Amachree and his deputy George Amachree. Although the substantive issues generating the dispute were undisclosed, these women were said to have held different views over the inauguration of the Christian mission at New Calabar. The dispute, however, escalated when the husbands (Princewill and George) got drawn into the matter; and, it was only the timely intervention and mediation of other chiefs that diffused the situation. Consequently, the inauguration of the Christian mission at New Calabar was delayed by two weeks.

Women married to powerful and wealthy merchant chiefs, like these wives, contributed enormously to the socio-cultural and economic growth of the society: they performed the vital role of foster mothers to domestic slaves incorporated into the houses ruled by their husbands. It may be recalled that it was New Calabar's policy to increase its personnel for defence and trade through the recruitment and assimilation of slaves into the community. The status, role and influence of *alapu-ereme* (wives of merchant chiefs), as foster mothers to slaves, become more obvious when we remember that 'over perhaps two hundred years, as many people were bought into this community as were born into it.'[19]

To fully place the contributions of *alapu-ereme* to New Calabar's socio-cultural and economic development into perspective, it is necessary, even at the risk of digression, to elaborate on the acculturation of slaves for integration into the house.[20]

Acculturation of domestic slaves and *alapu-ereme* in the house

The hallmark of New Calabar's socio-cultural history in the nineteenth century was the high level of success in the integration of domestic slaves into the house (or lineage) and the community. This integration followed upon their successful acculturation. Its effectiveness, which essentially involved the imparting of New Calabar's norms and values, including the language, to the domestic slaves, was demonstrated by the fact that New Calabar remained a monolingual community (the language is Kalabari, a branch of the Ijo language family), despite the massive integration of Igbo-speaking domestic slaves. Lineages with means competed in the incorporation of slaves because the overall lineage ideology, as a trading corporation, was to expand through reproduction and incorporation so that its workforce effectively surpassed those of competing lineages. This is what brings the role of women, and especially *alapu-ereme*, who domesticated the slaves, into the central picture of New Calabar's socio-cultural, political and economic transformation.

In the first place, slaves intended for integration into the lineage were bought at a tender age, preferably between ten and twelve years old. Horton has described the *rite de passage* for the newly bought domestic slaves.

> When the newly bought slave arrived in the community, the breaking-off of all his previous kinship ties and the assumption of a whole series of new ties was brought home to him by means of a dramatic rite de passage in which his new 'mother' (the merchant chief's wife) shaved his head clean and then gave him a ritual meal. From then on, the 'mother' was supposed to live up to her title in the fullest sense.[21]

The pertinent question is: how did the 'mother' live up to her title in the fullest sense?

Extant colonial and missionary records sufficiently illuminate the institution of domestic slavery in the Niger Delta. One view is that domestic slavery there was 'in its mildest form', because slaves 'can acquire property and are themselves frequently the owners of slaves.'[22] Evidence indicates that it was the slave's mother who created the atmosphere for his socio-economic mobility. De Cardi, a European palm oil trader who lived in the Eastern Delta (New Calabar and Opobo) in the mid-nineteenth century, wrote this account of the 'mother's' role in the economic survival and social mobility of domestic slaves in society.

The domestic slave began 'by carrying his master's (the merchant chief and husband of his mother) pocket-hand-kerchief and snuffbox, pockets not having yet been introduced into the native custom'. After some years of this duty the slave was:

> promoted to going down to the European traders to superintend the delivery of a canoe of oil, seeing to its being tried and gauged. The first assignment, if efficiently performed, would lead to his being sent on the same errand. The duty required a certain amount of intelligence, for he had to so look after his master's interest that the pull-away boys (these are the category of slaves who man the dug-out canoe) that were with him in the canoe did not secrete any few gallons of oil . . .; nor must he allow the white trader to undergauge his master's casks by carelessness or otherwise. If he is able to do the latter part of this errand . . ., that day marked the commencement of his upward career, if he was possessed of the bump of saving.[23]

At the end of these trying transactions, De Cardi went on, the slave received some presents in proportion to the quantity of oil sold. Presents were in the form of cloth cut in separate pieces, each costing about 2s 6d. If the sale amounted to about 15 puncheons of oil, the slave might get two pieces of cloth and a bunch of beads.

These presents were then handed over to the slave's 'mother', together with all subsequent gains, until he amassed enough property to buy his own oil. The permission to start his own trade was obtained for him by his 'mother' from her husband, the slave's master. Gradually, after this humble beginning, the slave soon became a man of means and could own his own canoe and slaves.

The history of the Eastern Delta trading states in the nineteenth century is replete with the names of powerful, opulent erstwhile slaves who rose through the social experience described above to great heights. Some of these were: George Amachree, the deputy to the king of New Calabar; Oko Jumbo, one of the co-leaders of the Manilla Pepple house at Bonny; and, the most celebrated of them all, King Jaja,[24] the founder of Opobo in 1870.

The critical point is that a 'mother' who had successfully seen a domestic slave through the process of acculturation, that is, from servility to nobility (or even kingship), became popular as a person of tremendous influence, authority, power and craft. Furthermore, she became admired by all in society as a woman with considerable creativity, ingenuity and foresight. Available evidence shows that women in this category enjoyed an elevated status and exhibited a life style characterised by an ostentatious consumption of European manufactures. Bishop Crowther once commented on the conspicuous display by New Calabar merchant chiefs and their wives. Occasions for such displays were the moments when merchants, having taken a break from their routine trading ventures, took out time to feast and to celebrate. At these celebrations, families displayed their acquisitions of European textiles. Since the beginning of contact between the Eastern Delta trading states and Europeans, the acquisition and consumption of European manufactures had been regarded as a symbol of status and success in society. Crowther, after observing a festival on 3 April 1875, described the men as wearing long shirts made of the best Manchester goods such as 'rich silks, silk velvets and damasks; their under wrappers being of the same materials; the head coverings are black or straw hats or caps decorated with coral beads of the best quality obtainable'. 'The females', he went on,

> appeared in the same drapery, but their dresses are cut into lengths of cloths about the size of a moderate table cover; many such are passed round in layers on their waist and bent in the front, till they became a large pile of folds, which make their gait awkward. In addition to the rich drapery, strings of large expensive real coral beads are suspended on the necks, both by the males and females, at the lowest rate to the amount of £50 and £60. The necks of some individuals are quite weighed down with them.[25]

A certain chief, according to the same source, had spent as much as £500 to purchase coins used as ornaments for himself, his two wives and children. These were paid for in palm oil to the European trader from whom the coins (probably Spanish dollars) had been bought. It may be recalled that palm oil, measured in units of puncheon or cask, was acceptable as a standard medium of exchange between Africans and Europeans in the nineteenth century.

The above evidence demonstrates that these women were not neglected and down trodden creatures whose lives were dominated by the absolute autocracy of their husbands. On the contrary, women are depicted as consuming a fair proportion of the wealth they helped to create. It also shows that in the period under review these women were far from being voiceless beasts of burden to be exploited by their tyrannical and inhumane male overlords. In view of this, we disagree with Leith-Ross's generalisation that, in traditional times, male chauvinism tended to make a husband see and treat his wife as being of 'little account' (see above).

The role, status and influence of women in socio-religious matters

The role, status and influence of women in socio-religious matters, as in political and economic matters, do not support this conclusion.

However, discussions on the role of women do still reflect, to some extent, the theme of 'the woman creator of a male-dominated institution'.

The New Calabar religious thought system revolved around three interrelated spirit-forces which influenced the lives of people: ancestors, communal gods and goddesses, and the water-spirits. Members of New Calabar society often pacified those spirit forces with lavish sacrifices and rituals, in order to procure assistance and cooperation in their daily and everlasting struggles for political and socio-economic survival. It is interesting to note that, in a male-dominated society, the most feasted and celebrated among these spirit-forces was the female goddess, Owamekaso, who instituted the export trade with Europeans and also introduced political centralisation. In spite of these achievements, women were made subordinate to men in trade and politics. The same is true of the cult organisation devoted to the worship of this goddess.

The cult organisation was (and still is) headed by a divine chief (*soalabo*). Throughout the first half of the nineteenth century, the divine chief or priest of Owamekaso enjoyed a pre-eminent social status above the secular king and house heads at New Calabar. For example, T. Hutchinson, a British consul to the Niger Delta in 1857, noted that:

> The social position of the juju king is before that of Amachree (the secular king) among his people. The juju king is the head high-priest and holds the same pre-eminence over the monarch as church does over state in other parts of the world. On public occasions the juju king always walks before Amachree, having an umbrella held over his head by an attendant slave.[26]

De Cardi also noted that the high priest was 'ranking higher than the king in any matters relating to purely native affairs'.[27]

This powerful high priest of a female inspired socio-religious institution was followed in the hierarchy by a priestess called *bibi aro* and a host of other female cult servants (*egbele-ereme*). According to oral tradition, the oracular utterances of the goddess *Owamekaso* were made through the mediumship of *bibi aro*, while the *egbele ereme* were the vigilantes monitoring the observance of the laws of the deity. There were also other women priestesses (*oru kuro apu*) who ministered to different water-spirits and divinities. All priestesses claimed some form of secret knowledge, including the knowledge of state governance. Hence they were politically very powerful and influential in society. According to Talbot: 'In the olden days the chiefs used to come to them for advice, and only by their counsel, supposed to be inspired, was any grave step taken'.[28]

Oral tradition supports Talbot's view; it tells us that some of the great nineteenth-century chiefs of New Calabar actively sought to incorporate prominent women priestesses into their households as wives.[29] These women then constituted the organisation around which feminine opinion on crucial national questions revolved. For example, available records indicate that these women inspired and championed the first resistance movement against Christianity at New Calabar in 1879.

Christianity was introduced to New Calabar in 1874. A scant few years after, Christianity had gathered some chiefs and youths around itself and was seriously influencing their opinions. To counteract the growing influence of this alien faith, these female devotees of Owamekaso and the priestesses of the innumerable water-spirit cults initiated an anti-Christianity movement. This movement was led by ten priestesses. To justify the campaigns, they castigated the male rulers of New Calabar for their injudicious decision to let the Church Missionary Society into the community. They argued that the values of western Christianity were inimical to the traditional social values of New Calabar society. To underscore their points, the leaders of the movement shrewdly attributed all the ills afflicting society since the inception of Christianity to the visitations of the offended gods and goddesses of New Calabar. One such ill was an internal uprising against the ruling dynasty in 1879, which created turmoil. The cult devotees urged that for New Calabar to appease the goddesses and gods, and to restore calm and harmony to the troubled society, there should be an immediate renunciation of Christianity by all converts, and the destruction of all Christian emblems, including the reading book for school pupils, the religious tracts and the hymn books.[30] Consequently, on the orders of King Princewill Amachree, Christian items were duly collected together and taken to the shrine of the tutelary deity Owamekaso. After this, the school pupils of the missionary boarding house, as representatives of the new faith, were especially singled out for attack by the anti-Christian movement. They were paraded round the town to make a confession of their errors and to renounce Christianity. It is interesting to note that, subsequently, these pupils and the confiscated emblems were only rescued from the depredations of the overzealous female priestesses after a special plea to the king by Rev. W.E. Carew, the CMS agent at New Calabar. To further demonstrate the point that priestesses constituted one of the important pivots around which feminine opinion revolved, it is pertinent to mention their role in the eventual acceptance of Christianity at New Calabar. According to Horton, a respected female medium of the water-spirits, having been overwhelmed by the Christian message, urged society to accept Christianity; this happened between 1900 and 1912. As he puts it: 'This woman possessed by her 'water husband,' is said to have travelled about telling everyone to go to church and abandon the spirit cults, because in the times that lay ahead the spirits were going to become very weak and would no longer be able to help people'.[31]

This reconstruction of female roles in the initial rejection and the eventual assimilation of Christian values presents a picture at total variance with the notion that in traditional African societies women constantly lived under the tyranny and overlordship of men. On the contrary, what has been demonstrated are the ways and means by which the weight of feminine opinion, once properly articulated and galvanised, could be brought to bear on society.

Traditional New Calabar attitude to western missionary education as it relates to women

Lastly, I shall examine the initial attitude of society towards female education. Around 1874, the CMS built a boarding school at New Calabar estimated to accommodate 50 persons. The idea of this boarding school was to remove young boys and girls from the 'traditional environment', with its pejorative connotations in the missionary mind of superstition, adultery, ancestor worship, savagery and polygamy. These were vices that the missionaries were most eager to condemn and to eradicate. It was hoped that by being in constant touch with the missionaries the young students would be inspired to emulate their example, at the same time making it possible for the missionaries to select the most promising youths for church work. The pupils, in effect, became the personal wards of the missionaries. This perspective was endorsed by Bishop Johnson of the CMS, who said:

> The boarding school system was in the early days of mission work in the
> Niger Delta a prominent feature because of the promise it gave and the hope it
> held out of being quickly very helpful in detaching the more youthful sections
> of the different communities from heathenism and its idolatry and winning
> them over to Christianity and through them influencing the different
> households which they severally represented.[32]

By 1876 there were 45 children in the boarding school, 40 of whom were boys. In 1844, the number of girls had increased to six, and there were 42 boys. The statistics relating to enrolment reveal a conspicuous prejudice against female education. Moreover, the CMS agent, W.E. Carew, tells us that nineteenth-century New Calabar social norms prohibited the education of females, so that the chiefs who chose to violate this taboo brought their daughters to the mission boarding house in the dead of the night.

However, New Calabar's attitude to female education can be explained in pragmatic and rational terms. New Calabar's principal aim in inviting the CMS was succinctly summarised in a reported conversation between a New Calabar chief (unnamed) and Bishop Crowther in 1875. The chief said, 'He did not want religious teaching, for that the children have enough at home, they teach them such themselves; that they want them to be taught how to gauge palm oil, and other like mercantile business as soon as possible.'[33]

As traders, the people of New Calabar sought a type of instruction that was strictly utilitarian or pragmatic. They wanted a commercial pedagogy that would produce artisans, clerks and men educated in the trading life and language of the coast. The medium in which they wished to receive instruction was English and, in this connection, the chiefs expected the missionaries to continue the tradition of those earlier European merchants who had taught traders to speak some English, and who had instructed them in part in the proper accounting and management of trade returns.

As earlier stated, the palm oil trade in the coastal states was not the province of women interested in commerce, unlike their counterparts in the primary producers' hinterland who participated fully in the production and sale of palm oil. The education of girls was, therefore, of no immediate practical appeal and was considered to be superfluous. According to Dandeson C. Crowther (an archdeacon of the CMS, and the son of Bishop Crowther), objections stemmed from the view that, 'They [females] were not expected to become clerks or to engage in other pursuits requiring some measure of book keeping'.[34]

Nineteenth-century Christian missionary education and the school curriculum did very little to prepare women for competition in the evolving colonial cash economy. For example, to enhance the skills of primary boarding school graduates, the CMS founded post-primary industrial institutions at Old Calabar, Brass and Bonny, all in the geo-historical area called the Bight of Biafra (now Bight of Bonny). Students of the industrial institution were taught elementary skills in engineering, tailoring, carpentry and home management; out of these, only the last course was for girls.[35] Thus, to a certain extent, early missionary education reinforced those traditional attitudes which consigned women to the household.

Women lagged behind men in the nineteenth-century transformation of traditional African societies as a result of structural constraints imposed on them by society. However, all of these began to change gradually at the end of the nineteenth century.

Endnotes*

I express my profound thanks to Professor Robin Horton of the University of Port Harcourt, Nigeria, for his comments on this paper after the symposium. The revised edition of this paper has benefited from these comments.

The abbreviation FO (Foreign Office) refers to archival papers deposited at the Public Records office, London; archival papers at the Heslop Room of the University of Birmingham Library are classified as CA3 or G3A3.

1. K.O. Dike, *Trade and Politics in the Niger Delta* (Oxford: Oxford University Press, 1956).
2. G.I. Jones, *The Trading States of the Oil Rivers* (Oxford: Oxford University Press, 1963).
3. E.J. Alagoa, *A History of the Niger Delta* (Ibadan: Ibadan University Press, 1972).
4. A.E. Afigbo, *The Warrant Chiefs: Indirect rule in Southern Nigeria 1891—1928* (Ibadan: Ibadan University Press, 1978). The references to women in this book relate to the 1929 uprising in the Ibibio and Igbo speaking areas of South-east Nigeria.
5. S.J.S. Cookey, *King Jaja of the Niger Delta: His Life and Times 1821—1889.* (New York: Nok, 1974)
6. O. Ikime, *Niger Delta Rivalry* (Ibadan: Longmans, 1973).
7. R. Horton, 'From Fishing Village to City-State' in M. Douglas, and M.R. Kaberry, (eds), *Man in Africa* (London: Tavistock, 1969).
8. J.C. Anene, *Southern Nigeria in Transition 1885—1906.* (Cambridge: Cambridge University Press, 1966).
9. J. F. Ajayi, *Christian Missions in Nigeria 1841—91: The Making of a New Elite* (London: Longmans, 1965).
10. W.I. Ofonagoro, *Trade and Imperialism in Southern Nigeria* (New York: Nok, 1979).
11. Horton, 'From Fishing Village' pp. 37—58.
12. Sylvia Leith-Ross, *African Women: A study of the Ibo of Nigeria* (London: Routledge & Kegan Paul, 1939) p. 21.
13. R. Horton, 'The Kalabari Ekine Society: A Borderland of Religion and Art', *Africa*, Vol. 33, No.2 (April 1963), pp. 94—95. See footnote 2 of Horton's article for comments on 'the woman creator of a male-dominated institution'.
14. *Ibid.*
15. Chief N. Princewill, oral interview, Buguma, 1983. Also see: W. Brown West (now Tienabeso) *A Short Genealogical History of King Amachree of Kalabari* (Yaba: Yaba Printing Press, 1965).
16. An apparent exception to this was Madame Orupumbu (*c.* 1820—1908), who seems to have participated in the palm oil trade. However, she was subject to a great deal of interference and harassment, and her attempts to become a chief were steadily resisted [communication with Professor Robin Horton, 16 March 94].
17. Jones, p. 51.
18. CA3/04/475 S.A. Crowther, *Miscellaneous Papers,* 3 April 1875.
19. R. Horton, 'Igbo: An ordeal for aristocrats', *Nigeria Magazine*, No. 90 (September 1966), p. 183.
20. At the community level, the organisation of *Ekine* built upon the work of *alapu ereme* in the acculturation of domestic slaves (see Horton, 'The Kalabari Ekine').
21. Horton, 'From Fishing Village'.
22. FO 84/2109: Major C. McDonald, *Administration of the Niger Company's Territories, Reports and Papers,* Chapter V (1890).
23. C.N. De Cardi, 'A short description of the natives of the Niger Coast Protectorate, with some account of their customs, religion, trade, etc.', in M. Kingsley, *West African Studies* (London: Rank Cass & Co., 1899), pp. 472—75.
24. For an elaborate account on King Jaja, see Cookey. (In addition to what men like Jaja accumulated with the assistance and support of their foster 'mothers',

they secured huge amounts of house loan to make a breakthrough in commerce).

25. CA3/04/479: S.A. Crowther, 'Brief Statement exhibiting the character, habits, and ideas of the natives of the Bight of Biafra, after ten years observation and introduction of Christianity among them', 31 March 1875.

26. T. Hutchinson, *Impressions of Western Africa* (London: Frank Cass & Co, 1970), pp. 101—02.

27. De Cardi, p. 501.

28. P.A. Talbot, *Tribes of the Niger Delta* (London: Frank Cass & Co., 1967), p. 32.

29. Communication with Professor Robin Horton, 16 March 1994.

30. CA3/010/14: W.E. Carew, 'Annual Letter', 20 November 1879. For a history of Christianity emphasising the role of the cult servants, see: W.E. Wariboko, 'New Calabar and the Forces of Change ca. 1850—1945', (unpublished PhD. thesis, University of Birmingham, 1991), pp. 152—61.

31. R. Horton, 'A Hundred Years of Change in Kalabari Religion', in John Middleton (ed.), *Black Africa: Its Peoples and their Cultures Today* (London: Macmillan, 1970), p. 204.

32. G3A3/1906/168: Bishop Johnson, *Journal Report*, December 1904-July 1905.

33. CA3/04/479: D.C. Crowther, *Miscellaneous Papers*, 31 March 1875.

34. G3A3/1907/51 D.C. Crowther, *Niger Delta Pastorate Church and Mission Work*, 1906.

35. G3A3/1908/70 *The Delta Pastorate Chronicle* (No. 3) (England, 1906).

20.

Women and Plantations in West Cameroon since 1900

Richard Goodridge

In February 1993 the following extract appeared in a widely circulated news magazine on western Africa:

> Even with a press card it is not easy getting to Mr. Fru Ndi's residence. Security check points are many and the security officers legion. A touch of your pocket, a curious cursory look into your bag . . . but you are nowhere near the palace [sic] itself. There is another check point ahead, this time manned by zealous elderly women of about 50 years or more. They are strict but they are only compassionate mothers who want to be sure that nothing fatal happens to their dear son, John [Fru Ndi].
>
> A few metres ahead, you see a large battalion of particularly old women huddled together like sacks of corn; they are stretched all over the area leading to the main gate. Some are warming themselves up with firewood fires, others are just dozing off, grey heads swing from left to right. These are the famous Takembeng Women who have vowed that anyone who wants to take Fru Ndi prisoner will have to do that over their dead bodies. They are about 70 years old. As you greet them, they all respond in unison. Their trembling voices give them up. They are tired and old; the spirit is willing but the body is weak.[1]

The writer of this piece appeared to be surprised at the level of commitment displayed by elderly women. Perhaps he was unaware of women's participation in riots at Kom, near Bamenda, 30 years before, or of the general involvement of Cameroonian women in the socio-economic life of their communities in this century.

This article is partly an attempt to examine the nature of this involvement in the face of the intrusion into the communities, of western colonial capitalism. It also seeks to assess the impact of colonialism upon the women of West Cameroon between 1900 and 1960. Some effort will also be made to outline developments before 1900 and the immediate background to the establishment of plantations. This is necessary since the argument is that the plantation provided the principal colonising agency and influenced the lives of West Cameroon women. It will become evident that despite the obvious social differences stemming from a historically different cultural evolution, the women of West Cameroon and their counterparts in the Caribbean shared a common existence in the six decades after 1900. This assertion is based upon the fact that both were subject to the pervasive influence of the plantation; and their lives were regulated to a greater or lesser extent by British colonial policy.

The central themes of the research on Caribbean women encompass the issues surrounding the sources of livelihood, emotional support and power and authority as these affected women. The Woman in the Caribbean Project (WICP) concluded, *inter alia*, that women's position in the Caribbean was characterised by a dual role which stemmed from their engagement in both household and extra- household work; that women were increasingly involved in the formal sector of the economy; and that increasing numbers of women were forced to assume the major responsibility for their households.[2]

Among the major concerns of the WICP was education. Research in this area clearly indicate the areas of convergence between the situations in the Caribbean and West Cameroon. In a study on official ideology and the education of women in Barbados, it was found that education policy rested on the premise that women's role in society 'was primarily a socialising one' and that policy changes after the Second World War stimulated changes in education of women. Hermione McKenzie's study of female education in the Caribbean clearly indicates the influence of Africa upon the formulation of British education policy for the Caribbean. It should come as no surprise then, that 'female education' in the Caribbean was equated with the teaching of needlework and domestic science, and that, as McKenzie records, 'policy initiatives in women's education may be interpreted, however, mainly as an effort to redress the overwhelming concentration on male education'.[3]

The web of intrigue, deceit and despotism that characterised politics in post-colonial Cameroon resulted in the obliteration by administrative fiat of the entity known as West Cameroon. The term West Cameroon as used in this article, however, refers to the former Cameroons and Bamenda Provinces of British Cameroons[4] (present-day South-West and

North-West Provinces respectively of the Republic of Cameroon). West Cameroon consisted of a forested southern portion, whose single dominant physical feature was Mount Cameroon, and a northern (largely) savannah region.[5] The plantations which the Europeans created provided the main avenue for the linking of the two in this century.

It should be pointed out here that the analysis is made against the background of other studies on women in Africa and their relationship to westernising and colonising agencies after 1900. In 1984 S.E.M. Charlton produced *Women in Third World Development* which was viewed as a major study of the role that women played in the economic life of the developing states. Before then, Ester Boserup's 1970 publication, *Women's Role in Economic Development* had helped to encourage the academic study of women's role in the third world by focusing on the distortions of the scholarship concerned. Even earlier, in 1963, Denise Pauline had edited *Women of Africa*, a study of women in Francophone Africa.[6] Few scholars, however, paid attention to West Cameroonian women during the colonial period. The exceptions were the direct result of government-sponsored studies of socio-economic problems and these were largely anthropological in character.[7] Yet they offer valuable information on the state and status of their object of enquiry, that is, the women of West Cameroon.

Ester Boserup and Walter Rodney have asserted that colonialism in Africa resulted in a deterioration of women's status vis-à-vis that of men.[8] Specific examples from Francophone Africa and Ghana, which respectively deal with the modification of traditional marriage law and the decline in status of the Asante queen mother, have been cited by L. Mullings, who focused on the economic changes introduced by colonialism, especially the efforts of the colonial regime to foster production that benefited the male at the expense of the female.[9]

The present analysis falls into the category of studies which concentrate upon the socio-economic impact on the women's response to colonising agents and institutions. H. Moore argues that this response, as a component of the response of women to capitalist transformation, is partly determined by women's ability to control, utilise or dispose of economic resources and the products of those resources; and that these are themselves determined by such socio-political practices as division of labour, organisation of households and patterns associated with kinship, marriage and inheritance.[10]

A major characteristic of studies of women during the colonial period is the emphasis on labour migration[11] and the concentration upon South-Central Africa. Colin Murray and Ray Bush suggest that in Lesotho and South Africa, an increasing number of households in rural areas were headed by women, as a consequence of labour migration.[12] To Moore, the phenomenon of the female-headed household was likely where urban poverty existed or 'where general insecurity and vulnerability prevail',[13] as in societies where there is a high level of male labour migration.

The conclusion of M. Lovett's examination of labour migration was that class formation can only be understood as gendered, that is, state or class formation had a differential impact on women and on men. Thus, for East, Central and South Africa, she found that: the colonial state intervened to largely determine the conditions under which the migrant labour force was procured and controlled; the state intervened in land tenure and usage systems; and promoted cash crop production. Consequent upon these three, the experiences of and the impact upon women differed from those of men.[14]

These different experiences were rooted in the gendered nature of class formation. Under colonial capitalism, based on male migrant labour remunerated at subsistence wages, production was increasingly gendered male and reproduction was gendered female. To Lovett, 'The strategic nature of woman's structural position as reproductive labourers both subsidized capitalist production and ensured the continuity of those pre-capitalist social relations on which the edifice of colonial rule was constructed.'[15] Consequently, both the state and capital sought to develop effective means of controlling women's movements and activities.

Situation in West Cameroon to 1916

Western scholars have tended to emphasise the importance of F. Engels to an understanding of the historical relationship of male to female. Engels established the social character of woman's relationship to man, particularly the change (to patriarchy induced by the move from kinship and the potential overthrow of patriarchy by socialism) in the relationship.[16] Engels was also important for his analysis of the subordination of women in terms of the emergence of private property and class inequality.[17]

In pre-colonial West Cameroon there was an important link between the social organisation of production and familial organisation and the marriage institution, 'the social control over access to women', remained the cornerstone of the system. Whether the individual society was patrilineal or matrilineal, marriage was a union between two groups which, through the marriage, started a complex system of interrelationships bound to operate for a long time. Finally, marriage was linked to a well-defined residential system where the rights and duties of women were clearly distinguished.[18]

There is a tendency in the literature to cite the role of women and women's institutions in pre-colonial Africa. In West Cameroon mention is made of the headwoman, known as *iya* in Banso and *mafaw* in the Fontem area. Among the peoples in the latter place females had their separate meeting house where *mafaw* presided.[19] The *jango* was the female equivalent of the male *basongo*, a society for those of free birth among the Bakolle, utilised in cases of emergency such as when there was a scarcity of fish.[20]

Marriage, land rights and inheritance were all closely related. Among the Bakweri, Bota and Bamboko, there was an emphasis upon patrilineal and matrilineal descent, although the core of the localised group was the patrilineage and succession was patrilineal. Yet, as Ardener notes, 'the matrilineage is of great ritual importance among the Kpe [ie Bakweri]' and, in practice, inheritance of land or goods was sometimes matrilineal,[21] that is, from mother's brother to sister's son. Nevertheless, West Cameroon societies in the pre-colonial period tended to be highly stratified and women ranked lower than men. Moreover, being a woman meant being a mother. In effect, the woman's status in society was determined by her fertility.

Pre-colonial West Cameroon was primarily agricultural and women were heavily involved in agriculture. It is true that tasks requiring heavy physical labour such as the clearing of farms and other activities were performed by men, but, according to Ardener, 'full-time devotion to agriculture by males is considered not quite manly' among the Bakweri.[22] It was generally true that while males did the bulk of the clearing of the land, actual planting/cultivation was 'women's work'.[23]

There was a close link between women and slavery. Among the Balong of Kumba a rich man could pay fines for judicial offenders and take in return either the offender's wife or daughter as a 'slave'.[24] The authors of the *Annual Report on Cameroons Province* (co-terminous with West Cameroon) for 1919 stated that trade in a European sense was of recent existence in Cameroons Province because before the First World War ivory and women were the staple articles of trade and wealth.[25] The introduction of European plantations ought to be viewed as a major catalyst to change in the activities and status of women.

Germany was responsible for the creation of plantations in West Cameroon. Major difficulties affected German-Cameroon trade and the Germans were convinced that plantation agriculture offered the best solution.[26] The All-Highest Decree of 1896 was the legal instrument that facilitated creation of the plantations.[27] By 1914 264,000 acres of West Cameroon had been formed into plantations. This may seem to be a small portion of the area but these plantations occupied the most fertile lands in Victoria and Kumba Districts and recruited their labour from a very wide area including Mamfe and Bamenda Districts.

H.R. Rudin offers detailed information on the ways in which German rule affected the lives of the inhabitants in West Cameroon, but the data tend to be gender-neutral (that is, pertaining to the general impact) or focused on male plantation labourers and male political figures. German rule is identified with brutality, as Rudin points out, and 'the climax is reached when women are flogged'.[28] Indeed the flogging of wives of African soldiers caused a mutiny in December 1893.[29] The creation of the plantations impoverished and expropriated the Cameroonians so as to force them to work for low wages on estates, but given the Bakweri hostility to agricultural labour, the Germans resorted to the forced recruitment of labour from Mamfe, the Bamenda Grassfields and other areas in their colony.[30]

The consequences of this movement were largely negative. There was a depopulation of certain districts, a physiological disaster for those who left a malaria-free zone (that is, Bamenda) to work in the swampy, malaria-infested area where plantations were established; and there was a high death rate of as high as 50 per cent in some plantations.[31] A further consequence, therefore, was the negative impact on women both in the area of the plantations and in the area from which the male labour came. In general terms, loose relationships were forged in the former, and this did little to advance social or family life throughout West Cameroon.

The period 1916—39

The effective colonisation of West Cameroon occurred in the period between the start of the First World War and the commencement of hostilities in Europe in 1939. The plantations were the principal instrument in the process of establishing British rule. In this period some effort was made deliberately to mould the West Cameroon women after the European fashion, but attention here will be focused on the contrasting influence of the plantations upon the women of West Cameroon.

The start of the First World War in Europe was followed by the speedy eviction of the Germans from West Cameroon and the inauguration of British rule. The first ten years were crucial to the development of colonialism as the British divided the German colony between the French and themselves, put in place the institutions necessary for the effective operation of a colonial system and resolved the issue of how to proceed with the German plantations they had seized. Thus the local administrative system was implemented, missionary bodies were reintroduced, plantations were once again acquired by their former German owners and the League of Nations Mandate that regulated the affairs of the British Cameroons, including West Cameroon, came into operation.[32]

While statistics for the plantation labour force are reliable only after 1926, the decade between 1914, the start of the First World War, and 1924, German repossession of the plantations saw a reduced labour force on the plantations.[33] After 1925 plantation activity was once again in full swing. Almost immediately, however, economic activity in West

Cameroon was adversely affected by global depression after 1929 and the results were clearly visible among the female population.

One characteristic of plantation labour between 1916 and 1939 was its poor treatment by management, manifested in several ways: late payment of wages and the related practice of paying workers in credit notes. These practices had been going on since the 1920s but became a major worry in the 1930s as a result of the depression and Germany's financial difficulties.[34]

Originally, labourers asked for an advance on their wages, but estates offered credit notes rather than cash and this soon became the general practice. The use of credit notes had been motivated by German firms' difficulty in acquiring West African currency; by the subsidiary, but clearly profitable, consideration of the profits on retail sales to labourers; and by the 'lack of any direct means of securing continuity of labour.'[35] Apart from the issue of credit notes, the plantations also paid their workers late. As the British informed the League of Nations:

> wages are at daily rates, but in order to discourage employees from leaving without adequate notice it is customary to pay them monthly, usually some two weeks after the last day of the month in which the wages were earned. There is little doubt but that on many plantations men who regularly insisted on receiving their full wages in cash would be considered unsuitable for permanent employment.[36]

This policy of enforced retention of labour affected women in two ways, both significant, with one more so than the other. In the first place the system of payment in credit was unpopular in cases where a male labourer was anxious to receive wages in cash to enable him to pay a debt or a bride-price instalment.[37] More significantly, however, the enforced keeping of labour belied the official claim enunciated since 1924 that the 'tribal organisation' (that is, including familial organisation) of West Cameroon was not adversely affected by the regime of plantation labour, as labourers could easily return to their homes.[38]

Family life was also being undermined by the emergence of child labour on the plantations. The 1938 *Report to the League of Nations*, the last major one and the most detailed, initially suggested that Cameroonian women would themselves have abused the labour of children at home, but it unequivocally acknowledged the deleterious effects of plantation use of child labour. According to the *Report*,

> On educational grounds their presence on the plantations seems fraught with undesirable consequences. In its native village the child is subject to the weight of public opinion and partakes of a traditional store of practical wisdom and morality instilled by daily precept and example: on the plantation every man is a law to himself and there are no generally recognised standards of behaviours . . . such an environment must, it is feared, have an adverse

effect on the upbringing and moral development of children exposed to it at an impressionable age.[39]

These negative social developments were somewhat offset by the fact that the plantations offered new opportunities to West Cameroon's women. Indeed it is a feature of plantation societies that whatever socio-economic amenities are provided tend to be concentrated in the area where the plantations exist. There were six government-run primary schools, which represented the most advanced type of education available locally. By 1930, there were four in the Victoria and Kumba Divisions where the plantations were found and one each in Mamfe and Bamenda Divisions. Total enrolment that year stood at 1,250, including a mere 172 girls, of which 113 were at the Buea and Victoria schools[40] located in the heart of the plantation zone. These statistics indicate an element of discrimination, which was made all the more distinct considering that there was a female predominance in the population of West Cameroon.[41]

The plantations offered the opportunity to West Cameroonian women to earn some cash from the direct sale of produce to labourers or to the plantations. In the early 1920s the Plantations Department, created to supervise the German estates during the war, claimed that the sale of palm wine, often women's work, was becoming 'a perpetual nuisance'.[42] By this it was meant that sales took place even during working hours, and that liquor sales by the plantations were in competition. The women were also afforded the chance to sell cocoyams to the estates to help feed the labour force. However, in January 1938 'a great number of 238 women from different villages of Buea District' complained to the District Head, Endeley, that 'regarding the selling of cocoyams to the plantations it is now a great difficulty to them'.[43] This complaint stemmed from a reduction in the price offered from 3s for a full basket to 1s 9d by Ekona Plantation, although the women suggested that all plantations made price reductions.[44] The Bakweri women responded in a firm — even aggressive — manner: they agreed to stop selling cocoyams to plantations until their grievances were satisfied (and 'one woman vehemently exclaimed that never under any circumstances would she sell cocoyams to a plantation again'); they threw cocoyams already bought by a plantation contractor out of a lorry containing them, and assaulted the driver of the lorry; and elected as their spokeswomen Emma Bekanga of Soppo, Namondo Likove of Buea and Namondo Liombe of Lysoka. The colonial official's response was to suggest that the women had exaggerated the price reduction, to fine them £1—3 sterling for throwing away the cocoyams, and to conclude a settlement to ensure the continued supply of cocoyams to the plantations.[45]

Women were exploited in non-monetary ways. The Permanent Mandates Commission of the League of Nations found that while there was no exact record of disease, itself a major shortcoming, 'it appeared that venereal disease had increased; that the people were underfed; that the women were overworked and child mortality was heavy. It was stated that one contributory cause of the spread of venereal disease was the high price of wives, a statement which indicated that women were regarded as chattels'.[46] Most of these health problems may be attributed in varying degrees to the development of a plantation wage-labouring class, although one member of the Permanent Mandates Commission posited that these problems would be solved merely by encouraging the people to grow maize to ensure a food supply and not to maltreat their wives.[47]

Given the problem of heavy infant mortality, British officials attempted to investigate the general level of health among West Cameroonian women, particularly with a view to ascertaining the fertility rate of women based on Carlyle-Johnstone's work in Kenya. The rate was found to be 3.4 children in Mamfe Division for both the direct method (the total number of women of aged 40 divided into the total number of their children) and the indirect method (mean age and average number of children per woman, then a further calculation[48] to show how many children a woman would have by the time she reached 40). The conclusion from Mamfe Division where 8—13 per cent of women were sterile was that there was a 'fairly high' infantile mortality rate as well as a high mortality rate before puberty.[49] In the Bamenda Division which supplied most of the male labourers to the plantations, by the 1930s cardiac disease was reported to be common in the hilly areas where heavy loads were carried by females.[50]

The proposed solutions to the various problems affecting West Cameroon women in the interwar years reflected the colonial ethos. Generally, the spread of western education and European influence were favoured, since the spread of education was said to possess a great effect on the moral and social welfare of the people. While acknowledging the need to ameliorate the conditions of West Cameroon's women, the British concluded that this 'can only be brought about by the gradual extension of missionary, educational and economic influences.'[51]

The British proposals for raising the 'singularly low' status of West Cameroon women included a concerted campaign of instruction in mothercraft and midwifery training; the introduction of special courses of instruction by European nurses and female missionaries; and the institution or expansion of classes in needlework, laundry, cooking, infant welfare and housewifery.[52] Thus one specific proposal called for the creation of a clinic-cum-centre at Buea, to be supervised by a Committee of European females under the chairmanship (sic) of the wife of the Resident of Cameroons Province, which would offer lectures and demonstrations on children's diet and the clean preparation of food.[53] Yet there was no thought given to dealing with the real source of the problems, that is, the plantations.

Amidst the problems and unimaginative proposals, West Cameroon women had the task of keeping the traditional sector of the economy going, for it was this sector to which the male labourers had to return in the depression. Faced with an unfavourable international market, the plantations in West Cameroon reduced their labour force and the labourers sought refuge in the operation of the traditional sector.[54]

During the 1930s, international agencies (that is, the International Labour Organisation, ILO, and the League of Nations) pressed for an amelioration of the lot of women worldwide. The pressure came from a League Assembly Resolution of 27 September 1935 which asked the ILO to examine the issue of equality under labour legislation as well as the existing, political, civil and economic status of women. As in West Cameroon, the emphasis in this international campaign was upon the curtailment of the practice of early marriage and the provision of education, so that women could take up their 'true vocation' as teachers, midwives and district and hospital nurses.[55] By 1939 the lot of the West Cameroon woman was not a happy one, and the war years and their aftermath exacerbated some of her problems.

The situation 1939-60

The period after 1939, but especially after 1945 is generally taken as the one during which the decolonisation of Africa occurred.[56] West Cameroon, as part of the British Empire, was subject to colonial development and welfare policy[57] in which labour and educational schemes figured prominently. In the period of two decades between 1939 and 1960 under review there was an expansion in plantation activity which, of necessity, had an impact on woman's socio-economic status. This expanded activity owed its origins to the peculiar demands of the Second World War. There also appeared to be a desire on the part of officials to tackle, if not solve, the many outstanding social and economic problems of West Cameroon, especially as these affected the women. Moreover, there were some changes in the role of the plantations: although their duty to promote external trade remained unaltered, they were made responsible for the development of West Cameroon, indeed, of the entire British Cameroons.

In 1939 British policy was that in the event of war, the German estates in West Cameroon were to become government property and would be kept in full production. So, on 13 September the District Officer of Buea District proceeded to the Ekona plantation to apprise labourers of the situation:

> I stated that there was war in Europe but that there was no war in the
> Cameroons. That the Government wished the plantations to go on and had

provided money for that purpose. That the planters would continue their work and would be the labourers' masters as before. That plantation discipline would continue as before, and that the Government wanted all men to go on with their work and do it properly.[58]

In practice, however, the Germans were expelled and until 1942 plantation production was scaled down. The policy of all-out production was settled in March—April 1942 by Captain Miller, the Custodian of Enemy Property:

palm oil kernels and rubber were to be produced to capacity, that banana estates were to be kept in a fair state of cultivation, that cocoa need not be harvested but that the best and most accessible estates were to be kept on a care and maintenance basis . . . In deciding that maximum production was essential the supply situation at the time was the overriding factor and no price was prescribed.[59]

Before the adoption of a policy of full-scale production in 1942, it was decided that production on the estates in West Cameroon was of little strategic value to Britain's war effort. The immediate result was a scaling down of production; and as a corollary, the labourers were sent home. Thus the plantation labour force, which had peaked at over 25,000 in 1938 and stood at 23,500 in 1939, plunged to 8,500 in 1940 and 7,700 in 1941.[60]

The large reduction in the plantation labour force was regretted by the Governor of Nigeria, Sir Bernard Bourdillon. He was uneasy about the socio-economic consequences of laying off 18,000 labourers, 'large numbers of whom, and their families, are undergoing hardship, if not privation, for want of work'.[61] It was to the traditional sector of the economy that these 18,000 returned. As had occurred during the depression, West Cameroon women were once again asked to reabsorb the labour force that had been ejected from the European economic sector.[62]

The return of the labourers posed problems for British officialdom, especially in Bamenda Division. In general, the British officials could not comprehend the fact that ex-plantation male labourers were 'idle' while women performed agrarian tasks.[63] As a result, all efforts at developing the agricultural potential of this Division had to incorporate women. Thus J.D. Browne, Senior Agricultural Officer, found that programmes for future agricultural development in Bamenda ought to be aimed at women and at making the younger generation of males favourably disposed towards agriculture.[64] The difficulties posed in Bamenda Division did have a positive effect: they resulted in a serious discussion on the need to educate the women of West Cameroon in general and those of Bamenda Division in particular. Before analysing this discussion, it must be pointed out that the emphasis remained on the role of education in promoting agriculture; for it was found that the main lines of educational development, as discussed and approved by the Cameroons Provincial Welfare Board, 'mainly concern an increase in the facilities for training teachers in primary subjects and rural science'.[65] The immediate backdrop to the discussion on women's education had been provided by the prevailing view of educational and other authorities that the fact that women were performing the bulk of agricultural labour was evidence of exploitation and this ought to be changed.

The Cameroons Provincial Development Committee, established to help plan development and welfare schemes, broached the subject of women's education in March 1944. The Committee viewed with alarm the backward position of women in the Cameroons; asked the Nigerian government to post a 'Lady Education Officer' to Cameroons Province and to send 'a woman anthropologist' to make a survey of women's economic position;and further asked for funds to inaugurate classes for adult women in conjunction with the domestic science centres.[66]

A year earlier, Miss G. Plummer, an Education Officer serving but not posted to West Cameroon, found that 'comparatively little' had been done to educate West Cameroonian girls, for there were only four government schools for girls, with 347 girls, and the proportion was even lower in the mission schools. For Plummer this detestable situation was the product of three conjoint forces, two of which were deemed peculiar to West Cameroon. According to Plummer, the deplorable state of women's educational opportunities stemmed from the general tendency of societies to educate boys first; from the generally depressed state of West Cameroon women and their physical exhaustion; and from 'the general poverty and ignorance prevailing in the country'. Thus, she concluded that an improvement in both education and the economic conditions was the 'real remedy'.[67] Similar sentiments were echoed by the Resident who tried to get the Provincial Development and Welfare Committee to accept his view that 'until we do something to educate the women of this Province, we will never improve the economic situation and thus create that wealth from which the general education of women will follow'.[68]

The view of the 1940s that education was a remedy to socio-economic backwardness was repeated in the independence period. Post-colonial Cameroon authorities sought through education to tackle the problems of women in society and took steps to upgrade their social standing. Although this approach was not likely to bring immediate changes, it represented an improvement over the colonial system whereby administrators often perceived the problem but were unwilling to tackle it due to their own perceptions of, and attitudes towards, women's role in society and due to their fear of antagonising the African male.[69] The importance attached by the British after the Second World War to the education of African women was reflected in the fact that the Colonial Office itself had from 1947 a Woman Assistant Education Officer.

West Cameroon did benefit from the services of Dr P.M. Kaberry, the 'woman anthropologist'. Her research concentrated on the ways in which colonialism affected the position of women in the Bamenda Grassfields. Her general conclusion was that:

> mission teachings, the operation of British law, schools, the increase in the use of money, the appearance of a considerable range of European articles in the markets — these, to mention only a few factors, are modifying the institution of marriage and are exercising a direct and indirect effect on the position of women.

However, Kaberry thought that the tendency for women to participate more regularly in trade than formerly, while they simultaneously continued to do the bulk of the farming, was the most radical change.[70] It seems reasonable to suggest that as men remained in estate labour, women were forced to continue agriculture, but the absence of the males created a vacuum in trade which women filled.

Indeed West Cameroonian women seemed to be holding their own economically in wartime. The increased plantation activity after 1942 led to a commensurate increase in plantation labour force and cheap supplies of food were required to feed the estate labour. Cocoyams formed a large part of the labourers' diet and Bakweri women producers dominated the market, partly as a result of their taking their produce all the way to Bota, headquarters of the plantations. The male contractors, in a continuation of the pre-1939 struggle, unsuccessfully petitioned the authorities and were brusquely informed that: 'cocoyams will be bought at the ruling market price, and no machinery will be set up to create an artificial price ... If you cannot compete with direct sales by producers ... your remedy is to retire from business'.[71]

That the plantations exerted a significant influence on women's livelihood cannot be discounted, when it is recognised that after 1942 a greater area had been cleared for farming and an increased quantity of foodstuffs was produced in the Kumba and Victoria Districts,[72] that is, the area where plantations existed.

Although there were increased opportunities for the education of females,[73] namely, the opening of the first secondary school for girls at Okoyong in the Mamfe Division, the main avenue to the socio-economic advance of women continued to be provided by plantation agriculture. During the 1950s an increasing number of women were taking up agricultural employment and one of the main centres for this was the Tole Tea estate near Buea, opened in March 1958, which employed 70—80 women weeding, pruning and plucking at a rate of 2 shillings 9 pence per day.[74]

One of the more enlightening features of the history of West Cameroon after the Second World War is that the plantations were legally required to foster its social and economic development after 1945. However, the new role of development assigned to the plantations must not obscure the perpetuation of social ills in the plantation zone. During the war, the German plantations were seized as enemy property by the Nigerian government, which in 1946 declared them to be 'native lands', and leased them to a newly-created statutory body, the Cameroons Development Corporation (CDC).[75] The corporation was charged with the responsibility of developing the entire British Cameroons, for under the ordinance which legally sanctioned its creation:

> the annual profits of the Corporation, after the Corporation have made such allocations as they deem necessary or expedient for meeting their obligations, and for discharging their functions under this Ordinance, and after they have set aside such sum or sums as they deem necessary or expedient by way of general or special reserves, shall be applied for the benefit of the inhabitants of the Cameroons under British Mandate in such manner as the Governor may decide.[76]

After 1954, the inhabitants of Northern Cameroons were excluded from sharing in the profits of the CDC;[77] but before then the male-dominated Bakweri Land Committee had unsuccessfully sought a retrocession of ownership of the plantation lands.[78] The postwar years were, however, dominated by increasing disquiet — official and otherwise — over the decline in moral standards in West Cameroon as a result of the operation of plantations.

It is generally agreed that developments affecting such issues as marriage, informal union and divorce were clearly distinguished among the Bakweri and Bakolle. This provides the justification for limiting discussion on them to the Victoria Division.[79] The introduction of labourers from Nigeria, for example, had helped to undermine morality as well as the powers of the traditional political authorities. The latter responded by calling for the eviction of all male Igbo labourers 'and any Bakweri lady whose indiscretions might be instrumental in their leaving progeny behind them was to be fined £5'.[80] This rather punitive action against the women in Victoria and Buea Districts was consistent with the trend in colonial Africa of native authorities imposing severe sentences upon any woman who contravened their rules or proclamations.[81]

In the 1950s a coincidence of the interests of the CDC (that is, the need to investigate the problems posed by a large labour force) and the Cameroons Development Corporation Workers Union (that is, the need for a sociological survey of plantation labour) led to a major investigation of the negative impact of plantation activity upon the moral and social life of the peoples of Victoria Division.[82]

The results of the investigation suggested that there was 'a drift of the women and girls of the indigenous tribes into prostitution and other irregular liaisons'; that there was an 'imbalance' in the population — most pronounced in the Bakolle area, in which there was 'the great excess of males over females'; that the fertility rate among the Bakweri female was low;[83] and that there was an interrelationship of these features. Thus Ardener found that in some Bakweri villages there was evidence of depopulation, partly due to a deficiency of females in the Bakweri population itself, and 'it is not unreasonable to assume that this represents a loss of women to the immigrant centres as prostitutes'.[84]

The view emerged in West Cameroon that the Bakweri woman was of low moral fibre, inclined to promiscuity and generally of 'easy virtue'[85] - a view which has emerged since plantations were introduced. During the period before 1960 there were changes in the level of bride-price: it was said to be too high at first, but by the 1950s it had fallen to a low level which allegedly made divorce easy. With the 'too high' rates, a woman was discouraged from divorcing her husband on account of the difficulty of repaying bride price. The Bakweri male complained that low rates furthered divorce since the availability of money, due to the presence of the plantations and their labour force, made repayment of bride-price in the event of divorce a relatively easy task.[86] Finally, Ardener's research found that over 60 per cent of the 'legitimate' unions completed in his sample of 1062 women and 40 per cent of all legitimate unions ever contracted had ended in divorce.[87]

Conclusion

The introduction of plantations is of tremendous importance to an understanding of the socio-economic evolution of women in colonial West Cameroon. The imperial tradition of African historiography might suggest that plantations were beneficial since they offered opportunities for women to take part in the modern economic sector through wage labour on or sale of foodstuffs to the plantations. Yet the West Cameroonian woman in the 60 years after 1900 was heavily exploited and discriminated against.

The role of women was altered as a result of plantation enterprise. In the Bamenda region, the women were forced to take a larger share of responsibility for ensuring the survival of the family and the traditional economic sector without the compensation of improved or increased socio-economic amenities. Their counterparts among the Bakweri bore the brunt of the impact of the plantations and found themselves 'liberated' from the traditional system. Yet it is a tribute to the women of West Cameroon that they were able to appreciate the changes which accompanied the operation of the plantations and to grasp whatever opportunities were available to them.

Endnotes

1. Dan Dzidze, 'A Call on the Chairman', *West Africa*, 1—7 February 1993, p. 144.
2. See *Social and Economic Studies*, Vol. 35, 2 (1986), for WICP's Overview and Conclusions.
3. See *Social and Economic Studies* Vol. 35, 3 (1986) for H. McKenzie, 'The Educational Experiences of Caribbean Women', pp. 65—105.
4. The German territory, Kamerun, was divided after 1916 into British and French portions called British Cameroons and French Cameroun; after 1960 the southern part of the former *and* the latter formed the Federal Republic of Cameroon. This changed in May 1972 to the United Republic of Cameroon and, again, in 1984 to the Republic of Cameroon. The republic is officially bilingual, thus the spellings Cameroon and Cameroun are both used.
5. Colonial Office (London), hereafter, CO, *Report on the Administration of the Cameroons under British Mandate for the year 1922* (hereafter cited as *Report on Cameroons*).
6. M. Buvinic *et al.*, *Women and Poverty in the Third World* (Baltimore: Johns Hopkins, 1983); A. Christian, 'The Place of Women in Ghana Society', *African Woman*, Vol. 3, 1959; D. Pauline, *Women of Africa* (California: UCLA Press, 1963, translated by H.M. Wright); E. Boserup, *Women's Role in Economic Development* (New York: St Martin press, 1970); J.H. Morrison, 'Boserup Revisited: Economic Restructuring and Gender Roles in Caribbean Agriculture' (University of Newcastle Upon Tyne Geography Seminar 46, 1986); S.E.M. Charlton, *Women in Third World Development* (Boulder: Westview Press, 1984); and Denise Pauline, *Women of Africa* (California: University of California Los Angeles Press, 1963).
7. E. Ardener, *Divorce and Fertility. An African Study* (London: Oxford University Press, 1962) and *Plantation and Village in the Cameroons - Social and Economic Studies* (London, 1960); P.M. Kaberry, *Women of the Grassfields*, (London: HMSO, 1952).
8. E. Boserup, *op. cit.*; W. Rodney, *How Europe Underdeveloped Africa* (London: Bogle L'Overture, 1972).
9. L. Mullings, 'Women and Economic Change in Africa', N. Hafkin and E. Bay, *Women in Africa. Studies in Social and Economic Change* (Stanford: Stanford University Press, 1976), pp. 239—64.
10. H. Moore, *Feminism and Anthropology* (Cambridge: Cambridge University Pres, 1988), p. 82.
11. S. Osoba, 'The Phenomenon of Labour Migration in the Era of Colonial Rule', *Journal of the Historical Society of Nigeria*, 4, 4 (1969), pp. 515—38.
12. C. Murray, *Families Divided. The Impact of Migrant Labour in Lesotho* (Cambridge: Cambridge University Press, 1981); P. Lawrence (ed.) *World Recession and the Food Crisis in Africa* (London: James Currey, 1986), pp. 283—99.
13. Moore, *Feminism and Anthropology*, p. 63.
14. M. Lovett, 'Gender Relations, Class Formation and the Colonial State in Africa', J. Parpart and K. Standt, *Women and the State in Africa* (London: Lynne Rienne, 1989), pp. 23—46.
15. *Ibid.*, pp. 23—24.
16. E. Leacock, Introduction to F. Engels, *The Origin of Family, Private Property and the State* (New York: International Publishers Co., 1972).

17. J. Kelly-Gadol, 'The Social Relation of the Sexes. Methodological Implications of Women's History', in E. Abel and E. K. Abel, *The SIGNS Reader. Women, Gender and School* (Chicago: University of Chicago Press, 1983), pp. 1—26.
18. M. R. Cutrufelli, *Women of Africa. Roots of Oppression* (London: Zed Books, 1983), offers a general introduction.
19. National Archives Ibadan (hereafter, NAI) CSO 26/1 06800, Ancient Tribal Machinery: Investigation by H. Cadman.
20. NAI CSO 26/1 06782, Bakolle Assessment Report.
21. Ardener, *Coastal Bantu of the Cameroons* (London: International African Institute, 1956), pp. 52—54.
22. *Ibid.*, p. 48.
23. Consensus derived from the many Intelligence and Assessment Reports in NAI, National Archives Enugu (NAE) and Cameroon Archives, Buea (CAB).
24. NAI CSO 26/1 11154, Balong Assessment Report.
25. CAB Ba 1919/1, Annual Report, 1919, Cameroon Province, Paragraphs 98—104.
26. Foreign Office (hereinafter FO), *Handbooks Prepared under Direction of the Historical Section of the Foreign Office, No. 114. Treatment of the Natives* (London: HMSO, 1920), pp. 20—21.
27. CSO21. CSO1179. 'All Highest Decree concerning the Creation, Occupation and Disposal of Crown Land and the Acquisition and Disposal of Landed Property in the Protectorate of Cameroons, 15 June 1986'; S. J. Epale, *Plantations and Development in Western Cameroon, 1885—1975: A Study in Agrarian Capitalism* (New York: Vantage Press, 1985) Chapter II; R. Goodridge, 'Society and Economy in British Cameroons' PhD. dissertation, (Ibadan, 1988), pp. 38—41.
28. H.R. Rudin, *Germans in the Cameroons 1884—1914 : A Case Study in Modern Imperialism* (New York: Greenwood Press, 1968), Chapter VII.
29. *Peace Handbook* 114, p. 13; Rudin, *Germans in the Cameroons*, pp. 193—94.
30. *Peace Handbook* 114, p. 23; CAB Ba 1916/1, for British criticism of forced recruitment; NAI CSO 26/1 01435, Vol I.
31. *Peace Handbooks* 111 and 114 contain the views and information of those critical of German colonialism.
32. Goodridge, 'Society and Economy'; Epale, *Plantations and Development*, Chapter III.
33. See the multi-volume files CSO 26/1 01435 and 01857.
34. CSO 26/4 34566; CSO 1/32/146 No. 29, Governor's Deputy to Secretary of State, 5 January 1939.
35. See paragraphs 187—91 of Draft Report on Cameroon 1938 in CSO 26/4 34566/1.
36. CO Annual Report to the Council of the League of Nations on the Administration of the Cameroons under British Mandate 1938, paragraphs 186—91.
37. CSO 26/4 34566, Vol. 1, pp. 135—40.
38. League of Nations, Permanent Mandates Commission, V1.1924. Minutes of 5th Session 3rd Meeting of PMC, 24 October 1924; CSO 26/2 13977, Vol. I.
39. *Report on Cameroon*, 1938, paragraphs 192—93.
40. CSO 26/3 23131, Vols. II and III contain educational data for W. Cameroon; the 1929 enrolment figures were 1,167 total, with 166 girls.

41. See *Report on Cameroon* for 1927—30.

42. CAB Qd/a/1923/90.

43. CAB Qc/d/1938/1, D.H. Buea to Asst District Officer, Buea, 15 January 1938.

44. Women claimed that prices of varying sizes of baskets of cocoyams in 1936 were 4s, 3s, 2s and 1s 6d but in 1938 these dropped to 1s, 9d, 6d and 3d respectively.

45. Qc/d/1938/1 D.H. Buea to Resident Cameroon Province, 7 February 1938; Resident to Division Officer, Victoria, 3 August 1938; Division Officer Victoria to Resident, 5 August 1938.

46. CSO 26/1 13977, Vol. I, pp. 68—71, 82—88.

47. LON, PMC (in French PCM), 190 (1). Observations with regard to B-Mandated Territories, 1924.

48. This calculation was based on the assumption that child-bearing is more or less evenly distributed over the entire reproductive period of 25 years.

49. CSO 26/2 13977, Vol. IV, pp. 377—96; *Report on Cameroon*, 1924, see Appendix IV for Biological Data on Mamfe Division.

50. CSO 26/3 23432, Vol. II; League of Nations. C.830.M.411.1931 VI.

51. CAB Ba 19233/1, *Annual Report Cameroons Province*, 1923.

52. CSO 26/3 26629/1; CSO 26/3 34566, Vol. I, pp. 102—07, *Reports on Cameroon* for various years.

53. CSO 26/3 28570. Cameron to Cunliffe-Lister 2 April 1935.

54. Personal Interview, Chief J. Ewule at Buea, 11 September 1985, and R.M. 'Papa' Lambe 8 October 1985.

55. LON A14. 1937.V. 26 August 1937; for discussion in Cameroon, see CSO 26/4 30302, Vol. II.

56. R. von Albertini, *Decolonization. The Administration and the Future of the Colonies 1919—1960* (New York: Africana, 1982); J. Hargreaves, *Decolonization in Africa* (London: Longmans, 1990).

57. *Statement of Policy on Colonial Development and Welfare. Presented by Secretary of State for the Colonies to Parliament by Command His Majesty. February 1940*, Cmd 6175.

58. CAB Qd/c/1938/1, pp. 65-67 D.O., Buea to Sen. D.O. Victoria, 15 September 1939.

59. CSO 1/40/6 #831 Officer Administering the Govt to Colonial Officer, 5 Oct. 1943 encl.

60. Figures, rounded to the nearest hundred, are obtained from various Annual Reports on Cameroons Province found in the Buea Archives as well as Nigerian Archives, Ibadan.

61. CSO 1/32/158 #611 Bourdillon to Moyne with enclosure, 14 October 1941.

62. On this point see Cutrufelli, *op. cit.*, Chapter 1.

63. In the post-1940 period Britain paid much attention to the prospects and problems of increasing agricultural activity in Bamenda Division; discussion on these offers much information.

64. Agricultural proposals found in CSO 26/2 16556, CSO 26/1 09052, CSO 26/4 38353; and for administrators' comments thereon see (NAE) EP10068, Vol. 1 CSE 1/85/5079.

65. CSO 26/4 44249, pp. 54—59, 'Report on Education Cameroons Province 1944.'

66. CSO 26/5 42150, pp. 1—2.

67. National Archives, Enugu (NAE) EP 19848 CSE 1/85/9872, 'Notes on Education of Girls in British Cameroons', by Miss G. Plummer (1943).
68. For the minutes of meetings of Cameroon Province Development and Welfare Committee see CSO 26/5 42150.
69. M. Azevedo *et al.*, 'The Status of Women in Cameroon and Chad', in M. Azevedo (ed.) *Cameroon and Chad in Historical and Contemporary Perspective* (New York: Mellen, 1988), pp. 155—56.
70. Kaberry, pp. 143—44.
71. CAB Qc/d/1938/1 for correspondence on the matter, including the petition.
72. CSO 26/2 16556, Vol. XIV, Cameroon Province Provincial Summary, 1942, 1943.
73. In 1956, for example, the first girls' secondary school was opened at Okoyong in the Mamfe Division; See United Nations Trusteeship Council (UNTC), T/1302 UNTC 19th session, 6 March 1957.
74. *Report on the Administration of the Cameroons under United Kingdom Trusteeship for the year 1958* (hereafter UNGA), paragraphs 650—65.
75. S. Bederman, *The Cameroons Development Corporation: Partner in National Growth* (Bota: CDC Press, 1968).
76. *Supplement to the Nigerian Gazette* (1946), pp. 1317—24.
77. See *Annual Report* of the CDC for 1955. These were published separately but often included in the annual report to the U.N.
78. UNTC.T/Petition 12. Petition from the Bakweri Land Committee, 12 August 1946; UNTC.T/461, *Report of the First UN Visiting Mission to the Trust Territory of the Cameroons under British Administration*, 13 February 1950.
79. H. N. Molua, 'The Bakweri Land Problem: A Case Study', MA History (Ibadan 1985).
80. National Archives, Kaduna (NAK), Yola Prof 4968 'A Study of Land Tenure in the Cameroons Province by C.W. Rowling, Acting Commissioner of Lands, 24 May 1948'.
81. Cutrufelli *op. cit.*, p. 23.
82. The survey was largely conducted by W. A. Warmington and the husband and wife team of Edwin and Shirley Ardener.
83. On this point see Ardener, *Divorce and Fertility, op. cit.* The study was based on a sample of 1,062 women.
84. Ardener *et al.*, *Plantation and Village*, pp. 274—92, the latter quotation is on p. 292.
85. I frequently heard such comments from Cameroonians living in Nigeria, 1982—89 and when on a field trip in North-West and South-West Provinces of the Republic of Cameroon 1985.
86. The issues of divorce, marriage and health occupied British and Cameroonian political forces; personal interviews E.M.L. Endeley and R.M. Lambe already cited and V.T. Lainjo, 1985.
87. Ardener, *Divorce and Fertility, op. cit.*, and his *Coastal Bantu* pp. 61—66; *Plantation and Village, op. cit.*, Chapter XV.

Notes on Contributors

Barbara Bailey is a Lecturer in the Faculty of Education at the University of the West Indies (UWI), Mona campus. She specialises in Curriculum Theory and Development. She is Campus Co-ordinator for the Centre for Gender and Development Studies and in 1994 co-chaired Jamaica's National Preparatory Commission for the United Nations 4th World Conference on Women to be held in Beijing, China, in 1995.

Hilary Beckles is Professor of History, Head of Department, and Dean of the Faculty of Arts and General Studies at the Cave Hill Campus of the UWI, and University Dean. He is author of several books including *Natural Rebels: A Social History of Enslaved Black Women in Barbados*, *Afro-Caribbean Women and Resistance to Slavery in Barbados*, *White Servitude and Black Slavery*, and with Verene Shepherd, co-edited *Caribbean Slave Society and Economy* and *Caribbean Freedom*.

Bridget Brereton is Reader in Caribbean Social History and has served as Head of the Department of History at the St Augustine campus of the UWI. She is President of the Association of Caribbean Historians and author of many articles and books including *Race Relations in Colonial Trinidad* and *A History of Modern Trinidad, 1783—1962*.

Digna Castañeda is a Lecturer in the Department of History, University of Havana, Cuba. She is the author of *La Revolución Haitiana, 1791—1804*, published in 1992 by the Social Sciences Publishing House in Havana City.

Mary Chamberlain teaches history at Oxford Brookes University. She is a Trustee of the National Life Story Collection of the British Library's National Sound Archives. She has written several books on women's history, including *Fenwomen*, *Old Wives' Tales*, and *Growing Up in Lambeth*, and has edited *Writing Lives*.

Jonathan Dalby is a graduate of the University of St Andrews, and the University of Manchester. He is Senior Lecturer in the Department of History at the Mona campus of the UWI where he teaches European history. His publications include *Les Paysans Cantaliens et la Revolution Française, 1789—94* (trans. Catherine Marion, Institut d'Etudes du Massif Central, Clermont-Ferrand, 1989).

Richard Goodridge is a Lecturer in African history in the Department of History at the UWI, Cave Hill campus, Barbados. He previously taught at the University of Maiduguri, Nigeria, and at the Mona campus of the UWI. His research focuses on the social history of Nigeria and Cameroon.

Catherine Hall is Professor in the Department of Sociology at the University of Essex. She is the co-author with Leonore Davidoff of *Family Fortunes: Men and Women of the English Middle Class 1780—1850* and the author of *White, Male and Middle Class: Explorations in Feminism and History*. She is on the editorial collectives of *Feminist Review* and *Gender and History*.

Paulette Kerr holds an MA degree in History from the UWI, Mona. She is a Reference Librarian at the Main Library, UWI, and is Vice-President of the Jamaica Library Association.

Felix V. Matos-Rodríguez is an Assistant Professor of History at Northeastern University, Boston. He was previously a Program Officer at the Social Science Research Council, and taught Caribbean history courses at City University of New York (CUNY) and Yale University.

Janice Mayers is a doctoral candidate in history at the Cave Hill campus of the UWI and Head of the Department of History at Combermere Secondary School in Barbados. She has served as a part-time tutor in history at the UWI, Cave Hill.

Patricia Mohammed is a Lecturer in the Centre for Gender and Development Studies at the UWI, Mona campus. She recently completed a PhD. thesis on Gender and History at the Institute of Social Studies in the Netherlands. She is co-editor (with Catherine Shepherd) of *Gender in Caribbean Development*.

Bernard Moitt taught at the University of Toronto for many years and is Assistant Professor of History and Black Studies at Utica College, Syracuse University. He has published several articles in international journals and chapters in books on the subjects of slavery and its impact on women and children in Africa and the French Caribbean.

Glory Robertson read history at the University of St Andrews. She worked for many years as Librarian at the UWI, Mona campus. Her paper in this collection is part of a larger work on dress in Jamaica to be published by the Institute of Jamaica Publications. She is former President of the Jamaica Historical Society.

Veront Satchell is a Lecturer in the Department of History at the UWI, Mona campus. He teaches courses in Caribbean economic history and specialises in quantitative methods. He is the author of *From Plots to Plantations*, published in 1990 by the Institute of Social and Economic Research (ISER), UWI, Mona.

Verene Shepherd is a Lecturer in the Department of History, UWI, Mona, teaching courses in women's history and Caribbean history. She is Fellow of the Cambridge Commonwealth Society and a former holder of the DuBois-Mandela-Rodney Fellowship at CAAS, University of Michigan. She is author of *Transients to Settlers: the Experience of Indians in Jamaica 1845—1950*, and co-editor (with Hilary Beckles) of *Caribbean Slave Society and Economy* and *Caribbean Freedom*.

Jean Stubbs is Senior Lecturer in Caribbean Studies and Latin American History at the University of North London, and 1993—95 Chair of the Society for Caribbean Studies (UK). She has published extensively on Cuba. She is co-editor with Pedro Perez Sarduy of *AFROCUBA: An Anthology of Cuban Writing on Race, Politics and Culture*, and author of *Tobacco on the Periphery: A Case Study in Cuban Labour History, 1860—1958* and *Cuba: The Test of Time*.

Rosalyn Terborg-Penn is Professor of History at Morgan State University, Baltimore. Her research interests include black women's history in the African Diaspora and oral history. She is co-author of *A Special Mission: the Story of Freedmen's Hospital, 1862—1962*, and co-editor of three books on African-American women, including *Women in Africa and the African Diaspora*.

Linnette Vassell is a Temporary Lecturer in the Department of History at the Mona campus. She has conducted research on Women's Voluntary Associations in Jamaica and has been involved in the women's movement for many years. She is the compiler of *Voices of Women in Jamaica*, published by the Department of History, UWI, Mona, in 1993.

Waibinte Wariboko is a graduate of the University of Ibadan and the University of Birmingham. He is a Lecturer in West African History at the University of Port Harcourt, Nigeria. He is currently Visiting Lecturer in the Department of History, Mona. He teaches West African history and has an interest in oral history methods.

Swithin Wilmot is a Lecturer in History at the Mona campus of UWI. He has published journal articles and chapters of books which focus on popular politics and protest in post-slavery Jamaica. He is the editor of *Adjustments to Emancipation* (Social History Project, Department of History, UWI, 1993).